COLONIAL URBAN DEVELOPMENT

COLONIAL URBAN DEVELOPMENT
Culture, social power and environment

Anthony D King
Departments of Sociology and Building Technology
Brunel University

Routledge & Kegan Paul

London, Henley and Boston

First published in 1976
by Routledge & Kegan Paul Ltd
39 Store Street,
London WC1E 7DD
Broadway House,
Newtown Road,
Henley-on-Thames,
Oxon RG9 1EN and
9 Park Street,
Boston, Mass. 02108, USA
Typed by Jeanne Bellovics
Printed and bound in Great Britain
by Unwin Brothers Limited,
The Gresham Press, Old Woking, Surrey
A member of the Staples Printing Group

ISBN   0   7100   8404   8

CONTENTS

ACKNOWLEDGMENTS

I should particularly like to acknowledge the help of five people without whom this work would not have reached its present form. The book originated early in 1970 in conversations with Bijit Ghosh, Professor of Planning at the School of Planning and Architecture, University of Delhi, and the particular approach gained much from discussions with Professor John Useem, Department of Sociology, Michigan State University. To both of these I owe much of my initial interest and many early ideas. To Professor Otto Koenigsberger of the Development Planning Unit, School of Environmental Studies, University College, London, for his continued interest and Jim Dyos, Professor of Urban History at the University of Leicester, and the Social Science Faculty, for supporting the research with a University Fellowship, I should also like to express my warm appreciation and thanks. In organising a richly stimulating conference on 'The Mutual Interaction of Man and His Built Environment' as part of the 9th International Anthropological Congress at Racine and Chicago, 1973 and inviting me to participate, Amos Rapoport, Professor of Anthropology and of Architecture at the University of Wisconsin-Milwaukee, provided a rare opportunity to exchange and develop ideas; to both him and other participants, I owe my thanks.

Many other people have read chapters, sent their comments or own papers and helped in numerous ways. In sociology, my thanks are due to Professor Yogesh Atal, Professor Janet Abu-Lughod, Dr Ashish Bose, Mr Malcolm Cross, Professor Victor d'Souza, Professor John Rex and Dr Fredj Stambouli; in anthropology, Professor Bernard Cohn, Dr T.S. Madan and Professor Adrian Mayer; in geography, Mr Deryck Holdsworth, Professor David Lowenthal, Mr Hugh Prince and Professor Paul Wheatley; in architecture and urban planning, Mr John Collins, Mr Satish Davar, Mr Jan Pieper, Dr Nigel Harris and Mr Michael Safier; in architectural and Indian history, Mrs Mildred Archer, Dr Ranajit Guha, Dr Susan Lewandowski, Dr B.R. Nanda, Professor Sten Nilsson and Dr David Page; in the history of medicine, Dr E. Clark. To my erstwhile colleagues in the Department of Social Science at the Indian Institute of Technology, Delhi, I owe my thanks for the many contributions to the inter-disciplinary context in which this study originated.

To Mrs Mildred Archer and the staff of the India Office Library for
their assistance in supplying many of the illustrations, Mr Ken Garfield
and his colleagues at the Central Photographic Unit, University of
Leicester for their very considerable skills in reproducing these and
to the Research Board of the Social Science Faculty there for grants
towards research expenses, I am greatly indebted. I should also like
to thank Professor M.P. Thakore of the University of Delhi, and the
Library of the University of London, for allowing me to use previously
unpublished material from his doctoral dissertation on the urban
geography of New Delhi, Dr Jaya Indiresan for some private research
on the development of communications in Delhi and Mr S.R. Gupta for
sending me recent books. I am also very grateful to Mr John Taylor
for helpful advice and to Jane and Alan Crawford for their hospitality
in the early stage of the research.

My thanks are due to the staff of numerous libraries including those of
the Indian Institute of Technology, the Indian Institute of Public
Administration, the School of Planning and Architecture, all of Delhi,
the Universities of Leicester and London, the British Library, India
Office, Development Planning Unit, University College, London, the
London School of Hygiene and Tropical Medicine and the Institute of
Royal Engineers, Chatham.

In producing this book as 'camera-ready copy' it has been a pleasure to
co-operate with Jeanne Bellovics whose interest and involvement in the
production has been as great as her expertise in typing and lay-out.

My greatest debt, however, is to Mrs Ursula King, Lecturer in
Comparative Religion, University of Leeds, for a generous research
subsidy; without this, as well as both intellectual and practical
assistance given in a more domestic capacity, and the enthusiastic
encouragement from Frances, Karen, Anna and latterly, Nina, the
book would not have been completed.

Whilst I have benefited from these and many other comments, the final
interpretation is, of course, my own.

The study developed out of a paper on 'Colonial Urbanisation: a
cross-cultural inquiry into the social use of space', first given
at the Nehru Library, Delhi, in May 1970 and revised for the Working
Group on the Sociology of Urban and Regional Planning, World Congress
of Sociology, Varna, Bulgaria, in September of that year. Part of
Chapter 1 was produced for an audio-visual unit on 'The social and
spatial structure of an Indian city: the case of Delhi' for the Open
University's Social Science course on *Urban Development* in October
1972 and is reproduced here by permission. Chapter 2 was first given
as a paper to a British Sociological Association conference on *Aspects
of Urban Sociology* at the University of Leeds in September 1972 and
subsequently abridged for the Open University's *Urban Development*
course; a revised version was read to a seminar at the Centre of South
Asian Studies, School of Oriental and African Studies, University of
London, June 1975. A more extensive version of Chapter 3 was read to
a pre-Congress conference of the IXth International Congress of

Anthropological and Ethnological Sciences, Racine and Chicago,
August-September, 1973, on *The Mutual Interaction of Man and His
Built Environment: A Cross-Cultural Perspective* and is included in
a book of the same title edited by Amos Rapoport (Mouton, World
Anthropology Series, 1976, forthcoming). An earlier version of
Chapter 4 was first given in the Urban History seminar at the Univer-
sity of Leicester in 1972 and subsequently revised and published in
Sociology, 8,1 (January) 1974; it is reproduced here with permission.
Chapter 5 was given in the Sociology and Anthropology Seminar on South
Asia in the School of Oriental and African Studies, University of
London, in April 1973 and a revised version presented at the Racine-
Chicago conference mentioned above. This also appears in the Rapoport
volume. An earlier version of Chapter 6 was published in the *Journal
of Architectural Research*, 3, 2, (May) 1974 and other versions in the
Indian Anthropologist and *Ekistics*, 39,234, (1975) and is reproduced
with permission. Chapter 7 is based on a paper first given to the
Staff Seminar, School of Social Sciences, University of Bradford
and subsequently revised for an SSRC conference on *Developments in
Indian Social and Economic History*, St John's College, Cambridge,
July 1975. Parts of Chapters 9 and 10 were given as papers in the
School of African and Asian Studies, University of Sussex, 1973, and
the Institute of Social Anthropology, University of Oxford, in 1974.
Part of Chapter 11 developed out of seminars at the Development
Planning Unit, School of Environmental Studies, University College,
London, 1972-3. I should like to express my gratitude to all those
providing me with an opportunity to exchange ideas on the above
occasions.

Whilst these papers have been revised for this book, substantial
alterations which subsequent literature might have suggested have
not been incorporated. To have done so would have resulted in an
already lengthy text being even longer and would have further delayed
publication. At the risk of occasionally over-burdening the text
with documentary quotation and explanation, footnotes have been
omitted in the interests of economy.

London and Leeds   Anthony King

PREFACE

The main aim of this book is to attempt an understanding of the social, political and especially, cultural processes governing a type of urban development and, more particularly, to develop appropriate theoretical and methodological tools to undertake this task. Though the work explores a number of issues, there is one basic theme which runs throughout. It is that the physical and spatial arrangements characterising urban development -. indeed, the entire man-made environment - are the unique products of a particular society and culture, operating within a given distribution of power. Only with a thorough understanding of a society's values, beliefs, institutions and social organisation is its built environment properly understood.

Nowhere is this proposition more apparent than in the 'colonial cities' of the nineteenth and twentieth centuries, whether in Africa, Asia or middle America, where the urban forms of a dominant, industrialising Western power were introduced to largely 'pre-industrial' societies. From Rangoon to Cairo, Luanda to Singapore, cities were laid out by the rulers not the ruled. Here, juxtaposed in the environment of the colonised society, were the urban forms of East and West, a unique type of social, physical and spatial organisation which this study identifies as 'colonial urban development'.

Political independence for many, if not all, these societies has brought change in their urban forms. In Africa, some inherited cities are currently being de-colonised by their indigenous elites: others, such as Durban and Salisbury, continue to embody the colonial and racist principles on which the societies rest. Yet whilst this process of colonial urban development took place in many countries of the world it was in colonial India, between the eighteenth and twentieth centuries, that the modern, industrial phase of colonial urbanisation was most patently worked out. Here, colonial life-styles and organisation, and the urban forms which contained them, established a pattern, aspects of which were transferred to colonial societies around the world. Here also was built the text-book example of the modern colonial city, twentieth-century New Delhi, the first of all such colonial capitals to present, in 1947, its newly independent inhabitants with the task of adapting it to the needs of a new, democratic and socialist nation.

Yet whilst the case material is largely drawn from India and other
colonial societies under British rule, and the colonial development
of Delhi forms a case study, the fundamental problems of how social
and cultural factors influence, within a particular distribution of
power, the nature of environments and how these environments relate
to social processes, are those which have a global dimension. To
this extent, the question of *where* such problems are studied and in
what context is irrelevant. The great advantage of the colonial city
as a locus of research is that, with its multi-cultural composition
and extreme distribution of power, it provides a laboratory
situation for examining three related dimensions of the book's
central theme. For the sociologist and historian, the case study
shows how the power structure inherent in the dominance-dependence
relationship of colonialism influenced urban development in the
colonial society. For the anthropologist, geographer, architect or
planner, it provides an ideal laboratory for comparing the cultural
forms of the European immigrants with those of the indigenous
population. For the student of man-environment relations, it
demonstrates how behaviour produces environments and environments
influence behaviour.

The aim, therefore, has been to attempt a comparative analysis of the
essentially cross-cultural data inherent in colonial urban development, and to do this within an inter-disciplinary framework. Where
appropriate, theory has been taken from sociology, anthropology,
social and cultural geography, planning and man-environment studies
to examine, what, for the most part, are historical materials. In
particular, extensive visual data, retrieved from the archives of
the colonial culture, have been used to investigate how environments
were perceived and modified according to the specific social, cultural
and temporal categories of the dominant colonial power.

In attempting such an inter-disciplinary exercise, I am aware that,
with the rapidity with which theory advances in all the various fields,
there is a danger of using obsolete concepts in any one of them.
This will be particularly apparent to readers interested in dependency
theory which has become increasingly explicit and developed in the
last few years and for which good bibliographies exist in Brookfield
(1975) and Oxaal, ed. (1975). The relatively 'undeveloped' dependency concepts used in this book are based largely on my own
observations and experience prior to starting it rather than a
detailed study of the literature. Yet a compromise must be arrived
at between 'research absorption' and 'research production' and that
compromise is embodied in the following pages. Whilst the theory and
methodology have been developed specifically for the purpose of this
study, if they have any wider application - for the understanding of
colonial urban development in other historic empires such as those
of Spain or Rome, for example, for other culture-contact urban
situations - then this would be an unexpected bonus of the research.

Although this book is also addressed to architects and planners, in
no way has it been conceived as a 'policy-oriented' study, least of
all in regard to the post-colonial urban phenomena the origin of
which it describes. It is not concerned with 'the problems' of the

so-called 'developing countries', despite the fact that the last
chapter does, in fact, rehearse arguments which those who deal with
such problems have sometimes put forward. To indulge in such discussion, and to add to the literature which already exists is, in
my view, simply to continue, at the cognitive level, 'colonial urban
development'. In other words, advantageous access to research and
publishing sources, together with finance from 'aid' (as in my own
case) enables studies to be undertaken and published which are not,
for obvious reasons, possible in the post-colonial society itself.

It is for this reason that the scope of this study is strictly limited
to the colonial period and concerns itself with the analysis of the
metropolitan culture (with which I am familiar) and the colonial
expression of this (which I have investigated) and not with post-
colonial indigenous development. If reference is made to this, it
is on the basis of studies undertaken by members of the indigenous
society.

The problems of any society are problems only to the people who
perceive them as such. The identification of such problems is based
on prevailing values and ideologies and the priorities which a society
decides. Implicit in this study is the viewpoint that cultures are
autonomous, to be evaluated only on their own terms.

The book is in four parts. Chapters 1-3 are mainly theoretical and
are based both on secondary works and formulations drawn from the
empirical work of the study. Throughout, an attempt has been made
to include just sufficient theoretical discussion to locate the
problem in its setting and provide a background with which to approach
it. Chapter 1 states the nature of the problems to be examined and
briefly describes the present-day structure of Delhi. It also discusses the theoretical relevance of colonial communities to the
study of larger issues of social and cultural analysis.

The second chapter provides a conceptual framework for examining the
impact of colonialism on urbanisation and urban development; within
this framework, the three main variables of culture, technology and
the power structure of colonialism are suggested as heuristic aids
for studying the structure of the colonial city.

In the third chapter, the variable of culture is examined in more
detail and the structure of the city related to the *institutional
system* of each cultural section in the city. The central concept
of the *colonial third culture* is also developed.

Chapters 4 to 7 (part two), provide a background to the case-study
by looking at the basic elements of colonial urban development and
by developing a methodology to examine them. In each chapter, a
methodology is discussed and then applied to the understanding of
one of such elements. Chapter 4, on The Language of Colonial
Urbanisation, aims to give an insight into the 'urban universe' of
the colonial community and into the physical-spatial urban forms into
which this was translated. It also discusses the structure of social,
economic and political relationships which such forms reflect.

Against this background, three key units are examined in greater detail. As the colonial relationship depended ultimately on armed force, the first of these is the 'cantonment' or military camp. This is discussed as a particular form of social organisation located in a culturally controlled environment the successful functioning of which depended on a code of culturally determined behaviour.

The largest part of most urban areas is taken up by residential units. Chapter 6, therefore, is devoted to a detailed examination of the values, beliefs and behaviour related to the modal dwelling-place of the colonial community, the bungalow-compound complex, considered in its larger setting of the 'civil station'.

The following chapter considers the 'hill station', the third element in the urban system of the colonial community, of which the other two are the 'civil station' in the colonial city and the urban centres of the metropolitan society. The 'hill station' is considered as a 'social place' whose environment resulted from distinctive forms of culture-specific behaviour.

The third part (Chapters 8-10), consists of a case-study of colonial urban development, namely, the transformation of the pre-industrial city of Delhi between the early nineteenth and the mid-twentieth centuries.

As Delhi is not one but a number of cities, at the heart of which are 'Old Delhi' and 'New Delhi', two factors make a study of its development both more difficult and yet more interesting than investigating the structure of a city in a society with a politically and culturally autonomous past. In the first place, at least two very different cultures, representing contrasting forms of social, political and economic organisation and development, were responsible for the creation of these two main areas. Second, the form of, and relationship between, these two areas emerged as a result of the distinctive power relationship imposed by modern industrial colonialism. It is these two characteristics which demand, on one hand, that the cultural variable in the development of the city be carefully examined and, on the other, that the sociological variable of power and the ensuing system of social relations between dominant and dependent sections be given serious attention. As there is no other study of Delhi - one of the world's most important capital cities - in this period, this final section utilises the theory, methodology and empirical data discussed earlier, to attempt a detailed history of the socio-cultural and physical-spatial development of the city, distinguishing implicitly between factors of 'modernisation' and 'Westernisation'. In terms of method, this last section provides the empirical data with which the theoretical propositions put forward in the study can be tested.

In conclusion, Chapter 11 examines briefly the nature of dependent urban development, aspects of the post-colonial city and discusses theoretical issues raised in the course of the research.

In the past there have been many cases in which the orientations of a 'colonial anthropology' have been used to study non-Western and relatively small-scale communities (Asad, 1973). In an attempt to redress the balance, this book uses the orientations of a Western and relatively small-scale anthropology to study the colonial community itself.

PART ONE

Chapter 1

COLONIAL URBAN DEVELOPMENT:
The problem stated

1 THE BASIC THEMES

The aim of this book is to explore a number of inter-related themes.
Some of these themes are primarily sociological and relate to urban
social structure, planning, race relations and, in connection with
post-colonial societies, cultural dependence, 'development' and
'modernisation'. Issues referred to in this context include:

1 The effect of power relationships on urban structure and
   particularly, the impact of Western industrial colonialism
   on urbanisation and urban development in non-Western societies.
2 The transformation, as part of this process, of a pre-industrial
   city.
3 The interaction between environment, social organisation and
   behaviour.
4 The relationship between 'colonial urban development' and urban
   planning for national development.

Because such issues clearly involve a cultural component, other
themes relate to questions of acculturation, pluralism and cultural
change, traditionally the province of anthropology and, in the
relation of culture to environment, of cultural geography. In this
context, other themes taken up include:

1 The effect of social, and especially cultural factors in influencing the man-made environment.
2 The diffusion of values and beliefs about the environment
   between cultures.
3 The development of a methodology and framework to investigate
   these phenomena.

As any one of these themes clearly merits a specialised monograph,
I am only too aware of the shortcomings evident in the following
chapters, each of which takes the form of an exploratory essay.
Why these themes have been taken up for investigation can best
be explained by examining the origins of the study.

2 THE ORIGINS OF THE STUDY

In what is known as the 'sociology of development' it is frequently
debated whether cities act as generators of economic development,
itself dependent on a larger and more comprehensive process of
'modernisation' (Hoselitz, 1969; Qadeer, 1974). Though variously
defined, this concept is usually taken to comprehend notions such
as 'the increase and spread of those values and institutions that
enhance the ability of a society to generate and successfully cope
with continuing change', a process with which urbanisation is
supposedly linked (Friedmann, 1968). The question of whether
economic development depends primarily on such institutional change
in the so-called 'developing' society or on the need for a fundamental restructuring of the international economy to eliminate basic
inequalities (Brookfield, 1975) is too large an issue to be entered
into here. It can none the less be argued that whatever the prime
mover of economic development, social and cultural change occurs
and this involves changes in institutions and values.

The way in which these changes take place, at what rate or whether
they take place at all are processes about which little is known.
Whatever else can be said, the probability of change in values and
institutions is closely related to the degree of social interaction,
information exchange and communication, and this in turn is affected by the physical-spatial structure of the city and the means of
communication within it.

This is not to say that 'spatial structure' is, on its own, a major
determinant of social relations or social structure as some of the
early urban ecologists would imply. Yet it is also true that 'all
social behaviour occurs in space' (Filkin and Weir, 1972, p.107),
and though sociology is primarily concerned with the study of
social relationships, research in urban sociology has too often
assumed that such relationships occur in a physical-spatial vacuum
(Harvey, 1973, p.24). It is clear from recent studies on man-
environment relations that socially and culturally learnt perceptions
of physical environments both influence behaviour and also influence
environments (Rapoport, 1971, 1976, forthcoming; Craik, 1973). It is
in this context therefore, that physical-spatial variables in the
city and the perceptions of them are assumed to have importance
for social behaviour.

Apart from the influence of such subjective factors as perception
on social behaviour, in cities where electronic and automotive means
of communication, such as telephones, television, automobiles and
forms of public transport, are relatively few, it can also be
assumed that spatial configurations of the inhabitants affect the
degree of interaction, and through this, the maintenance or avoid-
ance of social relationships.

Against this background we can examine the particular case of the
'colonial city', that non-Western city resulting from contact with
Western industrial colonialism. Here, as will be described in
greater detail below, two or more 'cities' exist, the indigenous

1   Indigenous walled city

2   Former colonial urban
    settlement of
    New Delhi

    Extent of developed or
    built up land in 1942
    (dotted line)

2a Civil Lines

3   Cantonment or
    military camp

4   Area of post-
    Independence
    expansion

5   Urban fringe

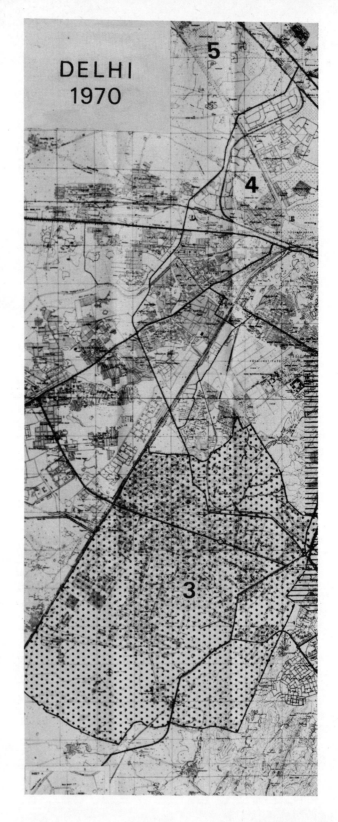

DELHI
1970

Figure 1.1 Delhi,
1970. Physical-
spatial areas

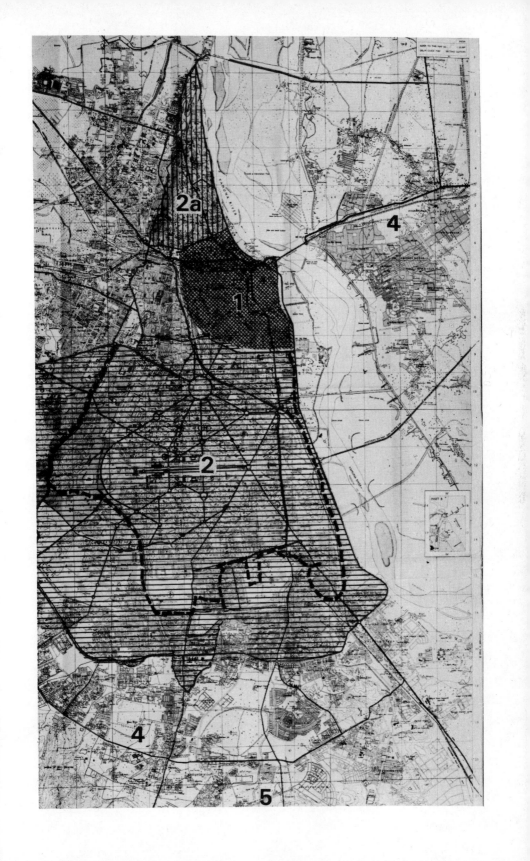

'tradition-oriented' settlement, frequently manifesting the characteristics of the 'pre-industrial city' (Sjoberg, 1960), and on the other hand, the 'new' or 'Western' city, established as a result of the colonial process. Around these two nuclei, to a greater or lesser extent, other urban development has taken place since the formal ending of colonial rule.

Whilst this is a widespread phenomenon, this particular study began as an investigation of one such city, namely Delhi. Stated in the broadest of terms, the original problem was one of examining the relationship between selected aspects of social change and the particular ecological profile of the city. A prerequisite for the investigation of this problem was a proper understanding of its socio-spatial structure. It was in attempting to gain this understanding that the focus of the research was moved and the problem re-defined.

3   THE URBAN STRUCTURE OF DELHI

In contemporary Delhi five main areas of physical growth can be distinguished which have, over time, helped to determine the present spatial structure of the city (Figure 1.1). Though this particular spatial analysis stems from a historically-conscious, Western viewpoint, it is clear that some 'Westernised' inhabitants of Delhi would agree with it though others would have different perceptions of areas in the city.

The first of these is the indigenous walled city of Old Delhi, dating from the seventeenth century. In Sjoberg's terms this is the physical-spatial form of a 'pre-industrial' city where technology was, and to a considerable extent still is, based on animate rather than inanimate forms of energy. The narrow streets (Figure 1.2) lead off the single main road (Figure 1.3) giving entry into shaded courtyards. The *mohullas* or - for want of a better word - neighbourhoods, are still to a large extent characterised by a particular language, religion or geographical origin of their inhabitants though, because of increasing social mobility, less by caste and occupation than was previously the case. Here, traditional crafts and customs can be found as well as very considerable small-scale industry. For the Western observer, residential densities are high, with over one thousand persons per acre in some wards of the old city, compared to less than twenty persons per acre in some residential parts of New Delhi. The place of work and place of residence are frequently undifferentiated.

Though the earlier, nineteenth-century colonial urban settlement was that of the Civil Lines and old Cantonment, north of the old city, the second spatial area is that of the twentieth-century colonial settlement of New Delhi, developed in the thirty-five years prior to Independence in 1947 (Figure 1.1). This was, and largely still is, an area of very low residential density, originally planned and built according to the values of the metropolitan society, as interpreted by and for the use of a colonial culture.

Figure 1.2

Figure 1.3

The residential section consists of what, according to European norms, would appear to be spacious bungalows situated in large, two-to four-acre 'compounds' (Figure 1.4) grouped round the old 'Government House' or 'Viceroy's House', now Rashtrapati Bhavan, and Secretariat. A large proportion of visual,symbolic or ceremonial space is incorporated in this lay-out (Figure 1.5). Roads, designed for a motorised elite rather than a pedestrian mass, are broad and long; in contrast to the indigenous city, climatic control is achieved by extensive tree-planting, illustrating a basic preference of the colonial culture.

Since the end of colonial rule, this extensive area has been modified, though not fundamentally changed, by further development. It remains the preferred residential location for political and Westernised business elites, senior members of the bureaucracy and a considerable international community. The main retailing centre of Connaught Place has undergone extensive re-development at much higher densities (Figure 1.6).

The third major area is that of the cantonment or permanent military camp, situated in the south-west of the city.

The largest spatial unit, if it can be accurately conceptualised as such, is represented by the vast growth of Delhi both between and around its earlier component parts since 1947. This has resulted from the accommodation of some 200,000 refugees after Partition and from the provision, in more than thirty large housing estates, of thousands of government employees (Figure 1.7). It also results from recent housing projects of the local development authority and extensive private development. In addition, many schools, colleges, specialised government agencies, national and international headquarters, and hospitals have been built as well as new educational institutions and hotels.

The sixth and last identifiable component is the constantly expanding urban fringe where an intermingling of urban and rural functions is frequent (Figure 1.8). Here Delhi has been more successful than many cities in low-income countries in accommodating some of the ceaseless flow of rural migrants who continuously fill up empty pockets of the city with temporary shacks or *jhuggies*, where they live whilst gaining a foothold on the urban economy. In Delhi, in 1970, some 25,000 of an estimated 150,000 families living in such shacks were provided with either 80 or 25 square-yard plots for 'do-it-yourself' housing in developed areas on the edge of the city. These are supplied with electricity, water, basic sewerage and some educational and medical facilities.

At the heart of this metropolitan area therefore which, in 1971, had a population of over 3,500,000, are two central, and contrasting areas, the old city, and New Delhi with its cantonment. It is around these, and the river and the ridge, that the present urban system of Delhi is formed.

Figure 1.4

Figure 1.5

Figure 1.6

Figure 1.7

Figure 1.8

These two central areas represent the urban product of two totally
different cultures, the first, Indian, originally an amalgam of
Muslim and Hindu but now predominantly the latter, the second,
the colonial form of a European and particularly British culture.
If the physical-spatial form of each of these two contrasting and
juxtaposed units is to be understood a new question has to be formulated. The problem which now needs investigation is that of how
two cultures, situated in the same geographic environment, but with
different forms of social, economic, technological and political
organisation and development, responded, under the conditions of
colonialism, to that environment and provided for human needs each
according to the values, beliefs and behaviour of its own social
and cultural system. In brief, we are examining, within a particular distribution of power, cultural responses to the environment. It is this problem which is central to our investigation.

4 CULTURE AS VARIABLE IN MAN-ENVIRONMENT STUDIES

Increasing interaction between architecture, planning and the
social sciences has, in recent years, resulted in a rapidly growing
literature on the behavioural aspects of environment. Though
valuable knowledge has accumulated on, for example, environmental
perception and the social use of space (e.g. Buttimer, 1969;
Goodey, 1971, 1972; Craik, 1973), empirical or theoretical studies
of the social, and more particularly, *cultural* variables in the
relation of behaviour to environment are still hard to find.

The major exception is the work of Rapoport, whose *House Form and
Culture* (1969) remains, with the work of E.T. Hall (1959,1966),
the standard introduction to the subject. For other studies of
cultural factors in the perception and use of space and on the
quality of the modified environment, one must turn to the relatively small place it occupies in standard anthropological mono-
graphs such as those of Evans-Pritchard (1956), Levi-Strauss(1963),
Herskovitz (1966), Hallowell (1967) and others whose work is
generally focused on so-called 'pre-literate' or non-Western cultures.

Yet studies at the cultural, as opposed to the social or personality level (Parsons, 1961,p.38), are of paramount importance if
we are to penetrate the underlying value-systems which influence
all forms of human behaviour and which transform the behaviour of
a common species man into a variety of different activities which
are clearly manifest in cultural terms. Moreover, if the value
assumptions of a society are to become the subject of analysis,
it is clear that the study of cultural factors in environmental
decision-making, and of the value orientations on which they are
based can only be undertaken within a broad, comparative and
cross-cultural framework which is itself based, if not on a utopian
'value-free', at least on a 'value-conscious' culturally relative
position (Bidney, 1968; Herskovitz, 1973).

The study of cultural factors in the utilisation of space and the
modification of built environments has both theoretical and practical importance. At the most fundamental level, members of all
human societies, irrespective of culture or location, share common
needs: food, shelter, reproduction, socialisation, security from
attack. How the members of a society provide for these needs
however, and modify their physical environment to obtain them, is
a process mediated by culture. Thus, the study of the provision
for shelter, for example, both synchronically, across cultures
distributed in space, and diachronically, through time, has value
not only in delineating the characteristics of any one particular
culture but, by identifying those attributes common to them all,
gives us an insight into those basic properties which are unique
to man as a human and social being.

For some, the most convincing example of the practical value of
such studies would be drawn from an area of concern to those
architects, planners and policy-makers whose primary problem is
the design of housing for the rapidly expanding urban areas of the
so-called 'developing' world. Here, as elsewhere, design solutions
must be congruent with the value-system and culture of the community being housed. According to a United Nations report, in
many cases minimum standards (including spatial specifications)
'emanating from a by-gone colonial era and representing an entirely
different cultural and climatic background are prevalent and even
promoted'. Such problems, it has been suggested, call for extended studies of social and cultural factors in the analysis of house
and community design to ensure that design solutions have the optimum degree of acceptibility (United Nations, 1971).

Though the need for cultural studies in relation to this particular
problem is obvious and easy to recognise, less recognition has been
accorded to the situation in countries of the more affluent Western
world. Here, it is well known that differing value-orientations
operate at various social class levels or between 'professionals'
and the public (Michelson, 1970). However, basic value assumptions,
specific to and shared by the vast majority of the members of a
culture irrespective of region or social class, have rarely - if
ever - been studied in a systematic, cross-cultural framework.
What constitutes a shared value-system across any given culture
and how such a system changes over time are still matters about
which too little is known in respect of housing and urban structure,
to say nothing of other social fields, in many societies. Despite
a vast literature in the fields of 'architectural' or 'urban
history', well-documented comparative, cross-cultural historical
studies which attempt an explanation of just *why* typical dwelling-
forms are those of the 'semi-detached' or 'terraced' house, rather
than, for example, the *apartement* as in France, or the Iroquis
long house, are still not available.

It is difficult, therefore, to disagree with Rapoport when he pleads
for a historical and cross-cultural point of view in the investigation of man's interaction with his 'natural' and built environment. Such an approach would provide the two basic matrices

of time and space within which any generalised statement can
be made (Rapoport, 1970,p.90).

5   THE COLONIAL CITY AS A LABORATORY FOR CROSS-CULTURAL RESEARCH

The understanding of any city presupposes an understanding of the
society to which it belongs. In the case of the colonial city,
this is the colonial society, of which an important though
numerically small component is the European colonial community.

As Smith points out (1965,p.xii), colonial societies provide social
science with problems and data of the utmost theoretical importance.
Colonial communities, originating in the metropolitan society, represent examples of social systems which have been established in
an alternative environment, developed mechanisms to maintain themselves and then have ultimately disappeared. Irrespective of any
influence which its members may have exercised on the host society,
the colonial community provides an opportunity for studying
fundamental social processes.

At the cultural level,an examination of such communities can tell
us of inherent, core characteristics of the metropolitan society
which, as Laslett points out in regard to the study of family
structure in the early American colonies (1965,pp.61,74), a study
of that society alone would never make apparent. On a different,
though related, aspect of the colonial community, Worsley has
written

> the style of living of the white colonial official is one
> of the neglected fields of research though much casual
> illustration exists... it is a fertile area for examining
> changes in ethic under changed social conditions: a central
> problem-area for sociological theory(1964,p.279).

In yet another context, Wilcox (1969,p.286) has affirmed that
'urban sociology... in Britain, the United States and Africa must
address itself to the nature of the relationship between coloniser
and colonised'.

With regard to the study undertaken in this book, it is evident
that whatever adaptations have to be made by representatives of
the metropolitan society as they establish a new community in
the host culture, each member carries with him his own 'conceptual
models' of his society and culture. Such conceptual models are
fundamentally important in structuring his new social world, whether
this relates to his own new community, his contact with the indigenous culture, his patterns of settlement or the means of shelter he provides for himself. The degree to which these models are
modified by contact with the host society and environment are
evidenced by the type of social order and new culture which, over
time, emerge.

It follows, therefore, that where colonial communities emanate from different metropolitan societies, having comparable levels of economic and technological development, and are established in the same host society and environment (for example, the British, French, Scandinavian, Portuguese or Dutch in India) the extent to which they differ can be attributed to the core cultural characteristics which they carry with them.

As far as general theories of urbanism and urbanisation are concerned, the colonial city provides unrivalled opportunity to examine other assumptions.

Until recently, our understanding of urbanism was dominated by theory derived from Western industrial and post-industrial models (Wheatley, 1969, p.3; Berry, 1973, p.xv; Bailey, 1975, p.53). Only in the last two decades, however, have urbanists begun to see that much of what was previously accepted as 'universally applicable urban theory' has been based on an ahistorical Western ethnocentrism. Increasingly we find that models or theories developed in the context of Western industrial urbanisation do not fit the majority of cities in the non-Western world and particularly, the 'colonial' or 'post-colonial' cities of Asia and Africa.

Here, as McGee (1971), Hauser (1965), Ginsburg (1965), Bose (1971), Qadeer (1974) and others have pointed out, neither general theories of urbanisation, such as those predicting certain types of relationships between demographic, urban and economic indices, nor of socio-spatial structure, nor of the socio-psychological characteristics of 'urbanism' are found to apply.

There is sufficient evidence to suggest that the colonial city might be treated as a distinct type. Wheatley has suggested that
the cultural hybrid of the colonial city, which typically subsumes elements of both the traditional and the modern world, and which consequently might have been expected to have excited the curiosity of urbanists, has in fact attracted little more attention than the traditional city proper... only (recently) has there been any attempt to particularise the specifically colonial features of this genre of city and to integrate it into a general theory of urbanism (1969,p.31).

Wheatley refers especially to Horvath's (1969) three models of urbanisation devised to compare types of urban development in time and space: the industrial city model, best illustrated by Wirth (1938), the pre-industrial city model of Sjoberg (1960), and a third model, the colonial city, of which the major explanatory variable is dominance. It is this latter variable which partially accounts for the fact that, in its pre-independence phase, the component sectors of the colonial city were kept separate, deliberately preventing the development of those characteristics of diffusion and interaction which are invariably assumed in any definition of the city.

The 'most important question in cross-cultural urban research', however, is most explicitly stated by Ginsburg.

The controversial issue, one that intrigues geographer, sociologist, and historian alike, turns to a considerable degree on the relationships between value systems and social organisation, on one hand, and the development of city systems and various types of urban morphological patterns, on the other....

What appears to offer greater promise by far for further study is the impact of colonially derived administration and transportation networks on the landscape and the consequence of areally differentiated economic development policies on urban structure, pattern and hierarchy....

Studies... suggest major differences between Indian cities and models of spatial arrangements hypothesised for Western cities. The nature, causes, and longevity of these differences provide an admirable field for both theoretical and applied research. One can speculate that technology, levels of living, capital available for urban improvement, caste and ethno-linguistic and religious diversity, and other cultural concomitants are involved, but to what extent and for how long?

Clearly, here is support for raising once again the most important question in cross-cultural urban research. To what extent are basic differences in culture, even given the spread of 'modern Western' technology and values, likely to give rise to different urbanisation processes and the creation of cities as artifacts that differ from culture to culture?... What kinds of cities can be expected to evolve in different societies as these societies make their decisions to select, adopt, and modify those elements that characterise Western city-building functions and structure? (1965,pp.311, 315, 319).

These and other factors suggest that the study of colonial urban development has considerable theoretical significance.

Our interest in such cities may, therefore, be purely academic. We may simply be interested in them as examples of distinctive urban systems.

On the other hand, interest may stem from the inter-related problems of poverty, housing, unemployment, and occasionally racial strife which, as elsewhere, beset such cities today. Whatever the interest, there is urgent need for an adequate explanation of the social, physical and spatial characteristics which are manifest in these cities. This study, therefore, arises from a belief that such cities have certain underlying characteristics in common and that explanations of their structure which restrict their scope to historically unique circumstances can be placed in a broader frame of reference.

6   METHODOLOGY

If one of the main objectives in studying the colonial city is
to isolate the cultural variable which helps to account for its
physical-spatial form, then, ideally, the approach to the problem
should be genuinely comparative and cross-cultural. As will be
suggested in Chapter 2, this would include a three-fold comparison
between urban and social structures in the metropolitan society,
in the indigenous society and in the colonial society. For a
number of reasons such a comprehensive approach has not been
possible.

As outlined in Chapter 3, an approach to the understanding of
urban forms in each cultural section of the colonial city can be
made by, investigating the *institutional system* of each section
and then by seeing how each institution is reflected in the physical-spatial form of the city. The reasons for limiting this
study primarily to a treatment of the forms of one section, namely
that of the European colonial community, are many. Initially, it
will be apparent that even a preliminary analysis of the urban
forms of one representative part of this cultural community (i.e.
the Europeans in Northern India) requires extensive treatment.
To undertake, even at the same level of analysis, a study of the
institutions of the indigenous culture and their physical-spatial
expression would go far beyond the scope of this present research.
This is not only because of the different religious and cultural
traditions in India, but also because of the multifarious regional
differences which exist.

A further reason for concentrating on the European colonial community is one of familiarity with its language and culture. To
investigate indigenous urban forms and the institutional system
on which they were based would require a detailed acquaintance
with the culture in question. If the treatment of indigenous
forms is to be investigated at the same level as that adopted
for those of the colonial community, then this must either be
undertaken at a later stage or left to the members of the indigenous, Indian culture.

A final factor has determined this mode of treatment. If, as will
be suggested, the culture-specific forms of the British colonial
community were diffused, not only to India, but also to other
parts of Asia and Africa, there is some justification for treating
the 'colonial urban settlement' as an ideal type. If a comparative framework is adopted, then one of the other units for
comparison becomes a generalised 'indigenous settlement area' or
'native town'. While acknowledging that each 'colonial urban
settlement' was in some way a product of culture contact processes
by which institutions of the metropolitan culture were modified
by those of the host culture with which it came into contact, as
well as the 'situational' circumstances in which this contact took
place, one may none the less recognise certain basic cultural as
well as structural characteristics which are common to the colonial
urban settlement whether it be in Africa, Asia or elsewhere.

It remains, in conclusion, to give some basic definitions of terms
already introduced and to say something about the data and
sources on which this study is based and the methodology used
to interpret them.

The following terms are used throughout

1   The *colonial city* is that urban area in the colonial society
    most typically characterised by the physical segregation of
    its ethnic, social and cultural component groups, which re-
    sulted from the processes of colonialism. It is to be dis-
    tinguished from the *ex-* or *post-colonial city*, the same urban
    area which results from modifications following the withdrawal
    of the colonial power. *Colonialism* in this context is under-
    stood as 'the establishment and maintenance, for an extended
    time, of rule over an alien people that is separate and sub-
    ordinate to the ruling power' (Emerson, 1968). The particular
    variety of colonialism relevant for this study is that as-
    sociated with Western industrial capitalism of the nineteenth
    and twentieth centuries and which emerged from what Ribeiro
    (1968) has termed 'capitalistic mercantile formations'.
        It is worthwhile noting at this point that Horvath(1972)
    has attempted to distinguish *colonialism* from *imperialism*.
    'Colonialism refers to that form of inter-group domination
    in which settlers in significant numbers migrate permanently
    to the colony from the colonising power. Imperialism is a
    form of inter-group domination wherein few, if any, permanent
    settlers from the imperial homeland migrate to the colony'
    (p.46). Although Horvath classifies India as part of an
    imperial rather than a colonial process on the basis of this
    definition, his view is not accepted in this book. First,
    because the British community in India referred to themselves
    as 'colonials' and to their society as 'a colonial society';
    second, because there were always a large number of permanent
    roles in the colonial system in India which were continuously
    filled from the metropolitan society. Note, for example,
    the observation of Buckland(1884,p.2).
        Though colonisation is usually spoken of in a different
        sense the British inhabitants of India are virtually a
        colony. The individual colonists may change but as fast
        as one man goes another steps into his place, and thus
        it comes to pass that over the whole length and breadth
        of India there is now a large and continuously growing
        colony of English families who endeavour to maintain their
        old home feelings and to keep all those old surroundings
        which remind them of their birth to which they all hope
        in due course to return.

Subsumed under the concept of the *colonial city* are

2   the *colonial urban settlement*, that sector of the colonial
    city occupied, modified and principally inhabited by represen-
    tatives of the colonising society. In India, this is typically
    referred to as the *Civil Station* (alternatively, the *Civil
    Lines)* and/or *Cantonment*, the military base.

3 The *indigenous city* or *indigenous settlement area* is that
   sector of the colonial city occupied by the indigenous
   population, and referred to, in the colonial culture, as
   the 'native city', 'native quarter' or by the Anglicised
   version of the indigenous name. This may be a traditional
   city ante-dating the coming of the colonial power or it may
   be an area of indigenous settlement, arising after, and
   usually as a result of, the establishment of the *colonial
   urban settlement*.

4 In all cases where it is clear that the experience of the
   British colonial community in India is being referred to,
   the terms *metropolitan society* and *indigenous society* refer
   to Britain and India.

5 The term *urban development*, as opposed to *urban growth*, is
   used to describe a planned or directed process, in contrast
   to one which is unplanned or 'organic'. *Physical-spatial* is
   used in a comprehensive way to include, in the first place,
   the actual built forms of an urban area housing basic human
   and social activities (habitation, economic activity,
   recreation, government, religion) as well as what is normally
   called 'architecture' (a term avoided in this study as
   generally having too limited an application). In the second
   place, it refers to the spatial areas taken up by such forms
   and relating them to each other within the entire urban area.

7 DATA

The basic data for the study were collected as a result of five
years intermittent field-work undertaken in Delhi, both consciously and sub-consciously, between 1965 and 1970. It also
includes material gathered on field-trips to some sixty major
'modern' and 'traditional' urban centres of India, including
those particularly influenced by Western contact, religious
centres, traditional North Indian fortress towns and hill stations,
mainly between 1967 and 1970.

The research is also based on material gathered as a participant-
observer of social processes in Delhi during these years and as
an observer of 'overseas communities'. Data for the pre-1947
situation has also been collected, largely at an informal level,
from informants representative of both the indigenous as well as
the metropolitan society with experience of the colonial situation.

The more historical sources, consisting of written, pictorial and
cartographic materials, have been drawn from public and private
collections. The most important of these are the India Office
Library, London (particularly, the Western Drawings Collection
and Photographic Archive) and the British Library. A comment on
the use of these is necessary.

One of the main objectives of this study is to examine the values
and assumptions relating to the natural and modified environment
of certain social groups of a particular culture and to trace
how these were transferred to another culture area.

Attitudinal and value research is a difficult enough task in
existing cultures; with those which have disappeared, the problem
becomes even more acute. As discussed in more detail below, the
method adopted in this study is to examine three types of data,
namely, the built environment actually created, the institutionally
related activities which it was meant to accommodate, and the way
the inhabitants reacted towards this environment as manifest in
the records they made of it.

Any understanding of the socially and culturally determined
responses to the environment requires, in the words of Prince
(1971,p.30), 'the ability to see the land with the eyes of its
former occupants from the standpoint of their needs and capacities'.
On an assumption that an understanding of 'how other people in
other times have perceived reality enables us to gain a fuller
knowledge of the world in which we now live'(ibid.,p.24), extensive use has been made of written and pictorial material. Where
accounts have been quoted this has been done not only to demonstrate the existence and selection of phenomena perceived but
also, how the process of perception has taken place. It is by
including such comments verbatim that values and attitudes inherent in the culture are demonstrated.

Similarly, the pictorial material in this study is included not
simply as 'illustration' of the phenomena discussed, although
it does of course fulfil this function. It is included primarily
as research data in itself, examples of existing artefacts which
in themselves are evidence of certain basic values of the culture
to which they belong. Publication costs have unfortunately prohibited more than a minute selection of over 200 illustrations
originally chosen from being included. These, however, have been
selected after an extensive search through relevant material in
the India Office collection of over 10,000 items. Such pictorial
data can be regarded as evidence of

1   the existence of the physical world as a primary category
    in the cognitive universe of the colonial culture;

2   the importance of selected 'environmental' phenomena for
    the members of that culture in their perception of this
    physical world;

3   the value of these phenomena in forming part of the *stored
    knowledge* of the culture, evidenced by the desire to *record*
    these phenomena in written and pictorial form;

4   the high value placed by culture members on this *recorded*
    knowledge, evidenced by its continued preservation in the
    'knowledge repositories' of the metropolitan society (i.e.
    libraries, museums and archives).

Whilst all graphic or photographic data is, by definition, a record
of an 'interaction' with an environment, the criteria governing the
final selection have been to include,where possible, records of
culture-specific behaviour taking place in particular environments.

The ability to undertake research of this kind has depended on
the existence of the historical data which has been drawn upon. The
sheer quantity of this, the nature of it, and the care bestowed on
its preservation are themselves evidence of fundamental cultural
attitudes to both the physical and built environment. The fact that
these data should be worth collating in a study of this kind, is
likewise evidence of the continuity of similar cultural values.

This research in the photographic archives of the India Office
Library, London,combined with experience of looking at 'snapshot'
photographs in India over a number of years,leaves clear, though
subjective and unquantifiable impressions. Photographic records
are evidence of what the photographer perceives as important phenomena
in his social and physical world. Houses, horses, kin, dogs, and
particular landscapes would seem to figure prominently in the universe
of the colonial community whilst people, particularly kin and
occupational groups,figure prominently in that of the contemporary
Indian amateur photographer. This is discussed at greater length
in Chapter 6.

In the collection of the colonial community, the sense of time
attached to a particular detail of place is often remarkable,
'Taken from the steps of the verandah, 9.15 a.m. December 15, 1935'.

The discussion of *spatial usage* in this study does not arise primarily
because the main focus of the research is that of the geographer or
physical planner. It is rather that physical form and spatial usage
are both identifiable and 'measurable' indices of inherent cultural
characteristics (Hazlehurst, 1970) as well as power relationships.
In examining these, fundamental cultural differences can be explored
and charted. In this sense, studying the material artefacts of a
culture is a means to arrive at the basic cognitive categories,
symbols, images and usages which are inherent in the culture itself.
In this context, the observation of Goodenough (1971) is worth noting
    Anthropologists have debated whether or not culture includes the
    things men make, such as the tools, bridges, roads, houses, and
    works of art, all the things to which they commonly refer as
    'material culture'. But the material objects men create are
    not in and of themselves things men learn... *What they learn*
    are the necessary precepts, concepts, recipes and skills -
    the things they need to know in order to make things that will
    meet the standards of their fellows... Here, then, we shall
    reserve the term *culture* for what is learned, for the things
    one needs to know in order to meet the standards of others.

And we shall refer to the material manifestation of what is learned as *cultural artefacts*.... *We must recognise that any cultural artefact, once created, may become a model for the creation of other artefacts, the idea of it being added to the body of standards in the culture* (pp.18-19, italics added).

Chapter 2

TOWARDS A THEORY OF
COLONIAL URBAN DEVELOPMENT

The major metropolis in almost every newly-industrialising
country is not a single unified city, but, in fact, two quite
different cities, physically juxtaposed but architecturally
and socially distinct.... These dual cities have usually been
a legacy from the colonial past. It is remarkable that so
common a phenomenon has remained almost unstudied. We have
no real case-studies of the introduction of western urban
forms into non-western countries... a knowledge of the
process whereby the former were introduced is of interest
not merely historically... but also as an example of culture
change. Anthropologists have long studied the process of
cultural diffusion of simple artifacts. How much more important to study the transplanting of man's most complex
artifact - the modern city (Janet Abu-Lughod, 'Tale of two
cities: the origins of modern Cairo', *Comparative Studies in
Society and History*, 7 (1965),p.429).

1 THE NEED FOR A THEORY OF COLONIAL URBAN DEVELOPMENT

Both before and since Abu-Lughod made these comments, many studies
have appeared relating to the phenomena she describes, though few
have been undertaken in the manner she implies. Studies exist of
'Dutch' cities in Indonesia, 'French' cities in Egypt, 'Danish',
'Dutch' and 'British' settlements in India, and especially, of
'British' cities in South-East Asia and in Africa. Sociologists,
historians, demographers, geographers and anthropologists have,
either directly or indirectly, referred to the distinctive morphology
of the colonial city, or to the equally distinctive life-style and
residential behaviour of the colonial community(Representative
studies would include Redfield and Singer, 1954; Cressey, 1956;
Murphy, 1957, 1969; Palmier, 1957; Kuper et al., 1958; Gist,1958;
Wertheim, 1964; Keyfitz, 1961; Brush, 1962, 1968, 1970; Abu-
Lughod, 1965, 1971; Hoselitz, 1962; Breeze, 1966; Kay, 1967;
McGee, 1967; Nilsson, 1968; Mabogunje, 1968a, 1968b; Gillion,1968;
Wheatley, 1969; Horvath, 1969; Swanson, 1969; Collins, 1969;
Pons, 1969; McMaster, 1970; Rex, 1970, 1973; Swanson, 1969;

Johnson, 1970; Banton, 1971; Southall, 1971; Stambouli, 1971;
Cruise O'Brien, 1972; Castells, 1972; Mitchell, 1972; Schwerdtfeger,
1972; Learmonth, 1973; Lewandowski, 1975.)

Apart from the fact that they all defy analysis in terms of Western
derived theories, such cities have other common characteristics.

1 Crudely speaking, they are all products of culture-contact
   situations between an industrialising or industrialised
   European colonial power and a 'traditional', agrarian or
   craft-based economy.
2 They all manifest certain comparable spatial characteristics,
   both in terms of the relationship between different cultural
   settlements and, within each settlement area, between its
   component parts.
3 The cities today are characterised by cultural pluralism.
4 Despite the fact that they were deliberately planned to
   promote residential segregation, they are now required to
   promote processes of integration, at the national, cultural,
   social, economic and ethnic levels.
5 In comparison with urban centres in industrial societies and,
   in many cases, according to their own administrators, these
   cities all have problems of housing, a shortage of economic
   resources, under-developed communication systems and a lack
   of the institutional infrastructure required to deal with
   social, administrative and political needs.

Though attempts have been made to develop a theory of the colonial
city (McGee, 1967; Horvath, 1969), no 'ideal type' construct has
been suggested comparable, for example, to that of Sjoberg's
'pre-industrial city' (1960). Where studies of individual cities
have been made, explanation of the spatial structure of the 'Western'
component and its relation to the indigenous city, has generally
been made in terms of unique, particularistic or culture-specific
criteria. Thus, New Delhi or Lusaka are said to be the result of
'garden city' ideas of 'town-planning', explanations which, for
the non-European social scientist, unfamiliar with the cultural
history of Europe and especially of Britain, convey little.

Such particularistic categories fail to account for the similarities
and differences identifiable in the 'Western' sector of the colonial
city and of the relationship between its component parts; nor do
they have a more universally comprehensible meaning outside the
culture in which they originate. An explanation of socio-spatial
structure is impeded, in the first place then, by an inadequate
explanation of spatial structure.

A conceptual framework is therefore needed which will

1 comprehend the essentially cross-cultural phenomena which
   are manifest in these cities,
2 permit an explanation of the similarities and differences in
   their socio-spatial structure and

3 provide some testable hypotheses which can be offered for
   empirical investigation. This is particularly important
   with regard to the theoretical issues suggested in Chapter 1
   and also, with regard to such policy-relevant, planning issues
   as housing, urban renewal, distribution of resources, communication systems and race relations.

The aim of this chapter is, therefore, to suggest an overall framework for studying the impact of colonialism on urbanisation and
urban development. By urbanisation is meant that process whereby
the proportion of a given population living in places defined as
urban increases at the expense of those living in non-urban areas;
crudely speaking, it means the increase in number of new urban
places as well as an increase in the size of existing urban
populations. Urban development implies the more limited process
of the directed growth of existing or new urban centres. The
distinction between urban growth and urban development made here
is that the latter is more consciously planned or directed.

Indeed, it is this distinction which is one of the main characteristics of the colonial city, distinguishing it from those cities in
politically autonomous, democratic societies. In these latter
cities, there was invariably a conflict of interest between those
who wished to direct urban form and the vested interests who
eschewed controls. For much of the nineteenth and twentieth
centuries - the most rapid period of growth for the industrial
city - vested interests prevailed in the competition for urban
space, with the 'planning authority' performing either a negative
or delaying function. In the colonial city there was rarely an
'urban management' problem as planning authority and vested
interest were one and the same thing (I am grateful to Michael
Safier for bringing this point to my attention).

Colonial planning affords an example of a comprehensive and positive
planning theory put into practice by government many decades before
this became feasible in the metropolitan society. As far as
British experience is concerned, prior to the 'New Towns' built
after 1945, the only other sphere where comprehensive urban development existed as an actual expression of urban and social theory was
in the private sector (e.g. Robert Owen's 'company town',
Bourneville, and other urban developments built on private,
ideologically-conceived schemes such as Welwyn Garden City).

Initially, this framework for analysing the impact of colonialism
on urbanisation is offered at a spatial or geographical level and
comprehends the study of global phenomena as well as those of a
micro-urban level. Second, within this larger spatial framework,
the more specific aim is to investigate and explain the socio-
spatial structure of the colonial and ex-colonial city and to
suggest various hypotheses which can be put to empirical investigation. The assumption in both these tasks is that physical-
spatial structure has meaning for the analysis of social structure.

In the previous chapter colonialism has been defined as 'the
establishment and maintenance, for an extended time, of rule over
an alien people that is separate and subordinate to the ruling
power', the particular variety of colonialism being that of modern
industrial capitalism.

The main conditions comprised in this form of colonialism are
threefold: first, a *contact situation between two cultures* and
the value-systems on which they are based. Second, this contact
takes place between two cultures which have *different forms or
'levels' of economic, social, technological and political
organisation and development*. Such differences result partly
from the differences in value-systems indicated above and partly
(see Balandier, 1951; Ribeiro, 1968; Hobsbawm, 1968; Brookfield,1975),
from the power structure of the colonial situation itself. Third,
the relationship in which this contact takes place is one of
dominance-dependence where the ultimate source of social, economic
and political power rests in the metropolitan society, with physical
force being the ultimate sanction in the colonised society. As
these three elements are extensively used as explanatory variables
throughout the study, some further elaboration is required.

It is clear that, initially, the first and overriding variable
is that of culture, out of which the other two variables or 'components' of colonialism, the *economic-technological order* and the
power structure of colonialism arise. Technology is a cultural
product and political systems depend, among other things, on the
values and beliefs of a culture and the political and economic
relationships they foster with other societies. Once the political
system of colonialism is effective, however, it is convenient, for
heuristic reasons, to treat the three different variables as inter-
related. The justification for this will, it is hoped, be made
evident during the course of the analysis.

Thus, the impact of colonialism on urban development in non-Western
areas is to be understood as the impact of a Western (i.e. culturally
'British'), capitalist-industrial (i.e. a form of economic-technological order) and colonial (i.e. politically dominant) power.
Support for the use of these variables in investigating colonial
urban development, derived independently in the manner outlined
above, is to be found in Sjoberg's essay on 'The modern city'
(1968). '(T)echnology, cultural values and social power appear
to be the most useful variables for predicting the changing patterns
within the modern city, that is, one built upon the industrial and
scientific revolution' (p.456). Additional confirmation exists in
Balandier's analysis (1951, pp. 54-5) in which he suggests that
the 'contact' between the colonial and metropolitan cultures arose
in the 'special circumstances of 'the colonial situation'. The
most obvious of these circumstances were (1) the domination by a
foreign minority, racially (or ethnically) and culturally different,
of an indigenous population, inferior from a material viewpoint;
(2) the linking of radically different civilisations in 'some form
of relationship'; (3) the imposition of an industrialised society

onto a non-industrialised society in (4) an 'antagonistic relationship' where the colonial people were 'subjected as instruments of
colonial power' and (5) with the need, 'in maintaining this
domination, not only to resort to force but to a system of pseudo-
justifications and stereotyped behaviour' (I am grateful to Susan
Lewandowski for drawing my attention to this reference).

In any explanation of the social and spatial structure of the
colonial city, or indeed, of the impact of colonialism on the larger
environment, it is essential that these three variables, briefly,
if somewhat inaccurately summarised as *culture*, *technology* and the
power structure of colonialism, implicit in the concept of modern
industrial colonialism, are acknowledged.

2   A CONCEPTUAL FRAMEWORK FOR THE STUDY OF COLONIAL URBANISATION

The underlying assumption in the following framework is that all
urban phenomena which it seeks to comprehend are part of a colonial
system, at the centre of which is the metropolitan power (c.f.
Balandier, 1951,pp.42,55). The notion of system implies that all
its component parts are inter-dependent and that an understanding
of any one of these parts requires that it be approached in terms
of its relationship to the whole.

The colonial system which is described here is one which, though
usually considered as primarily economic, political and administrative in character, has also significant social, cultural and
cognitive attributes.

With the definitions suggested above, the impact of colonialism
on urbanisation and urban development can be examined at six
discreet but inter-related levels (Table 2.1). Though it is clear
that the analysis at all these levels (with the exception of the
second) can be carried out both with regard to the metropolitan
as well as the colonial society, this study is largely concerned
with the latter. For purposes of illustration, the experience
of Britain and India is used to indicate the metropolitan/colonial
society relationship.

1   Global (inter-cultural)

This level is essentially cognitive and comprehends the knowledge
and assumptions regarding urban systems (particularly urban planning)
derived by members of colonial and ex-colonial societies from the
metropolitan society. This may result either from their experience of 'Western' colonial urban settlements situated in the
colonised society, from direct experience of Western industrial
urban systems or from institutions for planning education in the
metropolitan society. This might be alternatively expressed as
one aspect of 'cultural colonialism' where the cognitive processes
of decision-making in the colonial and ex-colonial society are

TABLE 2.1 A conceptual framework for the study of colonial urbanisation

Scale of geographic unit	Dimension	Scale of social unit	Type of phenomena considered	Illustration
1 Global	Macro	Inter-cultural	Cognitive	Knowledge of urban systems, planning theory
2 International or 'imperial'	Sub-macro	Inter-societal	'Centre-periphery', 'cultural pluralism'	'Third country urbanisation and urban development'
3 National	Major	Societal	Economic, organisational, spatial, cultural	Sea-ports, district towns, colonial capital, 'cantonments', 'hill stations' considered as a *system*
4 Urban	Intermediate	Urban	Social, spatial, cultural, economic, technological	'Colonial city' structure: 'native city'/'cantonment'/ 'civil station'
5 Sector	Minor	Community	Social, spatial, cultural, economic	'Colonial urban settlement' structure: 'indigenous city' structure, 'cantonment structure'
6 Unit	Micro	Institutional (domestic or public)	Built-form (architectural), social, cognitive, cultural, economic	Residential units: 'bungalow-compound', courtyard-house, church, mosque, temple, barracks

dominated by value-systems, models and 'urban solutions' prevailing in the metropolitan society. (See, for example, Fonseca's
analysis of the proposed re-development of the walled city of
Delhi (1971), subsequently questioned by Jagmohan (1975), in which
it is implied that 'Westernised' planners ignore or reject traditional
value-systems of the inhabitants and propose re-development of high-
density areas by low-density housing schemes.)

Logically, this level of analysis would also be appropriate for an
investigation of the processes by which knowledge and assumptions
about urban systems in colonial and ex-colonial societies are derived by members of the metropolitan society.

2   Inter-national or 'imperial' (inter-societal)

Analysis at this level examines the pattern of urbanisation and
urban development in those parts of the total colonial territorial
area (the 'Empire' or 'Commonwealth') which result from the economic
and political policies of colonialism and which were previously
either relatively uninhabited or, in comparison with the metropolitan society, at lower levels of economic development. These
include those areas where the prime colonial function was one of
agricultural or mineral exploitation such as, for example, of
sugar, cotton, tea, cocoa, rubber, rare metals and stones. In
those areas where such policies were practised (West Indies,
South and South-East Asia, South and East Africa), particular
patterns of urbanisation resulted and, as a result of the trans-
plantation of millions of people from one culture area to another,
particular configurations in the spatial and social structure of
urban development took place (e.g. Durban, Kampala, Hong Kong,
Singapore,Port Louis/Mauritius)(see also Amin, 1974, Introduction).

Other urban places developed as part of a colonial urban system
would include what Castells terms the 'centre d'affaires'
(Castells, 1972,p.65), in this case, links in the communications
network between various parts of the system (e.g. 'coaling stations'
such as Gibraltar, Valetta and Aden).

3   National (societal)

This level of analysis focuses on the characteristics of urbanisation and urban development, resulting from the processes
of colonialism, in the two societies concerned, the colonised and
the metropolitan. In the colonised society, such patterns can be
examined in terms of *function* or in terms of *scale and locality*.
In either case, the distinctive pattern of urbanisation and urban
development would be analysed in comparison to patterns in non-
colonial societies.

A *functional* analysis would classify towns in terms of their
major functions such as

a   Economic/commercial (sea-ports, e.g. Bombay, Calcutta,
    Madras; market centres)
b   Administrative (district towns, sub-district towns,
    provincial towns)
c   Political-administrative (provincial capitals, colonial capital,
    metropolitan capital)
d   Strategic (cantonments)
e   Residential/recreational (hill stations, 'sanitaria')

An alternative classification can be made in terms of *scale/
locality* (i.e. numerical size of 'colonial' population and distance from colonial capital)

a   Individual settlement area (planter, isolated official)
b   District town ('colonial' population including the district
    officer, judge, missionary, civil surgeon, engineer, district
    superintendent of police)
c   Provincial capital and cantonment (as in (b), but with
    larger civilian, military and private (commercial) population)
d   Major ports and colonial capital

At this level, particular attention would be paid to *inter-urban*
relationships, to the communication system linking the various
urban centres and to the economic and political policies of
colonialism determining the total pattern.

In the metropolitan society, the impact of colonialism on urbanisation and urban development is best examined in terms of
function.   This could be economic/commercial

a   Urban areas, such as industrial centres and ports (e.g.
    Liverpool) primarily dependent on the import and manufacture
    of colonially derived raw materials
b   Land and property development resulting from the investment
    of resources derived from colonial trading
c   The communications system (especially railways) developed
    as part of the colonial system

or residential

    Selected towns and semi-rural areas (e.g. coastal resorts,
    'Home Counties') preferred as residential locations by
    returned colonial ex-patriates, or benefitting by their
    patronage (i.e. in providing educational facilities for
    their children).

No sociological attention has been given to this latter phenomenon,
long recognised in the lay knowledge of society. For example, the
large number of 'returned ex-patriates' retiring in certain south-
coast resorts of the metropolitan society and the significance
of other urban places (e.g. Cheltenham) as preferred residential

and educational areas for the same group. Rex has drawn attention
to the stereotypes of 'colonial populations', based on the experience of large numbers of the metropolitan society in colonial
societies during military service, and the importance of such
stereotypes in structuring race relations situations(Rex,1973,p.89).

4   Urban

This level of analysis concentrates on the social, physical and
spatial development, over time, of the individual city within the
colonial system as modified by that system. Emphasis here is on
intra-urban relationships and the various characteristics of
those sectors of the urban area developed by their respective
inhabitants. In the colonised society these would include the
indigenous inhabitants, the non-indigenous or colonial inhabitants
and, where present, what Horvath terms the 'intervening' group
(i.e. those imported from a third territory in the colonial system,
such as the Chinese in Kuala Lumpur or the Asians in Kampala).

This level is represented by the 'colonial city' concept developed
by Horvath (1969) and McGee (1967) an understanding of which
demands 'an analysis of demographic, social, political, religious
and educational structures within both a temporal and spatial
framework (Horvath 1969,p.76). In India, the various parts of the
'colonial city' include the 'native city', the 'colonial urban
settlement' (the 'civil station' and 'cantonment') and occasionally
other functional areas.

The analysis of such a city would take place within a framework
which compared its social, physical and spatial development to
culturally comparable cities which had not been subject to the
colonial experience.

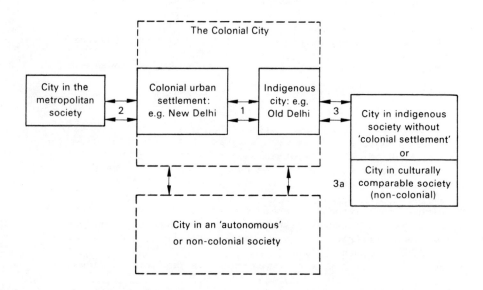

In the colonial city are 'the various social groupings brought together by the colonial situation' which, according to Balandier (1951, pp.46-7) are the representatives of the colonial power, other white 'foreigners', the 'coloured' and the colonised population. The 'ensuing social hierarchy is based on criteria of race and nationality'(ibid).

It would be an appropriate research task to examine how far the colonial city modifies the traditional social structure or even replaces it by a new class structure based on metropolitan or colonial social categories (ibid,pp.43-4). The case study of Delhi, for example, shows how the development of a colonial city resulted in the partial break-down of a traditional, territorial-based social structure associated with religious, ethnic, caste and socio-occupational criteria (in the old city) and the building up of a new, territorial-based system of class linked to occupational, socio-economic and racial groupings (see Chapter 10).

5 Sector (community)

At this level, the analysis concentrates on the social and spatial structure and social relationships related to both within each of the distinct areas of the colonial city as described in para- graph 4 above. Such an analysis would be undertaken within a tripartite comparative framework which took account of the social and spatial structure of cities in the 'parent' society of each of the two, or three main groups. For example, the social and spatial patterns manifest in the 'colonial urban settlement' of New Delhi would be examined in comparison,first,to patterns in the indigenous city of Old Delhi, as well as those prevailing in urban centres in the metropolitan society of Britain (1 and 2 in the preceding diagram). Similarly, patterns of the in- digenous city would be compared not only to those in the colonial urban settlement (cf.1) but also, to those in other cities in the indigenous society (if such exist) not subject to immediate colonial influence (cf.3). Additionally, indigenous city patterns can be compared to those of cities in culturally comparable societies which have not been subject to colonial rule (cf.3a). Likewise, the social and spatial structure of the settlement area of the 'intervening group', where it existed, would be examined in relation to patterns prevailing in the parent society of that group (i.e. the social and spatial structure of Indian communities in East Africa seen in comparison to their original structure in India).

The important point here is that the urban forms of the colonial urban settlement, whether in their social or their physical-spatial form, were not, as Castells, for example,maintains, 'reproductions of the towns of the metropolitan society' (1972,p.65). They are rather unique entities, the products of the three essential elements of industrial-capitalist colonialism which have been indicated above.

In the metropolitan society, analysis at this level would focus on
those parts of the metropolitan capital and possibly other urban
centres, developed as a result of colonialism. These might be
areas of urban development financed by colonially derived investment, or residential areas preferred by returning colonial ex-
patriates. In the early nineteenth century, for example, 80 per
cent of the 30 Directors of the East India Company lived within
an area of 1 by ½ a mile in the metropolitan capital of London
(Marylebone, Baker St, Harley St) (see Cohn,B.S. (1966)p.109).
In the later nineteenth century, large areas of the south side
of the metropolitan capital were developed as a result of the
colonial connection. The Horniman Estate (tea), the estate of
Sir John Tate (of the Tate Gallery and numerous Tate Libraries
in the metropolitan capital) (sugar), and that of Sir John Anderson
(founder of the Peninsular and Orient Shipping line) are all within
a radius of a few miles. The estates are now either public parks
or belong to educational institutions.

In the early twentieth century, South Kensington was known to
colonial ex-patriates as 'Asia Minor' on account of the large
number of 'colonial-returned' living there. In the 1850s, a
retired Indian civil servant invested £116,000 into building
houses on Kensington Park Estate (Reeder, 1972, p.64). St John's
Wood, in the north of the metropolitan capital, was a preferred
residential area for members of the Indian Army in the late
nineteenth century (Lambert, 1879,p.43).

6 Unit (institutional)

The last level at which the impact of colonialism on urban development can be examined is at the unit or micro level. This level
focuses attention on the comparative study of individual urban
units (such as the values, attitudes, behaviour and system of
social relations determining, for example, dwelling forms, residential space, institutional building) as conceived and constructed
by representatives of the various inhabitants of the city. In
the colonial city, for example, the bungalow-compound complex,
the basic residential unit of the colonial community, is compared
both to the 'house and garden' of the metropolitan society as well
as the 'courtyard house' of the indigenous community; spatial provision for recreation in the colonial urban settlement is compared
to similar spatial provision in the metropolitan society and in
the indigenous community; the church is compared to its counterpart in the metropolitan society as well as the mosque or temple
in the indigenous community.

In the metropolitan society, analysis of the impact of colonialism
on urban development at this level concentrates primarily on individual institutions resulting from the colonial connection.
These may be financial or administrative on one hand, or social
and cultural on the other. In the first category would come banks,
insurance companies, commercial houses, specialising in colonial
transactions; in the second, educational institutes (both schools

and colleges), clubs, as well as repositories of knowledge and artefacts (libraries and museums) which are found in the metro- politan society but are not reproduced in the urban structure of either colonised or non-colonial societies.

At all six levels, explanations of all urban phenomena are to be sought in terms of the three variables inherent in the concept of colonialism: culture contact, difference in forms of social, economic and technological organisation, and the dominance- dependence relationship of colonialism.

Having proposed, largely at a spatial level, these six categories for examining the impact of colonialism on urbanisation and urban development, the remainder of this chapter concentrates on this impact at the urban or colonial city level.

3   SOCIO-SPATIAL STRUCTURE IN THE COLONIAL CITY

An 'ideal type' colonial city consisted of either two or three major parts. The first was the area of indigenous settlement, sometimes pre-dating the colonial era and occasionally manifesting the socio-spatial structure of Sjoberg's 'pre-industrial city'. Alternatively, it may have been a small town or village which grew as a result of its proximity to the incoming colonial power.

The second element is what is variously described as the 'modern' 'Western' or 'European' sector but which this study terms the 'colonial urban settlement'. This may, or may not, include - as it often does in India - a cantonment, or military station. Many 'colonial' towns and cities might consist of this simple, twofold structure. Others, especially in East Africa or the Far East, incorporate a third sector or number of sectors, mainly occupied by migrants from other colonial territories brought in by the colonial power. In Africa, this description needs modification in that the area of indigenous habitation, the 'native town' might have been 'planted' by the colonial power.

Briefly, what we have in the colonial settlement is what one might mistakenly compare to an early twentieth-century upper, or middle- class European suburb: large residential plots containing spacious, one-storey houses, broad, tree-lined roads, low residential density (less than 20 persons per acre), and the generous provision of amenities (water, electricity, sewerage, telephones, open space). In the indigenous area, on the other hand, one has high residential density (upwards of 1,000 persons per acre in parts of Old Delhi), traditional, or modified traditional housing and, in contrast with the colonial urban settlement, very low levels of amenity. Com- pared to the colonial settlement area, transport is usually by foot. These two areas are frequently spatially quite separate, there being anything from one to three miles between them. In other types of 'colonial city' there may be other spatial areas occupied by other ethnic groups (Horvath's 'intervening inhabitants').

Post-independence developments have led to a spatial, if not a
cultural or social integration of these spatially separated units
by a process of residential and institutional 'infilling'. Lastly,
a permanent process of in-migration has added squatter settlements,
which, depending on the Asian or African context, are variously
known as *bustees*, *jhuggies*, *shanty towns* or *bidonvilles*, to the
urban fringe as well as vacant lots in the city.

The objectives, in attempting to account for this structure,
are

1 to show how each separate spatial unit of the original
   colonial city is related to its social structure which in
   turn is accounted for by a culture-specific system of values;
2 to show how the *total* urban system, comprised of all the
   elements listed, is determined by the overall social and
   political structure.

It is clear therefore, that to understand these various phenomena,
both physical and non-physical, a conceptual framework must be
evolved which comprehends all of them. Thus, if we are to understand the socio-spatial structure of the indigenous Indian city
we need a framework which will take into account basic value
orientations, the system of social organisation, in this case,
caste in its social and occupational dimensions, the religious
ideology which legitimises it, as well as the physical-spatial
structures which, on the one hand it produces and on the other,
in which it is contained.

The most satisfactory framework for understanding these various
elements is that provided by combining Brookfield's concept of a
'man-environment system' (1969) with Hallowell's notion of a
'culturally constituted behavioural environment' which is perceived and functions within the culture-specific categories of
its users (1967). The advantage of utilising these two concepts
is that each main area of the city can be treated as an independent and viable culture area, where expectations from the environment expressed in terms of a particular culture, are balanced by
returns derived from it.

4   THE COMPONENT PARTS OF THE COLONIAL CITY

Three variables, inherent in the concept of colonialism, have been
suggested as essential for understanding the socio-spatial structure of the colonial city, *culture*, *technology* and the *power
structure of colonialism*.

Culture. The first characteristic of the colonial city is that it
is the product of a contact situation between at least two different
cultures. The implication of this is that there exist, in the
indigenous and colonial sectors of the city, areas of urban space,
'allocated' by the power relations of colonialism, which are
perceived, structured and utilized according to value-systems

unique to the culture in question. It is these value-systems which
legitimize the religious, social, economic and political institutions of the culture and it is these institutions which determine the physical-spatial form of each settlement area. For
example, caste is a form of social organisation which can only be
explained in cultural terms. It comprehends, with its notions of
purity, pollution and hierarchy, a system of 'social space' which
partially accounts for the physical-spatial form of the city. The
belief-system of Hinduism requires that the dead be cremated:
those of Islam or Christianity, that they be buried. In one area
of the city there are no burial grounds, in others, there are.

Similarly, in the colonial urban settlement or 'European' sector,
though social and spatial patterns can be explained, as will be
shown, in terms of technology and the prevailing power structure,
certain forms of social organisation and kinds of culturally
preferred visual experience, unique to members of the metropolitan
society, account for particular physical-spatial characteristics
on the settlement area, both in India and elsewhere. In this way
the built forms and spatial morphology of each cultural section
can be explained in terms of the institutions of each culture,
understood as systems of values, ideas and behaviour.

Accordingly, with the variable of *culture* are explained those
characteristics of the indigenous or colonial areas which can
be put down to culture-specific values, and which cannot be
explained in terms of the two other variables. A more detailed
account is given in Chapter 3.

Technology is an inadequate abbreviation to indicate that the
colonial settlement is not only a product of cultural interaction
but also of cultures with very different forms of technological,
social, economic and political organisation and development. In
a grossly over-simplified way, it can be said that the colonial
urban settlement expresses the physical, spatial and social forms
of the industrial city which, in turn, result from the use of
inanimate sources of energy - steam-power, electricity, and, in
the twentieth century, the internal combustion engine, rather than
man and animal power. By the same logic, the indigenous settlement area is the product largely of an agrarian and craft-based
economy, based on animate sources of energy.

In the colonial urban settlement or 'European' sector of the city,
two physical-spatial characteristics have to be explained. The
first is the overall spatial character of the settlement itself.
The second, its location with respect to the indigenous settlement
area. As both of these are discussed in detail in Chapters 5 and
6, only the more general categories of explanation are touched
on here.

The socio-spatial structure of the colonial urban settlement can
be understood in terms of two reference models. The first of these
is to be found in earlier patterns of colonial settlement in the
indigenous society; the second, in the urban forms of the

metropolitan society already determined by an advanced state of
industrial urbanisation. The more important spatial, temporal
and social consequences of this process can be briefly summarised
as follows.

Spatially, it meant that functional specialization of land use
had taken place, resulting in the separation of place of work from
place of residence. Temporally, it meant a division of time in
which human and social activities were clearly organised into two
distinct categories, work and non-work. This in turn meant, for
the industrial urban population, that not only were work and
residence separate but also, place of residence was separate from
place of recreation. Socially, the elite-mass dichotomy characteristic of pre-industrial society had been replaced by a social
structure which was increasingly differentiated in terms of
occupation, income, life-style and, of particular importance
for our analysis, location, style and scale of residential expectation. There was, therefore, in the metropolitan society, as
part of this process of social differentiation, an emerging middle
and upper-middle-class elite from whose ranks the residents of
the colonial urban settlement were drawn.

It is in terms of these processes that the characteristics of the
colonial urban settlement can be at least partially explained.
With regard to residential provision, norms of accommodation and
'residential style' are those of the metropolitan middle-class
elite, though with two important qualifications. The first
results from the existence of another reference model, namely,
earlier patterns of colonial settlement in the indigenous society.
The second is explained by the third variable, the power-structure
of colonialism, to be discussed subsequently.

With regard to institutional provision on the colonial settlement,
these are the institutions required by the stage of urban development and accepted cultural norms prevailing in the metropolitan
society: the church, club, library, theatre, park, race-course
and, occasionally, the museum. Apart from the European barracks
on the cantonment, there is nothing on the colonial urban settlement which can be said to represent 'working-class housing' as
there is no 'working class', in its modern, urban-industrial sense,
their function being performed, albeit in a totally different
capacity, by inhabitants of the indigenous town or those in the
rural villages. The only other metropolitan 'working-class'
institutions existing in the colonial city are the 'canteen',
'Temperance Rooms', 'Presbyterian' or 'Wesleyan Chapel' which,
like the 'barracks', are confined to the cantonment.

A further outcome of the process of industrialisation was the increasing competence of the society, both in terms of knowledge as
well as organisation, in dealing with the kind of social disorgan-
isation which it generated. As far as organisation is concerned,
this meant new institutions (local government), new methods of
social control (police), new technologies (transport, communications,
energy systems), new occupational roles (civil engineers, sanitary

inspectors) and new systems for promoting and organising knowledge (institutionalised research, professional associations, scientific journals). Of the new knowledge that was promoted, the most important was the scientific and medical theory which explained - or purported to explain - the breakdown in the man-environment relationship which industrial-urbanisation brought about and which manifested itself in rates of mortality and morbidity which exceeded previous levels of tolerance.

These developments, both in organisation and knowledge, are reflected in the institutions and socio-spatial structure of the colonial city. Thus, in the indigenous city in India are to be found the town hall, police stations, public works offices, water works and library, to mention only the most common.

Of more significance, physical space in the colonial settlement and between it and the indigenous city, is organised according to mid- and late nineteenth-century scientific and especially medical theories which, in brief, assume a causal connection between aerial distance and bacterial infection. Such theories were a direct outcome of industrial urbanisation in the metropolitan society.

To summarise: one has in the metropolitan society an urban system which, in its socio-spatial dimension, is the outcome of a two-century long process of social and technical transformation. Fundamentally, it arises from a value system which generates the 'scientific revolution'; this, in its turn, produces the new energy systems which lead to industrialisation. Industrialisation, embracing a whole series of social, economic, technological and organisational processes, and taking place within an interdependent system of political-economic relationships, produces a unique pattern of urbanisation and urban development, with an equally unique social structure.

As far as this chapter is concerned, the importance of these processes is that the social structure and physical-spatial forms of the metropolitan city which they produced, provide an important reference model for the colonial urban settlement. It is these which partly explain the characteristic lay-out, the 'sanitary space' dividing individual units within the system as well as the system as a whole from the indigenous settlement area, typical of such cities as Delhi or Lusaka. It is these processes which also produce a particular social structure which has its origin, as well as its main reference group, in the metropolitan society. However, to understand why such spatial and social forms in the colonial settlement, whilst being comparable to those of urban systems in the European metropolitan society, are none the less quite different from them we must consider the last and most important variable, the power structure of colonialism.

Power structure of colonialism. The third element inherent in the concept of colonialism is the dominance-dependence relationship. This is a crucial explanatory variable, for it is clear that urban forms can result from processes of culture contact, even where such cultures manifest different forms and 'levels' of organisation and development without resulting in the particular patterns which characterise the colonial city. These patterns may be described as those of social, ethnic and spatial segregation and, in comparison with the 'organic' growth of cities in politically autonomous societies, of spatial distortion.

The dominance-dependence relationship intercedes at two levels. First, the colonised society is dependent on the metropolitan. One consequence of this is that the colonial settlement is primarily devoted to political, military and administrative functions. Their inhabitants keep order, administer justice, control aspects of the economy but not, as is the case in the industrial city, generate production. It is this kind of phenomenon which Castells (1972), has in mind in his concept of 'dependent urbanisation': urbanisation takes place in the colonial society but the industrialisation, which historically has generated urbanisation in modern, politically autonomous societies, takes place in the metropolitan society. Significantly, the colonial urban settlement in the Indian colonial city consisted of the 'cantonment' and the 'civil station'. In the 'civil station' of a typical, small town, lived those members of the colonial bureaucracy whose political, administrative and cultural function is manifest in their designations, the 'collector', 'magistrate', 'judge', 'district superintendant of police', 'civil surgeon', 'missionary' and 'teacher'. In addition, there were representatives of European business interests as well as, in the later stages, those members of the indigenous society who either belonged to the colonial bureaucracy or who subscribed, economically and culturally, to the values of the colonial system. In the cantonment lived the army, the ultimate means of social control. The colonial urban settlement then, contained the 'managers' of the colonial system.

The conception of India as an extension of the capitalist economic system is well illustrated by the following quotation from the *Report of the Parliamentary Committee on Colonisation and Settlement(India)*. (Parliamentary Papers, Session 3, December 1857 - August 1858, VII, part 1, paragraph 4). The Chairman (William Ewart) questions a witness (Maj. Gen. G.B. Tremenheere) with long experience of India

CHAIRMAN: You are aware that the object of the Committee is to inquire into the question of settlement by Europeans in India: do you conceive that on account of the peculiar desirableness of applying European capital to India there is a material distinction to be taken between colonisation in India and what we call colonisation in other countries?

WITNESS: There is a very great distinction. Colonisation cannot proceed in India as it does in Australia and Canada: *it must spring from the upper, rather than the lower ranks of society, by the settlement of capitalists; that is, from the capitalist, rather than from the labourer.*

CHAIRMAN: You consider that whereas emigration generally moves from below upwards, *in this case, it would have to move from above downwards, by the settlement of capitalists in the country who shall employ the labourers, not by the labourers who work for the capitalists?*

WITNESS: Exactly.

CHAIRMAN: *In fact, the employment of Indian labour by English capitalists?*

WITNESS: Yes.   (Italics added)

Second, the dominance-dependence relationship can be seen at the city level. Here, for a variety of reasons other than those already discussed,the indigenous and colonial parts of the city were kept apart. Such reasons were economic, social, political and racial. Banton has shown why ethnic segregation characterised the colonial city in Africa (1971). This was either explicit and legally enforced through the creation of distinct areas (or 'reserves') for different racial groups with separate (and unequal) facilities, or it was implicit (as in twentieth-century 'imperial' India), with residential areas so characterised by cultural characteristics or economic deterrents (for example, the cost of land and housing) as to effectively prevent residential infiltration except by those willing and able to adopt the attributes and life-style of the colonial inhabitants. Movement into such areas, as a mark of social mobility, meant that 'modernisation' was necessarily 'Westernisation'. These were the 'culturally constituted behavioural environments' of the colonial community.

The segregation of areas performed numerous functions, the first of which was to minimise contact between colonial and colonised populations (Balandier,1951,p.47). For the colonial community they acted as instruments of control, both of those outside as well as those within their boundaries. They helped the group to maintain its own self-identity, essential in the performance of its role within the colonial social and political system. They provided a culturally familiar and easily recognisable environment which - like dressing for dinner - was a formal, visible symbol providing psychological and emotional security in a world of uncertain events.

Segregation of the indigenous population provided ease of control in the supervision of 'native affairs'. It was economically useful in cutting down the total area subject to maintenance and development. The colonial environment offered a model for emulation by members of the indigenous society (ibid). Segregation was also an essential element in preserving the existing social structure where residential separation in environments differing widely in levels of amenity and environmental quality simply reflected existing social relationships. Segregation had many other functions and Wirth's essay on 'The Ghetto'(1927) provides a useful insight into many of them.

> The ghetto... indicates the ways in which cultural groups
> give expression to their own heritage when transplanted
> to a strange habitat; it evidences... the forces through
> which the community maintains its integrity and continuity...
> the spatially separated and socially isolated community
> seemed to offer the best opportunity for following their
> religious precepts, their established ritual and diet, and
> the numerous functions which tied the individual to familial
> and communal institutions.... There was the item of a common
> language, of community of ideas and interest, and the mere
> congeniality that arises even between strangers who, coming
> from the same locality, meet in a strange place.
>   The ghetto... was a self-perpetuating group to such an
> extent that it may be properly called a closed community....
> it is... a cultural community (and) can be completely under-
> stood only if it is viewed as a sociopsychological, as well
> as an ecological phenomenon: for it is not merely a physical
> fact, but also a state of mind (pp.85, 98).

It would, however, be misleading if no reference were made to the
contribution of the indigenous culture to the maintenance of this
system. Though the overall distribution of power was fundamentally
important in maintaining this system of social and spatial segregation, indigenous socio-spatial categories, inherent in the
system of caste, are not to be ignored. It is clear that
traditional values were important in preserving the structure of
the indigenous city, as well as the distribution of power.

The physical segregation of the urban population in the colonial
city on the basis, ostensibly, of political and socio-economic
criteria, but effectively, on ethnic and cultural criteria as well,
has numerous implications, not least of which is the tendency for
the behaviour of all ethnic groups to be explained in what Mitchell
calls 'categorical' terms. 'Thus, any person recognised as a member
of a particular race is expected to behave in a standardised way'
(1966,p.53; see also Balandier, 1951,p.48). It is clear that
this process of classification is greatly assisted by the fact
of physical segregation.

The colonial city was a 'container' of cultural pluralism but one
where one particular cultural section had the monopoly of political
power (Rex,1970,p.20). The extensive spatial provision within the
colonial settlement area, as well as the spatial division between
it and the indigenous settlement, are to be accounted for not
simply in terms of cultural differences but in terms of the distribution of power. Only this can explain why labour and urban
amenities were available in the spacious, cultivated areas in the
colonial settlement, but not in the indigenous town.

Chapter 3

THE SOCIAL AND CULTURAL CONTEXT
OF COLONIAL URBAN DEVELOPMENT

> In a culturally homogenous society, such institutions (as)
> marriage, the family, property, religion and the like are common
> to the total population... where cultural plurality obtains,
> different sections of the total population practise different
> forms of these common institutions....
>
> In a culturally divided society, each cultural section has
> its own relatively exclusive way of life, with its own dis-
> tinctive systems of action, ideas and values and social relations.
> Often, these cultural sections differ also in language, material
> culture, and technology (M.G. Smith, *The Plural Society in the
> British West Indies*, 1965, p.81).

1 INSTITUTIONS AS THE CORE OF CULTURE

An examination of the relationship between social and cultural factors and the physical-spatial form of the colonial city imposes two
preliminary obligations. The first is that of clarifying the terms
'social' and 'cultural' as they are used in this study; the second,
of describing the particular social structure in which colonial
urban development took place.

One of the most frequently quoted statements on the meaning of
society and culture is that of Firth.

> The terms represent different facets or components in basic
> human situations. If... society is taken to be an organised
> set of individuals with a given way of life, culture is that
> way of life. If society is taken to be an aggregate of social
> relations, then culture is the content of those relations.
> Society emphasises the human component, the aggregate of people
> and the relations between them. Culture emphasises the component
> of accumulated resources, immaterial as well as material, which
> the people inherit, employ, transmute, and transmit(1951,p.27).

More recent formulations of the meaning of culture,however, have
emphasised the cognitive and ideational, the sets or meanings and
symbols around which cultures are organised, the beliefs and

knowledge which are needed by an individual to be accepted by and function in any role of a particular cultural group (Goodenough,1971).

Since conceptualisations are many and varied, it is important to recognise that definitions are operational tools devised for particular types of analysis. It follows that conceptualisations such as these are not necessarily the most suitable for analysing the particular social and cultural context we are concerned with here, namely, the *plural* culture and society of colonial India, one in which two or more different cultural traditions characterise the population of a given society. Furnivall regarded a plural society as 'a unit of disparate parts which owes its existence to external factors and lacks a common social will' (Smith, 1965,p.80). It was because of a similar concern with the plural society of the British West Indies that Smith developed an alternative understanding of these basic terms.

For Smith, Firth's conceptualisation is unsatisfactory in that 'it implies that culture and society are always conterminous and inter-dependent', a view which 'obstructs the recognition of culturally heterogeneous units' as, for example, are presented by the co-existence of indigenous Hindu, Muslim and immigrant European cultures in the single society of colonial India.

Smith argues that the core of a culture is what he describes as its 'institutional system', an institution comprising 'set forms of activity, groupings, rules, ideas and values'. More particularly it is

a form or system of activities characteristic of a given population. Institutional activities involve groups.... Moreover, institutional activities and forms of groupings are also sanctioned by normative beliefs and values, and social values are expressed in institutional rules. The basic institutions of a given population are the core of a people's culture; and since society consists of a system of institutionalised relations, a people's institutions form the matrix of their social structure. Thus, the description of social structure consists in the analysis of the institutional system of the population under study....

As institutions combine both social and cultural facts equally, they have been treated as social forms by some writers and cultural forms by others. Their *social* aspects consist of set forms of groupings and relations. Their system of norm and activity, together with their material culture, properly belong to culture.

Having thus established the basic notions of *institution* and *institutional system*, Smith then shows how these may be used to illuminate both the nature of the plural society and the quality of relationships between its component parts.

When groups that practise differing institutional systems live side by side under a common government, the *cultural plurality* of this inclusive unit corresponds with its *social plurality*

and the network of social relations between these culturally
distinct groups is wider and more complex than those within
them....

In a culturally homogenous society, such institutions (as)
marriage, the family, property, religion and the like are common
to the total population... where cultural plurality obtains,
different sections of the total population practise different
forms of these common institutions.... By virtue of their cultural and social constitution, plural societies are units only
in a political sense.

The culturally distinctive components of a single society are its
cultural sections which are distinguished by practising different
forms of institutions. In such a culturally divided society each
cultural section has

its own relatively exclusive way of life, with its own distinctive systems of action, ideas and values and social relations. Often, these cultural sections differ also in language,
material culture and technology. The culture concept is normally
wider than that of society since it includes conventions, language and technology.

Whilst the basic institutional system of each cultural section includes kinship, education, religion, law, property and economy,
recreation, it does not include government for an obvious reason,
namely, that the continuity of plural societies as single units is
'incompatible with an internal diversity of governmental institutions'.

Given the fundamental differences of belief, value and
organisation that connote pluralism, the monopoly of power
by one cultural section is the essential precondition for
the maintenance of the total society in its current form....
When the dominant section is also a minority... the dependence
on regulation by force is greatest (Smith, 1965, pp.80-86).

Smith's account has been drawn on so heavily because of its heuristic
value in understanding those aspects of the social structure and
plural society of colonial India with which we are here concerned.

The theory can now be examined in relation to the central problem
of the study. Though it is recognised that what in colonial times
was called 'British India' did not, because of the existence of the
so-called 'native states', include the entire population of the
Indian sub-continent, the relative dependence of these states none
the less justifies the treatment of the entire population of the
sub-continent as one society, in Smith's terms. The cultural sections practising different forms of basic or 'compulsory' institutions were those of the indigenous population and that of the
European colonial community, referred to subsequently, as discussed
below, as the *colonial third culture*. It is this section which has,
of course, the monopoly of power.

2   INSTITUTIONS AS INSTRUMENTS FOR
   THE EXAMINATION OF URBAN FORM

For an understanding of the physical-spatial structure of the
colonial city, the most useful aspect of Smith's analysis is his
focus on institutions as the core of a people's culture. For it is
evident that any physical or spatial aspect of the colonial city,
in any cultural section, relates to the provision made for a particular institution in that section. As all structures or spatial
areas are related to some human, social or cultural purpose, to
understand these purposes requires the understanding of the institutions of the culture. It follows that to understand the institutions is to understand the particular built forms to which they
gave rise. Our task, therefore, is to identify the basic institutions and examine them with reference to the physical-spatial
urban form in each of the main cultural sections of the colonial
city. In doing this, each 'dimension' or 'level' of the institution
should ideally be considered, that is, its related set of ideas and
value, its associated forms of activity and behaviour and its pattern
of social relations.

In the following analysis, the basic institutions considered are
those of government, kinship, religion, education, certain economic
institutions, recreation and, among social institutions, patterns
of association. These are discussed selectively and primarily with
reference to the urban forms and spatial areas to which they gave
rise. Moreover, the institutions of all cultural sections are not
uniformly discussed. Rather, the study focuses primarily on *one*
of these sections, that of the European colonial community, and
refers to the others only where this is necessary to bring out the
distinctive features of the first. For heuristic reasons, two main
cultural sections are identified, that of the immigrant colonial
community and that of the indigenous culture. Whilst such a categorisation ignores the substantial differences between Hindu and
Muslim cultural traditions as well as between distinctive religious
and regional traditions such as, for example, those of Sikh and Jain
or Bengali and Tamil, the particular methodological approach will,
it is hoped, justify this initial classification.

Government

Central to the concept of the colonial plural society is the assumption that one cultural section monopolises the function of government; moreover, 'when the dominant section is a minority... the
dependence on regulation by force is greatest' (Smith, 1965,p.86).

As the structure of the colonial city reflects, on a smaller scale,
the structure of the colonial society, it follows that the main
institutions of government, both military and civil, which exist
in the city, are the monopoly of the colonial cultural section.
They are first *separate from* the settlement area of the indigenous
culture and second, they manifest the physical-spatial characteristics associated with the dominant cultural section. The most

important characteristic of the colonial city in India therefore is
its tripartite division into the 'native city', the 'cantonment'
and the 'civil station' (Figure 3.1). (This was the typical structure in northern India. In the south, the 'civil station' was
frequently spatially incorporated in the 'cantonment' although the
basic military and civil institutions were kept separate).

Within the 'civil station' of the typical small town are to be found,
in the form of built structures, the manifestation of other re-
gulative institutions of government; administration, in the combined
residence and workplace of the District Commissioner; the police, in
the residence of the District Superintendant of Police and the
'police lines'; law, in the 'Circuit House' and 'District Jail',
and occasionally the 'District Court'; social administration, in
the residence of the 'Civil Surgeon'. Each of these structures
manifests the basic form and visual characteristics associated with
the colonial cultural section (Figure 3.2).

As government is the monopoly of the European cultural section, it
follows that there is no comparable physical-spatial provision made
by the indigenous culture in the 'native city'. However, an exception must be made to explain the existence of the 'Town Hall' in
many indigenous towns. At the level of local government, members
of the indigenous society were enabled to participate, forming their
own 'self-governing' institutions, though under the supervision of
a representative of the colonial power.

The original 'pre-industrial' city had, of course, provision for
civil and military branches of government which were represented
by the palace of the king and his court, and the fort (of which
the palace was often a part) providing accommodation for troops.
Under colonial control both these places were taken over and used
by the military arm of government.

Kinship

Of the institutions shared by all cultural sections, that of kinship is one of the most important. The principal subsystem of
kinship is the family with its extended kin, and the primary need
for the family is a form of shelter (Parsons, 1966,p.12). As
cities are, at the lowest level of definition, aggregations of
people, the provision made for shelter forms one of the most important physical-spatial units in the city. It is therefore appropriate to consider the institution of kinship and its effect on
dwelling form and physical-spatial needs.

In the indigenous Hindu culture, the joint family consists typically
of three generations. Household units may thus consist of upwards
of fifteen members. The preparation of food, its consumption, ritual
observations, sanitation practices and system of social behaviour
are all governed by caste beliefs and practices. Recreation is
largely kin-centred and generally associated with certain religious
festivals in the Hindu calendar.

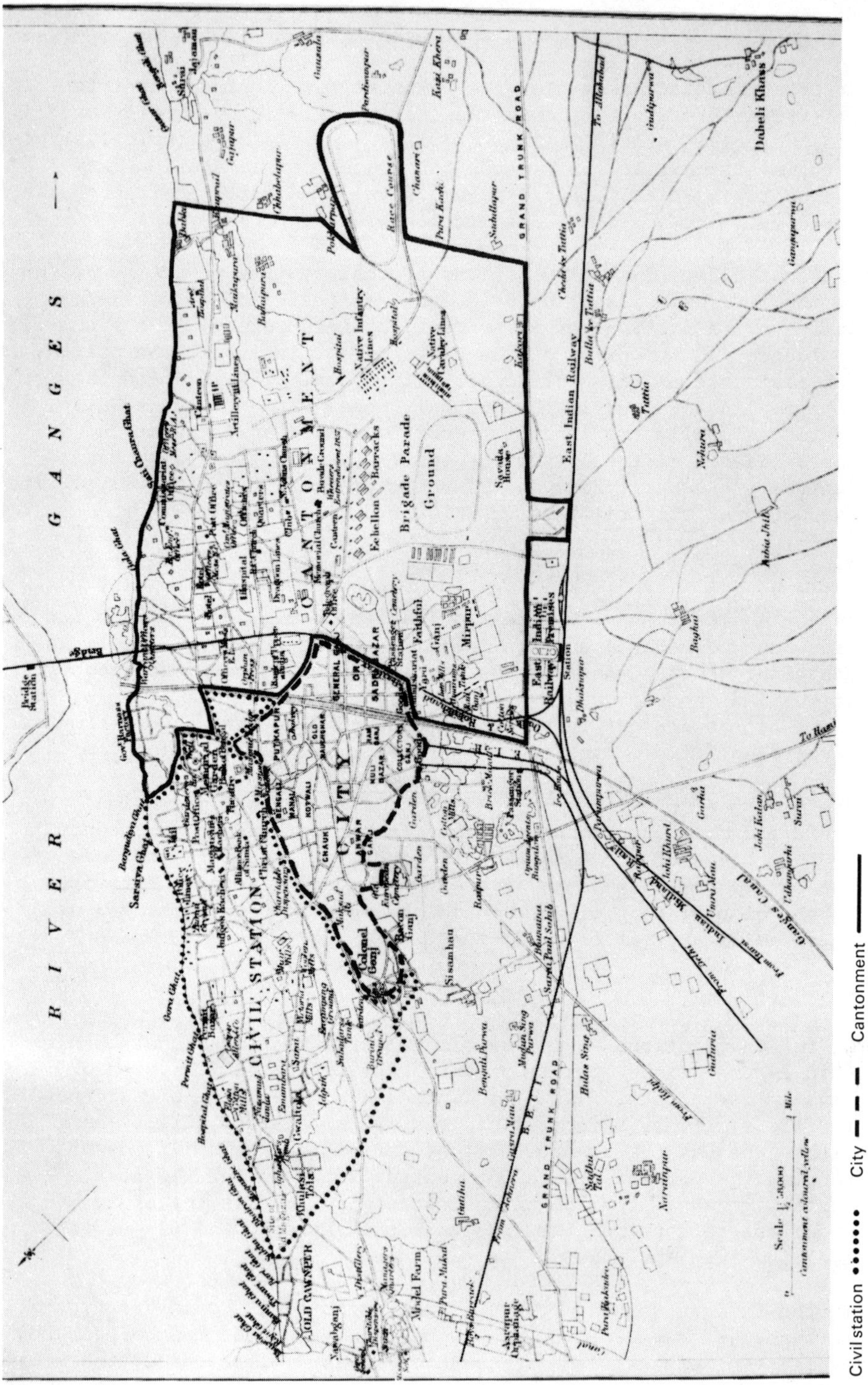
RIVER GANGES
CANTONMENT
CIVIL STATION
CITY
Brigade Parade Ground
East Indian Railway
GRAND TRUNK ROAD
Race Course
OLD CAWNPUR
Model Farm
Civil station
City
Cantonment

Figure 3.1

Figure 3.2

Such ideational and structural factors are obviously important in determining the form of the traditional urban courtyard house of three or four storeys, each containing numerous rooms and giving onto a central yard. Segregation of kin members on the basis of age and sex, the authority structure of the family and caste rules governing association with guests, servants or neighbours are dimensions of family activity which the traditional courtyard house is designed to accommodate. Equipment used for fundamental human needs is relatively little; such as exists, like the *charpai* (light cot), *masnad* (round pillow) and *gadda* (mattress) used for relaxation, are easily moved or stored in a built-in wall cupboard; sitting requires no specialised equipment and bathing is performed simply with the aid of a water tap and vessel with which water can be poured over the body. Because of this lack of 'furnishing', areas within the dwelling have considerable multiple use (see, for example, Unni and Oakley, 1965).

The corresponding built form provided for the family unit in the colonial community is the 'bungalow-compound complex'. This typically consists of a large, single-storey dwelling located in upwards of one, two or more acres of enclosed ground, the 'compound'. Each residential unit caters for one nuclear family, although functional constraints in the colonial community frequently mean that only husband and wife occupy the dwelling, with the two or three children of the occupants generally being absent in the metropolitan society or 'the hills'.

Within this dwelling, space is functionally divided according to middle-class norms in the industrialised, metropolitan society, with separate 'rooms' for 'sitting', 'dining', 'sleeping' and 'bathing', such rooms displaying in their names, the culture-specific equipment ('bath' and 'bed' rooms) they are designed to accommodate. Within these specialised rooms, the various functions are performed with equally specialised equipment such as 'cutlery', 'table ware', 'dining chairs and table', or 'sideboards'. Though the use of some of this equipment arises from situational rather than cultural reasons, cultural differences in postures adopted, for example, for relaxation, bathing, defecation or eating account for the use of many items.

The values of the occupants which have a bearing on this particular houseform are those derived from relevant reference groups in the metropolitan society, in this case, the upper middle class and 'landed gentry'. High value is placed on land-owning and property as symbols of status, on historically derived canons of 'aesthetic' taste derived from the past civilisations of Greece and Rome, and on a close attachment to the world of 'nature' (Glacken, 1967; Lowenthal and Prince, 1965). Hence, the external appearance of the bungalow is determined not merely by climatic and economic factors but frequently, also by the superimposition of symbolic 'architectural' features transposed from interpretations of Roman and Greek built form. In the 'civil station', ground surrounding the house is frequently modified according to culturally determined preferences,

with vegetation carefully arranged according to the prevailing norms
of what was known as 'picturesque' taste.

Apart from such culture-specific values and ideas, other factors
determine spatial use and built form, as discussed in Chapter 6.
The activity system of the occupants, as members of the colonial
community, governs the size, location and lay-out of the 'bungalow-
compound complex'. The typical occupational and recreational pursuits of the community are those of 'entertaining', the 'reception'
and 'garden party'.

Religion

The institution of religion finds different expression in each of
the cultural sections in the colonial city. These differences are
likewise reflected in the physical-spatial environment.

In contrast to the formally acknowledged Christianity of the colonial culture, the belief system of Hinduism is characterised by
a 'world-renouncing' or 'other-worldly' orientation. According to
Nakamura (1964,p.136) there is an Indian tendency 'to alienate the
objective natural world and to live in the world of meditation'.
Being an ethnic, rather than universalising religion, Hinduism
does not proselytise. The vast Hindu pantheon gives rise to a
variety of temples, large and small, which, unlike the church of
the Christian community, are god-centred, rather than community-
centred. In the external environment, certain rivers, rocks and
plants are sanctified. The cow enjoys a symbolic status as a
sacred beast and is permitted to wander freely through Hindu areas
of settlement (Sopher, 1967, pp.24-30; Basak, 1953).

In comparison to the world view of the colonial culture, that of
Hinduism emphasises adjustment of expectations to the environment
rather than the environment to expectations, a view which materially
affects activities and behaviour as they relate to the natural environment. In legitimising the caste system, traditional Hinduism
structures social relationships.

These beliefs are embodied in the physical-spatial form of the
built environment in the indigenous city. Typically, spatial areas
are occupied, inhabited and modified according to caste criteria.
Apart from the major festivals in the Hindu calendar, religious
observance is generally at an individual and family level rather
than at the level of community. This is reflected in the existence
of domestic shrines in each house, and the many small temples distributed throughout the city. The cyclical world-view of Hinduism
is associated with the practice of cremation rather than burial,
with its need for cremation grounds, generally by a river.

In the colonial community, religion is manifested in a formal ad-
herence to denominational Christianity, such as the Roman Catholic,
Anglican, Methodist and Baptist churches. In contrast to the
polytheism of Hinduism, the colonial belief system is monotheistic.

An idea central to Christianity and relevant to the man-environment
relationship is that the 'natural world' of animals, fish and birds
is subordinate to man, whose role as steward of the earthly domain
is legitimised by Christian theology. This permits not only the
domestication of animals but also, unlike in Hinduism, the right to
extinguish animal life in order to obtain food (Glacken,1967,p.157).
As Christianity is a universalising religion, not, in theory, recognising ethnic boundaries, it is a proselytising force, committed
to the promotion of 'missionary' activity.

The belief in the corporate, community worship of one rather than
many gods gives rise to the construction of 'churches' for each
congregation of the Christian denominations. As with other built
forms, these manifest the structural and visual characteristics of
the metropolitan culture. In comparison to religious beliefs in
the indigenous society, there is a greater distinction between
'sacred' and 'secular' activities. Formal worship and ritual in
the Christian community are therefore more specialised, both
spatially and temporally, with worship taking place generally only
once a week and only in 'church'.

The formalised role of 'priest' and his duty as 'pastor' (literally,
'shepherd') is reflected in the existence of special residential
accommodation in each 'parish'. The universalistic, proselytising
function of Christianity has its material expression, in originally
non-Christian culture areas, in the churches, schools, hospitals,
dispensaries or other urban institutions established as part of the
'conversion' task of the 'missionary' societies. Beliefs relating
to the 'resurrection of the flesh' and 'immortality of the soul'
account for the custom of burial, the place of which is visually
commemorated, and part of a larger community burial place whose
ground is sanctified.

Because of the legitimacy which Christian doctrine gives to conversion, as well as to material, 'this worldly' activities, conflicts
between its representatives and those of non-adherents or 'heathen'
could, according to the doctrinal interpretations of the nineteenth
century, be formally 'sanctified' with religious approval.

Consequently, both persons and places associated with upholding the
'faith' in the face of attack from opposing ideologies, are sanctified, take on symbolic, pseudo-religious meaning and are commemorated in the urban landscape. Most important here are those
places associated with the first major rising of the indigenous
against the colonial population in 1857, where significant numbers
of the latter were killed or where notable events took place. For
example, the 'Well' at Kanpur, commemorating the death of some forty
European women or the ruins of the 'Residency' at Lucknow, where a
siege of the colonial power took place, were carefully preserved
and developed as places of pilgrimage. Physical representations of
persons in the form of 'statues' also have sacred significance,
particularly where these represent the head of the metropolitan
and colonial government, combining, as he or she did, the dual roles
of 'head of state' and as 'defender of the faith', head of the

formal religious system. All such places and objects represent
sacred space in the colonial urban settlement.

Economic institutions

The main cultural sections also differ in their economic institutions. Taking saving, marketing, property, employment, as
illustrations, the various institutional forms and roles can be
clearly identified for each cultural section. In the colonial community, such functions as saving or credit facilities are provided
by the 'bank'; marketing, partially by the indigenous bazaar and
itinerant 'boxwallah' who brought goods to the house, but for more
specialised commodities, by the 'European shop' or by direct order
from the metropolitan society. Property is most usually in the
form of houses which, for members of the colonial community, might
be either in the metropolitan or in the colonial country.

In the indigenous society, saving is traditionally an individual,
domestic activity, with surplus wealth invested in jewellery or
gold ornaments, or, where it is of larger amounts, in land. Credit
facilities are supplied by the 'money-lender', generally a member
of a particular caste. Marketing is done in the bazaar, where
traditionally, prices are not 'fixed' but are arrived at as a
result of a complex and functional process of 'haggling'. Property
is most frequently held in the form of land.

In the colonial community, employment and occupation is decided by
criteria similar to those operating in the metropolitan society.
Recruitment to occupation is based partly on ascribed and partly
on achieved characteristics. Ascribed characteristics are mainly
social and relate to birth. Achieved characteristics are mainly
economic and consist of skills and knowledge which are either
self-acquired or gained through a formal system of education.

In the indigenous Indian society, employment and occupation are
typically decided by caste. Caste being at one and the same time
a social, economic and religious institution, it is difficult to
draw comparisons with 'parallel' institutions in the colonial or
metropolitan culture. Traditionally, each member of the indigenous
culture is ascribed, on the basis of birth, to a specific trade or
occupation or to a narrow range of occupations within a particular
sphere.

These few illustrations indicating the differing cultural expression
of basic economic institutions all have a physical-spatial dimension which is reflected in the urban plant of each cultural
section.

Thus, in the colonial urban settlement, saving, marketing, property
and employment are embodied in banks, the offices of 'insurance
agents', shops specialising in 'European' goods, housing of different types and sizes allotted according to occupational rank, and
status which is partly ascribed and partly achieved. On the cantonment are training institutions, and 'schools' are provided for the

children of non-military members of the colonial community though,
as will be discussed subsequently, these are not located in the
settlement area but are either in the metropolitan society or
in 'the hills'.

In the urban area of the indigenous culture however, the same
economic institutions find quite different physical-spatial expression. Credit facilities are reflected in the houses of the money-
lenders, saving, in the shops and godowns (warehouses) of jewellers
and the workshops of silver and gold-smiths who occupy a distinct
quarter in the indigenous city. Because of different styles of
marketing and retailing behaviour, the bazaar, with its line of
open stalls or shops giving directly on to the thoroughfare and
with constant movement along it, has a totally different physical-
spatial structure than has, for example, the European market (see
Figure 4.2). As a good example of this relationship between built
environment and culture-specific behaviour the functioning of the
bazaar is described in more detail.

The retailing activity consists in the retailer and his goods occupying a fixed location and the potential customer moving along
the length of the bazaar. In those shops where retailing activity
is spasmodic rather than continuous (for example, jewellers and
cloth-merchants rather than vegetable-sellers) the proprietor sits
cross-legged, towards the edge of the 'shop' floor which is raised
about one metre above the level of the main thoroughfare and opens
directly onto it. (There is, of course, no glass or other ob-
struction between proprietor and potential customer).

The initial stage of a potential transaction consists of a visual
enquiry: the passer-by looks at items displayed, only slowing down
his movement along the bazaar without actually stopping. Such semi-
'intention movements' provide the cue for the proprietor to extend
the visual stage of a potential transaction into a verbal one.
Following a visual appraisal of the purchasing potential of the
passer-by, the proprietor then offers to display more goods and
establishes the competitive nature of his prices.

Dependent on the passer-by's interest, the first part of this
verbal stage may lead to one of two procedures. He may either
remain as a 'passer-by' and continue his movement along the bazaar
or alternatively, he may become a potential 'customer', becoming
involved in further verbal stages of a transaction. Where the
passer-by leaves, the proprietor immediately returns to the task
of identifying further potential customers from among the passers-
by in the bazaar. The ratio of 'approaches' to completed transactions is obviously very high and this activity, demanded by a
situation where goods are looking for purchasers rather than vice
versa, occupies a large and important part of the entire retailing
behaviour of the proprietor.

For wealthier potential customers, an assistant is employed whose
task is to identify such customers as they move along the bazaar,
well before they reach the shop, and encourage them to move towards it.

The relevance of these procedures to the physical-spatial structure
of the shop and the bazaar is that, for the entire period of potential and real transactions, the proprietor remains in the culturally normal seating posture whilst having the minimum and optimal
amount of vertical and horizontal space separating him from his
potential customer. This behaviour is permitted only by the particular built structure of the indigenous 'shop'. The linear movement of potential customers inherent in this retailing activity is
embodied in the linear form of the bazaar. The process is well
described by a representative of the colonial community.

> The shop-keepers sat cross-legged, smoking hookahs, or lying
> on charpoys (rope-strung wooden cots) just inside the shop
> fronts but usually, one's arrival having been heralded im-
> mediately you set foot in the Chandni Chowk, they are ready
> to solicit you with: 'Come see, Memsahib, I give you very sheep,
> no want pay, you take and look'. His underling would then un-
> roll bales of silk and crepe de chine... shot silks... curtains
> of which were so frequently used in bungalows all over India...
> they start at a fantastic price and after much bargaining will
> drop say, from 50 to 20 rupees (Stokes-Roberts,1959,p.67).

Many functions in the colonial urban settlement which are part of
the economic system and are ultimately performed by the application
of technology, are undertaken as part of the social system of the
indigenous city. This is especially the case both with the supply
of water and the disposal of refuse. For both these tasks particular castes exist whose social and economic justification is
in the performance of roles which, in the later colonial settlement, have been replaced by the introduction of technology.

At different stages during the period of colonial rule, the different modes of technology manifest in each cultural section in
the city are important in affecting its physical-spatial structure.
During the earlier period of settlement, in the early nineteenth
century, each section largely shared the same technology. Later,
in the nineteenth and twentieth centuries, the technology of the
metropolitan society is introduced, making an immense impact on the
scale and form of the colonial urban settlement and modifying both
the physical and social structure of the indigenous city. Transport and communication is, in this later period, based on inanimate forms of energy; thoroughfares are therefore widened, intra-
urban distances magnified and specialised provision is made for new
means of communication such as the railway, telegraph, telephone,
motor-car and aeroplane.

This brief summary of economic institutions and the differences in
their cultural expression is obviously over-simplified, mainly to
highlight the difference between the main cultural sections. It
is acknowledged that, both over time and at different levels of

society, changes occur. Over time, members of the indigenous culture not only increasingly came to use the institutional forms of
the colonial culture (the banks, schools and retailing facilities)
but also created their own forms of these within their own cultural section.

Functional units within each cultural section need not necessarily
be provided by the same institutional subsystem. The hotel, for
example, an important unit in the colonial urban settlement, belongs primarily to the *economic* institutions of the culture. It
provided,against an 'economic' return, accommodation for culture
members moving between the metropolitan and the colonial society
as well as between different places within the latter. In the
indigenous society, the *dharmsala*, on the other hand, belongs
primarily to the religious rather than the economic institutional
system. In this case, the basic values of the religion require
that accommodation for pilgrims be provided as part of the religious duty of those sufficiently wealthy and pious to endow
such an institution. This fundamental difference helps to account
for the nature, quality and number of facilities provided in the
hotel and the *dharmsala*, as well as their respective locations.

Social institutions

So far reference has been made to such basic institutions as
government, kinship, religion, and economic institutions, all of
which form part of the 'institutional core' of the society. In
addition, there are significant differences in *social* forms and
activities between the different cultural sections of the plural
society. Differing associational patterns and recreational activities, for example, are particularly important in giving rise
to contrasting physical-spatial forms in the colonial city.

In the indigenous Hindu urban community, associational patterns
are based mainly on criteria of kinship, caste, sex, language
and to a lesser extent, age. Different parts of the indigenous
dwelling and its immediate area are associated with different
groups. For example, certain rooms are largely the preserve of
female members; 'unclean' castes are prohibited from entry to
areas where food is prepared. Traditionally, different sections
of the town are occupied by members of different castes, and
festivals or celebrations are one of the main forms of social
activity which, amongst kin, usually take place in the house.
Eating away from one's own kitchen is unusual owing to restric-
tions which caste rules place on this.

Criteria governing associational patterns in the colonial community
are related to kinship, occupational category, socio-economic
status and ethnicity. For those members of the community living
as part of a nuclear family, this acts as one basic unit for
association. Many members, however, are unmarried males or males
whose family lives in the metropolitan society. Shared social
and political values, a common culture and prevailing beliefs
discouraging intimate relations with members of the indigenous

society confine associational patterns of the colonial community
mainly to members of their own group.

Within this community, relationships cluster between the two main
sub-divisions, those of the *military* and the *civil* establishment.
Within these, associational patterns are governed by socio-economic
criteria, based on occupational rank. Sex is not an important
determinant of association, female members of the community participating according to the occupational rank of their husband.
However, other exclusively female groups do arise for purposes of
social intercourse and socio-economic activity (the 'coffee
morning', 'tea' and 'charity work' groups).

These associational patterns find their physical-spatial expression
in the modal type of colonial house, the 'bungalow'. Next in importance is the 'club' which, especially in a small community, is
the main centre for social intercourse for all community members.
Unmarried or 'unaccompanied' males also may live here or in the
'chummery', eating from a common kitchen.

Membership of the 'club' is confined to the higher ranks of the
occupational hierarchy. Though both civilian and military members
are admitted, similar facilities are duplicated on the cantonment
in the form of the 'officers' mess', whose membership is restricted to the 'commissioned ranks' of the military. For most
of the colonial period, the 'club' is generally not open to members of the indigenous society.

Those members of the colonial society whose occupational or
socio-economic status does not entitle them to associate, on
equal terms, with 'club members', such as 'non-commissioned
officers and 'other ranks' in the army, shop-keepers or clerks,
have their own forms of association, each with their own venue.
On the cantonment, the barracks, soldiers' canteen or sergeants'
'mess', provide the locale for social activities.

In larger urban centres, other settings accommodate the associational patterns of different sections of the colonial
community. The 'Masonic Lodge', the 'library', 'rackets court'
and 'theatre' all, however, share a common characteristic in not
being exclusively reserved for members of the colonial community.
Provided that they adhere to the norms of behaviour governing
the use of such places, indigenous society members also make use
of these particular colonial institutions. The social properties
of the club are discussed in Chapter 7.

Recreational patterns

It is in their recreational patterns that the two cultural sections differ most and it is these recreational patterns which
account for much of the contrast in the physical-spatial characteristics of the culture areas of the main sections.

In each of these, the pattern of recreational activities is closely
related to the nature and level of economic activity pursued.   In
the indigenous society, the predominant economic activity is
agriculture, with the urban area acting as a market and centre of
craft production.   In comparison to the metropolitan society,
neither the size of the economic surplus nor the amount of 'non-
working free time' permit regular, institutionalised 'leisure'
such as that associated with the limited working day or week of
factory production, with its institutionalised 'eight-hour day',
'lunch breaks', 'holidays' and 'weekends'.

Recreational activities are therefore family and community-centred,
and are frequently related to religious festivals.   Daily recreation is comparatively unstructured, consisting of social intercourse between groups of kin or caste members, groups frequently being formed according to criteria of age or sex.   Adult
male recreation generally takes place in small groups, with participants talking, sharing a hookah, or playing cards.   Children
play in relatively small, unstructured groups, with little
specialised equipment or 'toys'.   The kite is one of a small
number of exceptions.   Occasionally, larger groups gather for
'spectator activities' such as music, wrestling or dancing.   On
certain religious festivals, the entire community is involved in
watching a dramatic performance or the spectacle of a procession
passing through the streets.

Depending on the numbers involved, such activities take place in
the house, or, like the processions, in the main streets of the
city which serve multiple purposes for recreation, social intercourse, transport and economic activity.   Occasionally, a tent
or *shamiana* is erected in the street of a built-up area or on
one of the few open spaces or the *maidan* (parade ground) within
the city.

In the colonial community, recreational patterns are those generally associated with an urban industrial society.   In such a
society, time divisions are more structured and recreational
activities have become more formal and specialised, demanding
not only more specialised equipment but also specialised buildings
and spatial areas in which activity can take place.   Thus,
dramatic activity and musical performances require a 'theatre',
organised forms of sport such as 'football' and 'cricket' require
specially maintained 'pitches'; 'tennis', 'badminton' and 'squash
rackets' require purpose-built 'courts'.   Special 'tracks' and
'stadia' with stands for spectators and other facilities are
constructed for 'horse-racing' and 'polo'.

Though such developments are partly explained by the specialisation
of economic and social activities which accompanies industrialisation, ideological factors are also important.   Since the mid-
nineteenth century, values emanating from the 'public schools'
in the metropolitan society result in the concept of recreation
being interpreted as one involving physical activity and which
should preferably take the form of organised 'sport'.   The

'team games' associated with these developments are thought to foster particular moral attributes, referred to as the development of 'character' and the fostering of 'team spirit'.

Colonial 'sport' had also an important social function in providing a legitimate means by which individuals segregated by sex, social rank and race could interact and communicate without compromising their individual positions in a rigid system of stratification (Allen, 1975, p.109).

The consequences of these organised recreational pursuits, most of which were based on the principle of projecting solid or hollow spheres, of various sizes and weights, with or without equipment, in various directions but within a measured and limited area and according to institutionalised social rules ('cricket', 'golf', 'football', 'hockey', 'tennis', 'polo', 'rackets') on the physical-spatial needs of the colonial settlement, were clearly considerable.

A further recreational pursuit of the colonial community associated with the urban industrial values of the metropolitan society from the later nineteenth century was the practice of taking 'holidays' away from the usual place of residence. Although the origins of the 'hill station' in India were connected to the attempt made by the colonial community to find a healthier and more comfortable environment during what they perceived as the hot months of the year, it also depended on the notion of recreation being pursued 'away from home' (see Chapter 7).

Other values also affected recreational pursuits and resulted in modifications to the physical-spatial environment. A veneration of elements in the natural world such as flowers, birds, insects and other aspects of natural life was common to many members of the colonial elite (Archer 1962,1963,1967,1969). Such values supported their interest in investigating, reading, writing and talking about these phenomena. This shared sense of values helped to bond social relationships and led to the formation of organisations such as the 'Natural History Society' to pursue such interests at group level.

These values, and the activities to which they gave rise, 'gardening', 'walking', admiring specified 'views' in the landscape and recording these by 'sketching', painting and photography, had their physical-spatial expression in the existence of large 'compounds' and cultivated gardens attached to each dwelling, the parks, the botanical and 'Company' gardens, the 'reserved forest' of the colonial settlement, each with its consciously modified natural environment.

Criteria governing participation in recreational pursuits, like those governing associational patterns, were those of rank and socio-economic status. Socially small-scale activities such as 'entertaining', 'drinks' or 'dining out' took place in the domestic setting of the bungalow; those on a larger scale, such as 'amateur theatricals', social dancing and the 'children's party' took place in the club.

3   THE COLONIAL THIRD CULTURE

In discussing the various cultural sections of the plural society
of colonial India, reference has been made to the 'European
colonial community'. As this study focuses particularly on the
urban forms of this section and the way in which these affect
indigenous forms, it is essential to have a clearer conception of
this section and to know how it is constituted. A basic assumption
is that the culture of this community is a unique and distinctive
phenomenon. It therefore follows that the physical-spatial urban
forms which it produced do not simply reproduce those of the metropolitan society but are, in themselves, unique.

In considering the culture of the European colonial community we
are concerned with the process of acculturation. The contribution
of Malinowski to the understanding of this process - or culture
contact as he preferred to call it - is relevant here. The important factor which Malinowski brings out is that the product of
culture contact is not simply 'a combination of institutional
elements from both cultures' but a completely new cultural
phenomenon (Malinowski,1945,p.25).

As it stands,however, Malinowski's concept has two disadvantages
for the present analysis. Though he acknowledges that the 'institutions, intentions and interests' of the incoming (European)
culture may well be transformed by their contact with the institutions of the 'native' culture, his own focus of interest is
on the latter. In this study, we are concerned primarily with the
European colonial culture which results from the transformation
of metropolitan cultural institutions as they come into contact
with the culture of the indigenous society. In the second place,
Malinowski fails to differentiate sufficiently the structure of
the incoming culture.

In his discussion of the impact of 'Spanish' culture in Latin
America, Foster (1960,pp.10-12) shows that acculturation is a
selective process. Only *some* parts of European culture are bestowed and only *some* parts received by the host society. Is the
'conquest culture' as Foster calls it, that of the 'conquistadores,
the missionaries, the government administrators?' The two complete
cultural systems do not come into contact. Both the authority of
the donor as well as that of the recipient culture act as screening
devices.

A further refinement of this concept is that made by the Useems in
their conceptualisation of a 'binational third culture'. This
they define as
    the complex of patterns learned and shared by communities
    of men stemming from both a Western and a non-Western
    society who regularly interact as they relate their societies,
    or sections thereof, in the physical setting of non-Western
    societies (Useem and Donaghue,1963,p.169).

The Useems' concept refers to the zone of social and cultural
interaction between representatives of two different societies
in what might be described as a relatively politically neutral
situation. The emphasis in this concept is on the mutual,
bi-lateral nature of this *third culture* where, in theory at least,
each 'side' is capable of freely contributing to and sharing
aspects of it.

Though conceptually similar, the situational context of the
colonial third culture makes it operationally distinct. Here,
the cultural patterns and institutions which are 'created and
learnt' are, in the first place, not generally shared by representatives of each of the two cultures in contact. Second, the
politically neutral, 'free' situation implied in the Useems'
definition is absent. Instead, the *colonial third culture* is
one which depends on a politically charged situation which is
most adequately expressed as a dominance-dependence relationship.
This culture 'developed its unique social roles, ideology,
literature, folklore on what 'natives' were like, ideal norms
for administrative programming and even art and architecture'
(ibid,p.170).

In this concept, the first culture is that of the metropolitan
society, the second, that of the indigenous, pre-colonial society.
Clearly, each of these cultures have their own distinctive value
and belief system, their own system of institutions, social
structure and social relationships.

The content of the colonial third culture, whilst owing much to
its parent culture in the metropolitan society (particularly
in its belief system and most of its value orientations), is none
the less unique. It is a culture which emerges not simply as a
result of interaction with a second culture in a 'neutral'
diffusion situation, but necessarily, as a result of colonialism.

A further sociological refinement needs to be made,however,
before the colonial third culture can be represented schematically.
Who are the carriers of the metropolitan culture and with which
members of the indigenous society do they come into contact?

Two variables must be considered. The first relates to the
position in the social structure of each 'parent' culture occupied
by the 'agents' who create the new third culture; the second relates to their regional origin. From which particular social
class and from what regions in Britain did members of the British
community in India come? In which caste groups and from what
regions did those Indians originate whose culture was important
in contributing to the colonial third culture? Third, there is
a time dimension to consider, for clearly, the culture of both
societies changed over the two and a half centuries of contact
between them.

These are not simply academic questions. In considering the
evidence on colonial urban forms we need, above all, to know the
main reference groups, both in the metropolitan and the indigenous
societies, which are important as norm models for those members of
the colonial community responsible for urban development.

Whatever answers to these problems are suggested, they must be
relatively crude, being based on what little evidence is available.
First, we may deal with the temporal context of the colonial third
culture.

Though reference is made to the eighteenth century, it is the
period of settlement from the mid-nineteenth to the mid-twentieth
century, immediately prior to the formal termination of the
colonial third culture, which is primarily considered in this
study. Whilst it is recognised that changes occurred in both
cultures as well as in the relationship between them over these
years, evidence suggests that assumptions can still be made regarding certain underlying features of each culture which persist
during this period. Moreover, at the level of analysis undertaken
here, what is important are the differences between the two cultures in question, rather than the diachronic changes which may
have taken place in each of them in the time-span under consideration.

The second point of clarification concerns the social origins of
members of the colonial third culture and the type of social
structure which it gave rise to in India. Only brief reference
to this will be made here. To simplify, the social structure
of the European community in India consisted of four components,
each having its own system of stratification but with all four
forming an overall status hierarchy which comprehended the members
of the entire European community.

As all Europeans were, with respect to the total population of
India, an elite (at least according to their own perceptions),
it is difficult to find appropriate terms to describe the various
status groups within this community. The first component consisted of what might be termed the 'governing elite'. This comprised the senior-most members of the government, military and
judicial services who exercised (subject, in important matters,
to the approval of the metropolitan government), the main decision-
making powers in India. These included such persons as the
Viceroy and Governor-General, the Governors of the various provinces and Presidencies, the Commander-in-Chief and senior army
officers and the Residents in the 'native states'. Membership
of this top section was decided formally by occupational rank
and informally by social origins.

The second section consisted of the large number of government
'officers' including, along with the commissioned ranks of the
Army, the members of the various Indian 'services', such as
the 'Indian Civil Service', 'Indian Medical Service', 'Indian
Police Service' and others for engineering, forestry and education.

The third, semi-residual category, consisted of all other Europeans who, by virtue of social, economic or educational criteria, were deemed to be reasonably comparable to others of 'officer' status, but whose common characteristic was that they did not occupy official roles in the army or government and were therefore not 'gazetted officers'. The largest number of these were from 'commerce', including private businessmen, and agents of metro-politan concerns. In addition, there were non-official clergy or missionaries, school-teachers, bank managers and members of the professions, such as dentists, doctors or accountants.

The last section consisted of the 'non-officer' class represented by non-commissioned ranks of the army, minor shop-keepers, clerks and persons performing various technical roles in government service.

The little evidence that is available suggesting that members of the two middle groups were overwhelmingly recruited from the metropolitan 'middle' and 'upper middle class' (Cohn, 1966; Razzell, 1963; Compton, 1968; Otley, 1973; Allen, 1975) is of less importance than the fact that, with regard to life-styles and residential behaviour, the metropolitan middle and upper middle classes provided all three top sections with their main reference group.

In view of the importance of this question of social structure, it is worth including four contemporary observations as more accurately reflecting the perceptions of members of the colonial community at the date indicated.

> European society, like that of the ancient Hindoos, is divided into four great classes; the 'Judge... classes', the 'Military', the Commercial and the dependent.
>
> The first three classes, though by no means equal, are yet admitted into one pale; they all partake of certain sacred rites,... and they would appear to be that part of community who are bound by no laws; the fourth class are no farther considered than as they conduce to the advantage of the superior castes.
>
> A Judge is the Chief of all created beings; the world and all that is in it are his; through him indeed, other mortals enjoy life; he is exempt from punishment, even for the most heinous crimes. His offences against other classes are treated with remarkable levity; while all offences against him are punished with tenfold severity....
>
> The Military class, though far from being placed on an equality with the Judges, are still treated with honour. It is indeed acknowledged that the first class could do nothing without the soldiers, and that the prosperity of both depends upon their cordial unanimity.... The Military class enjoys, in a less degree, the protection against law, which is the privilege of the Judge....
>
> The Commercial class also stands high, though not as high as it might. Their time is passed in reading a sort of Shastra called Lejjar, and in studying the prophets.

The fourth class is, to a certain extent, in a state of
depression and dependence, being distributed in various
subordinate employments under the other classes....
Besides these, are Fakeers or Padres, and Hukeems (doctors),
who are considered to belong to the second class. It is to
be observed that the three first classes take their meals in
common, and that individuals even of the fourth class are
sometimes admitted to this participation....
It may be added that individuals of the fourth class often
rise into the third, and sometimes even into the second; while
members of the second class sometimes become Judges. This is
totally opposed to the principles of wisdom, which have made
the inhabitants of this country so wise and happy (*The Delhi
Sketch Book*, 1850-1855, pp.123-4).

Some sixty years later, another observer commented
Caste is very strong in Anglo-Indian society although its
rules for eating and marrying are not (unlike those of the
Hindu) made of cast iron.... The English communities in India
closely resemble one another in spite of the fact that they
are scattered over an area as large as Europe with Russia
left out.... Imagine an English community in India a rose,
and pick it to pieces. Pull out the yellow centre, which is
made up of the Governor and the Englishmen who hold the highest
positions. Tear off the leaves circling the middle of the
flower and lay aside the generals, colonels, majors and others
who hold India for England. Go on to the open leaves which
represent clergymen, lawyers, bankers, doctors, editors,
professors, planters and merchants: and finally, to the outside petals which are made up of shopkeepers, clerks, hotel-
keepers, actors, teachers, engineers, railway officials,
mounted constables, soldiers and others.
The caste system must be catching for there is in the English
community in India a strong tendency to fall into groups. Thus,
the Indian Medical Service is a close body and English people
who belong to it are satisfied to know the other members of
the IMS and no outsiders. Lawyers associate with lawyers,
missionaries with missionaries, engineers with engineers.
Enter one of these little groups and you will find in it much
social rivalry, egotism and debt.... Indian princes are almost
the only natives who mix freely with the ruling community in
British India (Law, 1912, pp.39-40).

According to Law, this rigid system of stratification resulted from
the absence of party politics (which) gives to Anglo-Indian
society an exclusiveness not found in self-governing parts
of the Empire. No aspiring hotel-keeper or shop-keeper can
force himself and his wife into Society in India by adding
M.P. to his name or becoming a Premier or a Minister. Trade
is rigidly excluded from Anglo-Indian society.... Money
cannot buy a place in (it) for a wealthy tradesman but the
poorest Lieutenant can write his name in the Visitors' Book
at any Government House and obtain invitations to the Viceroy's
Parties (ibid.,p.39).

The preponderance of ascriptive roles and the absence of roles which could be achieved, and the resultant forms of stratification which emerged, were a principal characteristic of the colonial culture.

The third comment is from 1933
> The white population of India - invariably referred to as Europeans and not British, although the non-British element has a very small majority -   numbers about 160,000 in British India. The non-official designation of the three castes in which the European population is divided is... the 'Heaven-born' (the ruling classes), the 'Services' (the Army and the Civil Service) and the 'Box Wallahs' (business men). The official classification, according to the Simon Report is: 'First there are the men of business... secondly, come the British members of the various branches of the Civil Service. These are found in the All India Services such as the Indian Civil Service, the Indian Police Service, or the Engineering Service; and again, there are numbers of Europeans engaged upon the railways.'
>
> It will be seen from the above... that... the men of business in India are put on the top of the basket. This does not correspond in the least bit with how matters are regarded in India, both by Indians and by Europeans. The businessmen themselves are divided into those who rank equally with the 'Services' and with those who may be frankly entitled the 'white untouchables' (Greenwall,1933, pp.103-4).

This rigourous sense of segregation, and the similarity in the ordering of the various social groups persisted into the last years of the colonial society. A representative middleclass spokesman, like his predecessor of over a century before, found a strong Hindu influence in the colonial hierarchy
> The Brahmins, the so-called heaven-born, were the members of the topmost British Government service, the Indian Civil Service. They were the *pukka* Brahmins and below them were the semi-Brahmins, the various other covenanted services - the provincial civil services and so on. Then you had the military caste, composed partly of members of the British Army and partly of members of the Indian Army.... The British businessmen, very wealthy and powerful in Calcutta but fairly low caste, were analogous to the wealthy but also low caste mercantile and moneylending caste, the *Vaisyas*. They were the *box-wallahs*, a term of contempt applied quite freely by the two upper British castes to the British mercantile community. They might be merchant princes of the very highest quality but they were quite inferior to the covenanted services and the military caste. This mercantile caste subdivided willingly - even strongly - into two. The upper people said that they were in commerce, the lower people said that they were in trade.... Then you went lower down to the menials, the so-called Eurasians and Anglo-Indians, people of mixed blood analogous to the des-pised Hindu lower castes. Another category here was the unfor-tunate domiciled community, the people of pure British race

whose parents, for one reason or another, had elected to stay
in India (Allen, 1975, p.84).

As far as contact between representatives of the two main cultural
sections was concerned, it followed that, at least in theory, all
members of the host society came into contact with the representatives of the metropolitan society. In practice this was not
the case for a variety of reasons. Over the entire period of
colonial rule, the majority of third culture members were more
likely to be located in Northern India than in other parts.
Politically, as well as economically, Bengal, 'Upper India' and
the 'Bombay Presidency' were of more importance to the colonial
community than was the south of India. Functionally, their prime
areas of concern being administration, military affairs and commerce,
they were most likely to come into contact with some regional,
religious, or caste groups than with others, for example, with
Bengali clerks in administration, Punjabi Sikh soldiers in the army,
Parsee businessmen in commerce, and with North Indian Muslims as
servants. With these four roles, for example, of clerk, soldier,
merchant or servant, the members of the colonial culture actually
worked; arguably, they became more familiar with the culture of
the particular groups in question. According to one informant,
'the only caste of Indian that (the British soldier) had the
opportunity of meeting or conversing with was that of the lowest
caste, whose members frequently performed the role of 'sweeper'
(Allen, 1975, p.156). At the other extreme the role of the
traditional Hindu priest was one with which the majority of members
of the colonial culture had little formal or informal contact,
except at a distance, when such roles were seen more as part of a
general 'cultural landscape'.

It is, in any case, arguable whether differences between members
of the indigenous culture which depended on regional, caste or
religious affiliation were of more significance than the overall
similarities between members of the culture which actually existed
or were perceived to exist by members of the colonial community.
In a political situation where the members of the indigenous
society were ultimately dependent on the dominant incomers, for
many if not all purposes, regional, caste, or religious differences
were disregarded or subsumed in the commonly perceived category
of 'Indian' or more usually, 'native', a perception well illustrated in the writings of a 'non-commissioned' member of the
military establishment (Richards, 1965).

It follows from the above that what has been termed the *colonial
third culture* can now be represented schematically as indicated
on the following page.

The first culture is that of the metropolitan society, in this
case, Britain. For part of our analysis, this might also be
seen as belonging to the larger culture area of Europe. The
'selected' first culture comprises those elements and institutions
of the metropolitan culture transferred to the indigenous society

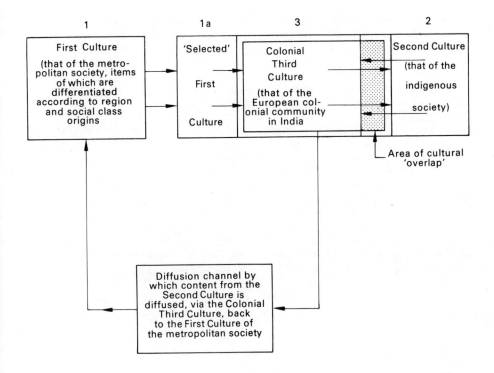

by a socially and regionally selected set of cultural agents recruited mainly from the middle classes of the metropolitan society.

The second culture is that of the indigenous society, namely India.
This comprises a vast range of individual variation comprehending
different religions and regions, yet, for the particular heuristic
purpose of this study, is taken as one culture.

The third culture is that resulting from the contact, in the
colonised country, between the selected first culture and the
selected second culture. Like all cultures, the colonial third
culture is centred round an institutional system which comprehends
ideational systems, meanings and symbols, social structure, systems
of social relations and patterns of behaviour. There are a form
of government, an educational system, a type of family organisation,
economic institutions, forms of knowledge, language and literature,
technology, and a whole range of social beliefs, groupings and
cultural artefacts - including built form and urban patterns -
which are unique to the colonial third culture. It is evident
that some aspects of this culture were, from the outset, shared
with members of the indigenous society (e.g. certain items of
dress, diet or language; these are indicated in the 'area of
cultural overlap'). Other items gradually became shared, over
the period of colonialism, such as aspects of government, administration, education, ideologies, knowledge systems, cultural
artefacts. However, other aspects of this colonial third culture,
such as particular social groupings, social and political ideologies,

literature, perceptions about the 'natives' and aspects of life-style remained largely unique to third culture members throughout its existence. With the demise of the third culture brought about by the end of colonialism, such items either disappeared, were transferred to the metropolitan society by third culture members or persisted as part of a Westernised indigenous culture sustained by the elite in the ex-colonial society.

It is the colonial third culture, the culture of the British in India, with which this study is mainly concerned and particularly, those aspects relating to urban development. These are the institutions of government, religion, law, kinship, economic and social institutions, systems of knowledge and value orien-tation, some of which have been briefly examined in the earlier part of this chapter. By investigating these institutions at the level of idea and value, activity and social relations, and by comparing them with the institutions of other cultural sections in the city, an insight can be gained into the way in which cultures are embodied in their built environment.

PART TWO

Chapter 4

THE LANGUAGE
OF COLONIAL URBANISATION

Human beings do not live in the objective world alone, nor in
the world of social activity as ordinarily understood, but are
very much at the mercy of the particular language which has
become the medium of expression for their society....The
fact of the matter is that the 'real world' is to a large
extent unconsciously built up on the language habits of the
group. No two languages are ever sufficiently similar to be
considered as representing the same social reality. The worlds
in which different societies live are distinct worlds not
merely the same world with different labels attached (Edward
A. Sapir, *Selected Writings in Language, Culture and Personality*,
1949, p.42).

This chapter is concerned with the relationship between language,
social organisation and physical-spatial urban form. It aims
first, to *use* language as a tool for the examination of social
and spatial organisation in a discrete culture and second, to
examine language as one element in a particular culture fabric
(Bright, 1968,pp.18-21). After considering certain basic concepts
in linguistic anthropology, the main body of the chapter utilises
some of these concepts to analyse the nomenclature of the *colonial
urban settlement* as well as those items in the terminology of the
colonial third culture which refer to patterns of settlement. By
examining perceptual phenomena, the object of the analysis is to
throw light on the ordering of some of the political, economic
and social relationships which characterise the process of colonial
urbanisation.

1 LANGUAGE AND CULTURE

A society's culture, according to Goodenough, consists of 'whatever
it is one has to know or believe in order to operate in a manner
acceptable to its members and to do so in any role that they accept
for any one of themselves.... It is the form of things which people
have in mind, their models for perceiving, relating and otherwise
interpreting them.' In brief, each member of a culture operates

with what Goodenough calls a 'conceptual model' of social reality
with which all phenomena are perceived, processed and organised
into a cognitive whole (quoted in Sturtevant, 1964,p.100).
Linguistic analysis provides one of the most effective means for
understanding these conceptual models, for how people talk about
their own world of experience and what names they give to it
gives us some indication of how they construe it.

Within such a framework, the study of vocabulary as a guide to
the way in which members of a particular culture divide up their
universe has been termed, alternatively, *ethnosemantics* or
ethnoscience, where 'ethno' refers to 'the system of knowledge
and cognition typical of a given culture' (ibid,p.99). A major
area for research in ethnoscience has been on terminological
systems, 'classifications as reflected in native terminology'
and although 'the analysis of a culture's terminological systems
will not... exhaustively reveal the cognitive world of its members...
it will certainly tap a central portion of it'(ibid,p.105, see also
Tyler, 1969). Cognitive features which are significant for a given
culture must be communicable between members of that culture and
language, as the major communication device, encodes these features.
Thus, on the assumption that what is named both exists and also,
is sufficiently important for it to be named, a study of the terminology in a particular cultural domain can give rewarding
insights into that particular aspect of culture.

The domain examined in this chapter is that which relates to the
terminological and classification system used to describe selected
aspects of settlement and the collective forms of social
organisation which, at the simplest level, are characterised by
the spatial concentration of population within a given geographical
area, for example, in the English language, town, city, metropolis.
Whilst it would be accepted that the word 'urban' denotes not only
a set of physical-spatial characteristics (i.e. population size,
density, concentration of built forms) but also a set of social
characteristics, there would clearly be less agreement regarding
the nature of these characteristics (the classical statement on
the supposed characteristics being that of Wirth,1938).
Nevertheless, most societies, whether 'traditional' or 'modern',
eastern or western, have terminologies to describe forms of socially
and spatially related organisation as well as lesser divisions
within these units. In India, there are *nagar* (city), *pura(m)*
(town), *gaon*, *grama* (village), as well as *mohulla* (ward or
neighbourhood); in English, city, town, village, as well as district,
neighbourhood, estate; in German, *Stadt* (town), *Dorf* (village), as
well as *Bezirk*, *Kreis* (district). The criteria used to distinguish
between these various terms (which will be called 'criterial
attributes') can generally be stated in terms of numerical size
of population, function, or forms of social or administrative
organisation.

However, as cultures differ in the way they classify experience,
it is clear that not only will forms of socio-spatial organisation
specific to one culture not invariably be found in other cultures

but also, the total range of a set of categories in one culture will not necessarily match a set in another culture. In short, social phenomena in one culture are classified according to a taxonomy derived from that culture and not, at least not accurately, according to one construed by and for, another culture.

It is the aim of the ethnoscientific method to discover the culturally relevant discriminations and categories used to define the objective world, and the principles on which they are based. By applying the method to what we may, from reasons of convenience rather than accuracy, call 'urban' nomenclature, insights can be gained into the nature of social organisation which would otherwise escape us (for the relation of language, culture and environment see Sapir, 1912; Boas, 1934; Whorf, 1956; Kuper, 1972).

The particular sphere in which these concepts are to be applied is that of the colonial third culture, discussed in detail in the previous chapter. Of the non-material aspects of this culture, one of the most important and without doubt, the most easily accessible items, is its language, much of which is collected and explained in the book by H. Yule and A.C. Burnell, *Hobson-Jobson*, 'a glossary of colloquial Anglo-Indian words and phrases, and of kindred terms, etc.' (1903). Though this source offers rich opportunities for research into numerous domains of the colonial third culture, that which is examined here concerns the particular set of *segregates* (i.e. 'any terminologically distinguished... grouping of objects', Sturtevant, 1964,p.104) relating to patterns of settlement and aspects of residential behaviour. As indicated above, this domain has been chosen for its heuristic utility in investigating the structure of relationships - social, spatial and ethnic as well as political and economic - in the colonial city.

2   AIMS, DATA SOURCES AND METHOD

It was stated at the outset that the aim of the chapter is to *use* language as a tool for the examination of socio-spatial organisation in a discrete culture and second, to *examine* language as one element in a particular culture fabric. Though these two approaches cannot be too sharply distinguished, the emphasis in the first part of the analysis is on using terminology as a guide for understanding socio-spatial arrangements and the economic and political *relation-ships* which they represent. The examination of terms in this first part, though still relevant for the understanding of these relationships is treated as a subsidiary task. In the second part of the analysis, the emphasis is on the examination of language. Here, the aim is to investigate the etymology and application of selected items in the urban nomenclature of the colonial third culture as a means of gaining insights into the social, economic and cultural *processes* of colonialism. It should be stressed, however, that these two approaches are not separate but complementary and frequently overlap.

The *corpus* of data selected for analysis is drawn from three sources. The first is that of current usage in the ex-colonial society and items from this source have been collected as a result of participant observation.   These consist of a set of linguistic terms used in contemporary India to describe physical-spatial-social elements in the urban system which are expressed in the metropolitan rather than the indigenous language (i.e. English rather than Hindi). Such terms however (indicated in italics throughout this chapter), are either not found in the system of urban nomenclature in the metropolitan society (e.g. *civil lines, civil station, cantonment, chummery, rest house, godown)* or, if they do exist, are used with different meanings to those prevailing in the ex-colonial society (e.g. *compound, bungalow, bazaar).*   The second source is that found in cartographic evidence belonging generally to the first half of the twentieth century prior to the termination of colonial rule. The final source is the extensive glossary provided in the book by Yule and Burnell.

From these three sources thirty-six terms have been selected with the following two criteria in mind. First, practically all of them (thirty out of thirty-six) are still in current usage in the ex-colonial society, some three decades after the formal declaration of political independence. Second, these examples are seen to be key terms in understanding the socio-spatial structure of the colonial city, and the larger phenomenon of colonial urbanisation. Verification that all thirty-six terms belong to the language of the colonial third culture (though clearly, not exclusively to it) is confirmed by their inclusion in either Yule and Burnell's glossary or by their consistent use in maps, guides and gazetteers produced by and for members of that culture. More powerful confirmation exists in that some 50 per cent of these terms, as a result of the presence of a British colonial third culture in Africa, can be found in the usage of ex-colonial societies there. (I am grateful to Michael Safier for this information. For some discussion of colonial terminology in African urban settlements, particularly 'boma' and 'bazaar', see McMaster, 1970,pp.340-1). Like other aspects of colonial culture, models of urban settlement and administration - including the terms and concepts of *cantonment* and *government station* - were exported from India to Africa as part of the colonial process. The terms *cantonment, government station* and *sanitary district* were discarded in favour of 'Urban District' and 'Township' (either of 'First', 'Second' or 'Third Class') in 1917. (See Lugard, 1970, (earlier editions 1906, 1919), pp.404-22).

3 KEY TERMINOLOGY IN THE LANGUAGE OF COLONIAL URBANIZATION

For purposes of analysis, the thirty-six terms are arranged into groups based on the scale of socio-spatial unit to which they relate. Those still in use in the ex-colonial society are marked by an asterisk. Those found in the colonial third culture of the British in Africa, are followed by a second asterisk (see Table 4.1).

TABLE 4.1

Inter-societal ('imperial' or macro level)	Societal	Urban	Urban sector	Unit or (micro level)
Home	Presidency	civil station*	bazaar**	barracks**
country	province	civil lines*	colony**	bungalow**
Europe**	division*	cantonment*	esplanade*	chummery*
native*	district**	lines**	Mall*	club**
	hills**	circuit house*	coolie*	compound**
	hill station*	dak (bungalow)*		gowdown**
	plains*	collector*		gymkhana**
		Residency		lodge**
				quarters**
				rest house**
				serai*
				verandah**

Words in the colonial third culture can be roughly divided into
one of four categories

TYPE 1:   originate in the metropolitan culture (though in turn, of
          course, derive from other cultures) e.g. barracks,
          station, club;

TYPE 2:   originate in the indigenous culture (again, these fre-
          quently derive from other cultures) e.g. dak, bazaar;

TYPE 3:   are hybrids, resulting from a combination between words
          from the indigenous and metropolitan cultures (e.g.
          gymkhana);

TYPE 4:   are diffused from the colonial third culture of other
          areas in the colonial territorial system (i.e. from
          South-East Asia, especially Malaya) e.g. compound,
          godown, verandah.

The method adopted has been to investigate the *meanings* of these
terms and their application, as used by members of the colonial
third culture. These meanings have been derived from a variety of
sources including descriptive accounts, handbooks and dictionaries
compiled by and for members of the third culture and reflecting
the 'conceptual models' represented by each term, pictorial and
cartographic data, as well as existing physical-spatial forms in
the ex-colonial city. The time-period during which these terms
were used in the sense described extends, for the majority, roughly
between the mid-nineteenth to the mid-twentieth century, immediately
prior to the formal termination of the colonial third culture as
it existed in the indigenous society.

Proceeding on the assumption that 'cultural categories are
lexically expressed' (Hymes, 1964,p.167), this chapter examines
the etymology of these thirty-six terms as well as their inter-
relationship as part of a culture-specific terminological system.
In this way, an insight is gained, not only into the overall
settlement pattern of the colonial third culture, but also, into
that part of the conceptual model of its members which pertained
to the organization of their socio-spatial urban universe. Whilst
the general rule of procedure will be to start with terms related
to the larger socio-spatial scale (the inter-societal or macro-
level) and move downwards to those associated with smaller socio-
spatial areas (the urban area, the urban sector, the unit or
micro-level) this rule is not rigidly adhered to, in order to
permit discussion of terms at appropriate points in the analysis.

4 PRINCIPLES OF CLASSIFICATION

The underlying principle of the language of the colonial third
culture is that of *dualism*; its analysis and description can best
be approached through what may be termed a *double binary structure*.

As implied by the definition, the third-culture concept arises from, and in relation to, the two cultures of the societies being related to each other. For members of the colonial third culture, there are, by definition, two reference groups, the first, ego with reference to the metropolitan alter; the second, ego with reference to the indigenous alter. This is what is implied by the term *double binary structure* which is basic to the cognitive schema of members of the third culture.

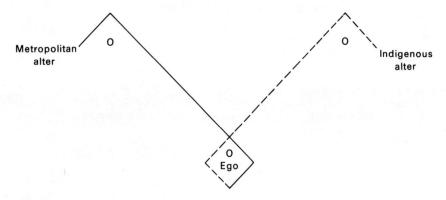

Thus, for the culture member, this *dualism*, or *binary structure* was fundamental to his orientation to the world (I am grateful to Ranajit Guha for this insight); one was either at *Home* or in India (or Abroad); goods were either from *Europe* or the *country;* the universe was peopled by *Europeans* or *natives;* actors in the universe were either black or white (if mixed, they were *half-caste, Eurasian,* eventually *Anglo-Indian,* all binary constructs). This dualistic orientation, required by the very concept of colonialism by which third-culture members were *in the territory* of the host culture but were not part *of* that culture, pervaded other spheres of perception and classification; it was a form of 'bifocal vision' which characterised their cognitive orientation to the world.

Home (like God, always written with a capital letter), as in Home Leave, in 'Anglo-Indian and colonial speech' always meant the metropolitan country of England. *Europe,* the racial connotation of which is discussed subsequently, was used adjectivally 'in contradistinction to *country*, as qualifying goods imported from Europe'. *European* was used to describe behaviour in the metropolitan society in contradistinction to that in the colonial third culture ('I took a "European morning" after having had three days of going out before breakfast', i.e. lying late in bed as opposed to the third culture norm of rising early). *Country* was used 'to distinguish articles produced in India (generally with a sub-indication of disparagement) from such as are imported, and especially imported from Europe'.

This notion of dualism, arising from the interaction of two societies, is, of course, fundamental to the concept of colonialism. In the words of Castells, it comprehends 'the penetration of one social structure by another' (1972,p.64), an idea which gives a valuable insight both into the function of the colonial third culture as well as the origin of its language. The process of penetration was *managed* by third-culture members. The areas, or domains of penetration - political, economic, administrative, social, cultural - tended to be encoded in third-culture terminology. This is clearly, if somewhat obviously, shown in the terminology reflecting the basic process of settlement and the division of the colonised territory into political-administrative units.

5 POLITICAL-ADMINISTRATIVE UNITS IN THE COLONISED SOCIETY

In the early stage of contact between the two societies, the relationship is primarily economic and is managed, not by the metropolitan government but by a commercial undertaking (the 'East India Company'). Thus, the first major territorial divisions in the dependent society (the three *Presidencies)* are described in terms of the authoritative head (the President) of each of the three agencies ('factories') of this organisation. With the further acquisition of territory and assumption of 'imperial' status by the dominant society, a relationship which had been primarily economic in nature became increasingly political and administrative. In this new relationship, the prime source of power lay in the metropolitan society with certain functions and authority delegated to third-culture members in the colonised society.

This political and administrative relationship between the dominant and dependent societies is reflected in the latter by the set of terms applied to the socio-spatial areas over which the metropolitan society assumed control. Thus, in addition to the *Presidencies,* further territorial acquisitions were divided into *provinces,* which were in turn split up into *divisions, districts* and *sub-divisions.* The term *province* is of uncertain origin but originates in the Latin 'pro' (for) and 'vincere' (to conquer). Historically, it was associated with earlier, Roman colonial systems, with the meaning of 'a country or territory outside Italy, under Roman domination and administered by a governor sent from Rome' (Murray, 1888).

As with other terms in the settlement terminology of the colonial third culture, such as *cantonment* and *quarter,* the words *division, district* and *sub-division* all originate in a military context. More significantly, the main criterial attribute common to each of these terms, is one related to separation or division, with the implication that first, something exists to be *divided* or *quartered* and second that authority is so distributed in this essentially superordinate-subordinate structure of relationships as to permit this division to take place. Thus, the socio-spatial unit immediately below the level of the *province* was the *division,* the origin of which is self-explanatory. Within the *division* there were a number of *districts* 'the respective portions in which a country is divided for the convenience of command'; within the *districts,*

a number of *sub-divisions*, again a self-explanatory term. Significantly, one of the last major acts of the colonial government
was that of 'partition', giving rise to the current terms
'pre-partition' or 'undivided' India.

The *district* and *sub-division* represented the lowest levels of
political, judicial and administrative authority under the direct
control of members of the colonial third culture. Containing as
many as one million people, the *district* was the responsibility of
the *Collector* or *Collector-Magistrate*, a term appropriately expressive of the financial, administrative and judicial role performed at this level by the incoming culture. Below the district
level was the *sub-division*, under the charge of an assistant
magistrate, or sub-divisional officer, the lowest rank in the
colonial bureaucracy. At this level, performance of the administrative role meant not only working with personnel from the
indigenous community ('native doctors', 'native lawyers', 'native
officers') but also being physically removed, both in terms of
work and residence, from the smallest socio-spatial unit of the
colonial third culture, the *civil station*. Below the *sub-division*,
authority was delegated, not to other third-culture members but to
members of the indigenous society in the service of the colonial
bureaucracy. Significantly, the administrative area for which
supervised indigenous culture members were responsible retained
its indigenous name, *tehsil*, a term deriving from the earlier
period of Muslim rule.

Those parts of the indigenous society left under the political and
administrative control of the indigenous rulers were known as
native states. The independence and autonomy implied by the term
state was, however, only relative, depending on the larger authority
system of which it was a part. The political relationship between
this system and that of the *native state* was embodied in the role
of the *Resident*, a designation which fully expressed his primary
task.

Apart from his advisory function, the first role of the *Resident*
was a representative one. By residing in the capital of the
indigenous state, the *Resident* was a permanent reminder of the
dependent relationship existing between the indigenous ruler and
the colonial power. The physical-spatial embodiment of this role
was *The Residency*, a complex of buildings and spatial area, carefully modified according to the distinctive values and 'aesthetic'
preferences of the colonial third culture (Figure 4.1).

Whilst the terms considered so far, at the inter-societal and
societal level, are perhaps better understood as those of a
language of *settlement* rather than of *urbanisation*, it is clear
that the former process is a prerequisite for the latter. Before
examining the latter, however, consideration must be given to the
political, economic and social process of colonialism itself and
its effect on urbanisation.

Figure 4.1

Figure 4.2

6   THE TERMINOLOGY OF COLONIAL URBANISATION: THE URBAN AND URBAN-SECTOR LEVEL

One of the more penetrating analyses of this effect has been made by Castells, who has described the phenomenon as 'dependent urbanisation'. Such 'dependent urbanisation' results from one or more historically experienced types of domination:

1   *Domination coloniale*, avec pour objectifs essentiels, l'administration directe d'une exploitation intensive des resources et l'affirmation d'une souveraineté politique.

2   *Domination capitaliste-commerciale*, à travers les termes de l'échange, se procurant des matières premières au-dessous de leur valeur et ouvrant de nouveaux marchés pour des produits manufacturés à des prix au-dessus de leur valeur.

3   *Domination impérialiste industrielle et financière*, à travers les investissements spéculatifs et la création d'industries locales tendant à controler le mouvement de substitution des importations, suivant une stratégie de profit adoptée par les trusts internationaux sur l'ensemble du marché mondial.

L'urbanisation dépendante exprime, dans ses formes et dans ses rythmes, l'articulation concrète de ces rapports economiques et politiques. (1971,p.64. Italics added).

Though Castells's primary interests are the economic and political manifestations of 'dependent urbanisation', it is clear that the phenomenon has also social and cultural, as well as physical-spatial dimensions. It is these dimensions which are being considered here and particularly, the terminology which is used to describe them at the urban, urban sector and unit level.

As already indicated, the relationship of dominance-dependence was based on the fact that ultimate power and authority lay in the dominant metropolitan society. In the dependent society, the final sanction used by the colonisers to maintain their authority over the colonised population was armed force. The urban manifestation of this relationship was expressed in a system of military *cantonments* situated at strategic centres throughout the colonised territory but generally close to the major centres of population. The political and administrative element in the colonial relationship was represented by the *civil station*, a distinct socio-spatial unit developed and occupied by civilian members of the colonial bureaucracy ('judge', 'collector-magistrate' 'superintendent of police') and supporting technical, medical and socio-cultural services ('engineer', 'civil surgeon', 'teacher', 'missionary').

The third socio-spatial area, representing the indigenous, dependent population and providing the only justification for the existence of the other two sectors, was the indigenous settlement, which, depending on its size and local circumstances, was referred to as the *native city*, *native quarter*, or by the anglicised corruption of its indigenous name.

Having largely used language to indicate political and administrative relationships prevailing at the inter-societal and societal levels between dominant and dependent societies, attention is now turned to examining language at the urban, urban-sector and micro or unit level.

It is evident from the above, that the urban universe of the colonial third culture consisted of three basic parts, the *cantonment*, the *civil station* (alternatively known as the *civil lines*) and the *city (native city or native quarter)* (see Figure 3.1). Considering that the ultimate sanction in preserving the structure of authority lay with the armed forces, it is appropriate to begin by examining the term *cantonment*.

The word, signifying a permanent army camp, is, amongst those cultures where English is used as the first language, peculiar to members of the colonial third culture in India. In the metropolitan society, the comparable term, though representing a dissimilar concept, is 'army camp', 'military station', or 'garrison town'; in the culture of North America, 'base' or 'army base'. The etymology of *cantonment* gives a valuable insight both into the physical-spatial organisation as well as its location in relation to other components in the colonial urban system.

The concept of a permanent military camp is represented, in the metropolitan culture, by a number of terms. Camp (from the Latin 'campus' - field) is 'used more particularly in a military sense' and represents 'a temporarily organised place of food and shelter in open country as opposed to ordinary housing. The idea of the camp being to keep troops together in a state of readiness and concentration rather than being scattered around' *(Encyclopaedia Britannica*, 1929). A military *station* (Latin, statio, onis: standing place, residence) is 'a place for the rendezvous of troops or the distribution of them'; 'garrison' (from the French 'garnier'- to furnish) implies 'the guard of a fortified place, or the place itself...,''garrison town' is 'a strong place in which troops are quartered and do duty for the security of the town, keeping... a main guard in or near the market place' (Stocqueler 1853). The main criterial attributes in these three terms are related to *location* (e.g. whether inside or outside a town) and to *duration* (e.g. whether permanent or temporary).

In the colonial third culture the concept of the permanent military camp is termed *cantonment*, a word which 'has become almost appropriated as Anglo-Indian, being so constantly used in India and so little used elsewhere. It is applied to military stations in India built usually on a plan which is originally that of a standing camp or cantonment' (Yule and Burnell, 1903). An equally authoritative source gives its meaning as 'the permanent military station in India... in that country a cantonment contains barracks

for European troops and native huts termed *lines* for the sepoys.
The European officers live for the most part in bungalows or
thatched houses. Regimental bazaars also form part of the adjuncts
of the cantonments'(Voyle, 1876). A further definition suggests
that it is a 'permanent station where troops of all arms are
massed together away from the native inhabitants' (Smith,1883).
The criterial attributes in these definitions are again in terms
of *location*, although in this case regarding the country of location
(i.e. India), *lay-out* (both with regard to the social and spatial
distribution of the occupants as well as the location of the whole
in regard to the indigenous population) and *duration* (cantonments
are *permanent* camps).

The term stems originally from the French 'canton' having the
meaning of to quarter, divide, divide land into portions, to part
or share, to divide a part *from*, or cut out of a whole, to separate,
or sever by division (Murray,1888). Like *division*, *district* and
quarter the word originates in a military context, and as suggested
above, presupposes an authority structure which permits the division
of spatial areas and their allocation to various functions and
social groups.

The separation concept implicit in the word cantonment is twofold:
the separation or division of spatial area within the boundaries
of the military camp; and the separation of the camp from the
indigenous city. The internal division arose from the well-defined
norms of military procedure regarding the demarcation of spatial
areas, the criteria of allocation, the relationship between various
units in the camp and the function of the whole. Separation from
the indigenous city resulted partly from accidental, partly from
strategic, but more especially from reasons associated with culture-
specific theories of medical science and the behavioural norms of
the military members of the colonial third culture, discussed in
Chapter 5.

This meaning of the *cantonment* as an enclosed area, separated from
other socio-spatial units and itself divided up into smaller
spatial areas is confirmed by cantonment plans. As the second
definition quoted above shows, residential accommodation was segregated according to three criteria, racial or ethnic group,
military rank and type of built structure. Thus, on a *cantonment*
racial segregation would be expressed in the existence of *European*
infantry lines and *native* infantry lines, a *European* hospital and
a *native* hospital, a *European* infantry parade-ground and a *native*
infantry parade-ground. Amongst *European* occupants, residential
segregation by rank provided one set of accommodation for *officers*
and another set for *troops;* segregation by building type provided
barracks for the *European* (if 'in line' also referred to as *lines),*
native huts (also referred to as *lines)* for the Indian troops
('sepoys') and individual *bungalows*, each situated in its own
compound, for officers. Though mentioning these distinctions may
seem unnecessary or trivial, the reason for doing so will become
apparent later in the analysis.

The duplication of spatial areas was brought about by the maintenance of separate functional and residential accommodation for
metropolitan *European* and locally recruited *native* troops. The
principle of division here, as in the larger society, was basically
ethnic or racial. By 1888, the term 'native' has such a connotation:
the original meaning, derived from the Latin adjective 'nativus' -
born, signified not only 'one of the original or usual inhabitants
of the country as distinguished from strangers or foreigners' but
also 'especially one belonging to a non-European and imperfectly
civilised and savage race', and was possibly equated with 'a
coloured person, a black' *(Oxford Dictionary*, 1903. The 1972
edition still lists 'member of non-European or uncivilised people'
as one of the main meanings of 'native').

The adjectival use of 'native' to express an ethnic category was
already firmly established by the mid-nineteenth century: 'the
Asiatic troops of the Company are called native troops... while
the British are called Europeans. These are merely local designations and, as such, the former term must be understood to mean
that the troops are natives of India, but not always of the provinces in which they are stationed' *(Royal Comm.*, 1863,p.25).   In
the early twentieth century, for the members of the metropolitan
culture, there were three 'races' in India: 'Europeans and Allied
Races', 'Eurasians (Anglo-Indians)' and 'Natives (Indians)'
(Murray, 1913, cxxii).

Whilst political and administrative services in the dependent
society were provided by members of the colonial third culture,
being represented by and located in the *cantonment* and *civil
station,* economic services, at least at the local level, were
supplied by the *native* population. These were provided by an
institution which was indigenous, not only in function, but also
in name and physical-spatial form, the *bazaar, sadr* (main) *bazaar,*
or occasionally, *native bazaar.* The origins of the term stem
probably from Persian or Arabic use; for third-culture members
generally it represented 'a permanent market or street of shops'
(Figure 4.2) or, in South India, 'a single shop or stall kept by
a native' (Yule and Burnell, 1903. See also McMaster, 1970).

However, it is clear from other evidence that where the *bazaar*
existed within a defined area of third-culture territory (generally
on a *cantonment),* it was not only an economic but also a social
area, where segregation on ethnic criteria was enforced. According
to the *Cantonments Code,* a *bazaar* was 'any land in a cantonment
which has been *set apart* for the purposes of trade *or the residence
of natives* or any other purpose and the boundaries of which have
been demarcated by pillars or posts... under the authority of the
General Officer of the Command' (Government of India, *Cantt. Code,*
1899,p.64. Italics added). The goods sold, the system of economic
organisation and the norms of retailing behaviour, as the word,
were those of the indigenous society; these contrasted with those
of the *Europe shop* whose wares, retailing norms, economic organisation and physical appearance derived from the metropolitan
society (Yule and Burnell, 1903).

Apart from the *bazaar*, the only other major indigenous institution
both in name and social-physical reality, permitted within the
cantonment boundaries was the *serai*, 'a building for the accommodation of travellers with their pack animals, consisting of an
enclosed yard with chambers around it'(ibid). Within the
cantonment however, the institution conformed to the same rules of
social and ethnic segregation as applied to the *bazaar*. Here, it
was 'a building in a *cantonment* ordinarily used, whether wholly
or in part, for the accommodation of *native* travellers and not
maintained by cantonment authority'(Government of India, *Cantt.
Code*, 1899,p.64).

Just as a distinctive institution existed for the provision of the
particular retail services required by the members of the colonial
third culture (the *Europe* shop), so also was provision made for
their temporary accommodation as they, or their kin from the
metropolitan society, travelled around the country. This was
provided, typically, by the *European* or *English Club*, the various
versions of the *Dak Bungalow*, or the one 'European-style' *Hotel*,
each of which is discussed subsequently. Here, the services,
amenities, dietary requirements and cultural environment of the
metropolitan society, or a third-culture approximation of them,
were available for the non-indigenous traveller.

The *Club* and *Hotel* were generally located within the second major
sector of the colonial urban system, outside the demarcated
territory of the cantonment. This sector was situated, and defined,
in relation to the first. The *cantonment*, being by definition
military in function, the names of the adjoining area, the *civil
lines* or *civil station*, derived also from the military terminological
system.

The *civil station* was situated in one of two places. With the
cantonment and *native city* it either formed part of a major provincial town or alternatively, it was a 'mofussil' or 'country station',
the 'capital' of a small, rural *district*. The *civil station*
represented and its inhabitants performed the major administrative
and cultural roles required in the colonial process. Here lived,
in the socially and physically segregated area which is inherent
in the term, those members of the colonial third culture whose roles
brought them into the closest contact with representatives of the
colonised society.

In the words of a third-culture member:
  A civil station is the capital of a district. The society
  consists principally of members of the Civil Service; there
  is the judge,... the collector-magistrate,... the joint-
  magistrate and deputy-collector, a sort of second in command
  to the collector-magistrate, and the assistant magistrate.
    Outside this nucleus of the Civil Service there come the
  police officers, the doctor, the clergyman and one or two
  other minor English officials and perhaps a few independent
  men employed in mercantile business or owning landed estates.
  If there is a railway running through the district, it may

> contribute an engineer to the little society, or there may be
> an officer of the Public Works Department located there. In
> Bengal, military detachments very seldom help to swell the
> numbers of a civil station. In fact, with the ladies of
> several families, a party of twenty can seldom be assembled,
> except on most important occasions.
>
> In a very small world such as this... the assistant (magis-
> trate)acquires his native designation as 'chota sahib' or
> 'little sahib' of the community (Buckland, 1884,p.93).

Apart from the light this late nineteenth-century description
throws on the occupants of a *station*, some insight is also
given - by the order in which they are listed - into its social
hierarchy, its sense of self-sufficiency as a social unit, its
acceptance of military third-culture members where they are
present, and into the means by which the sense of collective
identity was maintained.

Like other terms in the third-culture language, *civil station*
originates in a military context. As indicated above, a *station*
is 'a place calculated for the rendezvous of troops or for the
distribution of them' or 'any military post held permanently by
troops' (Stocqueler, 1853). The norms of residence for the
majority of members of the third culture being those of either
a military or a civil bureaucracy meant that all members were
assigned to or stationed in their place of role performance
within the system. 'To station', meaning to place, or to assign,
is a transitive verb which, like the verbs to quarter and to
divide, referred to above, indicates the existence of an authority
initiating action, an object on which action takes place and a
destination to which the object is assigned. Hence, a question
in the metropolitan culture taking the form 'which town do you
live in?' would, in the context of the military or colonial third
culture, become 'at which station are you posted?'. With usage,
the concept of place represented by the term 'station' became
synonymous with the particular form of social organization which
it contained. Thus, in the language of the third culture, the
term has the meaning of 'the usual designation of the place where
the English officials of a district or the officers of a garrison...
reside. Also, *the aggregate society of such a place'*, as in 'Who
asked the station to dinner?' (Yule and Burnell, 1903). (Similar
'military' usages persist in contemporary Indian English. A new
staff member at a university is asked 'When did you join?' or even,
'join service?'; a temporary address is indicated as 'Camp, Indian
Institute of Advanced Study, Simla' rather than 'c/o' or 'at' as
in current English usage).

The alternative term to civil station was *civil lines*. The adjective *civil* was, of course, used in contradistinction to military;
lines also has its origin in military terminology. This term
originally specified the physical demarcations of ground indicating
the relative location of the units of tented accommodation in a
temporary camp. The term clearly indicates the temporary nature

of the first phase of settlement, out of which the more permanent patterns of physical-spatial development grew. It also embodies not only a concept of planning but of planning on a linear prin- ciple. The word was subsequently adopted to refer to any planned and regulated built accommodation, generally provided for a service community such as police *lines*, coolie *lines*, dhobi *lines* (Figures 4.3a and 4.3b). (Compare also 'Line (Estate English) - an estate labourer's house'. See *Glossary* in Jain, 1970,p.444.)

The term *coolie* belongs to the language of the colonial third culture. It is 'the name given by Europeans in India and China to a native hired labourer or burden-carrier and is also used in other countries where these men are employed as cheap labourers'. The term originates either in the Tamil *kuli* meaning 'hire payment for occasional menial work' and hence, 'kuli', a 'hireling', a man who does odd jobs, labourer; or in Gujerat, in the name of an aboriginal tribe, the Kuli or Koli who, in the seventeenth century, were working as *coolies* in Western India (*Oxford English Dic- tionary*, 1910). In the metropolitan society, manual work of a kind done by coolies is performed by 'labourers' or 'navvies' (the latter originating from the 'navigators' associated with the digging of canals in the eighteenth and nineteenth centuries). In the language of the metropolitan society, *coolie* is associated with exploitation, cheap labour and the functioning of sectors of the colonial economic system (tea, rubber, sugar plantations).

The main thoroughfare in the *civil station*, *cantonment* or *hill station* was generally *The Mall* (Figures 4.4a and 4.4b). In *hill stations*, the roads higher or lower in elevation were the Upper and Lower *Mall* (each with its own social connotations). The concept of a 'mall', 'a sheltered walk or promenade' which was generally 'bordered with trees' (*Oxford English Dictionary*, 1910) clearly indicates its social function both as a centre of social interaction as well as for personal display. The reference point, The Mall, was (and is) located in the capital of the metropolitan society and forms the major avenue linking the residence of the official head of the political and unofficial head of the social system with the locations occupied by the major institutions of state and church (i.e. linking Buckingham Palace with Whitehall and Westminister). As such, the original Mall occupies the highest place in the physical communications structure of the social and political system of the metropolitan society. From this reference point, the colonial Mall derives its social and cultural significance.

Though shops were to be found on the *Mall*, they were relatively few in number. Retailing activity was largely the responsibility of the indigenous community; thus, neither in form nor function did the colonial *Mall* bear any resemblance to the comparable thoroughfare in the indigenous city, the centrally-located *chowk*. For members of the colonial third culture, this was 'an open place or wide street in the middle of the city', its origins as a market being clear in its derivation from the Sanskrit *chatushka* meaning 'the four ways' or crossing of streets at the centre of

Figure 4.3a The *lines:* nineteenth century

Figure 4.3b The *lines:* twentieth century

The Mall.

Figure 4.4a

The mall. Umballa

Figure 4.4b

business (Yule and Burnell, 1903).   Thus ,whilst the term for the
central thoroughfare of the indigenous city clearly indicates an
economically generative function, the comparable linear-spatial
element in the colonial urban settlement illustrates a function
that is primarily social.

The main focus of social interaction and the principal centre of
information exchange for members of the community in the *civil
station* was the *club*, occasionally termed the *European* or *English
Club* or *Gymkhana Club*.   The concept of the club, in this sense,
as a form of secular social organisation, stems from the mid-
eighteenth century; it is 'an association of persons... formed
mainly for social purposes and having a building appropriated for
the exclusive use of the members and always open to them as a
place of resort, or in some cases temporary residence... its
main feature is to provide a place of resort, social intercourse
and entertainment'.   It is also 'an association formed to combine
the operations of persons interested in the promotion or pro-
secution of some object, the purpose of which is often indicated
in the title' (*Oxford English Dictionary*, 1910).

Where the title was the *European Club* or the *Gymkhana Club*,
the object to be promoted was either the general interests of
the Europeans or, in the second case, a set of recreational
activities specific to the colonial third culture.   The word
'gymkhana' originated either from 'gend-khana' from the Hindi
'ball-house' and meaning the racket-court common to most *stations*,
or possibly 'gym-khana', from an abbreviated form of 'gymnasium'
(Yule and Burnell, 1903).   The term 'gend-khana' aptly summarises
the series of culturally-preferred leisure pursuits common in
the metropolitan society and central to the functions of the *club:*
cricket, squash rackets, badminton, tennis, billiards or polo.
The term, as the institution, gives a valuable insight into
basic forms of social interaction as well as the physical-spatial
demands of the colonial community.   Access to the *Club* was confined to members of the third culture.   Similarly, other 'sacred
space' such as the 'Memorial Garden' at Kanpur, was confined to
'Europeans and the caretakers alone' (Murray, J. *Imperial Guide
to India*, 1904,p.115).

The functions of the club, as a place for social interaction and
the reaffirmation of cultural identity, are well illustrated by
a representative member.
    The club, to which the whole European population belongs,
    provides a meeting place, and is a centre for all kinds of
    sports and games, as well as for dancing,... is one of the
    chief diversions of the British in India....The club is the
    centre of social life....It is the recognised meeting place
    of the station.   Most people manage to drop in during the
    interval between tea and dinner... almost everyone is to be
    met there during (this interval).   Much talk and gossip are
    heard - in a small station any news is appreciated.   Bridge
    enthusiasts gravitate to the card-room; the young and
    energetic play tennis; others, watching the game, or idly

turning over the last illustrated paper from home, find it
very pleasant to sit under the shady trees....
     Dinner parties and dances are frequent....Everybody knows
everybody else, the amount of income of each one is known,
and extravagence in entertaining or dress is not approved.
(Platt, 1923,pp.27,53).

A further significant illustration of the 'bifocal universe' of
the colonial community was the bifurcation of the host environment into two contrasting geographic regions, 'the *plains*' and
'the *hills*'.   In contradistinction to the '*stations*' on the plains,
those *stations* situated at the requisite elevation were known as
hill stations.   The term, like the concept it represents, exists
only in the colonial and ex-colonial societies, including other
parts of South and South-East Asia, as well as Africa.   In the
metropolitan culture, the closest comparable concept would be
represented by 'seaside town' or 'seaside resort', the place to
which members of an industrial society, given a minimum of
institutionalised leisure, would 'resort' for recreation.   In
North America, it would be 'mountain' or 'summer resort'.

The third main element in the colonial urban system was the *city*,
native city or, where it was of smaller dimensions, the *native
quarter*, describing that section of the colonial culture's urban
universe occupied by the indigenous inhabitants.   For the members
of the third culture, as also for the metropolitan society, the
native city was distinguished by a number of characteristics
which pertained primarily to its physical-spatial form, the
commodities sold in its markets, its inhabitants and particularly,
their norms of economic and social behaviour.   Here, within the
framework of values provided by the non-indigenous culture, the
architecture was perceived as 'picturesque' or 'quaint'; for
members of a society accustomed to the relatively geometric lay-
out of a city, by the twentieth century transformed by motorised
traffic, the pedestrian thoroughfares of the indigenous city were
'winding', 'tortuous' or 'labyrinthine'.   The minimum congruence
of values between indigenous and non-indigenous societies centred
round the norms of economic and social behaviour.   In economic
transactions, third-culture members were warned to be 'on one's
guard' and, of the most importance, particular attention had to
be taken in regard to health and sanitation on account of 'dirty
habits' of the 'natives' (ibid.,p.53).

Where troops of the metropolitan power were located in the fort
of the indigenous city, the ground between the fortress and the
native city was cleared as at Bangalore or Delhi in 1858, to form
an *esplanade*, 'an open space of ground separating the citadel of
a fortress from the town and intended to prevent any person
approaching the town without being seen from the citadel' (Stocqueler,
1853).   Like the park which frequently separated the *civil station*
from the *native city*, or the unbuilt-on open space which divided
the *cantonment* from both, the *esplanade* was yet a further device
for maintaining social and ethnic segregation.

7   THE TERMINOLOGY OF COLONIAL URBANISATION: THE UNIT
    OR MICRO LEVEL

If the urban world of the colonial third culture consisted of the
cantonment, the *civil station* and the *city*, the basic territorial
unit of that culture, whether in *cantonment* or *civil lines*, was
the *compound* within which stood the *bungalow*, complete with its
verandah, servants' *quarters* and *drive*. For effective insights
into the unique characteristics of the colonial culture and particularly, into its origin in the diffusion of cultural characteristics from a variety of sources, and to some central themes
in its social life, there are few better terms to examine than these.

In modern Indian English, as in the language of the third culture,
the enclosed ground area containing a single dwelling is termed
a *compound*, the main dwelling unit, a *bungalow*. In the. metropolitan society the ground area, if unbuilt on, is termed a
'plot' or, if partially covered by a dwelling unit or 'house',
is known as a 'garden'; in the English of North America, the
relevant term for the ground area is 'yard'. This difference in
terminology reflects a significant distinction in the origin and
use of what, at first sight, might be seen as comparable phenomena.
The origin of 'garden' is to be found in such languages as Old
Norse, Scandinavian, Latin and French, 'garo' denoting the
concept of enclosure and also forming the basis of the related
words 'yard' and 'garth'. The meaning of 'yard' is 'a comparatively small, uncultivated area attached to a house or other
building or enclosed by it, especially such an area surrounded
by walls or buildings within the precincts of a house, castle,
etc.'; a 'plot' is 'a piece of ground, especially one used for
a special purpose'. The criterial attribute which distinguishes
these two words from 'garden' is that related to function, 'garden'
being 'an enclosed piece of ground devoted to the cultivation of
flowers, fruit or vegetables' (Murray, 1888).

According to these definitions, there is no reason why the term
'yard' or 'garden' should not be in common use to describe, in
Indian English, the phenomenon which is in fact termed *'compound'*.
However, both the derivation and etymology of this term stem from
totally different sources. In the first place, it is defined as
'an Anglo-Indian word', i.e. one which, in this particular usage,
is confined to the colonial third culture. As far as can be
ascertained, its origin is in the Malay term 'kampong' or
'kampung'; its meaning 'an enclosure within which a residence or
factory (of Europeans) stands, in India, China and the East
generally'. Tracing the word's origins takes one significantly
into the languages of French, Portuguese, Spanish, Malay,Javanese,
Dutch and English, i.e. all languages of colonial culture contact
situations. The word was probably first used by members of the
metropolitan society
     in the early factories in the Malay archipelago and thence
     carried by them to peninsular India on one hand and China
     on the other. Subsequently, it was taken to Madagascar,
     East and West Africa, Polynesia and other regions where

Englishmen have penetrated and has been applied by travellers
to the similar enclosures round native houses (Yule and
Burnell, 1903).

Distillation of all the usages suggests that the most accurate
definition is that of Marré, 1875, who describes the *compound*
as 'a palisaded village, or, in a town, a separate and generally
closed quarter occupied by people of the same nationality'(ibid).
Sociologically and historically, it would be difficult to find
social situations fitting this description other than those of
the early colonies (Dutch, Portuguese, French, British), the
medieval or modern Jewish ghetto, the internment, detention or
concentration camp of the twentieth century or the diplomatic
enclaves housing some foreign communities in various parts of
the world, though most frequently found in ex-colonial countries.
As a relatively if not completely closed physical-social system,
the *compound* has unique sociological properties. It serves as
an instrument of control, both by those within it as well as
those without. It provides an isolating area in which one's
own culture can be developed and maintained.

From this origin therefore, the third-culture meaning of the word
compound came ultimately to denote 'the enclosed ground, whether
garden or waste, which surrounds an Anglo-Indian house'(ibid.).
In signifying that the ground surrounds 'an Anglo-Indian' house
rather than just 'a house', the earlier meaning of an enclosed
area occupied 'by a particular nationality' (or better, culture)
is reflected. Thus, one has a word which signifies both enclosed
physical space as well as possession by a particular nationality,
a unique concept for urban ecology.

A similar origin can be ascribed to the term *godown*, from the
Malay 'godong', having the meaning in India and other parts of
the East of a 'warehouse' or 'storehouse', the words used to
describe the phenomenon of comparable function in the metropolitan society. It is of some significance that two of the
most fundamental functions belonging to an urban form of social
and economic organisation, namely, the division and enclosure of
space for residential purposes and the provision made for storing
a surplus product are both designated by terms deriving from the
economic and political process of colonialism. In a small but
significant way the terms *compound* and *godown* indicate the impact
which colonisation has made on urban development in the indigenous
society.

Like *compound*, the term *bungalow* (with this spelling) was
originally unique to the colonial third culture. The anglicised
derivation is from Hindi and Marathi 'bangla', meaning 'of or
belonging to Bengal' (ibid). The term was used to describe the
dwelling form common to inhabitants of rural Bengal. The etymology
of the word indicates that the basic dwelling form is from Bengal
and the original term for it derives from non-Bengali Indian languages. The physical reality of the modern colonial *bungalow* was,
however, like the term used to describe it, the result of

modification by the colonial third culture. However, from being used
to describe a house-type which originally belonged to Bengal, the
term *bungalow* takes on the meaning of a particular house-type which
belonged to the colonial community, becoming, in the late nineteenth
century, 'the most usual class of house occupied by Europeans in
India'(ibid). It is not defined in terms of what it *is* but rather,
who it is *for*, which is, of course, the way in which the term
originated as 'bangla', 'belonging to Bengal'. Significantly,
however, as a result of the colonial process, ownership of the
term has been transferred. The term, as the concept, was 'adopted
by the French in the East and by Europeans generally in Ceylon,
China, Japan and Africa' (ibid. see also King, 1973a and 1973b).

The origins of *verandah* - 'an open gallery outside a house with
pillars along the front to support the roof' - is confused, though
it is likely to stem from Persian, Spanish or Portuguese (Yule
and Burnell, 1903). As with *compound*, therefore, the term
originates in colonial culture-contact situations. Like the concept
it represents, it was brought from India by the members of the
third culture and adopted widely in the metropolitan society.

As the members of the third culture were what might be termed
a 'vehicular elite', the link connecting the thoroughfare of the
station to the *bungalow* was, not a path, but a *drive*, 'a private
road to a house' (*Oxford English Dictionary*, 1910). At the rear
of the *compound*, lying leeward at some distance from the *bungalow*
were the *quarters* (not the house or even hut) of the servants, a
term derived, as indicated above, from the terminological system
of the military.

The significance of the colonial *bungalow-compound complex* lies
in the fact that the terms, like the reality, represent a physical-
spatial structure which embodies an entire life-style and system
of social behaviour unique to the colonial third culture. The
continuation of the *bungalow-compound complex* as one of the major
organising units of urban form in the modern Indian city, seen
against the previous urban tradition of the *mohulla*, represents
one of the most striking aspects of 'Westernisation' in the Indian
urban system.

The concept of the *bungalow-compound complex* is best understood
as an extended form of 'personal space', 'a small circle of
physical space with the individual at its centre, and a culturally
determined radius', the whole of the *compound* area being 'a
territorial unit' (Stea, 1969,p.324).

Whilst such 'territorial units', surrounded by a culturally controlled urban environment, were available in *civil stations*,
cantonments or *hill stations*, movement between these areas was
essential, either for the effective performance of roles (for
inspection or similar tasks) or between 'the *plains*' and 'the
hills'. In relation to the large number of indigenous inhabitants
over whom they had control, the number of colonial officials were
few, each being responsible for extensive socio-spatial areas over

which they had direct authority. Thus, touring the *district* or
province, administering justice, settling disputes or inspecting
personnel and public works was a major pre-occupation. It was,
therefore, necessary to have a section of 'moving territory'
(ibid.,p.325) in which the characteristics of the basic'territorial unit' were reproduced, situated at strategic locations
throughout the indigenous society. This was provided in a number
of physical-spatial institutions the names of which aptly illus-
trate their function in this system of supervision and control:
the *circuit house, inspection bungalow, canal and forest bungalows,
rest house,* and *dak bungalow.*

Dak, from the Hindi or Marathi, literally meant 'post' in the
form of transport by relays of men and horses and thence, the
mail or letter post, as well as the arrangements for travelling,
or transmitting articles by such relays. The system is old and
goes back at least to Moghul India. The *dak bungalow* however is
as essential an institution of the colonial third culture as is
the *bungalow* itself. It, and its numerous variations, provided
the third-culture members with their controlled 'culture area'
wherever they travelled.

Whilst the *club* and *hotel* supplied residential accommodation for
the few unaccompanied colonial males in the smaller *station,* for
the increasing number living in larger urban centres a new
institution developed. This was the *chummery* which provided
rooms and a common kitchen. The origins of the *chummery* lie in
the elite university institutions of the metropolitan society
where, in the eighteenth and nineteenth centuries, a 'chum' was
a 'friend sharing the same room' or a 'chamber-fellow'. In the
earlier days of colonial settlement, the practice of 'chumming'
or sharing accommodation was an obvious solution for newly-
arrived immigrants. Over time, this practice was institutionalised
and *bachelor chummeries* were constructed in larger cities, conforming both internally and externally to the norms of the third-
culture elite (Figure 4.5a).

In the twentieth century, these, together with other historically
and culturally evolved types of accommodation were incorporated,
as specialised housing types, into the new colonial settlement
of Delhi. Here, elite European males accompanied by their families
were allocated *bungalow-compound* units; unaccompanied elite
European males lived in the *hotel* or in rooms at the *club;* by
then, *chummeries* were for European male subordinates (Figure 4.5b).

The persistence of third-culture taxonomies in post-colonial Delhi
is demonstrated by a contemporary (1970) sign. This indicates twelve
separate systems of physical-spatial, social, racial, occupational
and cultural classification (see Figure 4.5b). The 'place' is a
particular kind of urban *spatial form,* usually circular or quadrangular, to be distinguished from other linear or quadrangular
forms such as the road, avenue or square; 'Alexandra' refers
to the joint head of the metropolitan society and distinguishes
the *location* of this 'place' from those designated by 'York',

Figure 4.5a The *chummery*: nineteenth century

Figure 4.5b The *chummery*: twentieth century

'Windsor' or 'Connaught'; 'chummery' is a *type of accommodation*
to be distinguished from those of the bungalow, club or hotel;
in its original use, it was also a *cultural* or *racial* category
in that it was for Europeans (and not Indians), a category of
gender (in that it was for male and not female), of *marital status*
(for unmarried males) and of *social class* (for those members of
the metropolitan society practising 'chumming' or the 'sharing
of chambers'). 'Block' is a term referring to a type of *built
form* containing, collectively, a number of dwellings, to be distinguished from other blocks according to *number*. 'Quarters'
(the full-stops are in error) denotes a particular *size, quality
and social class* of accommodation to be distinguished from 'lodge',
house or bungalow. 'Clerk' is an *occupational* category to be
distinguished from superintendant, assistant or secretary; 'upper
division' (the 'O' is a mistake for 'D') indicates a *status* in an
occupational hierarchy to be distinguished from 'lower division'.
('L.D.C.') Implicit is the distinction between these as 'government quarters' in the *public* sector and 'non-government', *private*
accommodation (see Urban nomenclature as a symbol of colonial
taxonomy, Chapter 10,9).

8   ETHNOSCIENCE AND URBAN ANALYSIS

In this chapter an attempt has been made to explore the urban
and social universe of the colonial third culture by using and
examining its language. It has tried to convey, both explicitly
and implicitly, the 'conceptual model' of that culture as it
operated, first, in regard to the perception and, at a different
level, to the ordering of social, spatial and physical reality
in the realm of 'urban development'.

Clearly, a more explicit and accurate picture could be obtained
if such an ethnosemantic approach could be made in a genuinely
cross-cultural and comparative framework. Indeed, the analysis
of the nomenclature of the indigenous Indian city - *mohulla,
haveli, gali, hata* - and of the sacred and secular names with
which these functional units are designated, may well give us
a better understanding of the social dimensions of 'urbanism'
(see above, p.69) than the application of demographic and other
indices, taxonomies for defining urbanism which stem from other
cultures.

In the cultural mix of the contemporary Westernised Indian city,
two aspects of urban labelling are significant. The first results
from the expression of cultural nationalism which replaces the
names of a colonial past with those of a new national future.
In Delhi, for example, Curzon Road becomes Kasturba Gandhi Marg
and Wellesley Road, Dr Zakir Husain Marg. Statues are removed
from imperial pedestals and new heroes installed. This is one
of the more obvious measures taken by the elite of new nations
to make their cities look and feel their own, a need, as Southall
points out, common to all ex-colonial nations in Africa (1971).

Traditions of an institutionalised bureaucracy however, are more difficult to erase. In all Indian cities where they existed previously, *cantonments* and *civil stations* remain, both in name and fact, separated from the city. In building residential sectors for (a Socialist) government's employees, the names and indeed the forms of different urban units reflect the attitudes of a colonial Works Department, sired by a military paternalism. Urban areas are designated as *colonies* (e.g. Lodi Colony, Defence Colony), 'the district or quarter inhabited by a body of people of the same occupation settled among others' (Murray, 1888). The campus of a modern institution of higher education in the nation's capital has some dozen types of housing: the Director lives in a Type I *lodge* ('a house in a forest, or other wild place serving as a temporary abode in the hunting season, now used for the solitary houses of sportsmen during the shooting season') (*Oxford English Dictionary*, 1910), a term popularised by its use for the *Vice-Regal Lodge;* professors live in Type II *bungalows;* assistant professors inhabit Type III *flats;* lecturers live in Type IV *quarters* ('stations or lodgings assigned to soldiers) (Stocqueler 1853); dhobies occupy *barracks* ('an extensive building, erected for the lodgement of soldiers which has usually a square or open place in front for the purpose of drilling or parade')(ibid). Servants look for *quarters* rather than 'rooms', 'accommodation' or 'houses'. The staff restaurant is not a 'cafeteria', 'snack bar' or 'restaurant' but a *canteen* ('a species of sutling or public house, kept in a barrack-yard, or fortified place for the convenience of troops')(ibid) or more recently, 'a provision or liquor shop in camp or barracks' (*Concise Oxford Dictionary*,1971).

According to Mittal, 'in providing residential facilities to its employees the government of independent India followed the same principle of segregation as the British government' (1971,p.39). Segregation of groups by incomes was so complete that in some areas the name of the locality indicated the position of the residents in the administrative bureaucracy.

> Shan Nagar and Man Nagar were thus named because the position of its residents in the bureaucracy denoted high prestige (*shan*) and high status (*man*) accorded to them; Vinay Nagar, because its residents were in a position of submission *(vinay)* and Sewa Nagar, because its residents were 'Class IV Servants' and were expected to provide a service *(sewa)* (ibid.).

Another contemporary Indian sociologist writes

> The most striking aspect of the social distance between different grades of government officials is their residential segregation. Different grades of government officials live in houses of different kinds, and these are generally located in different residential areas. Some amount of residential segregation between status groups comes about spontaneously in all societies. But in the case of government officials in New Delhi, this has been the result of meticulous planning....
>
> In New Delhi today, a commodious house in an exclusive neighbourhood is one of the chief perquisites of a government official. Houses, and the areas in which they are located, are graded in an elaborate hierarchy. Secretaries live in spacious

bungalows with front and back lawns, and for others, there are houses ranging from Type A to Type G. Type A houses, mainly for Additional and Joint Secretaries, have six rooms, garages and servants' quarters; at the other end, there is provision of two and one-roomed accommodation~for lower division clerks and menial staff.

Not only are the houses different in character, but they are located in different areas, whose very names often signify gradations of status. The most exclusive area is Hastings Road, where Secretaries live in spacious bungalows, cheek by jowl with Ministers. Akbar Road also ranks very high, and in it live Secretaries and people of similar status....(Béteille, 1969,pp.234-45).

Changing adjectival names is an easy enough task; even removing statues and buildings is not an insuperable problem. Yet as this chapter has endeavoured to show, names - linguistic forms - are not isolated phenomena. Language, as Sapir has well expressed it, represents a distinct social reality, a reality which, in urban terms, means physical forms on the ground and the spatial usages and relationships between them. Whether in probing the present social and spatial structure of the city, or in re-planning its future, an ethnosemantic analysis of its nomenclature provides us with a useful tool with which to begin.

MILITARY SPACE:
The cantonment as a system of environmental control

Cultural concepts do not just (or even necessarily) identify what exists in the objective world; cultural systems, in one sense, create the world. Reality itself is culturally defined and cultural constructs partition this reality into numerous categories. Cultural categories are thus conceptual categories (Gary Witherspoon, 'Navajo Categories of objects at rest', *American Anthropologist*, 73,1,1971,p.110).

1   THE CANTONMENT AS CULTURE-SPECIFIC ENVIRONMENT

The cantonment or permanent military station was the institution-alised form of settlement for the military representatives of British colonial power in India from the eighteenth to the twentieth centuries. In this chapter, the cantonment is examined as a culture-specific environment, a system of built forms and spatial arrangements organised by a particular culture for a particular purpose and at a particular time. In so far as it represents a limited area of territory modified by one culture, yet situated in the larger geographic area of another, the cantonment provides a unique example of how environments are modified according to culture-specific criteria.

In making this examination, three problems are explored.

1 How cultures perceive, explain and modify their physical-spatial and natural environment. This includes a consideration of how systems of knowledge, especially 'medical' knowledge, are developed to explain 'breakdowns' in the relationship between man and his environment and also provide the means for making good such 'breakdowns'.
2 How the knowledge of and explanations for the man-environment relationship in any culture leads to the development of a technology to improve it. The concept of technology used here includes any modification of the environment by means of built structures, the spatial arrangements between them, the clearing of vegetation or similar activity.

3   How the successful functioning of this technology - the physical-spatial built form of an urban settlement - depends on the acceptance of a code of culturally-compatible behaviour.

In examining the cantonment, particular attention is paid to factors governing its location within the larger culture area of India, its relationship to indigenous settlement areas and its overall lay-out.

2   LOCATION AND LAY-OUT

In the mid-nineteenth century, there were, according to the report of a Royal Commission from which most of the data in this chapter are derived, some 227,000 members of the colonial military establishment in the host society, 85,000 of them European, the remainder recruited from the indigenous population (*Royal Comm.*, 1863). These 85,000 - our major focus of interest - were located in some 114 purpose-built cantonments, situated throughout the country. The number of European troops accommodated in these cantonments ranged from 50 to over 4,000, the average being about 800. Thirty cantonments accommodated over 1,000 European troops, and two, over 4,000.

Over half of these settlements were located 'on the plains', some 5 per cent of them between 1,200 and 7,800 feet above sea-level in the so-called 'hill stations' and the remainder, a few hundred feet above sea-level. The location of many of these cantonments was largely fortuitous, decided by the historical circumstances of the contact between the two cultures. Where battles were fought or territory taken over, camps were set up. In time, what was once temporary became more permanent. Strategic considerations accounted for the fact that many were located near local population centres, or on the northern frontier area.

Cantonments were of two kinds. In the older places of settlement such as Madras or Calcutta, either an indigenous walled fort, typical of many pre-industrial cities, was taken over and adapted for accommodation or, where this did not exist, a new fort was built and occupied. Sufficient ground area outside the fort dividing it from the 'native city' was kept clear for tactical reasons. Alternatively and more frequently, a camp was set up next to the indigenous town. In comparison with this town, sometimes containing as many as a quarter of a million people, densely packed within two or three square miles of a defensive wall, the cantonment covered an extensive area. In the case of seven cantonments situated near the major cities in Northern India, the average ground area covered was from seven to eight square miles, accommodating, with European and indigenous troops and ancillary personnel combined, not many more than 5,000 inhabitants (Figure 5.1 and 5.2; see also 3.1).

Figure 5.1

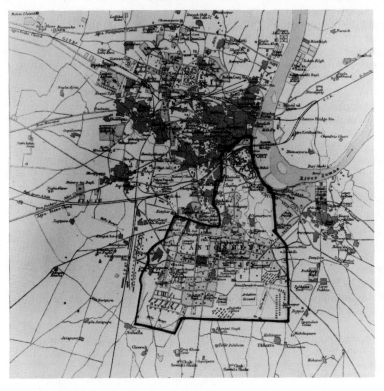

Figure 5.2

The lay-out of the cantonment depended on norms of social organisation in the metropolitan society as well as prevailing norms governing military organisation in the field.

> An encampment embraces the entire space of ground covered with canvas, of which the tents are constructed. The leading object in this arrangement is, that every battalion or squadron may be enabled to form with ease and expedition at any given moment. The extent of a camp is generally equal to the length of line occupied by the troops when drawn out in order of battle, and is usually calculated at the rate of two paces for every file of cavalry. The tents, both of cavalry and infantry, are arranged in rows perpendicular to the front of the encampment with intervals between them called streets; each row containing the tents of a troop or company. The companies are encamped in the order which they occupy when paraded in line....
>
> In the single rows for cavalry, an additional frontage must be given of 16 feet from the tent to the picket rope, 18 feet for the horse, and 4 feet for the manure, making a total of 19 yards for each troop. The breadth of the street is found by multiplying the frontage of each row by the total number, and subtracting the product from the extent of ground occupied by each regiment when drawn out; the remainder giving the space to be divided among the streets. The infantry tents open to the streets, those of the cavalry to the horses' heads.
>
> The tents of the captains and subalterns are pitched at the rear of their respective troops and companies, the former opening to the front, the latter opening to the rear. The field officers' tents are in rear of these, opening to the front and placed opposite to the outer streets of the battalion while that of the Commanding Officer is opposite to the centre of the street (Stocqueler, 1853).

Accommodation was divided into three basic categories: for indigenous troops, metropolitan troops and metropolitan officers (there were no indigenous officers). 'Native' troops were housed in self-constructed, temporary huts made from bamboo and matting and arranged in rough order in 'native lines'. Some distance away, European troops were accommodated either in tents or frequently in brick-built or wooden barracks. In earlier cantonments, these were often laid out in the form of a square and facing inwards onto it.

Officers' quarters were particularly distinctive and took up extensive areas. Each officer was housed in his own detached 'bungalow', centrally situated in a large plot or 'compound' of half an acre or more. Senior officers' compounds in some cantonments were five or ten acres in size, dimensions accounted for by the cultural preferences and activities discussed in the following chapter. Officers' quarters were grouped together, often along the 'parade ground', consuming a large proportion of the spatial area of the cantonment (Figure 5.3).

Other areas were taken up by the specific requirements of the institutional system of the European military community: religious institutions, in the form of Protestant, Catholic and nonconformist'

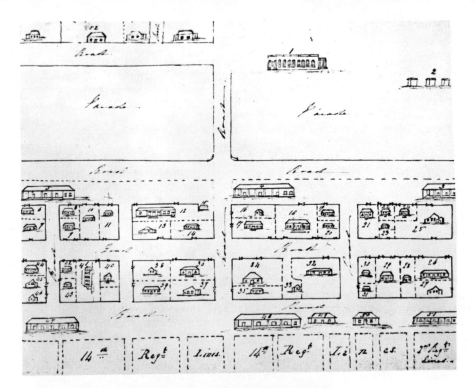

Figure 5.3

The annexed figure (1) drawn to scale, represents the 14 cubic feet of air which are used up per hour by each individual. This quantity of air, when returned from the lungs, exhausted of the vital element oxygen, is charged with carbonic acid to such an extent that it vitiates to a great and poisonous degree 100 cubic feet more of air.

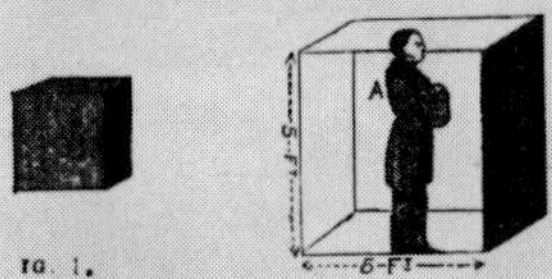

The adjoining sketch, drawn to the same scale as the former, contains 125 cubic feet of space, which is more than is provided for those living in Rose-alley and many other places to which we have directed attention. The figure A is a man of ordinary size compared with the cubic space provided in the dwellings in the alley ; and when we consider that in the St. Pancras dormitory, where 164 cubic feet were allowed to each person, Dr. Jones found that the air contained about thirty times its proper amount of dangerous carbonic acid,—as a matter of course the air in the dwellings in Rose-alley must be in a dreadful state of poisonous adulteration.

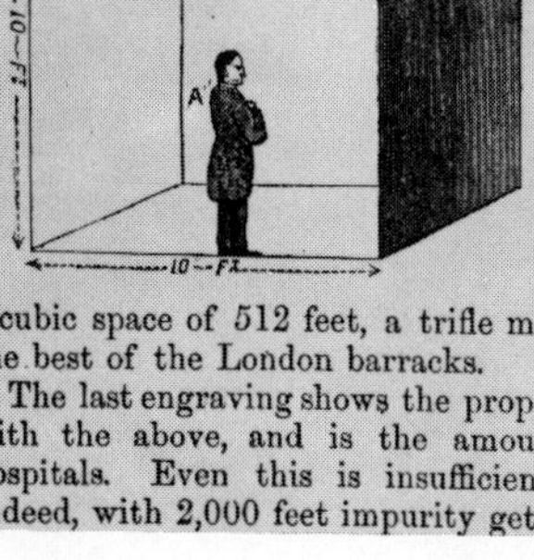

The next drawing represents a cubic space of 512 feet, a trifle more than the quantity allowed in the best of the London barracks.

The last engraving shows the proportion which 1,000 cubic feet bear with the above, and is the amount of space allowed in several hospitals. Even this is insufficient, without other arrangements : indeed, with 2,000 feet impurity gets in excess.

Figure 5.4

churches and burial grounds; social and recreational institutions in
the 'racket courts', 'public rooms' and race course for European
officers, and 'canteen', 'soldiers' gardens', 'ball court' and
library for European soldiers; economic institutions in the bazaar
and 'canteen', and separate hospitals for European and 'native'
troops. Extensive spatial provision was also needed for the
occupational and functional requirements of the military inhabitants.
These included separate parade grounds for European and indigenous
troops, camping and exercising grounds, shooting ranges, as well
as accommodation for a magazine, arms store, workshops, gunsheds
and horse lines. All units, though carefully related in space
according to military requirements, were widely dispersed across
the cantonment.

Although the cantonment occupied such an extensive area in the
early nineteenth century, an area accounted for by political,
cultural and technological factors, its spatial requirements were
to expand later in the century. This was due not simply to the
increased number of metropolitan troops accommodated after the
conflict between the two cultures in 1857, but to a changed perception of the man-environment relationship.

3   MODIFICATIONS IN THE MAN-ENVIRONMENT RELATIONSHIP

Towards the middle of the nineteenth century, a change took place
in the level of expectations from the modified environment of the
cantonment. The revised expectations were expressed in terms of
a higher life expectancy, decreased morbidity and lower death
rates for the inhabitants. As a consequence of these raised expectations, investigations were initiated, data collected and theories
put forward to interpret these data. On the basis of these theories,
changes were made in regard to the location of the cantonments as
well as their physical-spatial arrangements.

The change in expectations was brought about by the diffusion of
new forms of knowledge from the metropolitan society. Here, a
tradition of empirical investigation into natural phenomena, dating
largely from the seventeenth century, had led to the development
of various theories concerning the interaction of man with his
physical surroundings, particularly where it related to his physical condition and state of health. In the accelerated change
in man-environment systems brought on by processes of urbanisation
in the eighteenth and nineteenth centuries, these theories had been
developed, resulting not only in higher expectations but also in
new criteria for the accommodation of urban populations. A new,
science-based technology was developed with which these criteria
were put into practice. In addition to this new technology – the
provision of light, water, transport, waste-disposal systems –
new social technologies had been evolved in the form of administrative and governmental organisations. For example, 'local
government' was reorganised, 'improvement commissions' instituted,
and voluntary organisations coped with the increasing number of

problems generated by urban growth. New urban-industrial roles of
'public health inspector', 'civil engineer' and 'factory inspector'
were evolved as part of this process. These developments provide
the background against which the modifications of the cantonment
can be understood.

The changed expectations from the man-environment system of the
cantonment were brought about by comparing vital statistics from
the metropolitan society with statistics from comparable populations
in the colonial society. In the metropolitan society, annual
mortality for soldiers during peacetime was 17 per 1,000; in India,
not counting mortality from war, the figure was 58. At the age
of 20, expectation of life for European troops in the metropolitan
society of Britain was 59.5 years; in the colonial environment of
India it was 37.7 (*Royal Comm.*,1863,pp.15-18).

The investigation which took place had, therefore, the task of
explaining the causes of what were perceived as excessive rates
of morbidity and mortality and of recommending measures to reduce
them. If these could be reduced to levels comparable to those
in the metropolitan society, expectations would be met. In the
report of the investigation three basic explanations were offered.

The first cause of sickness was perceived as being *environmental*.
Diseases were thought to occur as a result of a combination of
factors such as air temperatures, humidity, the presence or absence
of particular types of vegetation, composition of the soil, quality
of water and the effects of elevation on these.

The two other causes of excessive morbidity and mortality were
seen to be *behavioural*, the first relating to matters of diet
(particularly the consumption of alcohol in quantities perceived
as 'excessive'); the second, relating to diseases stemming from
particular forms of social relations ('sexual diseases').

In considering these three explanations, and the modification of
the cantonment which results from them, attention is especially
drawn to their culture-specific nature. Not only did both
behavioural explanations apply mainly to the health of the
European troops, but also environmental explanations of disease
drew on culture-specific 'science' stemming from experience in
the metropolitan society. In this sense, therefore, we are discussing the ethnomedical explanations of the metropolitan culture
where expectations about health states are discussed primarily
in relation to value orientations and beliefs (see Polgar,1962;
Scotch, 1963; Fabrega, 1972).

4 LEVELS OF ENVIRONMENTAL CONTROL: A DESCRIPTIVE MODEL

The perceived causes of high mortality and morbidity rates and the
proposed response to them in this particular culture-specific environment can best be demonstrated by the use of the following
model (Table 5.1).

TABLE 5.1 Levels of environmental control: a descriptive model

I Types of available response (from McCoughlin, 1970, pp.39-40)	II Levels of Environment	III Illustrations of types of response	IV Case-study: nineteenth century recommended responses
1 LOCATIONAL	EXTERNAL 1 geographic region/area: elevation above sea level	move activity	1 1/3rd of activity moved to 'the hills' 2 activity moved to 'healthier' sites
2 DEVELOPMENTAL (modify environment to accommodate activity)	EXTERNAL 2 macro-environment (locality/area of services)	plant trees, build walls, construct sewers, drain lakes; prevent infiltration by non-culture members	increase extent of built plant, modify systems of water supply, sewers etc. Keep away from indigenous settlement
	3 intermediate environment I (building)	construct new, or modify old buildings	modify barracks, hospitals, etc.
	4 intermediate environment II (room)	modify rooms and internal divisions of space (raise ceilings, instal windows)	modify windows, floors, ventilation system, spatial distribution of activities inside building

5	micro-environment (body covering)	modify headgear and clothing (warmer and different design)	modify dress (especially headgear), flannel under-garment, uniforms
INTERNAL			
3 BEHAVIOURAL	6 physiological	modify behaviour, (e.g. sanitation practices, modify diet, modify physiological system by drugs) (biochemical)	'gymnasium' made compulsory, alternative forms of recreation encouraged, sale of alcohol controlled, reorganise activities
	7 cognitive	alter state of knowledge, (resocialisation); change value-system	teach medical hygiene, reorient goals and provide opportunities to transfer to Civil Service

The model is based on what McCoughlin has called 'dissatisfaction with place-related activities' (1970,p39). Such dissatisfaction may be overcome by three types of response, locational, developmental and behavioural.

One might, for example, consider the problem of a family needing to accommodate grandparents. The possible solution would be either to move house (locational), build an extra room (developmental) or re-programme activities and mealtimes (behavioural) to accommodate the new arrivals. In the model, the levels of environment are divided between the *internal* (the body), classified into the physiological and cognitive levels (6 and 7), and the *external*, a series of levels classified according to spatial distance or volume (5 to 1). The kind of response to a perceived dissatisfaction with the environment, available at these different levels, is shown in column III.

By distinguishing these seven levels of 'environment' we are able more easily to identify those levels and types of response which are (a) most effective and (b) least effective in dealing with a problem caused by dissatisfaction with a particular environment. To anticipate the outcome of the next few pages, it becomes immediately clear, in the light of current bacteriological theories of disease, that the most effective way of dealing with problems of disease is at the *internal*, cognitive and physiological level, that is to say, to understand the causes of disease and to modify our subsequent behaviour accordingly; second, by the use of preventive measures such as immunisation, inoculation and the use of curative and preventive drugs. In the light of present-day knowledge, the primary concern of the metropolitan power with developmental and locational (i.e. environmental) responses at levels 1 to 5, as a solution to the problem of disease can, therefore, be seen as basically erroneous, if not totally irrelevant.

The concern of the metropolitan power with the *external*, locational and developmental levels is well illustrated by the terms of reference of the official investigation into the perceived excessive rates of mortality and morbidity. These were
> to inquire into such causes of sickness and mortality; whether as relates to climate, locality, state of barracks, drainage, water supply, diet, drink, dress, duties or habits of troops... and into the subject of Healthy Positions generally with the view of recommending the most healthy for future occupation....
>   the best construction of barracks, huts, hospitals and tents for India....
>   the present regulations or practice for preserving the health of troops and enforcing medical and sanitary police....
>   the present organisation of the Army Sanitary and Medical Service....
>   the practicability of establishing a general system of military statistics throughout India and to ascertain whether any and what means exist of comparing diseases and mortality of troops with those of the civil population, English and native *(Royal Comm.,* 1863,p.iii).

Each of these factors and the order in which they are stated can
be shown to fit into the seven different levels of the model
as follows

TABLE 5.2

	Hypothetical explanation	Levels of environment
Locational	Climate, locality	1 Geographic location in terms of space or elevation
Develop-mental	Locality, drainage, water supply	2 Macro-environment (locality)
	State of barracks, huts, hospitals	3 Intermediate environment I (building)
	State of barracks, tents	4 Intermediate environment II (room)
	Dress	5 Micro-environment (body covering)
Behavioural	Diet, drink, duties, habits, regulations and practice concerning health	6 Physiological
	System of statistics to compare diseases and mortality rates between different sections of indigenous and non-indigenous populations (information/data)	7 Cognitive

The model also helps in understanding the indigenous, Indian
man-environment system. In brief, what made this work (with a
lower incidence of mortality and morbidity), were culturally-
learnt *behavioural* factors, for example, mores which determined
that defecation be performed at a distance from living and eating
quarters, strict caste rules governing the handling and consumption of food, as well as the interaction between castes
engaged on 'unclean' activities and the remainder of the community,
the use of separate hands for eating and perineal cleansing.
Physiological factors were also important such as the development
of relative immunity from bacteriological infection through constant exposure to risk. Finally, *cognitive* factors explained the
ability to accommodate what members of other cultures perceived
as excessive sickness or mortality, and explain these as part of

a totally different world view which held that 'life-on-earth' was, in comparison to the world-view of the metropolitan culture, a transitory experience.

In considering the locational, developmental and behavioural responses of the metropolitan power to the problem of 'excessive' mortality and morbidity, we are able to see how the cantonment environment was modified, especially in terms of built form and the utilisation of space.

5   LOCATIONAL RESPONSES TO DISEASE: THE CHOICE OF SITE

The major environmental variables affecting rates of sickness and health were perceived as the nature, quality and temperature of the local air and water, the presence of surrounding vegetation and the relationship between these and persons in the vicinity.

Excessive mortality was ascribed to what, in the mid-nineteenth century, were termed 'zymotic' diseases - diseases perceived as being caused by a process analagous to fermentation. The most common of these was malaria, literally 'bad air', 'that subtle unknown agent or rather that cause of disease known only by its effects'. Malaria was thought to be dependent on the interaction of three environmental elements, heat, moisture and vegetable decomposition. It was most intense in 'low, warm and moist locations where there was a super-abundance of vegetation and water', though it also occurred in dry situations without these conditions. It was thought that malaria could be checked by the 'withdrawal of any one of the three elements (i.e. heat, moisture or vegetable decomposition) 'on the coexistence of which it depends' (it might be added that the modern understanding of the cause of malaria was discovered some forty years after the period under consideration, in 1896).

Elevation was an important factor affecting these variables. It was believed that 'a certain amount of destruction of European health results from residence on the plains'. Carefully chosen sites, with settlements situated away from the wet, windward side of mountain slopes, where the air was cool and dry and vegetation scanty, at heights between 2,000 and 4,000 feet were thought to be healthier. However, certain hazards had to be avoided, such as 'ravines full of dead animals and the ordure of many thousands of natives' and what were perceived as 'malaria-laden mists rolling up the mountains'.

This explanation for the causes of malaria, and the belief that they were considerably reduced by moving to higher elevations where cooler air temperatures prevailed, had profound effects on the settlement pattern of the European army in India. Since the early nineteenth century, European 'hill stations' had been founded in the lower Himalayas and elsewhere for a variety of social, cultural and strategic reasons. Though it was also thought that they provided a healthier and more comfortable climate, the

particular ethnomedical theories of the 1860s now gave them increasing importance. From then on it was recommended that,
subject to strategic considerations, one third of the establishment of European troops in India should preferably be permanently
located in 'the hills'. On similar criteria, cantonments in
malaria-prone areas were to be moved to 'healthier' sites, defined
according to their characteristics of air, water and vegetation
(ibid.,p.87).

Similar environmental, and especially 'aerial' factors were perceived as affecting the health of troops at the 'macro' level.
This level includes the area enclosed by the boundaries of the
cantonment and that part of the adjoining environment (generally
understood to be about two to three miles radius from the
boundaries) affected by its presence.

In addition to the factors mentioned above, stagnant water,
excreta, decaying vegetable matter and 'exhalations' from the
human body were also considered instrumental in causing 'zymotic'
diseases. It was believed that the air given off from these
sources was in some way poisonous and carried the means of infection. The infectious quality of the air and the degree of
its pollution could be determined by olfactive criteria. The
consequence of such theories was that 'the mere fact that
(neighbouring native towns) are near to European barracks must
necessarily exercise an injurious influence on the healthiness
of both barracks and hospitals, if the native dwellings are in
an unwholesome condition.' The role of the prevailing winds in
carrying infection-laden air from the 'native city' to the cantonment was also perceived as crucial. In the early siting of
cantonments, 'no limit to the proximity by which these large
native populations may approach European barracks nor to their
position as regards prevailing winds' had been laid down. In
one main centre of European population, a high wall had been
built round the grounds of a major public building 'expressly
for the purpose of excluding noxious smells that may issue from
the drains'.

Apart from such 'noxious smells', indigenous sanitation habits,
evolved over centuries in accordance with prevailing norms and
a complex concept of physical and social pollution, as also with
prevailing levels of technology, were perceived as a further
source of infection to the immigrant European culture. In one
city, with an indigenous population of over 100,000, 'the environs
of the military cantonment are resorted to for the purposes of
nature' giving rise by 'the excessive accumulation of surface
filth, to offensive odours injurious to the public health'.

The belief in this 'aerial' theory of disease is well documented.
    Impure air and water may not be the only causes of cholera,
    dysentery, malaria... but when the source of these impurities
    is the exhalations from the human body, they are the most
    powerful exciting causes of those diseases'... 'I believe
    that the part which the excrementitious matters of the

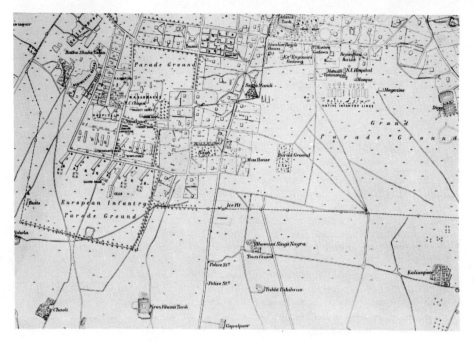

Figure 5.5 Levels of environmental control: 2. The macro environment. Boundaries are free of development; 'parade grounds' extend the zonal barrier. Barracks are 'en échelon' (p.114); officers' bungalows are isolated and dispersed round the 'parade ground'

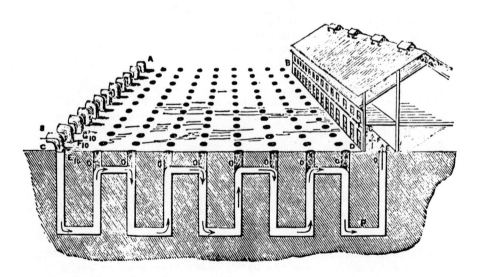

Figure 5.6 Levels of environmental control: 2. The macro environment of the locality.

affected play in the dissemination of epidemic diseases is
chiefly due to the gases given off by them immediately or
soon after they are voided, which gases enter the system
through the lungs (Clark, 1864,p.103).

The volume of air in barracks and tents per person was important
because 'organic matter given off by the lungs... tends to attach
itself to the walls of tents' (Duncan, 1888,p.58). The quantity
of air needed in such tents was culturally, or perhaps racially
defined, as also in all accommodation.

> European inmates in tropical climates to have a minimum of
> 72 superficial feet and more, if possible, with 1000 to
> 1500 cubic feet of air.... For natives, these numbers
> admit of reduction... with 42 superficial feet and 600
> cubic feet of air (King, 1875, p.220).

This concern with quantity and quality of air, a central theme
in the ethnomedical ideas of the metropolitan society (Figure
5.4), had significant spatial and locational implications for
the cantonment.

> The immediate neighbourhoods of large cities, especially
> in the leeward direction are not satisfactory localities
> for our troops. The sanitary condition of all Indian
> towns cannot be described as less than vile.
>
>   Localities not susceptible of easy drainage would be
> shunned and old graveyards and sites of ancient cities
> escaped. The whole cantonment would front the prevailing
> winds, native houses, bazaars, burial grounds, places
> of Hindoo incremation, in fact, all essentials excepting
> wells, would be placed rearward to European residences...
> the station should be surrounded by a zone of one or two
> miles radius, free from cultivation and irrigation. Such
> extent of country should be grass land with clumps of
> trees or occasional gardens... all refuse from the can-
> tonment should be removed by manual labour without these
> limits if not susceptible of being destroyed by fire within
> such space (Moore,1862,pp.117-18). (see Figure 5.5).

Similar considerations had led, in the eastern region of India,
to the prohibition of agricultural activities involving irrigation,
within five miles of military cantonments.

Two issues are relevant here. The first, the belief that 'polluted
air' is the main agent of sickness, a belief unsupported by modern
biological theories of medicine; the second, that olfactory experiences which are unfamiliar are an index of the 'healthiness'
of the air. As Hall points out, olfactory preferences are learnt
sensations, determined both culturally and socially (1959,pp.43-7).

Apart from helping to determine the geographical location of
the cantonment and also its position in relation to indigenous
centres of settlement, such theories also governed the design
of built forms on the cantonment as well as their spatial
distribution.

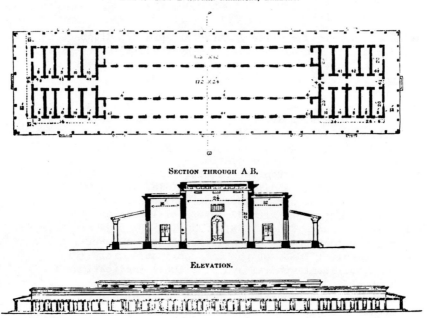

FIG. 3.—NEW EUROPEAN BARRACKS, BELLARY.

SECTION THROUGH A B.

ELEVATION.

Figure 5.7 Levels of environmental control: 3 and 4. The intermediate environment of building and room.

Figure 5.8 Levels of environmental control: 5. The micro environment of body-cover

6   DEVELOPMENTAL RESPONSES TO DISEASE: THE MODIFICATION OF THE
    LOCAL ENVIRONMENT

Within the macro environment, which included the area outside
the cantonment boundaries, the enclosed space of the camp is
considered, including the two intermediate levels of environmental control, the building and the room.

To improve the immediate environment of the barracks, proposals
aimed at reducing the temperature of the air. One such proposal
was a series of interlinking wells which, by lowering ground
temperatures, would,in consequence, reduce the temperature
of the air above. Combined with double-roofed barracks, this
meant that excessive heat, and the perceived threat to health
states which it posed, could be avoided (Figure 5.6).

As water supply, 'cleanliness' and waste-disposal were also
perceived as significant factors affecting morbidity, the re-
organisation of services was seen as essential. Again, this
had spatial implications. In the early cantonments, water had
been distributed in accordance with the practice of the indigenous
culture, delivered by the *bhisti* (water carrier) in leather skins.
Though some stations had 'plunge baths', no special accommodation
existed for washing or bathing, which was frequently carried
out in barrack rooms. 'Latrines' and 'urinals' were situated
in outbuildings at a distance from the barracks. These usually
had no drainage arrangements, the excreta being regularly removed
by indigenous 'sweepers' and buried.

Concern with environmental causes of disease now suggested that
these arrangements be changed. Barracks were to be supplied with
sufficient ablution and bathing accommodation and a constant
water supply. 'Drinking fountains' with filtered water were
to be provided. Iron or earthenware water latrines, drained to
an outlet were to be introduced, cesspits abolished and urinals
supplied. Extra structures involved in these proposals such as
filtration equipment, heating units, and pumping equipment made
increasing spatial demands on the total area.

The effect of the 'aerial' theories on the built environment of
the cantonment can best be illustrated with reference to the
barracks and hospital. In these, personal 'air space' became
the main criterion of design.

Though it varied in detail, one basic model of barrack accommodation
existed in most cantonments. This was a single-storeyed hut with
doors on opposite sides and walls protected by verandahs. Other,
less frequent, models were the 'casemented' variety, built on
two floors and another, with the centre portion carried higher
than the two sides, 'as in a Gothic cathedral', with air cir-
culating through windows in the 'clerestorey'. There being no
restriction on ground area consumed, single-storey structures
were common (Figure 5.7).

The size of such barracks depended on the size of military units.
These, in turn, were determined by tactical or strategic consideration. Consequently, a 'company' might be accommodated in
one large barrack, although the dimensions of these varied. The
largest, accommodating 400 men, was 100 yards short of half a mile
long, though only 20 feet wide. In this barrack, each man had 1,000
cubic feet of air space and about 64 square feet of personal ground
area. Smaller barracks, more recently erected and accommodating
only 16 men, measured 48 by 24 feet and gave 1,703 cubic and 72
square feet of personal space to each man.

Dissatisfaction with perceived health states, however, required
that new barrack accommodation be designed in accordance with
'medical' rather than strategic or administrative criteria. As
the main variable thought to affect health states was the nature,
temperature, quality and quantity of available air, it was important
to know where beds were placed in relation to windows, how air
entered the barrack room, the height of bed legs above the floor
surface, the height of barrack buildings above the surrounding
ground area, whether windows were with or without glass and whether
doors were closed at night. Throughout all cantonments, average
personal space for each European soldier was between 60 and 70 square
and 650 and 700 cubic feet.

Concern for improved health states led to the raising of these
norms. In future barracks, personal air volume was to be between
1,000 and 1,500 cubic feet, superficial areas, from 80 to 100
square feet, 'according to the airiness of the position'. In
future, beds were to be kept three feet apart.

The overall size of barracks was to be limited. Not more than a
quarter of a company were to be housed in one building. Small
barracks holding not more than 16 men were to be preferred. The
replacement of larger by smaller structures, together with the
arrangement of the new units 'en échelon' to encourage the cir-
culation of air around them was a further factor making more
extensive spatial demands on the cantonment. Hospitals were

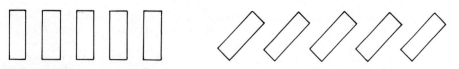

Early nineteenth-century pattern   Later nineteenth-century pattern

modified along the same principles.

A particularly apt illustration of the measured spatial demands
made on the culture-specific environment of the cantonment relates
to the mores associated with the disposal of the dead. Hindu

corpses were either cremated or disposed of, according to custom,
in a nearby river. If Muslim, they were buried outside the cantonment. As the norms of the Christian religion required that
European corpses be buried within the culture area of the cantonment, an appropriate area had to be provided. Because of the
potential health hazard which such an area was thought to create,
recommended 'dead spaces' were to be 7½ by 2 by 3 feet deep, each
divided from the next by a minimum 2 feet.

7   THE MICRO ENVIRONMENT

The fifth level of environmental control to be considered was the
micro environment of body cover. The most extensive discussion
was devoted to headgear. The protection of the head from direct
sunlight was considered the first and most fundamental prerequisite
of 'health', 'excessive heat on the brain produc(ing) moral depression'. The concern with this level of environmental control
is manifest in the credence given by members of the metropolitan
culture to the complex technology involved in the design of culture-
specific headgear for use in tropical environments (Figure 5.8).
According to the contemporary description, the 'essence of an
efficient head dress' was perceived as 'a copious and controllable
current of ventilation'. The helmet was 'stepped to avoid the
pressure of the wind.... Air enters... by numerous apertures,
sweeping up between the outer shell and the inner shell or crown
and washes away as much heat as it can from the interior surface....
The crown and outer surface are lined with tinned paper or aluminium
leaf'. The helmet was fixed on the head by means of a 'draw cap
of open canvas... made on purpose so open a texture as to transmit
perspiration freely'. This was connected to 'band clips (which)
held firmly at the back of the head at the same time permitting
the helmet to sit with military uprightness on the head'....The
band was attached to a cord, which in turn was fixed 'to a round
peg of hard wood... fixed on a wooden ratchet'. This 'prevents
any horizontal shaking of the helmet back, forwards or sideways'
(*Royal Comm.*, 1863,pp.322-325. For a comprehensive and interesting account of such theories, see Renbourn, 1961).

8   THE BEHAVIOURAL ELEMENT IN THE MAN-ENVIRONMENT RELATIONSHIP

The causes of what were perceived as lowered states of health on
the cantonment have been classified into the *environmental* and
the *behavioural*. Though such a categorisation may be heuristically
useful, it overlooks the essential inter-dependence between
environmental and behavioural factors in any man-environment
system. 'Environmental' elements, such as those of water, air or
vegetation only become significant in explanations of states of
health when examined in relation to the behaviour of actors in
contact with them; similarly, the significance of actors' behaviour
as it is thought to relate to health can be appreciated only if
related to the environmental context in which it takes place. Thus,
the presence of polluted water is not in itself a health hazard;

it only becomes so when the actor decides to drink it. Likewise,
the act of drinking water is not in itself a health hazard; it
only becomes so if the water is polluted. What is more important
here is a matter central to this case-study, namely, that health
states are dependent on behaviour and behaviour is determined
by culture.

Provided that this inter-relatedness is recognised, it is nevertheless convenient to treat the various variables perceived as
affecting states of health as those which are *primarily* 'environmental' and those which are *primarily* 'behavioural'.

The first behavioural cause perceived as resulting in lower health
states was a matter of diet, particularly the consumption of
alcohol in excess of culturally defined limits of tolerance, a
practice referred to as 'intemperance'. Officially prescribed
norms of the military establishment permitted each member to
purchase one twentieth of a gallon of raw spirit or one quart
of malt liquor each day. If, as was normally the case, this was
consumed, the annual intake of raw spirit was equal to some
eighteen gallons. The effects of this level of consumption were
thought to account for the prevalence of liver diseases, 'apoplexy'
and other disorders. It was usual for some 10 per cent of all
hospital admissions to be attributable to alcoholism.

The second behavioural cause of reduced states of health was
seen to arise from the particular social relationships established
with female members of the indigenous society, and which resulted
in 'sexual diseases'. Between 20 per cent and 25 per cent and,
in some cases, up to 50 per cent of all 'sick' admissions to
hospital were cases of venereal disease. Among European members
of the army, there were between 249 and 345 cases of venereal
disease for every 1,000 troops, a rate ten times that for indigenous troops. (In the indigenous society, syphilis was
referred to as *Feringhee*, the 'foreign' or 'European' disease.
See Reynolds, 1937,p.295).

Both 'intemperance' and 'sexual diseases' were perceived as
occupational diseases, consequent upon the system of supervised
inactivity which formed the customary behaviour for the army
in India.

> The soldier rises at gunfire, attends his parade or drill
> which is over soon after sunrise. He then returns to his
> barrack and during the hot season, he is not allowed to
> leave till late afternoon. At one o'clock, he consumes a
> large amount of animal food and vegetables, porter (perhaps
> a quart) and spirits. He has few or no means of occupying
> himself rationally. He lies on his bed and perhaps sleeps
> most of the day. He has his evening parade or drill, and
> his turn of guard duty once every 5, 7 or 10 days (*Royal
> Comm.*, 1863,p.68).

Over a century after these comments were made, a one-time member
of the colonial army in India, commenting on the volume of 'personal
space' available in the barracks, reported
> All he could lay claim to was perhaps one hundred cubic
> feet for ninety per cent of his life. He had his own bed
> and his own kit box. This bed was the centre of his life.
> He used it for everything... as a writing desk, as a
> cleaning room, as a work bench, as a card table, and when
> he wasn't doing anything on the bed he was sleeping in it.
> A great part of the time in India he slept, principally
> because he had nothing else to do (Allen, 1975,p.154).

Three solutions were recommended to solve these inter-related
problems. Each had important spatial implications for the cantonment environment.

In the first place, as indigenously produced liquor was seen as
the major source of 'intemperance', troops should be kept away
from the 'bazaars'. As bazaars were also accepted as the source
of 'sexual diseases' the separation of the cantonment from the
indigenous town was seen as a major deterrent. The segregation
of troops from indigenous sources of women and liquor was also
seen as a principal advantage of the hill station.
> In most hill stations, the difficulty of approach, except
> by authorized public roads would greatly facilitate the
> exclusion of two at least of the greatest banes of can-
> tonment life on the plains, the poisonous spirituous liquor
> of the bazaars and the venereal infection... a few sentries
> ought to be sufficient to guard a well-chosen hill station
> from these great evils (Royal Comm.,p.144).

The principle of strict segregation from the indigenous population
(as well, incidentally, as the civilian members of the colonial
community) was maintained to the end of colonial rule. For the
lower-ranking members of the military establishment 'the first
order that appeared when you got to a new station stated that
all Indian villages, Indian shops, Indian bazaars and the civil
lines were out of bounds to all troops'. 'As far as possible,
the military cantonment was self-contained, with its own approved
bazaar' (Allen, 1975,p.15).

The second solution was to encourage alternative modes of activity.
Many cantonments already provided space for 'recreational'
activities introduced from the metropolitan society. Here,
such activities had been developed, particularly since the
eighteenth century, to occupy the increasing amount of non-working
free time associated with the development of industrialisation.

Many of these activities had begun in a pre-industrial context.
Little specialised equipment had been used and they had taken
place in the open fields of an agrarian society. Increasing
industrial urbanisation institutionalised such 'leisure' activity,
leading to an increase in organisation, the formulation of rules
and the provision of specialised localities as part of the urban
environment.

Such activities, based on the use of a ball and other types of
equipment (see pages 56-7 in Chapter 3) took place on the cantonment and might include 'cricket', 'quoits', 'billiards',
'bagatelle', 'football', 'rackets', 'skittles' and in the later
nineteenth century, 'polo'. In addition, spatial provision was
made for pursuits which fulfilled both occupational and
recreational purposes such as 'horse-racing', 'horse-jumping'
and 'fencing'.

Dissatisfaction with the health-lowering levels of inactivity
suggested that such facilities were neither sufficiently available
on all cantonments, nor were they, in themselves, sufficient to
occupy the attention of the cantonment's inhabitants. It was,
therefore, proposed that 'the means of instruction and recreation
be extended to meet the requirement of each station'. Covered
sheds were to be provided for exercise and gymnastics, libraries
built or improved and reading rooms established. Workshops and
'soldiers' gardens' were to be introduced.

The third solution to the problems of 'intemperance' and 'sexual
disease' was thought to be an increase in the proportion of
married men on the cantonment. In terms of spatial requirements,
this demanded an extension of married accommodation in the form
of 'detached cottages' each within its own plot of land.

It is worth mentioning, in conclusion, that the fundamental reason
for the location of European troops in India was political. In
the dominance-dependence relationship inherent in colonialism,
armed force was the ultimate sanction. Yet where, in the
eighteenth and early nineteenth centuries, cantonments had been
located and laid out according to fortuitous or strategic criteria,
in the later nineteenth and early twentieth centuries, criteria
of 'health', interpreted according to culture-specific explanations
of the causes of disease, increasingly decided layout and location.
According to the *Cantonments Manual*, 1909, 'it should be carefully
borne in mind that the cardinal principle underlying the administration of cantonments in India is that *cantonments exist primarily
for the health of the British troops* and to considerations affecting
the well-being and efficiency of the garrison, all other matters
must give place' (Mackenzie, 1929,p.114).

9   THE INTER-DEPENDENCE OF ENVIRONMENT AND BEHAVIOUR

The successful functioning of any man-environment system depends
not only on a technologically modified environment but also, on
a learnt code of behaviour. Such behaviour consists of a set of
institutionalised norms, either internalised within a particular
culture, or enforced by a system of sanctions.

The cantonment was a culture-specific environment situated in an
alien cultural setting. European inhabitants could be expected
to follow their own norms of behaviour. For members of the
indigenous society, however, such norms were alien and had to be

learnt. It was, therefore, essential for a new code of behaviour
to be devised governing the operation of the cantonment environment and the interaction of members of the indigenous society
with it. The power structure of colonialism enabled such a code
to be enforced by means of penalties (including fines, imprisonment and occasionally corporal punishment) as well as example
and persuasion.

The rules of behaviour were formulated in the *Cantonments Acts,
Regulations and Codes* issued between 1864 and 1924 (1864, 1887,
1880, 1889, 1912, 1924). Many of these rules relating to sanitation
practices and embodied in the first Cantonments Act of 1864 were
modelled on metropolitan legislation, particularly the Public
Health Act, 1848, Nuisance Removal and Disease Prevention Acts
1855 and Local Government Act, 1858. Other sources were the
Bye-laws and Instructional Minutes issued by the Board of Health
and Home Department in Calcutta, the Indian Penal Code, the Calcutta
Municipal and Police Acts, the Bengal District Municipal Improvement Act (see *Cantonment Regulations* 1887,p.55. Much of French
municipal legislation for colonial urban development in the Middle
East and North Africa subsequently drew on British colonial models.
(Personal communication, Professor Janet Abu-Lughod).

A basic objective of these rules was to define the spatial area of
the cantonment and establish control over its adjacent region.
   Wherever it shall appear necessary for the protection of
   troops... it shall be lawful for the Governor General in
   India to extend the limits of any military cantonment...
   and to define the limits around such cantonment within
   which such rules... shall be in force.
Within this culture area, behaviour perceived as interfering with
the new man-environment system set up in the cantonment was
forbidden.
   Any persons... who sell or supply... spirituous liquor...
   for the use of an European soldier... or soldier's wife...
   without a license... shall be liable to a fine... or
   imprisonment... or to the punishment of whipping....
   The depositing of dirt, refuse... on public roads, wastes,
   or unoccupied ground, except in such manner and at such
   times (as permitted) is prohibited... no cart or carriage
   to be used not having a covering proper for preventing the
   escape of contents therefrom or stench therefrom.
Other punishable offences included carrying exposed meat, letting
fall 'nightsoil', carrying an 'indecently-covered corpse', failing
to bury a corpse within twenty-four hours, or storing any substance
emitting 'an offensive smell'.

Behaviour acceptable to the members of the indigenous culture outside the boundaries of the cantonment was not permitted inside them.
   No person shall perform the offices of nature in any other
   place within the cantonment than such as may be appointed...
   no person shall commit a nuisance by easing himself in or
   by the side of... any public road.... No bathing is to take
   place at places or times forbidden by the cantonment committee...
   no washing, cleansing by the side of any river, spring,

> tank, well, or source of water derived for public use... of
> any animal, wool, cloth, wearing apparel is permitted....
> No corpse is to be thrown in the river.

Most of the practices listed above were prohibited on account of
their perceived connection with the state of health on the cantonment. Other practices, however, were forbidden as being
instrusions into what was rapidly becoming a completely culturally
controlled environment.

> Every occupier of any ground within the limits of the
> cantonment shall trim or prune hedges and trees thereon
> in such a manner as the Cantonment Committee... shall
> prescribe... no persons shall cut down... any tree of
> mature growth... without the sanction of the Cantonment
> Committee.... No person shall beat a drum or tom tom, or
> blow or sound any instrument at any time or in any place
> prohibited by the Officer Commanding of the Cantonment.
> No person shall cruelly beat, abuse or torture any animal.
> The Officer Commanding, or Cantonment Magistrate... may
> order that boundary walls, hedges or fences... shall not
> exceed a specific height.

In this way, a total *culture area* was established where the
environment was modified not only according to culture-specific
theories of 'medicine' but also, to accord with equally culture-
specific olfactory, aural and visual preferences. The following
account gives some insight into this environment as it was perceived
by a member of the indigenous culture in the last two decades of
colonial rule.

> Somehow, the White Sahibs (really red) always saw to it that
> the best landscape in the town was reserved for the army.
> And, within a cantonment, they brought a discipline to bear
> which ensured that the roads were repaired as soon as they
> were torn up by the rains or too much traffic and watered,
> morning and afternoon, to keep the dust at bay, hedges trimmed,
> so as to set off the bungalows to effect; and there they
> lived,and moved and had their being, in a seemingly grim,
> awe-inspiring silence, only broken now and then by an
> occasional pink Memsahib's call for the 'Arderly' or the
> 'Bera'.

> The old guns captured from the Sikhs, or the Afghans, during
> the wars fought by the Angrezi Sarkar for the conquest of the
> country, decorated all four entrances of the bungalow of the
> Brigadier General and the Union Jack clung to a tall pole
> above for lack of air to make it flutter.... Ferocious bull-
> dogs, elegant spaniels and great danes, Irish terriers, as
> well as pekinese lapdogs, barked according to their various
> capacities from the verandahs to keep away intruders and
> trespassers, while the sentries, at every half a mile,
> insisted, in hush-hush voices, especially to the children,
> that we should be seen but not heard in the vicinity of the
> Sahib's bungalows...

> The hours of the day were struck on bells and the early
> morning and the last post bugles were blown, to punctuate
> the rigid routine of the sepoys, for parade, food, rest,
> parade, food and sleep (Anand, 1968,p.317).

(According to an indigenous informant in 1970, in the Delhi
Civil Lines between 1910 and 1920, 'fierce dogs' were kept by
the 'British sahibs' to keep watch over individual compounds,
rather than *chowkidars* or watchmen. Spitting, throwing of litter
and urinating were penalised by heavy fines. 'Officers' shopping
in Chandni Chowk, one of the two main retailing centres in Old
Delhi, were preceded by members of the military police.)

10   CONCLUSION

In the investigations of the metropolitan theorists into the
perceived 'excessive' mortality and morbidity of the cantonment
environment, it is worth noting that less than 5 per cent of
their evidence related to the mores and behaviour of the indigenous troops. These were accommodated in 'native lines' where
each constructed his own straw or bamboo and matting hut,measuring
some 10 by 7½ by 7 feet high with a volume of just over 500 cubic
feet and often containing the 'sepoy' and numerous of his kin.
These huts were 'without order or regularity', 'completely without
drainage or ventilation' and closely packed together. A hole in
the ground by the doorway was used to deposit refuse. No 'sanitary
supervision' was exercised by the European authorities.

Irrespective of these conditions, and with few hospital facilities,
the mortality rate was, at 18 per 1,000, much below that of the
metropolitan troops. Though some attention is given to these
facts, almost all of the 900 pages of evidence collected in the
investigation relates to the situation of European soldiers. On
the occasions when attention is focused on the indigenous civil
and military population it is within the framework of ideas and
theory drawn from the totally different environment and culture
of the metropolitan society. It was in this society where
> formerly, many people (had) doubted the practicability
> of diminishing epidemic diseases but a more rational mode
> of inquiry, pursued chiefly in this country, had led to
> the discovery... that there are certain well-defined con-
> ditions which influence... their intensity and frequency.

These conditions included 'soil drainage', 'cleanliness', 'fresh
air', 'diminished crowding' and 'better ventilation'. In transferring these essentially *environmentalist* explanations from one
culture area to another and in believing that 'zymotic diseases
have always been the chief causes of mortality in uncivilised or
imperfectly civilised countries', members of the metropolitan
society, convinced by the credibility of their own cultural
explanations, were inhibited from paying more attention to the
cultural context of indigenous behaviour. Yet as has been shown,
it is at this *internal,* behavioural and cognitive level that any
man-environment relationship is to be most fully comprehended.

At a more general level, the case-study suggests that in any system of man-environment interaction, expectations - whether relating to states of health, economic returns or 'aesthetic' satisfaction - are of an essentially relative nature, dependent on the inherent value system and world-view of a culture and the 'knowledge' which this culture brings to bear on the man-environment relationship.

Chapter 6

RESIDENTIAL SPACE:
The bungalow-compound complex as a study in the cultural use of space

I believe it both preferable and clarifying for us to speak
of the environment in which man lives as a 'culturally
constituted behavioural environment' rather than to say that
man lives in a 'social' or 'cultural' environment, without
further analysis (I. Hallowell, The self and its behavioural
environment, *Culture and Experience*, 1967,p.87).

We do not see the environment as though it were a photograph
or slide. Even when we consider sense modalities other than
vision, we do more than merely observe the environment. We
are immersed in it and participate in it with *all* our senses
and in different ways - as individuals, as members of ethnic,
social or cultural groups (Amos Rapoport, The study of
spatial quality, *Journal of Aesthetic Education*, 4,4, 1970,p.81).

1   THE BUNGALOW-COMPOUND AS A CULTURALLY CONSTITUTED BEHAVIOURAL
    ENVIRONMENT

The colonial bungalow, more accurately described as the colonial
bungalow-compound complex, is the basic residential unit of the
colonial urban settlement. Originally developed in India, the
concept of the bungalow was diffused, in the late nineteenth
century, to Africa and other parts of the Far East, becoming the
modal form of residence for members of the European colonial
community in the country of colonisation (King, 1973a, 1973b).

Using this example as the unit of analysis, the underlying aim of
this chapter is to demonstrate, for a particular culture, the
existence of what Hallowell has termed, a 'culturally constituted
behavioural environment' (1967,p.87). The analysis shows how
different behavioural environments are created for human individuals
reared in different cultural settings: each environment is 'unique'
for any member of a particular culture. Alternatively, it might
be said that any environment is only 'there' for the person who
perceives it and this perception is experienced through culturally
conditioned concepts and categories. In the words of Hall (1966b,
p.165) 'people raised in different cultures inhabit different

sensory worlds'.

The colonial bungalow-compound complex is taken as the basic behavioural environment of each member of the colonial community. The method adopted to investigate this unit is to describe, on the basis of written, pictorial and cartographic evidence, the way in which spatial areas of the complex were *used* and the way in which actors *behaved*, as determined by the value system of the culture to which they belonged.

In adopting the theme of space utilisation as a means to understand the functioning of the complex, it is recognised that *physical* space has multiple uses and can be conceived of in many different forms.   These uses have best been described by Rapoport(1970) whose categories of cultural, behavioural, social and experiental or sensory space are defined subsequently.

In examining the typical dwelling form and modified environment of the colonial community, insight is gained into two phenomena. The first is the extent to which the immigrants adopted traits and patterns from the host culture. The second is the extent to which solutions to the basic problem of shelter and the larger one of environmental control, were sought in terms of conceptual models of the metropolitan society of Britain. It is in this cross-cultural context that the most basic and immutable features of the incoming culture can be recognised.

It is clear that the most valid analysis of the colonial bungalow as a house-type could only take place within a tripartite frame-work which took into account the social and concomitant urban structures of the metropolitan society, the host society of India and the colonial society of the British in India, as suggested in Chapter 2. This analysis, however, is confined to a discussion of the main factors governing the site selection, lay-out and use of the complex as the residential unit of the colonial community; only where it is necessary to emphasise unique aspects of that community is reference made to the social and urban structure of the metropolitan and host societies.

2   THE SETTLEMENT CONTEXT OF THE COMPLEX

A house cannot be seen in isolation from the settlement but must be viewed as part of a total social and spatial system which relates the house, way of life and even landscape (Rapoport, 1969a,p.69).

The typical bungalow consists of a low, one-storey, spacious building, internally divided into separate living, dining and bedrooms, the latter with attached rooms for bathing. A verandah, forming an integral part of the structure, or alternatively, attached to the outside walls, surrounds part or all of the building. The bungalow is invariably situated in a large walled or otherwise demarcated 'compound' with generally one main exit to the road on which it is situated. For much of the period under discussion,

the kitchen, as well as servants' quarters, stabling and room for
carriage or car, are separate from and placed at the rear of the
bungalow.

The complex is situated in one of three areas: a rural, often
isolated or semi-isolated site, far removed from other members
of the colonial community. Such may be the house of the tea,
rubber or indigo planter, the 'traveller's bungalow', 'government
rest house' or 'inspection bungalow'; second, it may be one of
five or six such complexes located outside and away from the
indigenous settlement area and built to house the representatives
of the colonial political, administrative and technical system -
the 'district magistrate', the 'inspector of police', the 'civil
surgeon' and the 'executive engineer'.

The third location is in the colonial urban settlement, typically
formed by the civil station and cantonment. These areas are
characterised by low density, horizontal, single-storey developments and broad, tree-lined roads which give access to a system
of large compounds, each containing a roughly centrally-sited
bungalow. The general character of the settlement is, for a
Western observer, one of well-planted spaciousness with a high
proportion of trees and shrubbery both within and outside the
residential compounds (Figure 6.1).

The following accounts give an insight into the 'station' environment,
over the years, by members of the metropolitan and colonial
societies
     The European station is laid out in large rectangles formed
     by wide roads. The native city is an aggregate of houses
     perforated by tortuous paths....The Europeans live in
     detached houses, each surrounded by walls enclosing large
     gardens, lawns, out-offices. The natives live packed in
     squeezed-up tenements, kept from falling to pieces by mutual
     pressure. The handful of Europeans occupy four times the space
     of the city which contains tens of thousands of Hindoos and
     Mussulmen (Russell, 1860,p.140).

     Along the broad, straight roads, arcaded with trees, the
     dust (is) carefully laid by half-naked watermen, sluicing
     out water from the necks of goatskins on their backs. From
     time to time you pass gateways; but, unless it is evening and
     lamps are lit, you can only guess that there are houses behind
     the trees. Presently, you swing through one of these; there
     appears a broad house, too high it seems for one storey, too
     low for two, with pillared front, verandah on all sides and
     a *porte-cochère*....the house stands in a compound - even
     Government offices, banks and shops possess it. It is a
     large, walled or hedged enclosure, part garden, part mews,
     part village' (Steevens, 1899, p.277).

Figure 6.1

Figure 6.2

The larger stations have at least one church....The club is
the centre of social life... the recognised meeting place of
the station.... In the civil lines are the shops. Some of
the larger stations boast of one or more shops kept by
European tradesmen with European goods, chiefly drapery and
drugs. Every kind of tinned food, jams, cheese, needles and
other haberdashery, patent medicines, perfumery and all sorts
of unexpected articles may be found.... Cotton and silk
material can be obtained to advantage in the Indian bazaar
and in the European quarter there are usually one or two
shops which keep these, as well as general drapery (Platt,
1923, p.27).

As the first account indicates, the spatial characteristics and
environmental quality of the civil station are noticeable particularly in contrast to those of the indigenous city(Figure 6.2).
Here, especially in the major cities of northern India, the
predominant urban form is that of the 'pre-industrial city'.
In the words of the colonial resident

The Indian or native city is situated often at a considerable
distance from the European civil lines and military cantonments, in one or the other of which the Europeans live. (It)
is usually walled. The houses are closely packed together,
the streets being very narrow.... Even the main street, in
which the chief business is transacted, will hardly allow
of one cart passing another. The houses are high and most
picturesque, though very dirty. The bazaar is a feast of
colour. The booth-like open shops filled with many-hued
wares, gay silks and cottons, and piles of luscious fruits,
with the brilliantly coloured garments of the passers-by
and of the loungers (for in the East there is no hurry),
make the native city a joy to the lover of colour. The
effect would be garish, but with the background of closely
set fantastic buildings, the sunny lights and deep velvety
shadows, the picture gives joy and satisfaction to the
onlooker. True, a captious critic does not approve of what
he sees on close inspection, and the state of sanitation is
such that diseases when introduced spread with incredible
rapidity. It is not without reason that the European
residential quarter is built at a considerable distance from
the fascinating but dangerous native city (Platt, 1923,p.29)

3   STRUCTURAL DIFFERENCES IN ECONOMY, SOCIETY AND URBAN FORM: A COMPARISON

By the mid-nineteenth century, the two societies whose residential
urban forms were being juxtaposed in the early colonial city, were
organised around two different systems of economic production,
most simply described as 'industrial' and 'agricultural'. (This
is meant as a comparative generalisation rather than a statement
about the distribution of industrial and agricultural activity
in each society. There were many cities in India with craft-based

industry (Naqvi, 1968); there was also still a large metropolitan population involved in agriculture although industrial occupations were rapidly growing in number. In this society the census of 1861 recorded for the first time an excess of urban over rural population, whereas in India, in 1881, only 9 per cent of the population was technically 'urban', that is, living in places of 5,000 or more inhabitants (Cohn, 1971,p.92). Apart from any cultural difference, this economic distinction had considerable effects on land use, urban form and social structure.

Though well-developed urban centres with economic, military, political and religious functions, had existed in India for centuries, the overall economy which sustained them was primarily agricultural and rural-based. The physical size, form and population of the city were still governed by a technology based on animate rather than inanimate energy. In contrast, scientific and technical changes in Britain had led to the development of an urban-industrial economy based on new, fossil-fuel sources of energy. The development of transport technology - railways, steam carriages, new types of road surface - in this society was already pushing urban forms outwards; railways and suburban growth were rapidly eliminating boundaries previously marked, in some cities at least, by medieval walls. It is this distinction between agriculture- and industry-based economies which also helps to explain differences in the social structure.

Though contact with the West as well as other internal factors were already affecting the urban structure of the host society, the overall social structure was still relatively stable. The growth of cities, changes in the urban-rural distribution of the population and the emergence of a new class structure in India were largely developments of the early twentieth rather than the mid-nineteenth century.

In the metropolitan society, however, the same economic and tech- nical forces which were changing the physical form of cities were also revolutionising the social and political structure of the society. The rural-based agricultural labourer was giving way to an urban-industrial proletariat. More important for the purpose of this analysis, there grew up an increasingly sub- stantial middle-class whose residential expectations were deter- mined partly by the norms of the rural-based elites living in the city (the so-called 'landed gentry') and partly by the techno- economic possibilities prevailing in the cities themselves. It was from this growing middle-class, or from other sections in society who took this class as a reference group, that members of the 'officer class' of the colonial community were drawn.

This is significant, for apart from the European troops who were housed in barracks on the cantonment, the remainder of the colonial community were either mainly from, or adopted the life- style of, the urban middle class. In understanding the physical- spatial structure of the colonial urban settlement it is important to recognise that it was, in comparison to urban

development 'at Home', a one-class, suburban-style area where the
detached bungalow in its own compound formed the basic residential
unit. In the cantonment area, for example, all officers lived in
this style.

Apart from the mere physical growth of cities, and the changes in
social structure which accompanied it, a further change brought
by industrialisation relates to the growing specialisation of
land use and building type, particularly in urban areas. In order
to understand this specialisation of land use, it is necessary to
note that industrialisation brought changes not only in the *spatial*
but also in the *temporal* arrangements of society.

Industrialisation meant change in the daily living patterns of the
urban community, particularly for the emerging working and middle
classes. The most important aspect of the temporal change was
that life was increasingly organized in two different categories,
work and non-work. Societal patterns of urbanisation as well as
the emerging industrial city reflected these changes. Work,
whether in industry, commerce or government, was housed and located
in one set of structures situated in specialised sectors of the
city. Similarly, residence was provided for, not only in
functionally specialised 'houses' but also in increasingly
specialised 'residential' areas situated at some distance from
work places in the city.

These changes had been brought about, in the first place, by the
development of factory production and the increase of commercial
activity with consequent growth in specialised office accommodation.
In the second place, they were due to the development of suburban
areas made possible by innovations in transport (particularly
railways). Most significantly, in the residential sectors of the
city, between these and the work areas and in a whole new urban
system located around the coast, increasing spatial and institutional provision was being made for leisure-time and non-work
activities. At these differing spatial levels, redistribution of
land use accommodated varying periods of newly institutionalised
'free time': the public house or club took care of lunch-time or
'after-work' hours; the music hall, museum or park accommodated
evenings or the secular weekend; at a few hours' train journey
from the towns, a system of 'seaside resorts' catered for the
statutory 'bank holiday', the weekend or week-long vacation. With
increasing recognition accorded to the industrial town as the
dominant and future setting for social life there grew up a greater
awareness of the 'countryside' with the result that these two areas
(seaside and countryside) became increasingly utilised as appropriate settings for leisure activity whilst 'work' became concentrated in towns.

Within the town or city, increased spatial provision for non-working
time was either for *group* pursuits (public house, church, theatre,
park or sportsground) or *individual* activities. Consequently,
in providing housing in the new, middle-class residential areas
of the industrial town, spatial provision had to be made not only

for such basic human needs as protection from the elements, eating,
sleeping, and the socialisation of children but also, external
space around the house for use as a 'garden' was provided for
the occupation of leisure hours.   (On the growth of leisure
gardening, see Plumb,1973).

Moreover, irrespective of any cultural factors determining family
structure in the indigenous and metropolitan societies, by the
mid-nineteenth century, the norm of the nuclear family of parents,
children and occasional relative, resident in their own house,
was an aspiration if not an established fact in the metropolitan
society. (See Aries, 1962,pp.391-9; Anderson, 1971; Laslett, 1972).
According to Hall 'the concept of the nuclear family had to await
the specialisation of rooms according to function, and the
separation of rooms from each other' (1966,p.98).   This is in
contrast to the typical joint family house in the indigenous town.
In the industrialising metropolitan society, each dwelling was
expected to house one family, to have its own specialised room
functions with, at least for the middle class, separate sleeping
space for resident family members and guests, and separate areas
for eating, cooking, relaxation and subsequently, bathing.   Each
room had its own specialised furnishing and equipment.

It has been necessary to make these broad generalisations in
regard to the structure of the industrial town for two fundamental
reasons.   In the first place, members of the colonial community
were drawn from a society where these developments had taken or
were taking place.   Here were newcomers whose metropolitan-based
norms required that they live in separate dwellings, with space
devoted to specialised room functions, with further specialised
space for leisure activities and the whole situated in a functionally specific 'residential' area, separated from their place
of work.

Time-wise, they had expectations, not only of a day divided between
work and leisure, but of a year divided between work and (secular)
'holidays'.   Spatial recognition of this temporal fact had been
made in the provision of 'resorts' which catered specifically
for 'leisure'.   In any analysis of the development of hill-stations
in India and other areas of colonial settlement, this latter fact
is not to be underestimated.

Finally, these generalisations have been necessary in order to
emphasise that, for the largely 'pre-industrial' society of the
host culture, none of these characteristics applied.

4   THE COMPLEX AS CULTURE AREA AND TERRITORY

If the colonial compound is situated in an isolated site, it is
best understood as a particular *culture area*.   By *culture area*
is understood 'a territory inhabited at any given period by a
human community characterised by a particular culture' with a
landscape 'in which the choices made and changes worked by men

as members of some cultural community are manifested' (Wagner, 1962,pp.5,10). This culture area is a manifestation of the colonial community's *territoriality*, 'the taking possession, use and defence of a territory on the part of living organisms' (Hall, 1959,p.69). If the compound is one of a cluster, as on the civil lines or cantonment, the larger unit takes on the character of the culture area and territory and the single compound forms a basic unit within this larger whole.

5 FACTORS IN THE UTILISATION OF SPACE: THE SITE

The spatial needs of the bungalow-compound complex were not limited to the actual ground area covered but comprehended a much larger spatial environment. The extent of this was determined by the value-system and world-view of the colonial culture.

Though criteria for residential location held by the indigenous population have yet to be systematically investigated, various landscape features have particular importance in the cognitive schema of this culture (Basak, 1953; Sopher, 1967). Rivers, and especially the river Ganges, have religious significance and are essential for the performance of certain rituals at various stages of the life cycle. Settlement on river banks is therefore common. On the other hand, hill sites - preferred locations for the colonial community - apart from functioning as isolated places for spiritual reflection,as places of pilgrimage (Bhardwaj,1973) or the habitat of particular 'hill tribes', were not preferred areas of settlement for the indigenous society.

In siting colonial bungalows religious or economic considerations were replaced by other criteria. These were culture-specific concepts of 'sanitation' and preferred kinds of visual experience. Explanations of disease in terms of contaminated air and water ensured that, in site selection, high ground was preferable to low. Wherever possible elevated sites were chosen which gave 'facilities for drainage, healthiness of soil' and access to water (Goument, 1921,p.1). 'The site of the house should be high and dry, as far as possible from marshy land and the neighbourhood of a "tank" or pond should be avoided'. Conflicting theories of hygiene between the incoming and host culture required that
    Indian dwellings and servants' houses should be at a safe
    distance. Indian servants often have their families with
    them; their ways of living are not ours, and for hygienic
    reasons, especially in malarious and unhealthy districts,
    close proximity is not desirable (Platt, 1923,p.21).

The satisfaction of visual criteria was important, first,in providing specific kinds of visual experience from the bungalow - a 'view' or an 'outlook'; second, in ensuring that the bungalow and its compound formed part of such a 'view' when perceived from a distance. The site should be chosen 'to command the best view

possible... the outlook from doors and windows of sitting rooms
should be the best available'. In considering the contours of the
ground, 'an undulating site is often more interesting than a flat
one.' 'The external appearance should be pleasing to the eye, in
harmony with the surroundings and expressive of the use to which
the building is put' (Meadows, 1931,p.2).

6 FACTORS IN THE UTILISATION OF SPACE: THE COMPOUND

Where circumstances prevented the siting of the complex on elevated
ground, sufficient visual space around the actual bungalow had to
be provided within the compound for it to be seen, especially when
entering the drive
> We turn into the park, rattling up a deeply shaded avenue
> with lion-coloured grass reaching on either side, between
> the dark tree trunks... our home, long, low and friendly
> it looks, with its country tiles projecting out over the
> deep verandahs. Not in the least like 'Hulme Park', much
> more like the 'Commissioner's Bungalow' as indeed it is
> always called (Lawrence, n.d. p.26).

In satisfying these visual criteria, four areas of visual space
were ideally essential. These enabled the inhabitant, on occasions
to appreciate, on other occasions to record:

a the bungalow as seen from the bottom of the compound(front)
b the compound as seen from the verandah of the bungalow (front)
c the compound as seen from the verandah of the bungalow (rear)
d the bungalow and compound as seen from the distance
  (Figure 6.3a, b, c, d).

Enough space had to be allowed between the gate and the building to
permit the larger portion of the latter to be seen immediately on
entering the compound. More important, sufficient space had to
be provided round the house as a visual assurance for the occupants
to know that they were safely located in their own cultural
territory.

Compounds varied in size; in comparison with metropolitan plot
sizes they were, well into the twentieth century, of vast proportions.
In rural districts in the nineteenth, they could be between one and
fifteen acres (Woodruff, 1965,p.315); even in the centre of New
Delhi, built in the twentieth century, they were between one and
five acres. The actual ground area covered by the bungalow as a
proportion of the compound was rarely more than one-tenth. In 1925
the suggested norm for military officers' bungalows was about
one/fifteenth (Figure 6.4).

In terms of Rapoport's various categories (1970,p.81) some insight
is gained into the *multiplicity* of functions performed by physical
space on the compound.

Figure 6.3

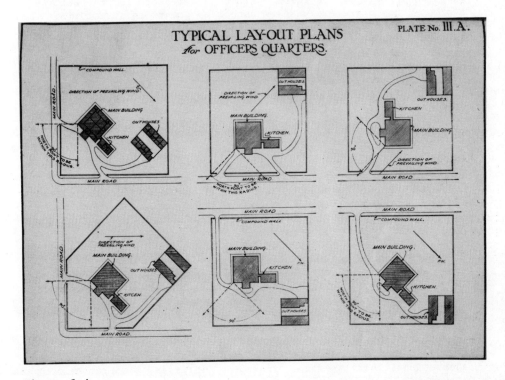

Figure 6.4

(i) *Cultural space. ('Space defined by various groups affected by training, previous experience, adaptation, memory and cognitive categories of the group'.)*

In this category belongs the 'visual' as well as the 'sanitary space' required by the culture-specific theories of disease discussed in Chapter 5.

For members of the colonial culture, generous provision of residential space, well above the norms obtaining for persons of similar status in the metropolitan society, was one of the major compensations for a life spent largely in exile. Moreover, usual market constraints on the economic use of land were inoperative in the political economy of colonialism; land was there almost for the taking. Income disparities between members of the colonial culture and the indigenous population ensured that manpower was available for the large number of service roles on the complex, including that of *mali* or gardener. It was assumed that there was no need for spatial economy.

In the early days of colonial settlement spatial expectations regarding both compound and bungalow had been defined in regard to two reference groups, the 'landed gentry' in the metropolitan society and members of the indigenous elite (see Nilsson,1968,p.115). In Shibutani's terms 'reference group' is used to describe 'that group whose perspective forms a frame of reference for the actor, a group whose norms are used as anchoring points in structuring the perceptual field' (1955,pp.562-9). To varying degrees such earlier members of the colonial community acted as role models for those following in later years (Figures 6.5). The expectations persisted to the last years of colonial rule: 'We brought with us in our home lives almost exact replicas of the sort of life that upper middle class people lived in England at that time. It was very homogenous in the sense that nearly everyone in official India sprang from precisely the same educational and cultural background' (Allen, 1975,p.72).

'Medical' theories required that compounds should provide optimum amounts of 'fresh air', the generous spatial distances acting as physical barriers between members of the community and particularly, against representatives of the indigenous society. As discussed below, such theories also affected the orientation of the bungalow in relation to prevailing winds.

A further spatial determinant was related to the balance of activities taking place on the compound itself and those undertaken in the larger urban unit of which it was a part. In the modern city, plant for services such as water supply, lighting and sewage disposal are part of the total urban system: the individual residential unit simply receives the product. Retailing centres cater for food and clothing needs, specialised markets supply fruit, meat and vegetables, laundries provide cleaning services for clothing. Recreational facilities are offered by libraries, theatres and parks, and transport is provided by private or public companies.

In the rural colonial compound and even in compounds on the
colonial urban settlement, all such services were accommodated in
the compound area.   One or two wells, the water drawn by bullocks
ambling up and down an inclined plane, might provide water in
rural locations.   Lamps had to be stored, maintained and lit.
Human waste had to be collected and disposed of.   Though an
indigenous bazaar existed in the locality, gardens provided
preferred types of fruit and vegetables, *dherzies* or tailors had
to be found space to sit and sew clothes, under supervision.
Individual transport had to be accommodated.   All such activities
needed locally employed manpower, of whom a proportion (with their
families) were usually accommodated on the compound.

In the indigenous city, shade and protection from the heat was
achieved by the close grouping of thick-walled houses in tall,
tightly packed clusters, in narrow, perpetually shaded streets
and inward-looking courtyards sometimes planted with trees or
shrubs.   Rooms were small and relatively dark, protected from
the heat of the sun both by further storeys above and by other
buildings close by.

However, perpetuation of the residential norms of the metropolitan
society in the colonial culture resulting in individual dwelling
houses for each member of the community, prevented this type of
climatic control.   Each bungalow had therefore to provide its
own solar protection by maximising the open area around and by
extensive tree planting round the edges of the compound.

Trees not only provided shade but, in the nineteenth century,
were held to be 'antagonistic to malaria... the oxygen they
exhale becomes electrified and converted into ozone and this has
disinfectant powers'.   Whilst deciduous vegetation round the house
should be cleared, large trees were to be left as they 'present(ed)
pleasant green to the eye, collect and condense vapours, equalise
the rainfall and prevent heating of the ground'.   However, trees
should not be allowed to overhang the residence as they 'retain
miasms in the foliage'.   It was also believed that trees
'beautified the town' (Moore 1862,pp.120-2; Sterndale, 1881,p.173).

Even in the twentieth century, when scientific knowledge had
become more sophisticated, visual values were still inclined to
conflict with concepts of personal safety and hygiene:
   A bungalow covered with climbing plants is no doubt attractive
   and picturesque, but it is not desirable to have creepers or
   vegetation too close to the house.   Even trees should be at a
   little distance.   Insects are one of the chief dangers in India;
   many of the most dreaded diseases are caused by insect-carrying
   germs and anything that harbours or encourages these should be
   sternly discouraged (Platt, 1923,p.25).
Because of this danger from mosquitoes, it was recommended that
where trees provided shade, they should be at least fifty feet
from the house (Meadows, 1931,p.25).

THE NEW HOUSE

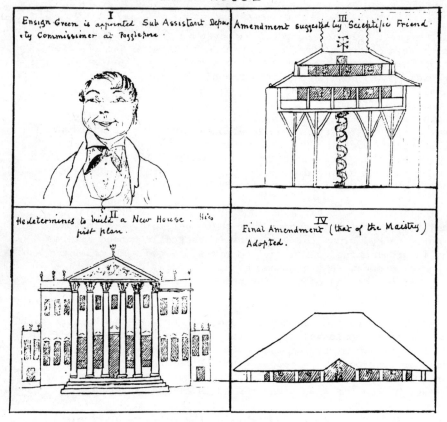

Figure 6.5 Conceptual models and reference groups in the housing choice of the colonial community, 1851.

IIa Housing model of earlier members of the colonial community, based on that of a metropolitan reference group, 1803.

IIIa European housing model based on 'scientific' theories prevailing in the metropolitan society, 1884. The floor of this 'Sanitary House' or 'Bungalow' is raised above ground level as a precaution against 'rising aerial sources of infection'.

IVa The 'Anglo-Indian bungalow': the vernacular house-type and environment of the colonial third culture.

The Residency, Hyderabad.

IIa

IIIa

IVa

(ii) *Behavioural space. ('Space which is available as a behaviour setting of a given individual or group').*

The bungalow-compound complex played a major role in the life of the total institution in the civil station. One of the characteristics of the total institution is 'the breakdown of the barriers which normally separate the three spheres of life in modern society - the arrangement by which individuals sleep, play and work in different places, with different co-participants, under different authorities' (Goffman 1970,p.17). The people living there were 'an occupational community' (Ness, 1970) whose work and social relationships overlapped. Formal and informal entertaining provided the main means of interaction. Receptions, lunches, dinners, breakfasts on the verandah, had to be provided for friends or visiting officials. Here, new members were welcomed and departing ones bidden 'bon voyage' (Figure 6.6).

For all such interaction, room had to be provided both inside the bungalow as well as the compound area. Space was needed for activities which 'broke the ice' in new encounters, or strengthened bonds between established community members. These took the form of 'croquet', children's games or the evening 'drinks'. Here, the race-specific practice of 'sun-bathing' occurred (Figure 6.7). Other activities institutionalised as a major means of information exchange in the colonial culture, such as 'morning coffee', the 'badminton' and 'garden' party as well as the 'reception' also took place there (Figures 6.8, 6.9, 6.10).

Further spatial provision was made necessary by the communication habits of the community. Like the elite of the indigenous society, members of the colonial community were carried, at first in manual or animal-propelled carriages (the 'palanquin' and the 'gharry') and subsequently in motor vehicles. Sufficient space on the compound had to be provided for storage and maintenance purposes (stables, carriage house or garage) as well as a 'drive', the dimensions of which were determined by the speed, length and turning radius of the vehicle.

The porch, though belonging properly to the spatial requirements of the bungalow, was also made necessary by the fact that the occupants were a vehicular-borne elite. Here, carriages and cars waited, visitors received, peons and *chowkidars* (watchmen) guarded interior territory and official messengers stood waiting for replies.

(iii) *Social space. ('The spatial arrangements reflecting patterns and regularities of various social groups, their hierarchies and roles').*

Compound space had numerous social functions. Its size was in accordance with the occupant's position in the hierarchy of the colonial community. Within the compound, servants' quarters were carefully separated and kept to the rear. The servants' quarters

Figure 6.6

Figure 6.7

Figure 6.8

Figure 6.9

Figure 6.10

and kitchen 'should be quite one hundred feet away from but not
directly behind the bungalow... as it is in servants' quarters
that fires most frequently originate' (Addis, 1910,p.26). Two
wells were preferable, one 'for the use of servants and native
staff', another 'for the exclusive use' of the resident. If
the garden were large enough, 'there should be one wide shady
path where persons in conversation may be able to walk two or
three abreast.' Even cn a small quarter-acre compound, the kitchen,
servants' quarters and stores were to be built thirty feet away from
the bungalow. This 'removes the noise and smell of cooking and
servants chatter from the house and allows both buildings to get
more light and air' (Firminger, 1918,p.18).

In bungalows of the senior colonial elite, the verandah steps
were used as a spatial device to express the occupants' status in
relation to that of indigenous guests: 'if you were greeting a
prince of a certain standing you had to go down to the bottom
of the steps outside to meet him. With one of less standing, you
would greet him on the top steps and one of no standing you would
probably greet while you stay in your study' (Allen, 1975,p.83.
See also Scheflen, 1976, forthcoming). Such norms of behaviour
were part of an 'elaborate code' which laid down where indigenous
visitors could be received, 'who should be seen only in the
courtyard, who on the verandah and who could be allowed to enter
the drawing-room' (Panikkar, 1965,p.118).

Space provided for servants might be categorised as economic space.
In the early twentieth century, a staff of between ten and twenty
servants was the norm. Some of these were made necessary by the
lack of services taken for granted in the metropolitan society.
The climate and lack of a laundry demanded a *dhobi* (washerman);
the lack of electricity and extensive premises, a lampman *(masal)*;
the absence of piped water, a water-carrier *(bhisti)*; the lack
of delivery services or prepared foods, a cook's helper *(chokra)*;
the absence of mechanical sanitation, a male and female sweeper;
the want of shops and supplies of 'European' clothes, a tailor
(dherzi). The need for other servants arose from the characteristics of the bungalow-compound itself: the bearers, to carry
objects within the bungalow; the *chuprassi*, to bear messages to
other station residents; the *coolie* to pull the punkah and modify
internal temperatures; the *malis* and grass-cutter to tend the
compound; the *chowkidar*, to guard the personal territory.

That manpower was available to perform these services was less a
result of 'surplus resources' than of the disparity of income
between members of the colonial and indigenous societies. In this,
as in other respects, the colonial immigrants were similar to the
indigenous elite; their spatial requirements, if not their life-
style, were comparable.

(iv) *Experiential or sensory space.* (*'This can be visual, acoustic, olfactory, thermal, kinesthetic, or tactile and the stress on specific sensory modes - and hence on sensory space - will vary from culture to culture'*).

Before all else, the compound was a *culture area*, an area modified according to the value-system of the metropolitan society as interpreted by the colonial community. In a situation of psychological uncertainty and exile from the parent society, the creation of a culturally defined 'personal environment' was instrumental in maintaining a sense of identity. Along with dress, language, expected behaviour and the collection of culture objects in the house, the cultivated part of the compound or garden was one of the main props in what Goffman has termed the *setting* for human behaviour (Goffman, 1971,p.32). It helped to identify the occupant with the community to which he belonged, distinguishing him from the culture in which he was located. Like 'dressing for dinner in the African bush' (Banton, 1971,p.24), the maintenance of a garden was one of the many ways in which an individual established and constantly reinforced his identity as a member of the group, distinct from the indigenous society. Departure from the norms of the colonial culture, whether in behaviour, dress or social relationships, was summed up in the brief, but sociologically seminal phrase 'going native'.

The principal way to establish this culture area was to modify the cultivated portion of the compound according to norms prevailing in the metropolitan society. In the later nineteenth century, these required flowing, curved lines and carefully placed planting (the 'romantic' or 'picturesque').

> Small beds... are easily designed and look well but many of
> the geometrical and contorted figures... when attempted by
> the rude skill of the malee... prove only ridiculous. Winding
> paths with clumps of shrubs planted at intervals at the bends
> and curves have a very fine effect (Firminger, 1918,p.20).

Equally important was the reproduction of species grown in the metropolitan climate, achieved by the careful cultivation of imported seed. Where this grew, the ensuing results had important associational functions in keeping the memory of other cultural landscapes alive, stimulated by sensory experience that was visual, olfactory and oral.

> My violets are in bloom: You cannot think how one treasures
> out here the quiet little 'home' flower.... Dear little English
> flower.... Carefully, one by one have I gathered enough to make
> me a buttonhole.... It is a great triumph for I have spent
> more care and thought on the violets than on all the lurid
> tropical flowers that patch the garden with colour (Anon,
> 1905,p.69. See also Allen, 1975,p.77).

In the celebration of ritual festivals, required by the religious belief-system of the colonial community, the 'cultural purity' of food grown from imported seed took on an almost symbolic significance.

> Our own *menu* on Christmas Eve was soup of tomatoes grown
> in our own garden from English seed, also French beans

and new peas, *not* the tinned article which pervades Indian
dinner-parties. My scarlet-runners are doing grandly. They
have gone on for two or three years from English seed, of
course much irrigated (ibid,p.120).

Whether in the nineteenth or twentieth centuries, species of flora
familiar from the metropolitan society, provided members of the
community with an opportunity to exercise olfactory preferences
learnt in the parent society. These contrasted sharply with
olfactory criteria of the indigenous culture.

The early mornings especially are as pleasant as anything I
can imagine: they have all the sweetness and freshness of
an English summer. The air smells of hay and flowers, instead
of ditches, dust, fried oil, curry and onions, which are the
best of Madras smells.... I saw a real staring, full-blown
hollyhock, which was like meeting an old friend from England,
instead of tuberoses, pomegranates... we have apples, pears
and peaches... (which) look like English fruit (Brown,1948,p.29).

Culturally defined canons of 'beauty' not only labelled unaccep-
table colours as 'lurid'; they also excluded the appreciation
of floral arrangements not conforming to the norms of the colonial
culture. 'The drawing room is now gay with balsams, asters,
nasturtiums, and chrysanthemums. These I arrange myself as
the native gardener's idea of a bouquet is too stiff for words'
(Anon,1905,p.17). (In the folk-culture of the 'native gardener',
flowers for presentation are traditionally arranged in small,
symmetrical 'bundles' and bound tightly round the stem, immediately
below the flowers.)

Although interest in gardens was a shared value in the colonial
community, it was intensified by other factors governing the
position of its female members. The absence of children in hill-
station or metropolitan boarding school and the presence of
numerous servants, deprived the colonial wife of her two
traditional roles of mother and housewife. New time-passing
activities had therefore to be found. The strong identification
of the male with his professional role, as well as the demands
made by the total institution of civil station or cantonment,
frequently left the female with an empty sense of frustration.

The heat of the darkness seems almost tangible... the other
sex lives and moves and has its being - on very early morning
parades, in stuffy court houses all through the hottest hours,
on the war-path after blackbuck over the plain at noon, on
the tennis court, or the polo ground at sundown. But we
women-folk seem simply to exist (ibid.,p.272).

The effect of this, for many women, was the direction of time and
energy to the culturally learnt pursuits common to their particular strata of society, the cultivation of gardens, writing,
painting, the collection of flora and fauna, and entertaining.
Consequently, the transformation and use of the immediate cultural
landscape, as well as its recording, was largely the province of
the women in the community. Only in the last two decades of
colonial rule did the pattern of women's activities change, with
a minority taking up roles outside the community in 'voluntary

work' legitimised by the belief-system of the metropolitan culture
(see Allen, 1975,p.177-8).

Whilst the compound provided *behavioural* or *activity* space, the
kind of transformation indicated above also ensured that it had
visual functions.

> Dr Anderson's house in Madras was built in a garden, beautifully
> laid out in the English taste; but from its abounding with trees
> and shrubs and flowers, such as are not known in Europe except
> in conservatories and hot-houses, it had to our unaccustomed
> eyes a very aristrocratic appearance (Brown, 1948,p.73).

Depending on the period, these visual experiences were recorded
either in writing, by painting (Figure 6.11), or in photographs.
Such records were an assurance of personal achievement, a source
of information for reference groups in the metropolitan society,
and an indication of status in a world that, for the parent society,
was largely unknown.

7   TERRITORIAL MARKINGS

The culture area of the compound was defined by clear territorial
markings (Martin, 1972), the boundary being demarcated by a low
wall, hedge or high bank. 'All over India fences appear to exist
for the purpose of marking boundaries than for any protection they
afford against intruders' (Trevelyan, 1894,p.4). The most important markers, however, were the two generally whitewashed gateposts.
In later times, gates themselves were often superfluous, their
function of excluding callers or animals pre-empted by the
enforcement of a strict code (the *Cantonments Code)* governing
activities on the colonial urban settlement (see Figure 6.1).

Despite the large number of servants in the colonial household,
there were generally neither servants' nor tradesman's entrances.
In this way complete control over the movement of persons and
objects into and, of more importance, out of, the compound could
be maintained.

The role of 'chowkidar' (watchman) was fundamental to this process.
Dogs were even more effective (see p.121, Chapter 5). In extreme
cases, authority over the area immediately outside and to the
front of the bungalow was exercised by requiring members of the
indigenous society to remove their shoes when walking by (see
Karve, 1963,p.233). A further means of ensuring that they recognised their intrusion into the personal territory of members of
the colonial community was by requiring that they wear the foot-
wear of the dominant culture.

> No sumptuary regulation to restrain extravagence in gilded shoes
> and enforce the use of plain black leather could be half so
> potent as the unwritten ordinance which permits an Oriental
> to retain a pair of patent boots on stockinged feet, and
> requires him to doff shoes of native make when in the presence
> of an English superior (Kipling,J.Lockwood, quoted in Punjab
> Government, *Gazetteer of the Delhi District,* 1883-4,p.125).

Figure 6.11

A corner of my compound. Arrah. May 1862.

Figure 6.12

Gate-posts were used as status indicators, not only because of
their size, but also by exhibiting a name-plate, bearing the
designation of the inhabitant.   Though compounds have been taken
over from their predecessors by the post-colonial indigenous
elite, the practice continues (Figure 6.12).

8   FACTORS IN THE UTILISATION OF SPACE: THE BUNGALOW

The 'ideal type' bungalow had a verandah on either one or two
sides and frequently all round the house, a large 'sitting'
room, 'dining' room, sleeping or 'bedrooms', each of which
usually had its own attached room for bathing, the 'bathroom'.
The size of the bungalow, and particularly, of the sitting and
dining rooms, was much larger than prevailing norms in the
metropolitan culture allowed.   In the early twentieth century
the wife of an army captain could write 'My drawing room is
twenty feet high by forty-five feet square, and the winds blow
through the house' (Anon.,1905,p.83).   Towards the end of colonial
rule when the norm for compound sizes had been reduced, it was
thought that the site for bungalows for private firms 'should
not be less than a quarter of an acre'.   No more than two thirds
of this should be built on and the bungalow should occupy about
two thousand square feet.   However,

> nothing adds more to the comfort of the occupants of the
> Eastern bungalow than generous open planning with plenty
> of air space in the bungalow itself.   The size of rooms
> are, as a rule, fifty per cent larger than rooms in a
> European bungalow... a room 25 by 16 feet large and 12
> to 13 feet high is a very convenient size for practically
> every purpose.... Rooms in the bungalow proper are usually
> of more generous proportions than the minimum stated... in
> planning the average bungalow it is usual in most cases to
> work on a basis in excess of the minimum sizes.... Dimensions
> of 10 by 12 feet are usually adopted for servants' quarters
> (Meadows, 1931,p.9).

From the beginning it was accepted that the behaviour and life
styles of the metropolitan society, though modified by the colonial
culture, should be continued.   This necessitated spatial provision
for a wide range of cultural objects and equipment to continue
these activities.   Sitting required three or four different kinds
of chair, dependent on whether the 'sitting need' was for eating
(dining chair), conversation (easy chair) or private relaxation
(chaise-longue).   Reading - a favourite pursuit - required storage
space for books, special cabinets and the 'occasional' table;
writing, a bureau, desk or table; time-passing activities such
as sewing, painting, or 'collecting' required storage places for
materials and relevant equipment.   Forms of social activity such
as 'cards' or the 'musical evening' required large tables and a
piano, with sufficient space to seat the audience and separate
it from the performer.   The practice of travelling led to the
accumulation of 'souvenirs' and these needed shelves or cabinets
for storage and display.   One item introduced by the metropolitan

society into India was the 'fireplace', whose function was largely symbolic; 'how often have I known people have a fire for the pleasure of seeing one and to make them think they were "at home" ' (Falkland, 1930,p.96). Though infrequently used for its original purpose, the 'mantelpiece' provided a focal point for the display of culture objects.

These culture objects, with their consequent demands on space, were needed by the inhabitant to establish his *front* and *setting*, essential for the actor's *performance*. This Goffmann refers to as
   all the activity of an individual which occurs during a period
   marked by his continuous presence before a particular set of
   observers and which has some influence on the observers....
   (*Front*) is the expressive equipment of a standard kind inten-
   tionally or unwittingly employed by an individual during his
   performance.... (Standard parts of the front include the
   setting) involving furniture, decor, physical layout, and
   other background props for the spate of human action played
   out before, within or upon it... (1971,p.32).

Thus, photographs of the interior of a hill-station bungalow in 1925 show, on the 'mantelpiece', two silver candlesticks, three ornamental plates, a framed picture of the head of state in the indigenous community. In other rooms can be identified a table in the form of a camel, a line of six carved white elephants, a large, empty silver bowl, a silver cup, three photographs of soldiers, drinking glasses, and pictures on the wall. In the 'hall' are seven 'walking sticks', five hats, a telescope and a specially constructed stand to hold them.

Such objects, seen from the viewpoint of the indigenous society, have no function outside the confines of the colonial culture. They include 'souvenirs' accumulated from journeys undertaken in the country; metal cups, utilised, not for drinking, but as symbols of achievement in culture-specific, leisure-time activities; signed photographs of senior members of the colonial elite, used as symbols of status; 'arrangements' of flowers indicating acquired levels of 'taste' recognised in the colonial and metropolitan society.

Apart from expressing 'aesthetic' values, such objects had impor-tant psychological meaning. Like the garden, they were links with the past, maintaining for their owner a continuous identity, a measure of achievement and a physical-visual record of activities undertaken and honours achieved. Such objects 'spoke' to visitors, immediately establishing a sense of shared values, indicating one's standing in the local and metropolitan society, establishing reference points for the deepening of social relationships. When inhabitants moved or were 'posted', official recognition was given to the need to transport, not only 'working tools' but the whole complement of 'culture objects' and 'effects'. The higher a person was in the social hierarchy, the greater the equipment allowance to carry his 'identity props' around. These included not only the objects referred to above, but also his clothes and other equipment essential for his personal setting. Thus, in the late nineteenth

century, a general was allowed forty, a colonel thirty and a captain
ten hundredweight of personal baggage to be conveyed at public
expense, at home or abroad (Murray, 1872,Appendix). These
belongings - clothes, objects of sentiment, furniture, a house and
a garden - provided assurance in a world that was strange, and on
occasion, hostile.

In terms of world-view, this concern for the garden, house and the
objects it contained, indicates a secular belief in the reality of
the lived-in, material world, whose artefacts have value, not only
for their original, functional use but as they become obsolete,
for their uniqueness and scarcity, having an economic exchange
value as 'antiques' or 'works of art'. Such an attitude is in
contrast to the world-view of the indigenous Hindu society, whose
view of life is one of transition, from one rebirth to another. It
is a view which traditionally puts little store on the value of the
material world and stresses the adjustment of man to the environment rather than the environment to man (Nakamura,1964).

Because of limited means of recreation, the demands of the
occupational community and the availability of servants,
entertaining was a frequent activity. 'India is the land of dinners,
as England is the land of five o'clock teas... all Anglo-India is
in a chronic state of giving and receiving this, the most delightful, or the most excruciating form of hospitality' (Brown, 1948,
p.134). Dining areas were large, accommodating, in the twentieth
century, anything from ten to thirty guests. Unlike eating practices in the indigenous culture which required little equipment
for sitting, holding dishes or transferring food from utensil to
the mouth, those of the colonial culture required special dining
chairs, a table, utensils with which to eat and receptacles on
which to keep the food. Such equipment had to be maintained and
stored in purpose-built 'sideboards' or cabinets. Dietary habits
such as the drinking of alcohol and the eating of meat, unaccep-
table for most members of the indigenous society, required special
utensils for their consumption and storage, and spatial provision
had to be made for these within the bungalow.

Though such practices, along with the equipment required to perform
them, were gradually being adopted by the indigenous elite, the
majority of residents in the indigenous city still ate without
furniture, at floor level, sitting on a cotton *dhurry* using a few
brass vessels for food and eating, as was customary, with their
fingers from a tray or dish or, in certain regions and at lower
levels of society, from 'plates' of banana leaves.

9   FACTORS IN THE UTILISATION OF SPACE: THE VERANDAH

Space on the bungalow-compound complex had various levels of
privacy, each part of the larger 'privacy system' of the colonial
urban settlement. Within the compound were:

1   the area between the verandah and enclosing compound wall
2   the verandah
3   the hall of the bungalow (where there was one)
4   the 'inner sanctum' of drawing, dining and bed room,

each with increasing degrees of privacy. On the compound, the well
   should be screened from view by shrubs and trees planted around
   it. As native servants have continuously to be going to the
   well both for performing their ablutions there and for drawing
   water... there should be a pathway to it made for them exclusively, cut off entirely from the rest of the garden by
   means of a hedge. This is desirable not only for the purpose
   of keeping the garden... secluded but also for the safety of
   its produce (Firminger, 1918,p.17).

Within the bungalow, privacy was needed both in relation to unexpected guests and to servants.
   Rooms are arranged so that visitors on arrival do not at once
   intrude on to the verandah, but are received in a hall which
   is screened off from the lounge. More privacy is thereby
   obtained from the occupants....
   The dining room leads off the lounge and is a separate
   compartment. This allows the servants to lay the table and
   prepare the meals out of sight (Meadows,1931,p.38).

Tradesmen might be required to wait outside the gate; if their
services were required, they waited inside the compound. The
following passage, from a work of fiction, gives an excellent
insight into the psychological effect of the culture area, if not
on the indigenous tailor which it purports to describe, at least
on the mind of the twentieth-century Indian author:
   In the big houses, carts carrying traders, servants and the
   like were not supposed to use the drive. It is not respectful,
   Apu had informed Ravi early in their association, for people
   like them to drive up as if they were great lords; they knew
   their position and must keep it. So at the gates the two of
   them dismounted....
   The house they were going to was owned by Europeans. Ravi
   could have told just by looking, for the gravel was swept,
   the clipped lawns green, giving a general air of tidiness
   that Indian homes lacked. Instead of a motley crew of servants
   there was only one peon visible, an important being in a khaki
   drill tunic and brass-buckled belt who sat like a guardian deity
   in a sentry-box next to the portico.
Here are the territorial markings, the uniformed peon 'defending
the territory'. The process of penetrating the territory takes
place:
   'Is the memsahib at home?'
   ... 'Yes, what is it?' The peon spoke testily,
   ... 'No hawkers, no hawkers allowed here',...
   'Memsahib's clothes are ready' he said. 'Is memsahib at home?'
   and at the same time he slipped a few coins into the other's
   palm - a procedure which Ravi resented but which he... accepted
   as expenses essential to the conduct of their business otherwise
   memsahib would never be at home.'

In this case the tradesmen wait in the porch. The house, as with
many 'bungalows' built in larger towns in the twentieth century,
had two storeys, a verandah running round each.

> Ravi and Apu waited, as they were used to doing, while Ravi
> gazed at the elaborate trellis-work along the walls that
> supported sheaf after sheaf of flame-coloured bougainvillea....
> In between he wondered... what memsahibs got up to while they
> kept them waiting one, one and a half, even two hours.
>
> Today they were lucky. Memsahib would see them at once;
> they were to go up. In some houses they were expected to use
> the back sweeper's staircase, but more frequently they used
> the main stairs, since most ladies disliked having their clothes
> trailed up the sweeper's way.

The verandah, whether upstairs or down, was an area for transactions,
for bargaining over prices and for doing those tasks of shopping
which in the colonial urban settlement, were transferred from
bazaar to house.

> They sat on the upstairs verandah overlooking the garden, she
> in her cane chair, they on the floor, and argued, item by item.
> 'Seven rupees for a shirt? Preposterous!'
> 'So much fine work, memsahib,... it took the lad many hours....'
> She beat him down.... It was all part of a game which both
> understood... Ravi... tried to pay attention but his gaze
> kept wandering to the garden which he could see between the
> verandah balusters... and from thence to the compound wall
> over which the children's heads kept bobbing. There were
> bits of broken glass... embedded on the top - they flashed
> like jewels in the sun.'

For the resident of the bungalow, the compound is an area of
cultural territory, situated *in* the indigenous culture, but not
being *of* that culture. It separated the occupant from the local
indigenous inhabitants, at the same time reassuring her of an
identity with 'countrymen thousands of miles away'.

> 'Your grandchildren', she said, 'I didn't know you had any'
> and her tone was a mixture of curiosity and disbelief, as if
> these people who appeared when summoned by her servants and
> disappeared when she was done with them, had no existence in
> between... she wondered whether, if they had skin like hers,
> they would become real to her, these people among whom she
> lived who were more faceless and alien than her own countrymen
> thousands of miles away (Markandaya, 1966,pp.157-61).

Other than its obvious climatic function, the main social purpose
of the verandah was one of relaxation. Unlike the indigenous
inhabitant who sat, either cross-legged on the floor, or lay on
a lightweight *charpai* (a simple four-legged cot, the supporting
part made from woven twine), or mattress, members of the colonial
society required a variety of purpose-built chairs, some of them
unknown either in indigenous or metropolitan culture.

> The verandah is spread with Chinese matting and littered with
> armchairs. India is the land of loll. There are chairs for
> each sex and size - long bamboo couch chairs; small grass
> chairs, cretonne-clad, corresponding to wicker ones in England;
> heavy, dark teak, or mahogany chairs, with wide cane seat and

tall curling backs, monsters, with great flat wooden arms
splayed out to receive the Sahib's extended legs when he is
weary, and with a hole in them to contain his peg tumbler
when he is a-thirst (Anon, 1905,p.26).
(Compare also Orwell (1955, p.68): 'As to the English in the East...
they lead unenviable lives; it is a poor bargain to spend thirty
years, illpaid, in an alien country, and then come home with a
wrecked liver and pine-apple backside from sitting in cane chairs...)

Such 'monster' chairs took up areas of fifteen square feet; with
space added to allow bearers to circulate, some insight is gained
into the spatial dimensions of the verandah (Figure 6.13).

For reasons of climate and health, the verandah was raised between
one and two feet above ground level, improving its function as a
place to supervise events. 'I am writing in my high-raised
verandah. Thence, eagle-eyed, I can oversee the scantily-draped
mahogany figure... and suppress any unlawful sneaking off...
on the part of my *malli'* (Anon.,1905,p.3).

Because drawing and dining rooms were often dark, their windows
permanently shaded by 'chics' or blinds, the verandah was used for
reading and writing; here, too, guests were received and children
allowed to play. In the heat of the summer nights, it provided
space to sleep. It was a place for the pursuit of hobbies, whether
painting or the stuffing of birds. The *chowkidar* (watchman) and
occasionally other servants slept there; it was a place for market
transactions (Figure 6.14) and there the *dherzi* (tailor) sat and
sewed. It provided the setting for the exchange of gifts between
servants and employer; on the steps, photographs were taken.

Most important, the verandah was a place to cultivate, whether in
climbing or potted form, the flora so favoured by members of the
colonial community.
    At this time of the year my verandah serves me for a drawing
    room. Between each pillar it is enclosed with bamboo-trellis,
    called *jaffri* work. This answers the twofold purpose of tem-
    pering the outside glare to the rooms within, and of supporting
    the creepers, which are now rapidly running up and clothing it
    from the beds below. Inside, against the wall of the house,
    stand flower pots on stages, wherein flourish palms and ferns,
    and my English seedlings, coming on fast. (Anon,1905,p.5).
An equally important function was to provide the place from which
experiential or sensory space could be enjoyed: in that of the
colonial community, this was especially subject to stimulation
from the flora of the compound. With other stimuli, these provoked
responses at the visual, acoustic, olfactory and thermal level
creating a total sense impression that was unique to the colonial
compound; with its spatial arrangements, its location in relation
to the indigenous city, its vegetation, and careful arrangement of
bungalow, kitchen and 'quarters', the sense data of the compound
created an almost mystical experience.
    After dinner we go onto the verandah.... It's very hot, and
    from the hot darkness hundreds and hundreds of crickets are

Figure 6.13

Figure 6.14

shrilling. It is exciting somehow, like the Venusberg music,
and away down in the bazaar there is a constant tom-toming and
squealing of native pipes. I feel over-excited. There is such
lots of everything. The garden is full of plants and trees
and ferns hidden in the darkness (Lawrence,n.d.,p.28).
One set of cultural values, however, was likely to clash with another
  Here in India sunset, or half an hour after sunset is a time
  when the natives of all castes are busy cooking their one and
  only meal and the atmosphere of the compound is laden with the
  peculiarly offensive smoke of their cow-dung fuel (Anon.,
  1905,p.7).

It is from these descriptions that an insight is gained into the
uniqueness of Hallowell's 'culturally constituted behavioural
environment', an area in which the elements and controls are so
arranged as to produce the desired 'mix' of sensory experiences
for individual members of a culture group. Thus, the colonial
compound was modified visually to accord with visual preferences.
If possible, a site was chosen, not out of sight of the 'native
town' but with sufficient distance between to ensure that, if it
were seen, it should appear only as a distant element in a 'view'.
The ground area, and particularly the trellissed verandah, was
planted with flora which scented the territory. Trees and shrubs
attracted the fauna, insects, animals and birds whose call added
the acoustic element to this modified cultural territory.
  This fair building stood in a pleasure ground in which were
  some very tall trees, amongst whose branches was the habitation
  of many doves. Never to this hour can I hear the voice of the
  dove without feeling myself carried back in memory to that
  beloved abode in Cawnpore (Brown, 1948,p.74).
Penetration into or interference with this acoustic cultural space
by members of the indigenous culture was tolerated, possibly welcomed, provided the sound was low: the distant drums, the far-off
music, the faithful mullah. This provided a sense of the romantic,
an exotic reminder of one's presence in distant lands. Should
these sounds come too close, the response was quite different,
first of anger, then of fear.

10 FACTORS IN THE ORIENTATION OF THE BUNGALOW

Two factors governed the orientation of the bungalow: the direction
of prevailing winds and the sun's course during the colonial day.

Thermal tolerance limits determined that the main living area
should be kept out of the direct rays of the sun for most of the
day. 'Living rooms should face north if practicable and verandahs
of bedrooms should preferably have an eastern aspect (Stokes-Roberts,
1910,p.1.). At different times during the development of the
bungalow, the direction of prevailing winds was important for any
or all of three reasons: for the effect they had on health, on the
thermal environment of the bungalow and compound, and on the quality
of olfactory experience which they helped to create.

As discussed in Chapter 5, the 'zymotic' theories of disease current
in the mid-nineteenth-century metropolitan society held that infection was present in the atmosphere; diseases were therefore
spread by prevailing winds. As indigenous areas of settlement were
perceived as potential centres of infection, it was important that,
in siting any buildings, 'the immediate neighbourhood of large
cities, especially in the leeward direction, are to be avoided as
the sanitary condition of all Indian towns cannot be described as
less than vile.' In Western India, it was often that 'outhouses,
stables, servants' rooms etc. are found between the wind and
dwelling houses. It was impossible for pure air to be breathed in
such a situation' (Moore, 1888,p.118).

Such theories explain first, the location of the house or entire
settlement area in relation to the indigenous town and the prevailing wind; second, the location of servants' quarters and
stables. These were generally separate from the main bungalow
and situated at the rear of the compound.

Though a more sophisticated understanding of disease and its
origins prevailed in the twentieth century, with winds no longer
being accepted as a source of infection, acquired olfactory preferences still governed the location of servants' quarters in
relation to the bungalow. In the suggested layout of officers'
quarters in 1925, north point and wind direction are the only
factors determining the orientation of the bungalow; outhouses lie
leeward of the main building (Figure 6.4).

11   CONCLUSION

   We are all interested in our bungalows, families, gardens,
   horses and dogs (Lawrence,n.d.p.39).

   The Englishman lavishes the same sort of care upon his house
   and his car, that we Indians lavish on our wives and
   children (Sharma, 1971,p.65).

In this chapter an attempt has been made to demonstrate how socially
and culturally derived values affect the development and use of a
particular dwelling-form and its immediate environment. Though
the practical implications of this study are many - the light
it sheds, for example, on the immensely varying densities in the
ex-colonial city - the concluding comments are restricted to more
theoretical aspects of the discussion.

The inherent advantage of studying the colonial bungalow as it
exists within the contrasting indigenous culture of India, is
that it clearly demonstrates how responses to environment are
determined by social and cultural factors. Ultimately, these
responses are affected by the world-view of a particular culture,
and by the cognitive categories and schemata with which its members
perceive the physical world. As Goodenough puts it, each member
of a culture operates with a 'conceptual model' of social and

physical reality, with which all phenomena are perceived, processed and organised into a cognitive whole.

Two points emerge from this analysis. The first is the existence of this 'conceptual model' as it affects the modification of the physical environment. The second is the insight the study gives into some characteristics of the particular 'conceptual model' of the British colonial community in India, and indirectly, into that of the metropolitan culture.

The most important aspect to note about this second issue is the comparative ease with which these characteristics can be investigated. This arises from the abundance of source materials relating to residential behaviour and environmental modification in the colonial culture. The large quantity of printed, painted and photographic records of this environment is itself evidence of certain basic values of the colonial community, and of the metropolitan culture of which it was a part. The significance of these statements becomes more apparent when making diachronic or synchronic, mono-cultural or cross-cultural comparisons.

Though existing sources allow the construction of a detailed model of the colonial culture's residential environment, it is much more difficult - if not impossible - to construct a descriptive or pictorial record of, for example, their image of God. On the other hand, the abundance of literary, theological or pictorial data for, say, the fifteenth century, would make this a feasible task to undertake for members of the metropolitan culture at that time.

Likewise, for the indigenous Hindu culture of the nineteenth and twentieth centuries, the profusion of written, pictorial or sculptural records would easily permit a description of the vast Hindu pantheon. 'Religious' beliefs therefore exist and their values and assumptions can be investigated. In comparison, literary or pictorial evidence illustrating attitudes to the physical environment are rare in that particular culture.

The very existence of these 'metropolitan' and 'colonial' source materials - of which those used in this chapter represent a minute proportion - indicates a long-range, cultural continuity in a man-environment relationship which dates back at least to the seventeenth century. It is evidence of a process which includes acts of perception, recording, record preservation, as well as the interpretation and application of these records. The process is itself evidence not only of an attitude towards the *physical-spatial* world but is also indicative of its *temporal*, historical dimension. In discussing these attitudes, as they were transplanted to other culture areas, this study provides a further illustration of a long-established cultural tradition.

Chapter 7

SOCIAL SPACE:
The hill station as a cultural community

There in the sight of the snows, are collected in the midst of
the green and the trees and the flowers, all the fair women of
Anglo-India who have been driven up by the summer heat
(L.C. Ricketts, 'English Society in India', *Contemporary Review*,
lOl, (May 1912),p.684).

I saw God, not with fleshy eyes, but with the inner vision, from
the Himalaya hills, the holy land of Brahma (Devendranath Tagore,
Autobiography (translated 1916,p.92).

1 THE HILL STATION IN THE COLONIAL URBAN SYSTEM

If the local urban universe of the colonial community was the 'civil
station', 'cantonment' and 'city', their larger socio-spatial world
was represented by 'Home', 'the Plains' and 'the Hills'. The hill
station was the third element in the urban system of the colonial
community; its function, institutions and form are to be understood
within a framework which includes the civil station 'on the plains'
and urban developments 'at Home'.

The appearance of Mitchell's study of the Indian hill station (1972)
makes an extensive description of the phenomenon unnecessary. In
what is otherwise a valuable account, however, the importance of
political, social and cultural factors, without which the hill
station would not have been developed, is seriously underestimated.
In the belief that the most important features of an environment
are the cultural and social characteristics of the population for
whom it exists, this chapter puts forward other explanations to
complement Mitchell's thesis. The first section suggests that the
development of 'hill stations' can be explained by reference to the
three main variables of culture, technology and the dominance-
dependence relationship of colonialism: in the second section, the
hill station is considered as a 'social place', a culture-specific
environment whose social and physical forms both resulted from and
contributed to the maintenance of the social structure and social
behaviour of the British colonial community in India.

156

Between 1815 and the end of colonial rule, some eighty urban
settlements located at elevations between 4,000 and 8,000 feet, were
established by representatives of the metropolitan power on the
lower mountain ranges of India. The main ones were clustered in
four regions, each accessible to the major European centres of
population. The largest number, the Simla-Mussoorie group, were in
the lower Himalayas, within reach by rail of populations from Delhi
and Calcutta. The second group, in the north east of India and
including Darjeeling and Shillong, were within closest range of
Calcutta. The third, Poona-Mahabaleshwar cluster, catered primarily
for a Bombay clientele and the Southern group, including Ootacamunde,
Kodaikanal and Coonoor, lay in the Nilgiri hills closest to the
fourth major colonial city of Madras.

The main characteristic of the hill station was the temporary patronage of its occupants. Apart from those with large military or
indigenous populations, the remainder catered for an annual influx
of inhabitants, their period of stay, between one and seven months,
coinciding with what the European population perceived as excessive
summer temperatures on 'the plains'.

The origin of these settlements, and the motivation for them, is
complex. Ostensibly, they began as 'health sanitaria', functioning
'as part of a British colonial ecosystem' (Mitchell, 1972,p.1).
According to this view, they were the product of European cultural
perceptions which held that expected states of health could be
attained more satisfactorily at higher elevations in 'the hills'.

Such an explanation is only partially correct. A more comprehensive
explanation lies not in one but a number of inter-related cultural,
social, political and psychological factors. Taken together, they
suggest that the hill station in India was a form of socio-spatial
organisation peculiar to colonial urban development. It is surprising, therefore, that apart from Mitchell (1972), Spencer and
Thomas (1948) and Withington (1961) it has received so little
attention.

2   EXPLANATORY VARIABLES: THE POLITICAL SYSTEM

Two factors characterise the hill station as a form of colonial
urban development. In the first place, it was developed by a non-
indigenous population; second, the relationship of this population
to the indigenous inhabitants was one giving them the monopoly of
power. It was not simply that the British, with a set of cultural
preferences for settlement in the hills, were located in India. It
was rather that their command of political power permitted these
preferences to be expressed.

As in all cases of colonial settlement, the initial acquisition of
territory and the organisation of resources to exploit it, depended
on the distribution of political and economic power. This was
especially the case in hitherto underdeveloped, physically
inaccessible areas where people and material had to be transported
up steep and difficult terrain.

The first modern hill stations of Simla and Mussoorie were established
in 1819 and 1826, in territory conquered from adjoining states.
These stations had immediate strategic purposes in acting as bases
from which the military could protect the frontiers of the colonised
society. In addition, though hill stations were used as recreational resorts and 'sanatoria' by civilian members of the
colonial community and subsequently, by members of the indigenous
elite, many were initially built as cantonments for European troops.
The communication system (particularly roads) was constructed
primarily for their benefit. Without the existence in India of a
European military force, the modern hill station would not have
developed. Significantly, the only other 'pre-modern' settlement
of comparable, though different, function was also established by
an alien invading culture, the Moghul 'hill town' of Srinigar
in Kashmir.

From an economic viewpoint, the construction and maintenance of the
hill stations, particularly in the early stages, required investment from regionally and nationally derived rather than local
sources. The construction of roads, railways, bridges and barracks
was financed from revenues gathered on a national basis. Apart
from the farming which some stations subsequently developed, their
major economic activity was, as in the tourist resort, to generate
a large tertiary sector of employment. The temporary patronage of
military and civilian populations was followed by the establishment
of other 'European' institutions such as hospitals,'convalescent
homes', orphanages, hotels and missionary headquarters. In some
cases, the hill station acted as an alternative 'summer capital'
for provincial centres on 'the plains'.

Apart from European troops, the main patrons and beneficiaries of
the hill station were the women and, to a lesser extent, the children
of the colonial community. Freedom from the normal domestic and
economic roles of the metropolitan society which such women enjoyed
depended on the distribution of economic power in the colonial
society and particularly, on the availability of indigenous
servants. According to Edwardes (1969,p.91) 'a hill station was
the only place in India where there were often more women than men'.
The predominance of women and the lack of what were perceived as
purposeful social or economic roles for them is a recurrent theme
in the literature of the colonial community. It influenced both
the nature of social behaviour in the hill station as well as the
type of social records which it produced.
    Hilda at Darjeeling wondered if there were any country where
    it was so useless and ineffective to be a woman - at any
    rate, an English woman.... The men she knew were busy all
    day, and every day, in work that was steadily, inexorably,
    building their minds away from hers' (Thompson, 1938,p.186).

Like other colonial administrative towns, the hill stations were
largely 'service' centres whose economic cost was borne by more
productive areas of the economy. (Other Asian hill stations were
also the result of settlement by European colonial powers, particularly the French and Dutch. Spencer and Thomas (1948) list

115 hill stations in India, China, Burma, Indochina, Malaya, Sumatra,
Java, The Phillipines, Celebes and Japan).

3   EXPLANATORY VARIABLES: CULTURE

If the political variable accounts for the existence of the non-
indigenous population in India and its command over resources, the
rationale for the hill stations, as well as their location and
form, results from particular aspects of the culture to which the
colonial power belonged.

The cultural variable is important in three respects. It explains
the particular 'settlement choices' available to the colonial
community in the early nineteenth century; it accounts for certain
ideological factors legitimising these choices; and it explains
the particular ethnomedical theories which were central to the
hill station's development.

The principal hill stations were established between 1815 and 1870.
At the beginning of the nineteenth century, the number of Europeans
in India was already substantial. In the 1830s it was about 41,000
including some 37,000 troops. By 1859 it had risen to 126,000 of
whom 85,000 were troops. In 1930 there were approximately 165,400
Europeans of whom some 63,500 were troops (Edwardes, 1969,p.12;
Royal Comm.,1863,p.28; *Times of India Yearbook*, 1930,p.30). The
question arises, therefore, not only why such settlements were
not developed earlier by the indigenous elite (other than Srinigar,
mentioned above) but why they were developed at this particular
time.

A central premise underlying the study of colonial urban development
is that the origins of particular phenomena in the culture of the
colonial society are to be found, at the cognitive level, in the
conceptual models of that culture as they originated in the metropolitan society. Accepting that metropolitan categories of
thought and action were used as means of organising behaviour in
the colonial society, it follows that the 'settlement choices'
available to European inhabitants of India in the early nineteenth
century were related to models of residence and types of urban
development prevailing in the metropolitan society at that time.

By the early nineteenth century, three major, inter-related
developments had taken place in this society which had significance
for colonial urban development in India. These are best described
in terms of the social, spatial and temporal models available to
members of the metropolitan society and which largely dictated
their social and geographical behaviour.

At the social level, there had emerged a large, socially differentiated urban population which included a substantial 'middle class'.
At the temporal plane, 'agricultural time had been replaced by a
new urban, social time' (Davidoff, 1973,p.38); the year, week, day
and hour were increasingly differentiated into temporal units

defined according to new social and economic criteria. As Davidoff
puts it

> as the century wore on, very slowly, the calendar of events
> in the pursuit of gentlemanly life, sport, social intercourse,
> entertainment and dining, was formalised, enlarged and organised
> into separate activities, pursued at specific times.... Very
> slowly, the business of pleasure and government took on the
> habits - and hours - of business (ibid.).

Although Davidoff's original analysis of the new social processes
and organisation prompted by industrial-urbanisation identifies
the *temporal* dimension of their operation (i.e. the 'Season') it
stops short of locating their *spatial* dimension. For every new
form of social behaviour there is a place where it occurs. Thus,
related to these two phenomena, of social and temporal differentiation, a spatially-differentiated urban system developed containing a range of socially and functionally specialised urban
places (see also Chapter 6, pp.127-30).

What these essentially inter-related developments meant can be
briefly summarised. They meant that new social groups, with new
types of social activity and behaviour, had developed during the
previous century, each associated with its particular time or
season of performance and each with its associated geographical
location and spatial demands. One of the most important aspects
of these developments was the emergence of an institutionalised
form of non-work or 'leisure' activity, an activity increasingly
accommodated into a revised temporal calendar (the 'Season' and,
later in the century, the 'week-end'), new physical-spatial and
urban forms (the 'hotel', 'boarding house' and 'resort') and
new forms of economic activity and occupation (the 'holiday'
industry and 'entertainment' profession).

A significant part of this emerging urban system were the so-called
'resorts', a development from the earlier 'spas' which had
originated in England in the sixteenth century and which had been
founded on the basis of the perceived medical benefits of the
mineral waters existing at their sites. By the early eighteenth
century the social, as opposed to the pseudomedical function of
the 'spa' was well-established (see Pimlott, 1947,pp.24-65;
Patmore, 1968; Martin, 1971; Neale, 1973. The most explicit statement on the system of social segregation inherent in the development of these specialised urban places is in Cosgrove and Jackson,
1972,pp.34,40). This function, as a place where an elite and
others aspiring to enter it could meet and participate in established social rituals was recognised in the institutions to which
they gave rise. The move of the 'spa' and its functions away from
inland locations, where opportunities to expand were restricted,
to coastal places in the mid- and late eighteenth century, permitted
an expansion in the size of the clientele (Patmore, 1970,p.53).

The establishment of such 'resorts' (e.g. Scarborough, Brighton,
Margate) served to extend a system of social stratification and
residential differentiation in the metropolitan society, already
existing at the level of neighbourhood and town, to a larger
urban and regional scale.

Such places not only supplied the supposed physiological benefits
thought to derive from 'the air', 'the waters' and 'exercise';
they also offered social returns in the access they gave to elite
circles and the opportunities afforded for furthering personal
relationships. Here, opportunities were sought for extending
economic and social influence, exchanging information, or promoting
social mobility, through acquaintance, friendship or marriage.
Here also, 'Society' (sic) as 'a system of quasi-kinship relationships... was used to "place" mobile individuals during the period
of structural differentiation fostered by industrialisation and
urbanisation' (Davidoff, 1973,p.15. The institutionalisation of
leisure associated with these developments is discussed in Plumb,
1973).

By the early nineteenth century, the concept, as well as the reality
of the 'resort' was fully established, along with the ideologies,
forms of activity and institutionalised behaviour which accompanied
it. The ideology was contained in an extensive literature on the
supposed merits of 'the air', the 'waters' and the benefits of
'exercise' and 'bathing'. The activities and social behaviour
were most clearly manifested in the new physical-spatial forms
characterising the built environment at such 'resorts'; it was
these which demonstrated their essentially *social* purpose, establishing their distinct functional identity in an increasingly
differentiated hierarchy of urban places.

Such forms included the 'Pump Rooms' where 'the waters', mechanically
raised, were made available for the rituals of bathing and drinking,
behaviour providing the setting for the exchange of 'Society'
gossip; the 'Parade', a centrally located pathway designed for
social interaction and the accommodation of personal display; the
'promenade', a level walkway bordering the sea which simultaneously
accommodated the activities of 'exercise', social interaction and
the inhalation of 'bracing' 'sea air'; the 'pier', an extended
platform projecting at right angles into the sea, which, in
addition to providing unrestricted exposure to 'sea air', by its
single access and terminal form, doubled the possibility for its
users of social encounters taking place.

Socially, however, the most important structure of the 'resort',
as of the 'spa' from which they had come, were the 'Assembly Rooms'.
With their regular programme of social dancing, entertainment and
community activity, the 'Assembly Rooms' provided a single,
socially approved meeting place which, for the essentially temporary inhabitants of the 'resort', served both to accelerate the
rate and increase the probability of social interaction taking
place. Other institutions patronised by a section of the urban
population sufficiently leisured, literate and affluent to use
them were also introduced to the 'resort' such as the 'library',
'theatre' and 'race course'.

Thus, for a particular social class in the metropolitan society, a
model of 'dual residence' emerged comprising a permanent, usually
winter, residence in the town and a temporary location, ostensibly

for health but in reality equally for social-recreational reasons,
in a 'resort'. The urban plant embodying this ideology and behaviour had been institutionalised well before the end of the
eighteenth century.

The originators and early patrons of the hill station shared these
social, temporal and spatial models. Thus, a rudimentary activity
analysis of a representative female member of the colonial community
between 1830 and 1870 indicates the following pattern of places
visited:

    1830–1849   (childhood and adolescence) Movement between London,
                Sevenoaks, Switzerland (Geneva), Broadstairs,Brighton,
                Dorking, Chichester, Bath ('coming out', 'first season')
    1849–1858   (married residence in India) Movement between Madras
                Calcutta, Benares, Lucknow, Delhi, Agra, Allahabad,
                Kanpur, Amritsar, Lahore, Karachi, Bombay and the
                hill stations of Simla, (several visits) Kasauli.
                (Relatively long periods were spent at these places).
    1858–1859   ('home leave' in Europe) Movement between London,
                Reading, Bath, Chew Magna, Midhurst (Kent) and
                Switzerland (Lausanne).
    1859–1861   (India) Movement between Calcutta and Simla.
    1861–1862   ('home leave' in Europe) Movement between Dartmouth,
                Maidenhead, Reading, Weston-super-Mare, Clifton
                (Bath), Broadstairs.
    1863–1866   (India) Movement between Calcutta, Simla, Mahasoo
                and other hill stations of Naini Tal, Almora.
    1866–1870   ('home' for permanent residence) London, Tunbridge
                Wells (Becher, 1930).

The 'resort', therefore, was the reference point for this new-found
habitat of the 'hill station'. In the 1830s, Mussoorie, begun in
1826, was compared to one of the more prominent of these metropolitan 'resorts' (the Isle of Wight) and in the seventies, the
function of the hill station generally compared to that of Brighton
and Scarborough (Edwardes, 1969,p.91; Mitchell, 1972,p.54). In
Ootacamunde, the first hill station in the south, developed from
the 1820s and likened to what in the metropolitan society was known
as a 'watering place' some few years later (Panter-Downes, 1967,
p.7), the 'Assembly Rooms' formed a key community institution.

The second cultural factor behind the development of the hill
station was of an ideological nature. This was the place which
the elevated terrain of 'mountains' and particularly, the Himalayas,
occupied in the world-view of the European colonial society in
India. We are therefore concerned with a set of environmental
attitudes and their social distribution within the colonial
community.

In the early nineteenth century, the principal indigenous inhabitants of those mountainous regions subsequently used for hill
stations were the so-called 'hill tribes'. For the indigenous
population on the plains, apart from a rare journey of pilgrimage,
there was neither economic, climatic nor cultural reason to

penetrate into nor create alternative settlements there.

Where the indigenous elite had sought to mitigate the excesses of heat experienced in the hotter plains of India, they had achieved this not through 'locational' but 'developmental' decisions, i.e. by modifying the environment rather than moving the location (McCoughlin 1969,p.106).   Climatic control was achieved by the 'summer palace', located outside the city.   Built form solutions to excessive heat included thick walls and underground chambers (the *taikhana*) or the creation of cool, shaded areas by the use of open-walled pavilions and light-repellent white marble, large expanses of water and well-irrigated gardens, as manifest in the Rajput palaces of Rajasthan.

In the Hindu world-view, the Himalayas have religious rather than aesthetic or geographical significance.   As Bharati suggests, 'to all Hindus except those who live there, the Himalayas tend to be ascriptive rather than actual.'   Mount Kailash is important more as the abode of Lord Shiva than as a potential place of settlement. 'The Himalayas of the *rishis* (priests) and *yogis* is more important as an ideal to (Hindus) than are the actual rocks and the miserable huts of the people there' (1973, pp.3,9).

> According to Hindu philosophy a spot of beauty is no place for
> social enjoyment or self indulgence.   It is the place for
> self-restraint, for solitary meditation which leads the mind
> from Nature to God.   Nowhere else is this concept more exem-
> plified than in the Himalaya.   Thus, religious cities have
> developed around the famous holy shrines which have been set
> up by saints at sites of exquisite natural beauty where devotees
> could perform their penance and meditation in a calm and serene
> and sublime atmosphere. (Singh, 1971,p.462.   See also Basak,1953;
> Bhardwaj, 1973).

Such twentieth-century views, portraying the phenomenon of the Himalayas as an image rather than a reality are likely to have been even more widespread in earlier times when communication between 'the hills' and 'the plains' was virtually non-existent.   Road-building began in the 1820s; a railway to Darjeeling, largely patronised by Europeans from Calcutta, opened in 1872. (Mitchell, 1972,p.66).

In the European world-view, the Himalayas, as other mountains, were quite differently perceived.   Amongst the educated elite, revolutions in philosophic, scientific and theological thought from the end of the seventeenth century had brought about a fundamental change in attitudes concerning the physical environment.   By the last quarter of the eighteenth century, mountain regions, previously feared or simply ignored as a conscious category of environment, assumed a new, positive significance (Nicholson, 1959).

Such ideological changes had important effects on elite behaviour. Mountain regions, hitherto avoided, were now visited and records, both pictorial and written, were made of reactions and attitudes towards them.   Amongst those sectors of society subscribing to such

beliefs, the practice of travelling was re-oriented to take in visits
to 'newly discovered' mountain regions in Europe such as the Alps.
In the metropolitan society, the mountainous area of the north
('The Lakes' and Scotland) assumed new roles as 'picturesque' environments (Nicholson, 1972).

Such attitudes, increasingly shared by members of an urban-based
middle and upper class in the metropolitan society, were most fully
embodied in the so-called 'Romantic' movement in literature and
pictorial art, with its associations with particular preferences
for 'landscape' and modifications of the physical-spatial environment. The existence of such ideas combined with increasing technological control over this environment to enable an increasing
number of this growing social elite to visit and ultimately settle
in the preferred 'mountain' localities.

Whatever other motivations were present for the creation of hill
stations, these ideological beliefs, common to elites in the metropolitan society, were shared by middle-class members of the
colonial community throughout the nineteenth and twentieth centuries.
Both descriptive and pictorial accounts provide ample evidence in
support of this hypothesis. Thus Baikie (1834), refers to 'the
beautiful and picturesque mountains, forming a majestic and extended
amphitheatre' to Ootacamunde. In the eyes of another observer
in 1854
    were the pine to be seen here... the landscape of Aboo with its
    lake and neatly thatched cottage peering through the pendant
    boughs of the shade, on conical hill and rocky declivity, would
    be very similar to the general landscape of Switzerland (p.304).
This account also indicates that
    prior to the erection of the Mess Room of the 8th Regiment,
    there was no place of general assembly, consequently the social
    hour had to be spent in the private dwellings of residents. Now
    inhabitants go to the Mess Room for dancing and also take
    exercise in the open air (p.307).
The conflicting cultural perceptions of the Himalayas are well illustrated in the comments of one of the earliest observers to make a
pictorial record of the 'newly discovered' environment between
1829 and 1832
    The mountains are considered very sacred, consequently temples
    dedicated to Krishna, Siva and other Hindoo deities are found
    in all parts and Brahmins are numerous. In many parts, the
    forests and woods present an appearance scarcely differing from
    the most splendid and luxuriant British scenery....
        Musoorie contain(s) private houses, and is usually termed
    the civil, as Landour is the military station. But the houses
    are rising so fast on every spot that can safely be built on
    that the exact limits of the depot station cannot easily be
    understood (White, 1836).

The third cultural reason behind the development of the hill station
were the particular ethnomedical beliefs of the colonial society
which held that certain diseases, particularly cholera, malaria
and typhoid, were less likely to occur in the elevated regions of

the hill station. The theories associated with this view are discussed in Chapter 5.

4 EXPLANATORY VARIABLES: TECHNOLOGY

If these were the beliefs and settlement models which motivated the
development of hill stations, it was the technological superiority
of the immigrant community which, particularly after the introduction
of a system of railways into India after the 1840s, allowed the
aspirations to be realised to greater effect. Whether in relation
to the sciences of geology, surveying or cartography or the technologies of road, bridge or railway construction, knowledge and
techniques originating in the urban-industrial processes of the
eighteenth and nineteenth centuries were first introduced, and then
developed, in the colonial environment of India to enable a European
population to live, at up to 8,000 feet in the Himalayas, at a
level of 'civilisation' reasonably comparable to that they
experienced 'at Home'.

5 SOCIAL PLACE: THE HILL STATION AS ALTERNATIVE ENVIRONMENT

As the civil station was a cultural response to the indigenous city,
so the hill station was a social response to the colonial settlement
on 'the plains'. There, members of the colonial community were
separated from 'the natives'; in 'the hills', they were temporarily
separated from each other. In this and other ways, the hill station
performed a social role, providing in its modified cultural environment an opportunity for new relationships and alternative patterns
of behaviour. It also accommodated the particular kinship and
community needs unique to the colonial society.

The significance of the hill station was that it functioned not
simply as a 'resort' in the dual residence model familiar from
the metropolitan society. It also provided, in its physical, social,
psychological and 'aesthetic' climate, the closest approximation
to conditions of life 'at Home'. Of all areas of settlement, it
was the hill station which most easily permitted the reproduction
of metropolitan institutions, activity patterns and environments
(Figure 7.1).
    Having seen (Ootacamunde) I affirm it to be a paradise. The
    afternoon was rainy and the road muddy but such beautiful
    English rain, such delicious *English* mud. Imagine Hertfordshire
    lanes, Devonshire downs, Westmoreland lakes, Scottish trout
    streams and Lusitanian views (1877) (Brown, 1948,p.27).

    The climate of Sonawar (near Simla) is thoroughly English...
    here it is possible to raise a population thoroughly English
    in habits, in physical constitution and in mental vigour
    (*Royal Comm.* 1863,p.4).

Isa.—Is not this delicious, Louisa? This fine, pure, bracing mountain air? Dear, dear, darling Simla!

Louisa.—Oh! indeed it is, dear Bella; and it is *so* delightful to be able to resume all our *active English habits.*

Figure 7.1

Figure 7.2

The use of national-cultural categories as a means of identifying
items in the indigenous environment occurs frequently in the records
of the colonial community. Where a combination of environmental
attributes matches up to particular perceptual categories in the
culture of the metropolitan society, the response is to label the
phenomena with the generic term used for all cultural items in that
society, i.e. 'English'. Effectively, this is a shorthand term to
express a combination of environmental characteristics existing in
and available for any member of that society sufficiently socialised
into these particular cultural modes of perception. For example, the
'country house' (outside Madras) 'is the most delicious place I have
seen in India. It stands in the middle of a delightful garden,
exactly like a big English garden.... It really is the most English
place I have seen' (Halifax papers, India Office Library, MSS.
Eur.C. 152,p.27: Lord Irwin to Lord Halifax. November/December
1929, no.172. I am indebted to David Page for this reference).
For such a context Harvey refers to 'cultural appraisal': 'individuals
must possess value systems which motivate them to want to make use
of (particular) resources' (1973,p.82).

The associational function of such environments had been recognised
at an early stage of their discovery. For example, in 1828 a
military member of the colonial society observed of Subathoo in
the Himalayas:

> European shrubs and trees greeted the eye, giving rise to emotions
> at once gratifying and regretful; the wild cherry and pear; the
> pine of different kinds, and many less prominent bushes appeared...
> the modest violet reared its head.... The recollections of home,
> and the many kindred associations which possess the mind, and
> arouse those undefinable feelings of love, of hope, desire and
> regret and which are not less forcible by being called into
> existence through the medium of such humble instruments as simple
> wild flowers - these make the heart yearn with tenfold eagerness
> to retrace the distance between it and the objects of its
> earliest and best remembrance(6 April 1828)(Archer 1833,vol.1,
> p.207).

Apart from these climatic and topographical similarities, the attraction of the hill station lay in the absence of the three major constraints which restricted social life on 'the plains': the unfavour-
able climate, 'official' authority and, most important of all, large
numbers of the indigenous population.

To understand the social significance of the hill station,further
insight is needed into the nature of the colonial community and
the character of its social world. Some of this may be gained from
the comments of a female member of that community writing in the
early years of the twentieth century.

> Anglo-Indian society... the Society of the dominant race, is
> exceedingly small and very much scattered... and exists in a
> state of perpetual motion.... Parents, deprived of their children,
> occupy themselves with alternative social activity. Mothers
> particularly have little outlet for sympathy and energy in
> charitable works as have their sisters at home as the annual

exodus to the Hills... constant moves between stations, and
the periodical year's leave at home frustrate any kind of
routine work.

There was in the colonial society

a consciousness of exile which is always with them. Their life
and work may be in India, but their treasure, the memories of
their youth, the parents and friends of their youth - these are
all 'at Home'. And so it happens that they all, quite
unconsciously perhaps, make an effort to forget it and draw
together in every way likely to distract one another from dwelling
on this idea. With this object in view, all but the very latest
arrivals from England contrive to make their houses as little
oriental and as much like an English home as possible. The
idea too doubtless originated 'the Club' which figures in every
station....

For all the internal stratification within the community, there was
none the less a greater consensus of a society

representing a family on a larger scale.... There, set against
the background of the diversity of type of the dark-skinned
races of Hindustan, the strong kindred likeness of the great
white family stands out conspicuous. British born and bred,
having imbibed the same traditions, acquired the same prejudices,
trained in the same schools and universities, been subject to
the same laws and customs and worshipping the same God, their
differences and divisions appear only as a matter of degree.
Living under the peculiar conditions of their exile, such
differences as there may be have a tendency to sink out
of sight....

   Chief among the influences which might help to unite the
members of this unique family is the fact that all are working
for the same object, and all are animated by the same spirit of
pride in ruling and keeping their vast and splendid dependency
for the honour of the larger family, the Nation.

   Anglo-Indian society is thus bound together by... community
of interest and experience... where all enjoy the same advantages
and labour under the same disabilities, and where nobody is
regarded as a stranger whose name, position and pay is seen at
a glance in the lists of the Army or Civil Service... there
exists a bond of fellowship which unites alike the tried friends
of yesterday and the barest acquaintance of today.

The considerable sociological insight which this particular member
reveals in the understanding of the bonds within the community are
paralleled in her comments on factors encouraging social cohesion
on a smaller scale.

For the majority

nothing is more binding than separation. Their long enforced
absences from each other seem only to awaken a longing for
reunion which serves as a perpetual stimulus to love. These
men and women faithfully attached to one another... devoted
to their children, have been welded the more firmly together
by the very circumstances that have made shipwrecks of others.
The fact of their exile, their separations, and of the exigencies
of the climate, have only served as incentives to closer

comradeship whilst the laxity of public opinion, the exceptional
temptations of opportunity, and of a gay and unconventional life,
have created in them an unwholesome fear which keeps them constantly alive to dangers (Ricketts, 1912,pp.683-7).

Though such racial and political views are more characteristic of
the earlier decades of the twentieth century than the later years
of colonial rule, and represent female rather than male perspectives,
the 'domestic' viewpoints have a more lasting validity. The value
of these comments is in the insight they give into the nature and
strengths of the social bonds operating at the level of both community
and family. Separation from the parent society strengthened commitment to it in the same way that separation from kin strengthened
the ties between them.

Such beliefs and attitudes are most easily associated with, and are
reflected in, the hill station. Here was a physical and social
environment most obviously created by, and according to the values
of, the colonial community. Temporary residence in the hills
provided not only a cooler and 'healthier' climate but also an
opportunity to strengthen one's cultural identity and participate
in familiar community roles. Here were localities with 'a marked
holiday atmosphere and absence of officialdom' (Allen, 1975,p.133),
where inhabitants could temporarily relax from the strains of
government, 'let their hair down' and, irrespective of their
attitudes towards them, be far away from the indigenous population
whom they governed on 'the plains'. 'On my part it was the over-
powering desire which takes possession of me at intervals in India -
to be alone. Alone, not only from one's fellow sahibs, and
mem-sahibs... but also from the ubiquitous native'(Anon, 1905,p.89).
Residence in the hills was a chance to escape the constraints of
formal colonial life and participate in behaviour which the controls
of this life, on one hand, prevented and on the other, made
necessary. It was this aspect which accounts for what would have
appeared, in the metropolitan society, to constitute bizarre if
not deviant forms of behaviour.

> It was colossal! Reverend gentlemen, renowned hitherto for their
> eloquence in the Legislative Assembly or the Council of State -
> or for their dignity of demeanour during interviews with the
> Viceroy - raced the length of the ballroom on cushions - danced
> in solitary defeat blowing gold bugles - tore round the room in
> teams of four to the strains of John Peel - bleated like sheep
> or roared like lions and laughed without ceasing.... Since then,
> (the guests) have enlarged, on the telephone, on the road, to
> each other and all and sundry, that never in their lives have
> they had such an evening (from an account of a party at the
> Vice-Regal Lodge, Simla, 1926, by the private secretary to the
> Vicereign, Butler, 1969,p.49).

Because each hill station fulfilled this essentially social role,
each developed a social as well as geographical image. Simla, the
official summer capital of the colonial government, was avoided by
those wishing to be free of the constraints imposed by their social
position. Mussoorie, more tolerant of deviant behaviour, provided

an alternative setting.

The absence of the three constraining influences of 'the heat',
'the station' and 'the natives' combined with the opportunities
for recreation and social intercourse to make the hill station
an important locale for courtship and the extension of personal
relations. For the space of a summer, the small, closed community
of 'the station' on 'the plains' would be exchanged for the new,
open community in the hills, whose population stemmed from a variety
of places

> 'Darjeeling!' he said... 'It's just a long street on a hill-side.
> You can go *up* the hill - or you can go *down* the hill. But you
> can't do anything else.'
>
> Mrs Nixon was out of temper.... 'There's the Club there',
> she replied. 'I get sick of this hole, and long to meet some
> people.'
>
> 'Damn the Club!' growled Nixon.... 'I never met a man who
> didn't detest the hills.'
>
> Mrs Nixon turned... indignantly....'Percy Fowke told me he
> loved them. So did Freddy Furnevaux'.
>
> 'They're not men, they're just dancing-partners' (Thompson,
> 1938,p.186).

Here, chance encounters on the sea passage from 'Home' could be
more deeply explored. The absence of spouses 'at Home' or on duty
in 'the plains' encouraged alternative social relationships for the
one who remained in 'the hills'. According to one observer, 'Simla
is a hotbed of flirtations and more, where every Jack has someone
else's Jill' (Butler, 1969,p.86. See also Allen, 1975,p.134).
The hill station was deemed a suitable environment for childbirth
(Thompson, 1938,p.107), matrimony and the burial of kin, the central
rites de passage of the colonial community. Not without cause was
one of the most percipient comments on the colonial social world
called 'Plain Tales from the Hills' (Kipling, 1915).

6 INSTITUTIONS AND THEIR PHYSICAL-SPATIAL ENVIRONMENT

For those hill stations functioning as summer capitals or cantonments, institutions of government were represented though their
physical manifestation was never so prominent as in the settlement
on the plains. As there, however, residential accommodation for
the head of government, such as the 'Vice-Regal Lodge' in Simla,
symbolised in scale, elevation and form, the authority of the
dominant culture (Figure 7.2). 'There can be few places in the
world where the upper ten were so literally upper; the Viceroy and
Commander-in-Chief naturally had the best peaks' (Spate and
Learmonth, 1965,p.218). Provision was made for the military in
the form of barracks and hospitals, and extensive modifications
of the terrain were carried out to accommodate the distinctive
military, religious and recreational needs of the colonial military
establishment (Figures 7.3, 7.4).

General view of Subathu.

Figure 7.3

Figure 7.4

For the majority of hill station inhabitants, however, the main
function was that of residence, the core institutions of kinship,
religion, association and recreation represented in the dwelling,
church, club, 'Mall' and a variety of recreational spaces.

The values underlying the social and cultural purposes of the hill
station were embodied in the irregularly scattered dwellings of
which it was largely composed. Typically, each bungalow was dug
closely into the hillside, occupying a separate compound and
isolated from neighbouring sites. The criteria of location were
those of seclusion, access to 'views' and conformity to a
'picturesque' landscape ideal. Though less substantial and more
sparsely equipped, the colonial hill dwelling conformed in its
form and lay-out to its counterpart on 'the plains'.

> At the top we saw a wooded hill-top before us, through which
> gleamed white bungalows here and there. Then we came out on
> a fine hard new road, which led us through pleasant forests
> of pine and patches of rhododendron of great size. Right and
> left and on all sides were the waving forests and a toppling
> sea of hill-tops....Above me, on the hillside, and below me
> in the valley, were rows of detached bungalows standing amid
> flower-gardens and neatly laid-out compounds, with English
> names on the gateways (Russell, 1860,l,p.92).

In contrast to the uniformity of the 'official' and public landscape of 'the plains', the private environment of the hills was
consciously varied and utilised for individual expression.
Dwellings were personalised by names invested with social and
cultural meaning. Thus, social identity is expressed in terms
with prestigious associations 'at Home': 'The Manor', 'The Grange',
'The Manse' or 'The Priory'; visual criteria of settlement are
made apparent in 'Vale View', 'Prospect Point', 'Snow View' or
'Bella Vista'. The significance of natural elements, particularly
trees, in influencing environmental choice is reflected in 'Willow
Bank', 'Oak Cottage', 'The Acorns', 'The Firs', 'The Saplings' or
'Holly Mount'. Preferred locations are evident in 'Hill Top',
'The Knoll' or 'Eagle's Nest'; commitment to prevailing metropolitan
literary categories in 'Kenilworth', 'Westward House', 'Bleak House'
or 'Waverley'. For others, the commemoration of comparable environments result in 'Glenelg', 'Dunedin', 'Interlaken', or 'Vermont'.
It is some indication of the social importance of the various hill
stations that the names, and locations, of the individual dwellings
are clearly shown on the maps of all the major stations included
in the various editions of Murray's *Guide to India*.

The institution of religion was most clearly expressed in the church,
in all hill stations the most visible symbol in the cultural landscape. Prominently located, the church adopted a form closely
approximating to models in the metropolitan culture, most frequently
assuming that of what was known as the 'Revived Gothic', the other
major alternative of 'Classical' being reserved for secular use.

As on 'the plains', the centre of social activity was the club.
In view of the importance of this institution in the social

structure of the colonial community it is appropriate at this point
to discuss some of its social properties and the meanings associated
with membership.

The station club was a private cultural environment in which were
reproduced the institutions of 'Home' as transformed by the
colonial community.

> Here there are green lawns, cooling drinks, a multitude of
> English papers, a library, tennis, racquets and badminton courts,
> bridge tables, billiard rooms. Here, at the end of a busy day,
> those who are socially inclined, or who want games or books,
> gather till dinner time. Here are given occasional dances,
> concerts, private theatricals or the much rarer lecture
> (Ricketts, 1912,p.633).

Membership of the club was decided by election which in turn, was
restricted by social and racial criteria. Senior members of the
European elite were invariably admitted, 'as also are usually
those who by birth, education and general social qualifications
are regarded as belonging to the "club set"'(Indicus,1919,p.321).
In smaller stations, for economic or social reasons (such as
providing the requisite number of participants for 'bridge' or
'tennis') Europeans of lower status were allowed. In the larger
and more prestigious clubs, a member of the indigenous society
would be occasionally, though rarely, admitted, provided his status
in the colonial system (such as that of 'judge') was sufficiently
high. In general, however, all members of the indigenous society
were excluded,'almost all members being pure European even Anglo-
Indians finding it hard to get in' (ibid).

The objection to indigenous membership stemmed from inter-related
social, racial and political reasons. Socially, the club represented the one community private space, the major locale for
its cultural behaviour and rituals (Figure 7.5). It was 'the one
place of general meeting for English society after the day's work
is done and to a great extent replaces the home'. Because of the
frequent absence, either 'at Home' or in 'the hills', of those kin
whose presence most commonly provided the opportunity for informal
communication and the relief of occupational fatigue, much of the
intercourse which in the metropolitan society would take place in
the 'family setting' of the home, in the colonial society took place
in the club (ibid.,p.323). It provided the single setting where
public postures could be relaxed and the mask of authority removed.

The basis of the club's exclusiveness rested in the divisions of the
larger society. The colonial community lived separately, had
separate kinds of behaviour and shared separate forms of knowledge.
The very lack of privacy between them was essential in the maintenance of their collective identity. The club, with its familiar
surroundings and established rituals, provided the setting for the
exchange of this social knowledge, the place where community beliefs
and sentiments were continuously reinforced and modified, the context
in which newcomers were socialised into the folkways of the colonial
culture. Any hindrance of these processes could undermine social
cohesion.

Figure 7.5

Figure 7.6

SKETCHES FROM INDIA—AN AFTERNOON IN THE HIMALAYAS

All our private life, our gossip, shall we say our scandals,
centre round the club. We know where we are with our own people;
we are not always quite so certain as to whether we would like
our more intimate affairs to be discussed by those, so to speak,
outside the family circle (ibid.).

The minutiae of social behaviour by which those admitted to club
membership were distinguished from those not so admitted are well
illustrated in a particular artefact of the colonial culture, a
copy of A.W. Chester: *Wertheimer's Law Relating to Clubs*, 1913,
existing in the Bowring Institute Library, Bangalore, in 1970. The
chapter which bears the most underlining and thumbprints is that on
'Expulsion'. The most heavily-underlined sentence reads 'none but
the members of the club can know the little details which are
essential to the social well-being of such a society of gentlemen'
(p.145).

As the central social form of the colonial community, acting as
social gatekeeper and arbiter in questions of status and behaviour,
held together by the shared social knowledge of its members
(c.f. Allen, 1975,p.105), the club in the colonial society has not
received the sociological attention it deserves.

In the hills, however, the club could afford to be less exclusive.
Here, its social functions were reduced, for the cooler climate and
selectively modified environment expanded the capacity for movement
and, in contrast to behaviour on 'the plains', interaction took
place out of doors. Moreover, as the hill station was largely
separated from the indigenous populations on 'the plains', it
embodied in itself the principal properties of the club, being an
exclusive environment where people with similar aims gathered
occasionally to pursue them. The physical characteristics of the
hill station confirmed this analogy. As a form of settlement, the
Himalayan hill station such as Mussoorie had unique socio-spatial
properties. Like the metropolitan 'pier', it was a social and
physical 'terminus'. As the noble Duke of York, 'once you were up,
you were up'; being up, there were two alternatives: to stay up, or
to go down. Through roads to other places were either few or non-
existent. Typically, the central thoroughfare of the Himalayan
hill station was 'The Mall'. From here, other 'cart roads', or
rather tracks, either branched off, to make a circuitous route
round the peaks on which the settlement was sited and then returned
to 'The Mall', or to peter out on the uninhabited slopes.

The function of such roads was not simply 'recreational', supplying
the need for preferred activities transferred from the metropolitan
culture such as 'walking', 'admiring the view', 'riding', 'collecting
flora' or 'taking the air'; they were also instrumental in generating
social interaction. Unlike in the settlement on 'the plains', roads,
both in width and distance, were geared to pedestrian and equestrian
use. When cars arrived in the twentieth century, they were usually
only permitted to a certain elevation from which rickshaws and
'coolies' carried visitors and belongings to their various destinations. The hill station was a pedestrian-equestrian precinct
(Figure 7.6).

The effect of this modified environment was to produce a location
where it was difficult, if not impossible, without staying indoors,
to avoid regular social interaction. Either 'by accident or design',
on the confined thoroughfares or in the limited places of recreation,
inhabitants were constantly in contact. In moving out of the house,
destinations were less important than encounters.

> There is no station in India where two people who wish to meet
> often may not have the opportunity for doing so every day, and
> more than once in the day, in the natural course of events.
> And when the leave season comes round and the stream of society
> begins to flow towards the hills, there ceases to be any limit
> to the constant daily intercourse of those who, by accident or
> design, find themselves in the same hill station (Ricketts, 1912,
> p.684).

It was this behavioural quality of the environment which was
commemorated in the designation of preferred locales as 'Charing
Cross' and 'Scandal Point'; by encouraging social interaction, it
simultaneously discouraged any form of privatised behaviour.

> (Lady Reading) constantly says how much she longed to 'slip away'
> into the bazaars incognito.... In Simla, it would have been
> utterly impossible because everything that happened there became
> common knowledge in club and bazaar at great speed, owing to the
> constriction of society dictated by the lie of the land. As you
> went along the Mall you were visible to the bazaars several hun-
> dred feet below you, just as movements below could be spied upon
> from above (Butler, 1969,p.30).

The lay-out of the hill station, 'plastered against the side of one
of the lower range of the Himalayas', with its community 'jam(med)
on to a series of ledges at 8,000 feet' produced a 'claustrophobic
and enclosed society' where inhabitants 'were always meeting the
same people. Everyone knew rather too much about everyone else's
affairs... what was going on, who was going out with so-and-so'
(Allen, 1975,pp.130,132). To enable the upper echelons of the
colonial elite to avoid excessive contact with members of their
own community, a further metropolitan residential model was introduced into the hill station environment. 'At Mashobra, the
Viceroy had a weekend cottage', situated some six miles away from
the main centre of population (Butler, 1969,p.31).

The centre of social activity was 'The Mall' which typically ran
mid-way through the station, giving access to the major institutions
of the church, principal hotels, library, club and the few European
stores. Apart from the occasional rickshaw, this was primarily a
pedestrian thoroughfare, the starting point for social encounters
and avoided by seekers of seclusion and peace. Like the boulevard
in France, 'the Mall' offered 'a socially sanctioned opportunity...
where one can see and be seen' (Michelson, 1970,p.137). Here,
the young, female and sick processed in a performance of competitive
display.

> In front of Mussoorie, you are in high public, the road called
> the Mall is from eight to ten feet wide, covered with children,
> nurses, dogs and sickly ladies and gentlemen, walking about
> gaily dressed. I always avoided the Mall; I go out for enjoyment
> and health and do not want to talk to people (Brown,1948,p.28).

Unlike the indigenous population whose leisure activities were still dictated by a pre-industrial economy and calendar, the colonial community had recreational expectations associated with the upper class of an increasingly leisure-conscious industrialising society. In the 'resorts' of this society such recreational expectations were fulfilled in a variety of institutions, the ballroom, theatre, race-course or library, and these were similarly reproduced in the hill station of the colonial society. The specialised and increasingly professional activity of 'entertainment', however, which grew rapidly in the metropolitan 'resorts' of the nineteenth century, was absent in the colonial society. For a variety of social and cultural reasons, indigenous forms of entertainment, patronised in the eighteenth century (Spear, 1963), were either unavailable or, during the course of the nineteenth century, rejected by the colonial community. Hence, for the duration of colonial rule, 'entertainment' was a non-professional activity. Provided gratuitously by civilian and military members of the community and developed in the closed social environment of 'the hills', it was the subject of comment both in the early and later stages of colonial rule.

> In Europe there are separate classes of people who subsist by
> catering for the amusements of the higher classes of society,
> in theatres, operas, concerts, balls, etc. etc.; but in India
> this duty devolves entirely upon the young civil and military
> officers of the Government, and at large stations it really is
> a very laborious one, which often takes up the whole of a young
> man's time. The ladies must have amusement; and the officers
> must find it for them, because there are no other persons to
> undertake the arduous duty (Sleeman, 1915 (first published
> 1844), p.638).

'There was no radio or TV, or even talking films. Entertainment (in Simla and Delhi) and culture had to be on a do-it-yourself basis and some of it was really very good' (Butler, 1969,p.33). Provision for recreational needs, therefore, required extensive modification of the hill station environment. Horse-racing and polo required the construction of a suitably even plane; sports, such as 'cricket', and 'fetes', the smoothing of uneven terrain (Figures 7.7, 7.8); sailing and boating (as at Ootacamunde or Naini Tal) the creation of a lake or diversion of existing water source. Reading, a favoured pursuit among an educated and leisured elite, meant the provision of well-stocked libraries, their contents providing a valuable insight into the preoccupations of the colonial culture (King, 1970). 'Assembly Rooms' offered accommodation for 'theatricals' and social dancing; on warmer days, the 'band stand' provided the venue for additional entertainment on the 'Mall'

> Mussoorie is purely a summer resort.... Most of the buildings,
> the Church included, lie along the Mall under the Camel's Back,
> at the back of which a circular road runs passing the Cemetery.
> The Library is beyond the Church at the end of the Mall. When
> the band plays, society (sic) gathers here and has tea, etc. on
> the verandah of the Criterion Restaurant. The (Skating) Rink
> is the great place for amusements, concerts, theatricals etc.
> Excursions to Mossy Falls and Kempti Falls may be taken (Murray,
> 1904,p.144).

Figure 7.7

Figure 7.8

Hardly less important than the provision for group entertainment were those individual activities which depended on interaction with the environment itself such as 'walking', 'riding', 'climbing', even 'looking', as well as the culturally favoured pastimes of 'painting' or arranging a 'picnic'.

A further socially important function of the hill station was in providing for the educational needs of the community. Where children were not at home, they were 'boarded' in hill station schools, fashioned after metropolitan models. As parents, particularly mothers, moved up to spend the summer months with offspring in the hills, such schools further supported the family-maintaining function of the hill station. In catering for the young of officials operating in other parts of the colonial system, in Africa and the Far East, some of the hill station schools fulfilled more than a local role in sustaining the socialisation requirements of the larger colonial society.

Day-to-day retailing and market activity was, as on 'the plains', provided by the indigenous population, the 'native bazaar' being generally out of sight, lower in elevation than 'The Mall'. Other 'European stores' catered for the particular dietary requirements of the colonial inhabitants and in larger hill stations, major retailers from the principal urban centres on 'the plains', such as 'tailors', 'photographers' or 'caterers', found it worth while to have branches there. Similarly, the major 'hotels', whose names ('Grand', 'Metropole', 'Elysium', 'Savoy', 'Waldorf', 'Cecil') reproduced the image if not the reality of the metropolitan models on which they were based, were managed by concerns from the major cities on 'the plains'.

Like the 'bungalow-compound complex' the hill station was a 'culturally constituted behavioural environment' (Hallowell, 1967,p.87). It functioned as an integral part of the social world and urban system of the colonial community, providing the setting in which metropolitan institutions could be maintained. As a 'social place' it admirably demonstrates the mutual interaction between man's behaviour and his culturally modified built environment.

PART THREE

Chapter 8

DELHI:
A case study in colonial urban development

Social life was, of course, exclusive, and from hotels and
even from certain parks, *unwritten rules* excluded Indians,...
the Europeans in India, however long they lived there,
remained strangers in the country. An unbridgable chasm
existed between them and the people.... They lived in two
countries, Anglo-India and India, and the two never met.
The one governed the other (K.M. Panikkar, *Asia and Western
Dominance*, 1965, pp.116-19).

1 INTRODUCTION

In the previous chapters, a methodology and framework have been
developed to examine the process of colonial urban development. In
considering the social and cultural context of the colonial city
(Chapter 3), we have shown that an understanding of its physical-
spatial structure can best be gained by examining the *institutional
system* of each cultural section in that city. We have assumed that
the cultural section which holds power in the colonial society has
a monopoly over the institution of government, and that government
comprehends a system of military and civil administration which
includes the police, and such legal institutions as the courts.

It has also been suggested that other institutions representing
the core of a people's culture, namely kinship, religion, education
and various economic and social institutions such as marketing,
property, associational forms and recreation, although extant in
each cultural section in the city, are expressed differently in
each section, as also are their forms of technology and language.
The ideas and values, forms of behaviour and patterns of social
relationships associated with each institution are unique to the
culture in question. Consequently, the cultural artefacts which
each section produced, and especially, the physical-spatial forms
manifest in the colonial city, reflect the culture-specific system
of values, behaviour and social relations in each of the cultural
sections, as well as the overall distribution of power.

Chapters 4 to 7 have aimed to demonstrate this analysis by examining the physical-spatial forms of the British colonial culture on the basis of evidence drawn from over one century of the culture's existence in India. With this method and framework the investigation and explanation of the urban structure of Delhi is approached.

2 DELHI AS CASE STUDY

For many reasons, Delhi represents an ideal case for studying 'colonial urban development'. Following the independence of the American colonies, India became the first large society outside Europe to come under the impact, through the colonial process, of Western industrial capitalism. The process of urbanisation and urban development which accompanied these events provides a detailed case-history of the transformation, under the impact of Western indus-trialism, of an indigenous urban tradition. With the possible sole exception of China, not subject to the same kind of Western imperial experience, India represents one of the oldest and most highly de-veloped civilisations whose known history of continuous urban settlement goes back at least four and a half thousand years. When Western institutions and urban forms were introduced they were, from the start, 'competing' with a highly developed and integrated urban system, itself a fusion of Hindu and Muslim culture. That this 'competition' took place in a situation of colonialism, with re-sources and authority, particularly after the nineteenth century, heavily weighted in favour of an industrialising colonial power, is taken for granted.

If India provides an ideal example of a civilisation brought under the domination of a Western industrial power, Delhi, of all Indian cities, represents a textbook case of colonial urban development.

The first major urban centres of what was to become the colonised society were those of the three ports, Madras, Bombay and Calcutta. Each of these had reached an advanced state of economic maturity as centres of trading activity under the mercantile colonialism of the eighteenth and early nineteenth centuries, long prior to the formal absorption of India into the British colonial system (Brush,1970). With India part of this system, the political and administrative machinery of an imperial state, both military and civil, was set up throughout the country. A system of strategic and administrative centres, including, in the 1860s, some 175 major 'cantonments', and increasingly linked after 1850 by a communications network of rail, road and telegraph, was established.

In each of these centres, located at the main foci of population, the basic apparatus of the colonial urban settlement was installed: the military 'cantonment', containing the army, and the 'civil station', providing accommodation for administrative and occasionally commercial activities. The basic pattern was to be found, on a large scale in the major towns or, on a smaller scale, in the pro-vincial or 'up country' stations. In South India, the civil station was often incorporated in the cantonment.

The significance of Delhi is twofold. In the first place, its
development prior to 1911 is typical of the 'classical' provincial
or district town in that it contains the three fundamental,
functional parts of 'native city', 'cantonment' and 'civil station'.
In addition, its post-1911 development gave the colonial power the
opportunity to utilise half a century and more of experience, and to
provide what was perceived as the optimum planning solution for the
administrative capital of the largest territory of the colonial
empire. To this extent, therefore, *New* Delhi not only embodies all
the functions of the typical nineteenth-century district or provincial
town with its 'cantonment', 'civil lines', government buildings, club,
race-course, and arrangement of residential accommodation according
to status, it also represents the most advanced ideas on the planning
of a colonial capital of its day. Moreover, as New Delhi was built
from scratch, 'without hindrance' from metropolitan or indigenous
'public', colonial theories of social, ethnic and occupational segregation were permitted free expression on the ground. Breeze
(1966,pp.71-2) has indicated the typical and atypical characteristics
of Delhi in comparison to other large Indian urban areas and Indian
urbanisation in general. Though it differs in significant respects
from Calcutta, Bombay and Madras, he suggests that Delhi and other
very large cities are comparable in terms of very rapid growth;
high mixture of land uses in older areas; wide ranges in density
of population; large housing and amenity deficits; except for heavy
rail commuting in Bombay, many similarities in transportation and
communication problems; historically, heavy foreign influences on
form and structure; low levels of public participation in the
planning process; multiplicity of governing units in the metropolitan area. Breeze concludes

   all generalisations for Delhi have been checked against the
   main features of Bombay, Calcutta and Madras and found to
   hold. Such checking, together with the judgement that the
   similarities among these very large cities are more significant
   for planning than the dissimilarities, suggest that, for the
   very large urban areas of India, Delhi is as nearly representative
   of all as any of the others. Any one, however, would inevitably
   be imperfect for this purpose.

Apart from being, in these respects then, representative of other
cities in India, Delhi is also, in some ways, representative of
other cities in so-called 'developing' economies in that it
contains within its two or more cities polar extremes between
'tradition' and 'modernity'. Within the boundaries of Delhi, an
immense range of values and behaviours are to be found, ranging
from the orthodox, traditional mores of 'village India' to the most
'modern' patterns of the secular, industrialised state. It is this
juxtaposition which makes a study of urban and social structure in
Delhi of special importance both for social scientists interested
in social and cultural change as well as the planner responsible
for its social and urban development.

A final set of criteria make Delhi an appropriate case-study. India
was not only the first large territory to come within the web of
Western industrial colonialism; it was also the first of many nations

in Asia, Africa and middle America, to achieve freedom from that web
in 1947. In addition to being a classical 'colonial city', Delhi
was also the capital city of the first state to gain formal
independence from the metropolitan power and be fully taken over
by representatives of the indigenous population.

The city has now experienced almost three decades of independence.
Its development over this last period and the next three decades
has both theoretical and practical significance. Theoretically,
investigations of the emergent social and spatial structure of
Delhi should help to generate more effective theories of the city
or promote new models. Practically, the experience of those
responsible for Delhi's urban development in these years, particularly for the task of integrating, in a social, political,
economic and cultural as well as a physical and spatial sense, two
previously separate though inter-dependent cities, should be of
relevance not only to planners in societies most recently 'de-
colonised' but for others in the larger planning world. The
difference in the urban forms and structure of Delhi between 1947
and, say, 1977, measures the extent to which a new, nationally
autonomous government has been able to modify the policies of
colonial urban development.

3 PHASES OF DEVELOPMENT

In examining the development of the physical-spatial structure of
modern Delhi as a product of acculturation through colonialism,
three phases can be distinguished. In each phase, the different
roles occupied by representatives of the incoming culture must be
clearly distinguished.

In the first place, their political role as members of an incoming
colonial power must be recognised. Second, they must be seen as
representatives of an industrialising society whose forms of
economic, technological, social and political organisation were,
particularly after the mid-nineteenth century, based on the increasing application of inanimate forms of energy. Finally, they
must be distinguished as 'colonial British', that is, as representatives of a particular cultural group, with certain culture-specific
values and preferences, within a larger cultural tradition of Europe.
In the three main phases of the city's development, any one of these
roles may assume more importance than the others.

The first phase begins with the arrival and permanent settlement
of a relatively few representatives of the colonial culture in
1803. In this phase, explanations of their impact on the physical-
spatial structure of Delhi can largely be made in political and
cultural terms.

In the second phase, between 1857 and 1911, numbers are larger and
changes in the form of Delhi are due primarily to political and
technological influences.

The boundaries of the third phase, between 1911 and 1947, are
defined by two major political events. The first is the decision to
move the political and administrative capital of colonial India from
Calcutta to Delhi. The outer limit of this phase, 1947, marks the
formal ending of colonial rule. In this third phase, technological,
political and cultural factors are equally important in influencing
the structure of the city.

In each of these three phases, the structure suggested in Chapter 3
is used to organise the approach. Physical-spatial forms are seen
to result from the accommodation, first of the military and civil
aspects of *government*. This invariably includes a cantonment and
accommodation for the official civilian representatives of the
colonial power. The institutions of this cultural community in
turn require specific accommodation. These are discussed in the
following order.

Kinship gives rise to a *residential* requirement. As the city is
fundamentally a permanent aggregation of people, the residential
requirement of kinship, namely the house or dwelling, is an
essential unit in determining the physical-spatial structure of
the city.

Religion necessitates the provision for the performance of rituals
and the exercise of religiously legitimised activities. *Education*
requires the provision of 'schools', 'colleges' or equivalent
means for socialising the young. *Economic* institutions, particularly
retailing, marketing and communication, need to be provided for;
technology forms part of this provision. *Social* institutions, such
as *associational patterns* generate purpose-built structures;
recreational activities frequently give rise to specialised structures or spatial areas.

For the sake of brevity, the institutions are not discussed
methodically at the level of idea and value, activity and behaviour
and social relations, sufficient insight into these various levels
having been demonstrated throughout previous chapters.

4   THE INDIGENOUS CITY AND ITS ENVIRONS

The indigenous city of Delhi, which, in the early nineteenth century,
was to form the nucleus of urban development over the following
150 years, lay on the west bank of the river Jumna. Situated at
the northern end of a strategic triangle formed by the tip of the
Aravalli range running north-east towards the river, a spur of the
same range running due East, and the river itself, the city had been
constructed in the first part of the seventeenth century by
Shahjahan, Moghul Emperor and grandson of Akbar the Great. Within
this triangle, situated on the main and only route into India from
the north-west, lay the remains of some thirteen previous cities
whose founders had appreciated the strategic significance of the
site. A map, produced by a member of the incoming culture some
four years after their arrival, indicates those features significant

for its members: the walled city, within the triangle of river and the ridge (rising to some 800 feet above sea-level at its highest point); the Moghul canal, running in from the north-west; some of the 120 villages lying within a ten-mile radius of the city, and the remnants of medieval urban settlements. In the city, the main gates and 'cantonment' locations are clearly indicated (Figure 8.1).

Average temperature extremes, then as now, contrasted sharply with those of Europe, ranging between 9-21°C (45-70°F) in January and 28-38°C (83-103°F) during June. Occasional day-time summer temperatures reached 47-49°C (115-120°F).

The city of Delhi, built between 1628 and 1648 and named Shahjahanabad after its founder, was referred to as Modern Delhi, in contrast to the many Delhis abandoned within its vicinity. Its physical structure was typical of the pre-industrial city. The central feature was the walled palace of the King, connected by bridge to the ancient fort of Selimgurh. The heavily fortified palace, its rear facing directly onto the river, gave access at the front to the central spine of the city, the main commercial and market centre, the bazaar of Chandni Chowk ('Silver Street').

The main manifestation of the Islamic religion was the Jama Masjid, the great mosque, immediately south-west of the palace, with a main road leading off each side to connect it to the four main sectors of the city. These three points, representing the major political, economic and religious institutions of the Moghul culture, are clearly indicated in an indigenous plan of about 1800 'reduced from a large Hindostanny Map of Dehly' existing in the Survey of India archives, Delhi. This also indicates the main thoroughfares leading, via Chandni Chowk, to Lahore Gate in the west and from the palace via Faiz Bazaar to Delhi Gate in the south (see Bhatia,1956).

Circumscribing the entire city, a wall, 5½ miles in length, enclosed an area of approximately 2½ square miles which, in 1803, contained some 130,000 inhabitants. Extra-mural suburbs brought the total to about 150,000. The main roads linking the central institutions of the city each led to one of the eight main gates located around the walls, the more important ones named after significant places or cities within the Moghul empire to which the routes eventually led, Kashmir, Lahore, Ajmer, or to ancient Delhi.

At one time one of the largest cities in the Eastern hemisphere with a population reputed to be almost half a million in the fourteenth century (Thakore, 1962), Delhi had suffered severely from attacks by various invaders in the seventeenth and eighteenth centuries. None the less, in 1800 it was still a major commercial and trading centre famous for its jewellery, embroidery, silverware, ivory and wood craftsmanship and its own school of court paintings.

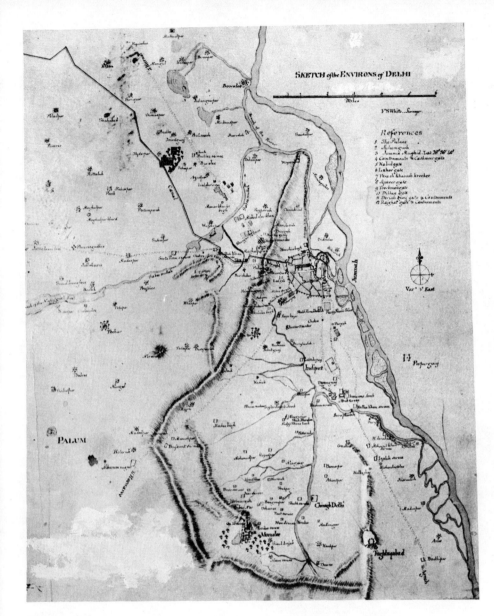

Figure 8.1

Figure 8.2

5   THE ACCOMMODATION OF A COLONIAL CULTURE 1803-57

The impact of European influence on Delhi begins effectively in 1803
when the city was captured by the British from the Mahratti invaders.
Its first role was that of military and strategic post for the
metropolitan trading concern (the 'East India Company') in northern
India.

The titular head of a now much weakened and rapidly declining Moghul
power lived in the enclosed area of the royal palace. Here he
was permitted to stay with his large court and the use of some two
square miles of territory north and south of the city. Within half
a century, however, the last representatives of this empire were to
disappear and the cities which it had created, including Agra and
Lahore, to become transformed by contact with a new, industrial
imperial power.

6   GOVERNMENT: MILITARY AND CIVIL PROVISION

The first effects which the incoming culture had on the structure of
Delhi resulted from its monopoly of government. Although the British
took over most of the city, the titular authority of the Moghul
Emperor remained, under the effective supervision of the 'Resident'
and the troops of the metropolitan power (see Spear,1951). The
presence of the new culture resulting from military conquest rather
than trade or diplomacy, it followed that the city had first to
accommodate the incoming troops and the head of military and civil
government, the 'Resident'.

There being still a military threat to troops encamped outside the
walls, they were located within the city. The elite sector lay
along the Eastern wall. Here, north and south of the royal palace,
following the typical structure of the pre-industrial city in being
close to the traditional centre of authority (Sjoberg,1960,p.49)
were the large mansions of the indigenous nawabs. Set in spacious
grounds, these were relatively cut off from the densely populated
and tightly packed buildings of the remainder of the city. This was
the obvious area to accommodate the needs of the incoming power.

A military plan of 1812 in the archives of the Survey of India
indicates the areas taken over. Both for reasons of space and
security, the European troops occupied two areas north and south
of the Emperor's palace. One battalion was located just inside the
Kashmiri Gate to the north, along with accommodation for guns,
stabling, and a small hospital. A small bazaar grew up to supply
basic requirements. Next to this was the 'Residency' and to the
south were the 'timber lines', the magazine and powder store.

Two other battalions were accommodated in 'lines' south of the
palace, an area occupied by the mansions of the nawabs. Here too
were the 'pioneer lines', sheds for camels and bullocks, more
gunsheds and a bazaar.

C Chownee Daryaganj
  (Daryaganj Cantonment)
1 Christian church
2 Hospital
3 Dak bungalow
4 Godown

5 Bungalows (three)
6 House of Padre Thomson
7 Surgeon's bungalow
8 Bungalow

9 Bungalow James ? sahib
10 Hospital
11 Sergeant's (?) or
   Surgeon's (?) bungalow
12 B (?) Company Barracks

(Original captions in Urdu)

Figure 8.3

A more detailed indigenous plan of the city (Figure 8.2), probably
produced under European supervision about the mid-nineteenth century,
indicates that as the small military colony became more established
separate 'bungalows' were provided for the accommodation of
officers.   These were located opposite the residences of the local
nawabs.   Two hospitals were also built as well as a small church
(Figure 8.3).   Military requirements also led to the modification of
the fortifications.   'Martello Towers' and 'bastions' were constructed
and named after the contemporary military and political leaders
associated with the taking of Delhi (Burn, Garstin, Ochterlony, Lake,
Wellesley).

The other major requirement of government was a dwelling and workplace for the 'Resident'.   As this was to be within range of the
indigenous titular head of state, the Moghul Emperor who, though
under the 'protection' of the new order was still held in esteem
by the local population, it needed to be sufficiently impressive
to establish the relative standing of the new elite.   A substantial
palace, situated in some ten acres of ground to the north of the
royal palace and close to Kashmiri Gate, was taken over.   To mark
the change in ownership, the building was drastically modified
according to the 'architectural' and social norms of the immigrant
culture.

Like subsequent accommodation for the colonial community, the new
'Residency' adopted the same external features characterising the
major items of built form in earlier phases of colonial settlement
in Madras, Calcutta and Bombay.   These so-called 'Classical'
features had, after a four-century long process of diffusion and
adaptation, been adopted as the cultural property of Europe from
earlier empires of Greece and Rome.   Such forms were to continue
as the main identifying symbols in the built environment of the
colonial culture for the next one and a half centuries.

An extensive colonnade was built on to the front of the building
and the inside adapted to incorporate 'banqueting rooms', a
'ballroom' and other facilities in keeping with aristocratic norms
in the metropolitan society (Figure 8.5).   At the rear were large
gardens 'laid out with the stately formality... of oriental
pleasure-grounds'.   For the metropolitan visitor, these modifications
gave it 'a solemn and imposing air' (Anon, 1835,pp.9-10).

Other dwellings belonging to members of the new community were
situated in the vicinity.   'Skinner's House' stood in some twelve
acres of carefully-modified grounds.   Close to the northern walls
of the city, immediately east of Kashmiri Gate, were the 'bungalows'
of three or four leading European inhabitants (Keating, Metcalfe,
Colonel Smith).   South of the 'Residency' a more permanent, walled
arsenal, the 'Magazine' was constructed (Figure 8.4).

Thus, within at least four years of the conquest of Delhi, the
pattern of European settlement centring on the Kashmiri Gate area
and extending southwards to the Delhi Gate, had been established.

1 Bungalow (?) sahib	7 Bungalow (?) sahib	13 Post Office
2 Bungalow (?) sahib	8 Foster Sahib's compound	14 Hospital
3 Kashmiri Gate	9 Guard	15 Kutcherry
4 Stable	10 Treasury (?)	16 Residency
5 House of Sekundar	11 House of Smith Sahib	17 Residency house
(Skinner) Sahib	12 Printing House	18 Graveyard
6 Company barracks		

(Original captions in Urdu)

Figure 8.4

(Explanation is appropriate at this point on the use of quotation marks in this and the following two chapters. The analysis has been undertaken from a viewpoint 'outside' the culture being examined; in anthropological terms, at the 'etic' or observational level. Hence, culture-specific items such as the 'Residency' and 'banqueting rooms' as well as places and activities particularly featuring in the universe of the third culture such as 'the Ridge' are indicated in quotation marks.

However, to pursue this policy logically, it is clear that all culture-specific items and categories would need to be in quotation marks and this would be unnecessarily confusing, e.g. the 'cantonment' was moved two 'miles' 'north' of the original 'barracks'. Moreover, as many items have subsequently been absorbed into the environment of the indigenous culture, the 'etic' level of analysis is not always appropriate. In the following pages, therefore, a pragmatic solution has been adopted of indicating those items, places and activities especially connected with the third culture in quotation marks, particularly at the start of this analysis. In this way, the geographical feature of a ridge in the vicinity of the old city becomes 'the Ridge' when forming part of the colonial environment and invested with the historical and symbolic meaning given it by the colonial community, and finally, the Ridge (as today) as it gradually loses its colonial symbolic meaning, becoming merely the most prominent geographical ridge in the area. In later pages, quotation marks are indicated only where the non-indigenous origin of the item or activity is to be stressed. If there is inconsistency it is regretted).

With the increasing sense of security and the establishment of a working relationship between the 'protected' Emperor in the royal palace, the 'cantonment' was moved, in 1828, to a new site just over what was known as 'the Ridge', some two miles north of Kashmiri Gate (Archer, 1833,p.105). Here, a large triangular tract of territory stretching between 'the Ridge' to the Grand Trunk Road and occupying 1,500 acres (some 2½ square miles),slightly more than the 1,437 acres enclosed by the city walls, was taken over and used, till 1857, for the principal military requirements. The camp, occupied by indigenous troops and their European officers, was seen as 'a cooler and more agreeable residence, free from the numerous plagues and nuisances, inseparable from an Indian town; not to say smells, dust and flies, each of which is almost a death to nature, certainly to comfort' (ibid.). Here, each officer lived with his family or on his own, in an individual bungalow situated on its own larger compound. The troops were accommodated in huts or tents, symmetrically laid out in lines. North-west of these and the parade ground on which they faced, was a further extensive area which included a 'race-course', of some 1½ miles circumference, a 'government garden', an exercising ground for a field battery, 'rifle range' and accommodation for sappers and miners. Beyond was the old Moghul Shalimar Garden, re-named as the 'Ochterlony Garden'. Within the cantonment was the European burial ground as well as a bazaar, located at the western foot of the Ridge (see map, 1867-8,Figure 9.1).

Taking advantage of the movement of the troops to their new 'cantonment', subsequent 'Residents' and 'Agents', as well as lower-ranking
officials, moved outside the city walls. Here, in the triangle
bounded by the north wall, 'the Ridge' and the river, increasingly
fertile since the opening up, in 1820, of the long-blocked Moghul
canal running into the west of the city (Anon, 1865,p.9), they
built dwellings in keeping with conceptual models of earlier third-
culture members and conforming to the image of the rural aristocracy
prevalent in the metropolitan society.

The first of these, an alternative 'Residency', was constructed about
1828. This occupied one of the highest points of 'the Ridge' and
commanded extensive 'views' over the surrounding territory. Described by a contemporary as 'an immense house which is a kind of
Gothic fortress' it was in fact built in the 'Classical' manner,
though adopting the so-called 'Gothic' features currently favoured
by the metropolitan elite (the house was subsequently occupied by
an Indian *nawab* and named after him, 'Hindu Rao's House'). Its
conception by a British 'Resident' as well as its accommodation,
siting and external features, were to bring it back into use for the
colonial community in 1855, first, for the 'District Treasurer' and,
between 1863 and 1912, as a 'sanatorium' for European troops. In
1912 it became a hospital for the exclusive use of Europeans (see
Spear, 1951,p.146; Chopra, 1970,p.141; Prasad, 1918). Shortly after,
in 1830, a larger dwelling was built by another member of the new
elite, Thomas Metcalfe, who was later to occupy the role of 'Agent'
(replacing that of 'Resident') between 1835 and 1853.

In keeping with prevailing norms this house was sited on a knoll
overlooking the river, one mile north of the city walls. The vast,
single-storey mansion was surrounded on all four sides by a verandah,
supported by immense pillars and set in a large estate. Complete
with underground *taikhana*, 'billiard' room, library, swimming bath,
extensive rooms containing collections of books and 'objets d'art',
'Metcalfe House' represented the most typical symbol of the new local
aristocracy (Spear, 1951,p.161).

The construction of these two dwellings, both less than one mile from
the walled city, marks a significant break in the history of its
urban development. As these new members of the elite now lived and
carried out their official roles outside the city, activities previously confined within the walls were now pursued beyond them.
(Though the Moghul elite had built summer palaces outside the city
walls, these were temporary, secondary dwellings, with the main
palace permanently in the city.) The trend begun by the incoming
colonial 'Residents', understandable within the metropolitan models
at the time and irrespective of any 'health' reasons, was that of
having a permanent 'country' residence away from the 'town'.

A similar process had already taken place in Madras.
     Very few Englishmen live in Madras; they live in country houses
     scattered for miles through the interior, and even the shopkeepers
     who can afford it have detached bungalows for their families.

> Fort St George is about three quarters of a mile from the Black
> Town of Madras; no houses are allowed to be built on the inter-
> vening esplanade which is intersected with excellent roads
> (Bevan, 1839, vol.1,pp.16-17).

With the exodus of the European elite began the suburbanisation of
pre-industrial Delhi.

Despite the 'Resident's' move outside the walls, other, though not
all, administrative functions remained inside, situated within the
cultural enclave at the rear of the old Residency compound. Here,
judicial and financial functions of government were carried out
in the *kutcherry* (office) and 'Court House', the 'Treasury' and in
the two or three bungalows of the European officials. Here also,
the local head of the judiciary had his private house. Another
function exercised by this still small community was that of the
taxation of goods, a task of sufficient magnitude to merit a large
'Customs House', situated in its own 25-acre compound, some 200
yards distant from the northernmost part of the city (see Figures
8.8, 8.9).

7   THE ACCOMMODATION OF KINSHIP REQUIREMENTS

In these early decades, Delhi's European inhabitants were relatively
few. As the settlement grew, other Europeans came in to provide
services and mediate between it and the local population. These
included officials of the 'Delhi Bank', 'missionaries', doctors,
teachers at the 'Delhi College' (discussed below) and printers
and publishers associated with the two papers, the *Delhi Gazette*
and *Delhi Sketchbook*. Lower in status were the European merchants
and shopkeepers who took up premises around Kashmiri Gate, the
few clerks working in government offices and European soldiers
(Spear, 1951,pp.140-2). In 1846 out of a total city population of
some 138,000 only 327, or some 90 families, were 'European and native
Christians' (Roberts, 1847,pp.153-7).

The Europeans of lower status and Christians of mixed European and
Indian descent lived in the area of Daryaganj, south of the palace
(Spear, 1951, ibid.). Other Europeans lived in the *thannahs* (police
districts) of Rajghat (25 families), Nigumbode (21 families),
Etkadkhan (19 families) each of which lay immediately next to the
palace, away from areas of indigenous population. In all, the
Christian population included 111 men, 115 women, 58 boys and 53
girls (Roberts, op.cit.). The area of Daryganj was enclosed on one
side by the city wall, and on the other two, by the main road from
Delhi Gate in the palace to the south-east corner of the wall, and
by the south wall of the palace. A number of army officers occupied
houses directly along the wall, and adjoining them to the south were
the smaller palaces of indigenous nawabs. Wealthier Europeans (a
further 16 families), lived around Kashmiri gate (Roberts, op.cit.;
Hearn, 1906).

With the lead provided by the elite, more European inhabitants took
up residence outside the city. Between 1830 and 1840, a European
doctor added a large house, with five 'reception rooms' (Murray,
1882,p.316) whose name, 'Ludlow Castle', and external characteristics were in keeping with elite suburban developments taking place
in the metropolitan society (Figure 8.6). Some years later, a
visitor, impressed by the transfer of metropolitan life-styles and
artefacts, described it as 'a fine mansion, with turrets and clock
towers, something like a French château of the nineteenth century...
with large, lofty rooms, soft carpets, sofas, easy chairs, books,
pictures, rest and repose within' (Russell, 1860, vol.1.pp.54-5).
The location, size and visual symbolism were later to recommend its
use as a dwelling for the 'Commissioner' in the 1850s and, as the
'Delhi Club', for use as the main centre of the European community
later in the century (Prasad, 1918,p.52). Lower down 'Ludlow Castle
Road' a senior administrator and soldier (Sir John Lawrence) took up
residence from 1831 to 1838 (Spear, 1951, p.146). Higher up the
ridge, a combined signal and 'Flagstaff Tower' was constructed
fulfilling a dual role as means of communication and symbol of
cultural and political control.

Now that the military station was established close by the growing
suburb became known as the 'Civil Station'. Its distinctive character as an area of culturally modified territory was manifest, not
merely in the built environment with the 'Flagstaff Tower' looking
down over the growing suburban dwellings, but also in the broad,
tree-lined roads and cultivated compounds to which they led. Their
names, based on local topographical features, helped to give the
'station' its particular cultural identity: 'Court Road', 'Racquet
Court Lane', 'Underhill Road', 'Ludlow Castle Road' and 'Alipur'
and 'Rajpur' Roads leading to local villages. By 1835, a metropolitan observer could write
    The modern capital of the Moslem Kings... (is) surrounded on
    every side with the ruins of Old Delhi, curiously contrasted
    with a new suburb, the villas belonging to Europeans attached
    to the Residency and with the Cantonments lately erected for
    the three regiments of sepoys (Anon, 1835,p.5).
It is clear from contemporary written and pictorial evidence that
one of the motivations for moving to the 'Civil Station' once the
security situation had improved, was - apart from that of 'health' -
what were perceived as the 'visual' attractions of the site. These
appealed to the inherent cultural categories of a middle-class
European elite.
    Modern Delhi... is enclosed by a splendid rampart of red granite
    and entered by gateways the most magnificent which the world
    can boast.... From the outside the view is splendid; domes and
    mosques, cupolas and minarets with the imperial palace forming
    like a mountain of red granite, appear in the midst of groves
    of clustering trees, so thickly planted that the buildings have
    been compared, in oriental imagery, to rocks of pearls and
    rubies, rising from the emerald sea.
        In approaching the city... the prospect realises all that the
    imagination has pictured of oriental magnificence; mosques and
    minarets glittering in the sun, some garlanded with wild creepers,

Figure 8.5

Figure 8.6

others arrayed in all the pomp of gold, the exterior of cupolas
being covered with brilliant metal, and from Mount Mejooon,
over which a fine road now passes, the shining waters of the
Jumna, gleaming in the distance (ibid.,p.6).

These reactions are confirmed by pictorial accounts. These reify
the indigenous settlement, suitably representing it within a category
of visual experience familiar to the colonial elite (Figure 8.7).

Increased traffic, in the form of horse and gun carriages, camels,
horses, elephants, foot soldiers and 'palanquins', generated by the
'cantonment' and the new residential developments, opened up a
network of roads based on four new highways constructed between
'the Ridge' and the city in the years prior to 1840. Along these,
before the mid-nineteenth century, some seven or eight bungalows
had been built, each within a compound of two to two and a half
acres (Map 'District of Dehlee', 1840). By 1857, there were between
twenty-five and thirty, mainly between the Alipur and Rajpur Roads
(Figure 8.9). These developments, indicating a separation of workplace from residence,represented a fundamental departure from the
residential pattern typical of the pre-industrial city.

8   THE INSTITUTION OF RELIGION

Further modifications to the city arose from accommodating religious
needs. The first of these was for a burial ground; this was established just north of the palace walls, adjoining the south end of
the military 'Magazine'. This functioned as the main place for
interment till 1855 when a new cemetery was established south of
the 'Civil Station' (Hearn, 1906).

The second requirement was a setting for community worship. With
the removal of the troops to the extra-mural cantonment in 1828,
more space had become available in the area of Kashmiri Gate. Here,
between 1829 and 1836, was constructed the community's 'church'
(Spear, 1951,p.149).

Standing in its own ten-acre grounds, the 'church of St James' provided a locale for the performance of rituals and the expression of
religious beliefs. It acted as a centre for social activity,
serving to cement a sense of identity within the group. It provided for the interment and visual commemoration of the community's
dead and, for indigenous and immigrant inhabitants, it was an
important visual symbol, signalling the presence of the new colonial
elite. The church was to become the natural focus of the community,
strengthening the claim of the Kashmiri Gate neighbourhood to be
the principal European section of the city. Shops began to be
established here and the area, with its arcades and wrought-iron,
increasingly took on the character of a comparable metropolitan
environment.

The institution of religion gave rise to other modifications in
the city. These arose from the activities of organisations engaged

Figure 8.7

in promoting cultural change among the indigenous population, namely, the 'missionary societies', associated with branches of the metro- politan religion.   The earliest of these, arriving within ten years of British entry into the city, were the 'Baptists'.   Active in the bazaars of the old city, in 1845 they set up their own 'chapel' at the eastern end of Chandni Chowk (Hearn, 1906).   The leader of this community ('Padre Thompson') lived within the European enclave of Daryaganj, with Muslim nawabs and European officers for his immediate neighbours (Figure 8.3; Spear, 1951,p.165).

9   THE EDUCATIONAL REQUIREMENT

No specific accommodation was provided for European educational needs. However, other manifestations of education can be found in the 'Delhi College and Institute' which, like the activities of 'missionary societies', became a centre of cultural change for the indigenous community.   Originally an indigenous institution, founded in 1792, the 'College' was supervised by a European principal after 1825 and assisted by indigenous and European staff.   Organised primarily for the local population, an important role was to teach the language of the incoming culture and, through this, new concepts of science and learning (Ahmad, 1969,p.60).   Like the governmental, residen- tial and religious institutions of the community, it was located in the colonial culture area, taking over the old 'Residency' for its premises in 1832.   The 'Institute', with its library and facilities for scientific, literary and social meetings, was eventually provided with its own premises in the central area of Chandni Chowk some thirty years later.

10   ECONOMIC INSTITUTIONS

Little provision had so far been made for the specialised economic needs of the immigrant culture.   The main exception was the introduction of Western banking and credit facilities in the early part of the century.   By 1842 the scale of these had become sufficiently large to require accommodation in the 'Delhi Bank'. For this purpose, another palace, located close to the main retailing area of Chandni Chowk was acquired and modified according to symbolic 'classical' forms.   The retailing needs of the European population were largely met by the markets in Chandni Chowk.

In the first half of the century, the representatives of the two cultures shared the same technological system in the city, the Europeans using indigenous devices and methods.   Thus, for transport, along with the native camel, horse and bullock, the animate-powered vehicles of the palanquin and carriage were utilised with European models of the latter being increasingly introduced (see below).

Communication between Europeans relied, for long distances, on a modified version of the Moghul system of the 'dak', the terminus of the European-owned 'North-Western Dak Company' being located in Chandni Chowk.   For short distances, it depended on the written transmission of messages by means of the *chitti* or note carried by 'peons' and 'bearers'. The fact that communication could be maintained among the spatially-dispersed units of the colonial urban settlement such as the Civil Lines, without such modern means of contact as the telephone, depended on the literacy of the immigrant inhabitants. Distance and climate discouraged their own movement between places; inadequate acquaintance with the immigrants' language by indigenous servants prevented the accurate verbal transmission of communications. The command over literacy and indigenous manpower enabled distances between neighbours to be bridged by means of the 'chit'. The writing of such 'chits' formed a preoccupation of early members of the colonial community and the practice is extensively documented.

For more long distance communication, a 'post office' was established and located in the European sector, outside the south end of the palace. This was later used as the 'Dak bungalow' (Spear,1951,p.149).

Methods of house-cooling such as the 'punkah', and ice-making were adopted from the indigenous society (Spear, 1963,p.96). Water was obtained from wells and carried short distances by the *bhisti* in goatskin containers. The canal system, developed two centuries earlier prior to the Europeans' arrival, was restored in 1820. Sanitation and the disposal of refuse in the city was the responsibility of low-caste members of the indigenous community.

Three important communications devices were brought into Delhi in this first phase of cultural contact. A printing press was established and utilised for printing newspapers, a magazine and occasional books and pamphlets. This was located in the cultural enclave behind the church. Sometime in the decade before 1857, the electric telegraph was introduced. The line ran down through the Civil Station to the 'Telegraph Office' (Spear, 1951,p.147).

The third communications innovation introduced was photography. This appeared about the middle of the century in Delhi and was soon to have important and subtle influences. By the more exact reproduction of visual images from both the metropolitan and colonial societies, along with the improved systems of printing, it accelerated the rate of cultural change in India, particularly as it affected the nature of the built environment.

11 SOCIAL INSTITUTIONS

As the European community grew, accommodation was made for group social activities. The 'Assembly Rooms', constructed in the 1840s, were situated at the northern limits of the small but developing 'civil station' at the furthest point from the indigenous city. Within some hundred yards, another opportunity for association was provided in the 'Racquet Court'.

The second purpose-built centre for social activities constructed
about this time was the 'club'. Because of the small size of the
community and the relatively few people living outside the city
walls, this was modest in size and was situated just north of
Daryaganj, on the *maidan* outside the royal palace. A contemporary
painting, existing in the archaeological museum of Delhi Fort,
indicates that the club, like other buildings of the incoming
culture, also adopted the external features of 'Classicism'.

Interest in 'social improvement' in the metropolitan society was
also present in the colonial elite. Trevelyan, a 'Deputy Resident',
made a conscious attempt at planned suburban development west of
the walled city, in the late 1820s. 'Trevelyanpore',later known
as 'Deputyganj', was built south of the village of Pahari

> to supply habitation for the increasing population of the city.
> ... The plan has been much approved for its elegant simplicity
> .... The centre, a large quadrangle called Bentinck Square, is
> entered by four streets, opening from the middle of each side,
> and not at the angles, according to the usual European custom.
> The whole extent of the streets, which are 90 feet in width,
> and the facade of the square, present an unbroken front of
> Doric columns, supporting a piazza behind, in which are commodious
> shops and dwelling houses, ranged with great regularity. The
> four triangular spaces at the back, formed by the arms of a
> cross, are intended for stables and courtyards for the cattle
> and bullock carts belonging to the inhabitants. In the event
> of Trevelyanpore becoming a place of native resort, a plan for
> increasing its extent has been laid down and a native gentleman
> of great wealth is constructing a magnificent gateway... which
> will lead to a circus ... this new quarter has not yet, however,
> been much sought after as a residence by the native population
> (Anon., 1835,p.12).

This probably was situated south of the road leading from Lahore
Gate (now Sadr Bazaar Road) and north of the Idgah. In addition,
another metropolitan institution, a 'Lunatic Asylum', had been
introduced in 1840. Like the near-by 'Jail', this was situated
outside the city walls, some few hundred yards south of Delhi Gate.

12 THE ACCOMMODATION OF RECREATIONAL ACTIVITY

Apart from the 'club', 'Assembly Rooms', 'Racquet Court', 'Institute'
and the 'race-course' on the cantonment, the main location for
social intercourse and recreation were the individual dwellings
and their compounds. For most of the year, the climate was thought
to be too warm for much active recreation which consequently tended
to be concentrated into the winter months. With the development of
the hill stations of Simla and Mussoorie in the mid 1820s, social
and recreational activities were increasingly pursued in this new
setting. As numerous cartoons in the *Delhi Sketch Book* (1850-5)
indicate, this was particularly the case for the wives and daughters
of army personnel.

The mixture of fear, racial antipathy, social exclusiveness and
concern with health which characterised the colonial population of
Delhi in the later nineteenth century and which helped to account
for their increasing physical segregation from members of the
indigenous society, were less evident in the first half of the
century. The elite, such as the early 'Residents', formed a new
'official aristocracy', their recreations and tastes not departing
significantly from those of their indigenous counterparts. As a
major pastime was the hunting of wildfowl, deer and hog in the
wilderness surrounding the city no further spatial provision was
needed for recreation either within the city or its environs other
than their own spacious dwellings and compounds. Here, house-
centred activities such as entertaining, scholarship and the supervision of their estates occupied their leisure hours.

Further influence on the immediate built environment of Delhi at
this time can be understood with reference to metropolitan
intellectual pursuits. The first 'Resident', Ochterlony, not only
provided a 'Classical' mansion for himself in Delhi but, representative of current taste 'at Home', built other dwellings outside
the city (Spear, 1951,pp.155-6). Charles Metcalfe, 'Resident'
for most of the second decade in the century, inhabited what
approximated to the metropolitan concept of a 'country retreat'
near the abandoned Shalimar Gardens, north-west of the city. His
brother Thomas, 'Agent' between 1835 and 1853, adapted a Muslim
tomb as a 'retreat' some ten miles south of Delhi at Mehrauli and
had a 'picturesque ruin' constructed on a near-by outcrop to complete
the modified environment according to prevailing metropolitan norms.

One of the greatest attractions of Delhi for this and later elites
was what they perceived as its 'historical' associations, evident
in its abandoned cities, tombs and Moghul gardens. These provided
the 'picturesque' landscape which they favoured and gave them ample
opportunity to exercise their 'antiquarian' and 'archaeological'
pursuits.

Such interests were expressed in the investigation, recording and
restoration of 'ancient monuments'. Pictorial evidence shows that
the Kutb Minar, a thirteenth-century tower built by earlier inhabitants of Delhi, was restored and modified in 1826. Measure-
ments, drawings and investigations were made and maps marking
sites of earlier, 'historic' structures produced. Local craftsmen-
artists were engaged to adapt their talent to the environmental,
'antiquarian' interests of their new patrons, producing paintings
of buildings in the Delhi area, many of them depicting members of
the incoming culture actively exploring the sites. Between 1847
and 1850 an 'Archaeological Society' was active in the colonial
community, consisting of the social and intellectual elite of Delhi.
This met monthly in the 'Assembly Rooms' 'to investigate ancient
remains in and around Delhi and also communicate any other information especially statistical researches, likely to increase the
general stock of knowledge of the country' (Journal of the
Archaeological Society of Delhi, 1850, vol 1,1).

Such phenomena were drawn to the attention of visitors from the
metropolitan society.

> The... inflictions of the climate are amply compensated by
> the endless gratification afforded to intellectual minds, by
> the number of interesting objects which greet the spectator on
> every side. A life might be spent in rambling over the ruins
> of old Delhi and subjects of contemplation still remain.
> Next to the palace... is the Jumma Masjid, a magnificent mosque.
> ... From the interstices of the piazza of this fine square, very
> picturesque views are obtained.
>
> The grand object of attraction in the neighbourhood of
> Shahjahanabad is the Kootub Minar, a magnificent tower, two
> hundred and forty feet in height, which rises in the midst of
> ruins of old Delhi at the distance of nine miles south of the
> modern city....From the summit,... the view is of the most
> sublime description, a desert covered with ruins full of awful
> beauty surrounds it on all sides, watered by the snake-like Jumna,
> which winds its huge silvery folds along the crumbling remains of
> palaces and tombs... the eye wandering over the stupendous and
> still beautiful fragments of former grandeur, rests at last upon
> the white and glittering mosques and minarets of the modern city
> closing in the distance, and finely contrasting by its luxuriant
> groves and richly flowering gardens, with the loneliness and
> desolation of the scene below (Anon.,1835,p.12)

Such intellectual categories were evidently not shared by all members
of the community. For others, recreational behaviour took different
forms, making alternative uses of the environs of Delhi. Occasionally,
the interests of this socially differentiated community conflicted.

> The few intellectual pilgrims who wander amidst the wrecks of
> bygone splendour must make up their minds to endure sights and
> scenes of the most incongruous nature - pic-nic parties,
> bivouacking in tombs; and being entertained at their repasts by
> the performance of a set of nautch (dancing) girls; young men
> amusing themselves with a game of quoits, and groups of flirting
> unimaginative women, speculating on the probabilities of getting
> up a game of quadrille (ibid.,p.14).

Recreational pursuits of non-elite groups were provided by the indigenous city. Chandni Chowk, with its central canal and tree-lined
pavements, was 'used as a Mall by European residents, particularly
those from the cantonments' (Cooper, 1863,p.34).

By 1835, after three decades of daily cultural contact, European
influences had made a noticeable impact on the city. In the view
of a contemporary observer

> In no other part of our Eastern possessions do the natives show
> so earnest a desire to imitate European fashions ... the houses
> are of various styles of architecture, partaking occasionally
> of the prevailing fashions of the west. Grecian piazzas,
> porticos, and pediments are not infrequently found fronting the
> dwellings of Moslem or Hindoos....

The shops are crowded with all sorts of European products and
Manufactures, and many of them display signboards, on which
the names and occupations of the inhabitants are emblazoned in
Roman Characters, a novel circumstance in a Native City. The
introduction of this useful custom is attributed to Budruddeen
Khan... patronised by the reigning emperor Akbar the second....

The English placards have a very curious appearance, mingled
with the striped purdahs or curtains which... supply the place
of doors, and the variegated screens.... The houses are for the
most part white-washed, and the gaiety of the appearance is
heightened by the carpets and shawls, strips of cloth of every
hue, scarfs, and coloured veils which are hung out over the
verandah or on top of the house....

The multitude of equipages is exceedingly great, and more
diversified perhaps than those of any other city in the world.
English carriages, altered and improved to suit the climate
and peculiar taste of the possessor are mingled with the palanquins
and bullock-carts, open and covered, the chairs,and cage-like and
lanthorn-like conveyances of native construction. Prince Baber,
the second surviving son of the reigning monarch, drives about
in an English chariot drawn by eight horses in which he
frequently appears attired in the full-dress uniform of a British
General Officer, rendered still more striking by having each
breast adorned with the grand cross of Bath....

Regular English coaches, drawn by four horses and driven by
postillions, the property of rich natives, appear on the public
drives and reviews, and occasionally a buggy or cabriolet of a
very splendid description may be seen, having the hood of black
velvet embroidered with gold (Anon.,1835,pp.5-9).

13   SUMMARY

The colonial culture had been accommodated in two main areas of Delhi.
Within the walled city, two relatively small cultural enclaves
existed, north-west and south of the royal palace. Though exaggerating
the symmetry and underestimating the density of building in the city,
a contemporary representation (Figure 8.8) indicates the royal
palace (1), the main mosque (2), the central bazaar (3) and conveys
a convincing concept of a walled city to members of the metropolitan
society for whom it was produced. Particular attention has been
drawn to the institutions of the immigrant culture represented by the
Customs House (4) located north of the city walls, the community
church (5), the 'Magazine' (6), 'Bank' (7), and in the distance,
south of Delhi Gate, the 'Jail'(8) and 'Lunatic Asylum' (9).

Northwest of the city, an area of some four to five square miles was,
by the middle of the nineteenth century, developed for the military
and civil administrative needs of the colonial power (Figure 8.9).
The main highway system for this area, as well as the highway 'grid'
on the cantonment which was to provide the base for further military
accommodation, as well as for three major demonstrations of imperial
power in the form of the 'durbar' and ultimately, for the campus
of the University of Delhi, had all been laid out by the 1850s.

1 'Palace and
  Gardens'
2 'The Jumma
  Masjid'
3 'Main Street of
  Delhi, Chandni
  Chauk'
4 'Custom House'
5 'English Church'
6 'Magazine and
  Store Houses'
7 'The Banking-
  house'
8 'Gaol'
9 'Lunatic Asylum'

Figure 8.8

DELHI
1857

Cantonment — — — Civil station ————

Figure 8.9

We may now summarise these early developments in the urban structure
of Delhi examining the relative importance of the three major
variables: the power structure of colonialism, the introduction of
new systems of technology and the impact of culture-specific values
and behaviour.

Before the conflict of 1857, the social and political structure of
Delhi was accurately reflected in its spatial structure. The prime
spatial needs of the newcomers were those of the military, situated
in the cantonment. Their location outside the city was recognition
of the comparatively stable political situation which existed inside
it. Most members of the two cultures residing in the city, though
spatially segregated, lived as neighbours in adjoining neighbourhoods.
The head of the indigenous population, the Moghul Emperor, occupied
the palace, surrounded inside by a court and outside, by the
mansions of the elite. To the south, in Daryganj, members of the
indigenous and colonial communities lived on opposite sides of the
main thoroughfare (Daryganj, now Ansari Road). By Kashmiri Gate,
the houses of leading Europeans stood close by the mansions of the
indigenous elite.

Western technology had so far made little impact on the physical
structure of the city. Unlike their counterparts in the West, the
'suburbs' to the north of the city had not developed as a result
of new forms of transport, indigenous cultural preferences and the
uneven distribution of wealth but by the introduction of new cultural
values and an allocation of resources made possible through colonial
control. The relative closeness of the indigenous and colonial
communities, particularly in the city, was a reflection of the
comparatively little social, political and technological distance
between them.

Chapter 9

THE TRANSFORMATION OF A PRE-INDUSTRIAL CITY, 1857-1911

1 INTRODUCTION

The main variables affecting Delhi's physical-spatial development in the second half of the nineteenth century are those of the power-relationship of colonialism and the introduction of in-animate-powered technology. The period is characterised by five inter-related developments, three of them the outcome of the con-frontation between representatives of the two cultures in 1857 (variously described as the 'Indian Mutiny' and 'First War of Indian Independence').

The first was a drastic modification in the structure of the walled city and its immediate environs. Two culturally and functionally specialised areas were created, one colonial, and primarily military and administrative, the second indigenous, and primarily residential, commercial and industrial.

Related to this was the effective segregation of representatives of the two cultures, with the city wall, as well as extensive physical space, acting as the barrier between them.

The third development is the emergence of the colonial urban settle-ment of the Civil Station as a relatively independent, self-sufficient culture area, supplied with most of its essential requirements.

The fourth results from the introduction of metropolitan technology into the indigenous city and its immediate region. This technology, including the railway, electricity, water supply and waste disposal systems, and a road system suitable for automotive transport, was selectively introduced, priority being given to specific areas of the city.

Finally, partly resulting from these technological innovations and partly from the political processes of colonialism, the immediate urban region of Delhi was greatly extended. In analysing these developments, attention is initially paid to the effects on the

city resulting from what now became the total monopoly of government over the entire walled city and its environs by the colonial
power.

2   THE INSTITUTIONS OF GOVERNMENT: THE EFFECTS OF TOTAL CONTROL

Although the titular head of the Delhi population, the Moghul Emperor,
had been dependent on the occupying power, he had retained control
over the royal palace and what was practically a self-contained town
within its walls. In earlier decades, the indigenous ruler and
incoming 'Resident' had been on cordial terms. Treated with respect,
the Emperor had commanded support in the city and the loyalty of the
Muslim elite.

His willing or unwilling involvement in the conflict formally ended
the Moghul empire in India. The Emperor was exiled, the palace
confiscated. The slaughter of Europeans prior to the siege was
matched by the slaughter of the indigenous population once entry
to the city had been gained. The entire population, both Hindu
and Muslim, was driven out and only gradually allowed to return.
In 1859 a visiting journalist referred to the 'miserable sheds in
which the outcast population of the city, forbidden to return to
their houses, are now forced to live.... For miles they stretch
along the roadside' (between Delhi and Safdar Jang's tomb) (Russell,
1860, vol. 1,p.77). The total population, some 160,270 in 1846,
had fallen to 141,709 by 1863 (Gupta, 1971,p.63).

The monopoly of government by the incoming culture was now based,
not on the 'acquiescence' of the indigenous ruler, but on the
presence of military force. The first requirement, therefore, was
military accommodation in the most strategic, visible and hitherto
most prestigious sector of the city. This was the royal palace.
Within this, most of the buildings were either demolished or occupied
by European troops until their own four-storey barracks were built
some years later. The official designation of the complex was
changed from the 'Royal Palace' to 'Delhi Fort'.

Round the Fort a strip of territory, 500 yards wide, was zoned for
military use. To provide a clear firing range from the ramparts,
the built-up area, previously existing between the main mosque and
the palace, was totally demolished to provide an extensive 'esplanade'.
Open ground to the rear of the mosque was laid out in gardens and a
500-yard security zone set up round all the city walls (ibid.,1971,
p.72). Here, building was prohibited and agriculture restricted.

The cantonment, established in the city in 1803 but removed three
miles away in 1828, was now brought back into the city. As re-
established in 1859, it occupied an area enclosed on three sides by
the city wall running from Kashmiri Gate, down the eastern wall and
round to Delhi Gate (Figure 9.1). On the west, the boundaries took
in the entire area of garden surrounding Delhi Bank (previously
Begum Bagh) and the cleared ground fronting the Jama Masjid. South
of the Fort, property was confiscated and cleared so that the

Cantonment ———— Extended colonial culture area — — —

Figure 9.1. Delhi, 1868.

occupied area, previously bounded by the Daryaganj road running
diagonally through the neighbourhood, now reached as far west as the
Faiz Bazaar which ran between the two 'Delhi Gates', in the southern
wall of the palace and the city wall. Mosques and houses were also
taken over for the accommodation of troops. The *maidan* in front of
the Fort was used as the cantonment parade ground. Effectively, the
cantonment occupied one third of the spatial area of the city, some
468 out of a total of 1,437 acres enclosed by the city walls (Figure
9.1). In 1882, some 1,260 troops were stationed here with accommodation
for a further 250 European soldiers in the fort barracks (Punjab
Government, *Gazetteer*, 1883-4,p.158).

These developments had important effects on the socio-spatial structure of the city; tendencies already apparent before 1857 were now
given full expression. Within the cantonment, European troops were
strictly segregated from indigenous troops, the latter being located
in the 'native infantry lines' outside the Fort. Many, though not
all, European civilians moved out of the city to the Civil Station
and those members of the indigenous elite who had survived the outbreak were moved away from Daryaganj into the city on either side of
Chandni Chowk (Gupta, 1971,p.66). Occupants of dwellings demolished
for the Military Zone either crowded into the indigenous sector of
the city - now compressed by the western boundaries of the cantonment
- or joined the rapidly-growing, extra-mural 'squatter settlements'
in the suburb of Paharganj. These, including Sabzi Mandi and Pahari,
had existed in embryonic form since at least the 1830s. Maps of
1867-8 show that they were still relatively small at that time.

The most important component defining the structure of the city was
the wall. Analysis of the factors affecting this essential con-
straint on the city between 1857 and 1912 confirms the significance
of colonialism as a key variable affecting the development of the
city in this period.

In Europe during the eighteenth and nineteenth centuries, the pre-
industrial, walled city underwent its most substantial period of
change. As the result of industrialisation, population growth and
the introduction of new forms of transport, the medieval city was
transformed, its walls demolished or made ineffective as containers
of the modern industrial city.

In Delhi the situation was different. Between 1857 and the end of
the century, despite suggestions to demolish various sections, the
only openings in the wall were made for railway developments. The
reason for its retention was that of 'military security'. When with
the continued expansion of the city outside the wall, this reason
became obsolete, other factors intervened. Not only was there no
pressure from the colonial power to demolish the wall but members of
the indigenous community also restricted its destruction(ibid.,1971,
p.75). Though demolition of a large section was again considered
in 1927, as a solution to problems of overcrowding, the proposals
were over-ruled by the government (Delhi Administration, *Report on
the Administration of Delhi Province*, etc. 1929-30,p.33 subsequently
Delhi Report). As a physical barrier around the indigenous culture

area of Delhi, most of the wall remained intact until the formal
ending of colonial rule. It was not substantially removed till 1950
(Thakore, 1962,p.158).

3   THE ACCOMMODATION OF RESIDENTIAL REQUIREMENTS

The effects of the military aspects of the monopoly of government
were mainly on the indigenous city. The results of the civil
dimension of colonial power were to be seen, over the next half
century, in the expansion of the Civil Station.

Responsibility for the colonised society had been formally transferred
from the 'East India Company' to the metropolitan government in 1858.
As a result, the number of members of the metropolitan society in
India, including the region of Delhi, increased. Out of a total city
and suburban population of some 160,000 in 1847, Europeans had
probably numbered about 300, less than 100 families (see above,p.195).
By 1864, in a city population of some 142,000, this had grown to
between 1,000 and 1,500. By 1881, of a population of 173,000
(Bopegamage, 1957,p.33) there were some 1,800 Christians, of whom
just less than 1,500 are likely to have been European. About 500
of these were military personnel (Punjab Government, *Gazetteer*,
1883-4,pp.157,207; Cooper, 1863, Appendix). (Bopegamage,1957,p.33
gives the following population figures for the metropolitan city
of Delhi.

Year	Population	Decennial increase(%)
1847	160,279	
1868	154,417	-3.7
1881	173,393	+12
1891	192,579	+11
1901	208,575	+ 8
1911	232,837	+12

There is some discrepancy between these figures and those of Roberts
(op.cit.) for 1847, probably due to the inclusion of suburban
populations).

For many of the civilian members of this community, the main residential sector increasingly became the Civil Station, separated from
the indigenous city by the north wall, the 500-yard military security
zone, a newly established 'Government Garden', the Qudsia Garden and
a new burial ground established in 1861. The nearest houses were a
third of a mile north of the city wall.

Ten years after the outbreak of 1857, some thirty European bungalows
had been established in three small groups (around the old Racquet
Court, the west end of Underhill Road and south end of Alipur Road),
each with its characteristic two- to three-acre compound, drive,

stables and servants' quarters. All were solid masonry structures.
The 'mud dwellings' which characterise the other two extra-mural
developments to the east, in Sabzi Mandi and Paharganj, were entirely
absent from the Civil Lines area. For the convenience of the inhabitants and for access to the old former cantonment at Rajpur,
all major roads had been metalled and shade trees planted on either
side (Map, 1867-8 Delhi... and Environs).

The growth of the Civil Station, and the improvement of service roads
after 1860 served to strengthen the north-east section of the city,
behind Kashmiri Gate, as the principal European sector of the city.
Here, particularly with the establishment of the cantonment in 1861,
further provision was made for the religious, educational, economic,
social and recreational institutions of the immigrant community now
resident in the Fort, Civil Station and to a lesser extent, in
Daryaganj. The extensive formal gardens, watered by the canal and
laid out according to the geometrical preferences of the seventeenth-
century Moghul founders of the city, were now re-modelled according
to the values of the metropolitan society and re-named the 'Queen's
Gardens' after the head of state (compare map of 1857 with that of
1867-8, Figures 8.9 and 9.1). New roads were laid out: Hamilton
Road, slicing off the northern area of the city; Queen's Road,
running parallel and north of the 'Queen's Gardens'; Lothian Road
running north-east from Kashmiri Gate to the Fort; Elgin Road,
cutting straight across the Fort to join up with Daryaganj; Nicholson Road, marking the southern extremity of the occupied area;
Esplanade Road, typically dividing the military zone from the area
of indigenous occupation. The new occupants of the Fort now
manifested their cultural supremacy by changing the names of the
two main gates, from 'Lahore' and 'Delhi' to 'Victoria' and
'Alexandra' (Map, 1867-8, Delhi... and Environs).

4   THE INSTITUTION OF RELIGION

The main religious building, the church of St James, catered only
for the 'Protestant' section of the European community, of whom
there were some 1,500 Indian and European adherants in Delhi in the
1860s (Cooper, 1863, Appendix). With the increase in total numbers,
as well as the intensification of 'missionary' activity, by 1865
provision had to be made for some 700 'Roman Catholic' inhabitants,
in a 'chapel' constructed within the cantonment area, north of the
gardens surrounding Delhi Bank. Just south of here, another 'chapel'
had been constructed by the 'Baptists' in 1845, mainly for the use
of its indigenous 'converts'. 'Missionary' activity was stimulated
rather than diminished by the conflict of 1857 and a small 'mission
house' was established south of Paharganj. The Delhi branch of the
'Society for the Propogation of the Gospel', founded in 1853, was
combined with the 'Cambridge Mission' in 1878. A further agency
of the 'Methodist Episcopal Church Mission' was introduced in 1892
(Delhi Report, 1921-2,p.67 et seq.). Much of this activity was
promoted by 'Fellows' of the two principal metropolitan universities
(Punjab Government, Gazetteer, 1883-4,p.64). As a result of these
developments, further provision was made in 'St Stephen's Memorial

Church', situated at the west end of 'Queen's Gardens', to accommodate
efforts in cultural change.

Religious values were also instrumental in bringing further changes
to the indigenous culture. The first was in the socialisation of
the young; the second, in the definition and treatment of the sick.
In education and medicine, systems of ideas and behaviour were introduced which had significant influence on the built environment of
the city. By 1883, some thirty-two small 'schools' had been established for the 'lower orders' and provision made for an 'industrial
school' and the training of teachers (ibid.,p.153).

This process of directed cultural change was intensified after 1877.
The 'Cambridge Mission to Northern India' became particularly influential in the spheres of education and medicine. As the 'Baptist
missionary' had lived separately from his 'congregation' in the
European enclave of Daryaganj, so the representative of the 'Cambridge
Mission' occupied a bungalow-compound unit in the cultural environment of the Civil Station. In addition to the schools, a 'college'
catering for the indigenous community was established in 1865 and
purpose-built accommodation provided in the form of 'St Stephen's
College' in the European culture area of Kashmiri Gate in 1891.
The so-called 'Moghul' style in which this was built was seen as
an abandonment of the symbolic forms normally used for religious
buildings(the 'Gothic') and criticised as unsuitable for 'Christian'
purposes (Monk, 1935, p.40).

The use of education in the language and culture of the colonial
society had long been recognised as an instrument of cultural change
(see Spear, 1965,p.127). In addition to 'missionary' schools, other
'Government Schools' and 'Colleges' were introduced as part of
government policy, the largest being set up in the old Residency and
in Chandni Chowk.

To compete with traditional 'Vedic' and 'Unani' medical systems,
Western medicine was introduced. A 'civil dispensary' had already
been created and the 'Lock Hospital', opened in 1870, catered for
the needs of those female members of the indigenous community engaged
in prostitution (Punjab Government, *Gazetteer*, 1883-4,p.153). Under
the *Cantonment Acts* of 1864, all public prostitutes were required to
be registered; those unregistered were prohibited from prostitution
and 'Lock Hospitals' were established for the treatment of women
suffering from venereal disease (see *Cantonment Regulations* formed
under Act XXII of 1864 and Act III of 1880, Superintendant of
Government Printing, India, 1887,p.92). The rules provided for two
categories of prostitute, 'those who are and those who are not
frequented by Europeans'. Means were adopted for the detection of
venereal disease only in the former group, who were then entitled to
treatment, against payment, at the Lock Hospitals.

The 'historical' orientations of the colonial community combined with
religious beliefs to affect the built environment in other ways.
Localities associated with the conflict of 1857 were commemorated
with 'monuments' whose function was both religious and political.

The most prominent of these, the 'Mutiny Memorial', was erected in
1870 on the highest point of 'the Ridge' where intense fighting had
taken place during 1857. Symbolically, the 'memorial' was made one
and a half feet higher than the highest landmark of the indigenous
culture, the 'Ashoka Pillar', in the area (Map 1912. Delhi and
vicinity). The road connecting this 'memorial' to the city was
designated as 'Mutiny Memorial Road'. Stone markers were installed
at places where'batteries' had been located during the conflict and
commemorative markers attached to other objects or areas associated
with the events such as 'Kashmiri Gate' and the 'Magazine'. A
'statue' of the principal military commander was placed in a specially
built 'Nicholson Garden'.

Over the decades, these and similar places, hallowed in the colonial
culture, identified and described in maps, 'guides' and by physical
markers on the ground, acted as centres of pilgrimage for the
colonial community and visitors from the metropolitan society. Not
only were they important landmarks in structuring the perception of
physical-spatial areas but, as symbols in the evolving mythology
of the colonial community, they helped to pattern activities and
were instrumental in determining future directions of urban development. Thus, when the new city was being planned in 1912, it was
decided that 'the Ridge' would not be built on because of its
'historic' associations. As each city makes its own cultural history
and embodies it in the creation and preservation of significant
physical-spatial areas, so the colonial city of Delhi increasingly
incorporated the collective past of its new occupants, incorporating
their history into its urban form, rather than that of the indigenous
inhabitants.

5 GOVERNMENT: THE EXTENSION OF CIVIL AND MILITARY PROVISION

In addition to accommodation for European and indigenous troops in
the Fort and Daryaganj, a new magazine and 'godowns' were established for the commissariat and ordnance in the Fort. In Daryaganj,
a magazine and hospital were built and 'soldiers' gardens' laid out.

Since 1857, the local representative of the colonial power had been
the 'Commissioner'. An appropriate dwelling already existed for
him in the form of Ludlow Castle, taken over for government use.
The 'Commissioner's Office' lay inside Kashmiri Gate, to the rear
of St James's Church. Next to this, provision was made for the
judicial functions of government in the 'civil court'. Close by
was the residence of the 'Magistrate' (Cooper, 1863,p.135). Other
means of social control were the police whose two main quarters were
strategically placed on the 'frontier', as it were, between the
cantonment and the indigenous sector of the city. One lay half way
along the Faiz Bazaar and the other, on the south side of Chandni
Chowk, both on the edge of the indigenous area. As the police
establishment increased later in the century, accommodation was
provided in 'police lines' (1890) placed, significantly, out of the
influence of the indigenous population, a quarter of a mile north
of the city wall at the south end of the Civil Station. Here,

under the supervision of European officers, they were available for
the protection of its inhabitants (Punjab Government, *Gazetteer*,
1913,p.219).

6   ECONOMIC INSTITUTIONS

The economic needs of the European community were mainly met by the
indigenous society. Culture-specific furniture or clothing were made
by indigenous craftsmen using imported items, or pictures of these,
as models. At first, such craftsmen were located in Chandni Chowk.
As the European population moved to the Civil Station, they increasingly occupied premises in the area of Kashmiri Gate.

Two important economic services not easily supplied by the local
community were those of providing accommodation and prepared food
for the use of itinerant visitors. For both these purposes, the
European institution of the 'hotel' was introduced.

In the early days of European settlement in Delhi travellers had been
accommodated in private dwellings. Increasing government control
after 1857 increased the flow of short-term visitors and therefore
the need for accommodation. To meet this need, the building earlier
used as a post-office located in the cantonment at the south end
of the Fort was converted into a 'Dak bungalow' (Spear, 1951,p.149).
The 'ever-increasing number of travellers' (Stephen, 1876,p.ii),
evidenced in the proliferation of printed 'guides' in the second
half of the century (Cooper, 1863; Anon, 1865; Harcourt, 1866;
Cole, 1872; Stephen, 1876; Keene, 1882; Murray, 1882; Fanshawe,1902;
Hearn, 1906), led to the provision of hotels, the first of which,
typically, was located in the European sector behind the church.
One of the earliest of these took over the premises of the *Delhi
Gazette* press (Cooper, 1863,p.135). It was important that such
hotels had European names and were run under European supervision.
'Mr Roger's Hamilton Hotel' was behind the church; 'Mrs Benn's
Hotel' was close to Kabul Gate, with an annex behind Ludlow Castle
in the Civil Lines. Where it was not indicated in the name, it was
made known that such hotels were 'under European management'. For
lower-status 'native and European travellers' a new 'Government
Serai' close by the newly-opened railway station was available from
the 1860s. By 1888, the 'Northbrook Great Eastern' and 'United
Services' hotels, both to the rear of St James's Church had been
established (Punjab Government, *Gazetteer*, 1913,p.206).

Apart from the immense impact made by the military needs of government, the most significant influence on the physical-spatial
environment arose from the diffusion of metropolitan technology.
Of this, the most important item was the railway. The railway had
been introduced into India just before mid-century. The events of
1857 had accelerated the need for extending this new means of
communication and control to the major cities of India. By 1862,
the Calcutta Gate on the north-east side of the city had been
demolished to permit the East India line to enter, over the Selimgurh
Fort.

A swath of urban land was cleared, north of the Queen's Road and as
far as the eastern wall, to accommodate the line, sidings and the
station. With the modified area containing the Queen's Gardens,
Bank, the Delhi Institute, Government College and chapels, the
introduction of the railway greatly extended the influence which the
incoming culture made on the physical form of the city (see Figure
9.1). As had happened with the creation of the intra-mural cantonment, the displaced population were pushed further into the south-
east of the city or helped to bulge the suburbs west of the city walls.

With the new bridge over the Jumna completed, the first regular train
from Calcutta entered Delhi in 1867(Hearn, 1906). In the same year,
the Sindh, Punjab and Delhi Railway penetrated the wall to the north
of Kabul Gate. This was followed by the Rajputana Railway linking
Delhi to Bombay in 1872; the Delhi-Kalka-Ambala line, significant,
among other reasons, for easing the journey of Delhi's European
inhabitants to the hill stations of the Himalayas, opened in 1890,
the South Punjab Railway in 1900 and the link between Agra and Delhi
in 1906 (Gupta, 1971,p.67). Though these developments breached the
walls at two places, causing the demolition of Kabul, Mori and Ajmeri
Gates to permit the increased flow of traffic generated by the new
stations, the remainder of the wall remained intact. Only in 1906
was the eastern wall, between Kabul and Ajmeri Gates, demolished.
By then, an equally effective barrier had risen in its place, the
railway sidings.

The railways had other effects on the city's structure. Once through
the city, the obvious site for the lines was on the undeveloped
500-yard wide military zone, running down the western city wall. By
1911, a solid wedge of main line and sidings had been driven north-
south down the western side of the city. On the opposite side of
the city, first the river, then the wall and then the occupied area
of the cantonment held the city's inhabitants in on the east. To
the north, a wedge of railway, a second Europeanised sector of the
city (ibid.,p.72), the northern wall and a series of gardens, police
lines and a cemetery separated them from the culture area of the
Civil Station (see Figure 9.8). In the next decades, the remaining
open flank to the south was to be blocked by the next phase of
colonial urban development.

Other urban technology was introduced from the metropolitan society.
Between 1890 and 1910 a new water distribution system was installed.
Storage tanks and a pumping station were constructed north of
Metcalfe House and water pumped from here to the reservoir on the
summit of the Ridge (Punjab Government, *Gazetteer*, 1913,p.195).
Within the city, its European population equally affected by the
consequences of pollution, a new sanitation system was introduced
which,by 1910, was bringing sewers into the suburbs of Sabzimandi
and Pahajganj (ibid.p.221). The canal in Chandni Chowk was built
over some time before 1882 (Keene, 1882,p.62).

Electricity had been introduced before the end of the century. Though
this was available to both private houses and for public thoroughfares in the Civil Station, in the city it was confined to the main

streets. An electric tramway, begun in 1908, connected Sabzimandi,
the railway station, Chandni Chowk and the Jama Masjid.

The main symbol of this technological transformation, and the new
institutions of urban government introduced in the 1860s, was the
'Victoria Clock Tower' erected in the most prominent thoroughfare
in the city, Chandni Chowk, in 1873. This embodied, in its name
and external form, a symbol of the metropolitan presence, a constant
reminder of a new orientation to time.

The effect of these transport developments was to link up Delhi both
with its immediate region as well as the larger national whole. By
1911, the introduction of motorised transport had helped to extend
metalled roads to distances of over a mile round the walled city,
particularly in the south, to Gurgaon and Mehrauli.

7 SOCIAL INSTITUTIONS

As the European community grew, patterns of association and behaviour
characteristic of metropolitan cities were introduced. Between 1832
and 1857 the old Residency, as the Delhi College and later,Institute,
had functioned as the main centre of literary and scientific activity.
Here, a small library had been established, lectures held and classes
given in the metropolitan language. During the conflict, however,
it had been extensively damaged and its occupation by the military
between 1858 and 1862 (Cooper, 1863,p.136) combined with the creation
of new 'municipal institutions' to stimulate new urban development.
Between 1862 and 1864 the 'Delhi Institute' was built, situated in
the centre of Chandni Chowk, at the heart of the indigenous city
(Harcourt, 1873,p.21). Described in 1873 as 'one of the largest
buildings in the European style in India', it was symbolic of the
new awareness of urban government. Within the building, in addition
to the offices of the new municipality created in 1863, were a
'Durbar Hall', the 'Station Library' ('reserved for European residents')
(ibid.), rooms for social activities and a 'museum'. Like the
institutions it was built to contain, the physical form of the
'Institute' (later the 'Town Hall') made few concessions to the host
culture, contrasting starkly with surrounding forms.

The museum, an institution arising from the historicist values of
the metropolitan society, had been started by the European elite of
Delhi earlier in the century. At first lodged in the College, the
artefacts had later been transferred to the 'Audience Hall' of the
Fort. Typical of metropolitan middle-class values, the museum consisted of 'objects of science, art and commerce' and was perceived
as being of interest 'alike to the Antiquarian, Archaeologist, student
of botany, Geology and History'. Items of local craft, industry and
art were also included (Cooper, 1863,p.137). As European residential
preferences increasingly favoured the Civil Lines, it was natural
that the Club should follow. Suitable premises existed in Ludlow
Castle which, towards the end of the century, were taken over
for the Delhi Club.

By 1868, members of the immigrant culture had sufficiently adapted
almost half of the indigenous city to cater primarily for their use
and for that of those indigenous inhabitants whose life-style and
values had undergone sufficient change to benefit from the
modifications (see Figure 9.1   The extended colonial culture area
is indicated by the dotted line.)

8   THE ACCOMMODATION OF RECREATIONAL ACTIVITY

Within this same area, recreational accommodation increased.   In
addition to the opportunities created for social and intellectual
exchange at the Delhi Institute, a library was built, just south of
the new Masonic Lodge.   Behind the Institute, the Queen's Gardens
were further adapted to meet the expectations of the immigrant
culture.   In 1873 the area was seen as being 'very tastefully laid
out in the English style'.   Provision was made for metropolitan
recreational pursuits in the form of a 'well-kept cricket ground'
and 'band stand'.   Unfamiliarity with indigenous animal life combined with the prevailing taste for natural history to create a
'menagerie' where local animal species were exhibited to indigenous
and immigrant inhabitants.

Apart from such specialised recreational provision, the city itself
and its environs provided opportunity for leisure pursuits.   The
remnants of previous cultures appealed to historicist values in
the colonial community.   Moghul tombs and Hindu monuments provided
subject-matter for painting or the growing practice of photography.
Economic disparities between colonial and indigenous inhabitants
ensured that 'leisure time' could be spent in comfort and relative
seclusion. (Figure 9.2).   In the city, the 'native bazaars' were of
special interest, particularly those of Khanum, Fatehpuri and
Dariba, offering
      a comb maker, cutting and filing, ghee vendors, 'punsari' or
      native chemist, sellers of fruit and vegetables, lacemakers,
      a toyman, dyers, a retailer of native pamphlets, silversmith,
      maker of looking glasses, bheesties.   In the Khanum Bazaar
      were 'looking glasses, sandal wood boxes, Benares and Delhi
      toys'.   In the street to the north of the Jama Masjid were the
      makers of cot-legs and wedding boxes, fireworks, and con-
      fectioners' shops.   The street leading from the Jama Masjid
      to Ajmir Gate was 'one of the best in the city'.   Where this
      street branched off from the Mosque were many bangle-workers,
      and further west, brass and iron merchants, stores with 'lotahs',
      bar, rod and sheet iron, screws and nails.   Between Fatehpuri
      Mosque and Lahore Gate, on either side of the road, were stores
      of dealers in grain and druggists.   Opposite the north gate of
      Fatehpuri Mosque was the gateway leading to 'the principal market
      for European piece goods'(Cooper, 1863,pp.34-5).
The Civil Lines provided a suitably restful environment, with its
own complement of parks and gardens.   By 1865, the influence of this
area on the city had led to the Kashmiri and Mori Gates in the
northern wall being those 'principally used by Europeans' (Harcourt,
1866,p.19).

Figure 9.2

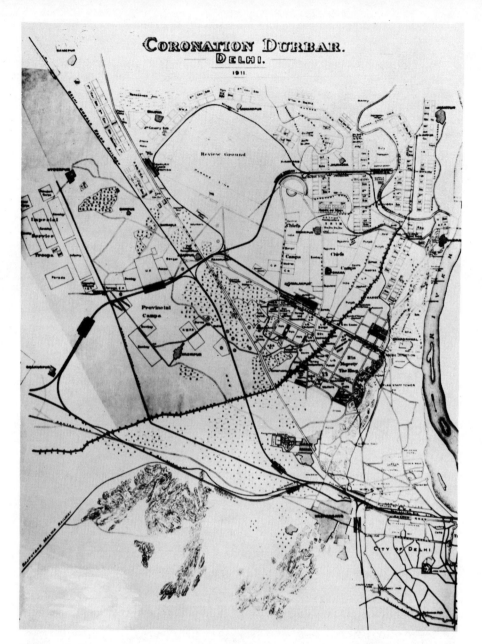

Figure 9.3

9   EXTENSIONS OF GOVERNMENT: THE POLITICAL SPACE OF THE DURBARS

By the early 1870s, the requirements of the colonial government had
resulted in the extension of Delhi's spatial boundaries by an area
roughly two and a half times the size of the indigenous city. Over
the following four decades, another thirty square miles were to be
added as a result of three imperial 'durbars'.

The assumption of responsibility for India by the metropolitan
government in 1858 was followed, in 1877, by the declaration of the
head of that government as ruler of the 'Indian Empire'. The
'durbars' which followed may be seen as forms of institutionalised
ritual to legitimise the new relationship. According to Weber,
leaders may claim legitimacy for their rule on three grounds,
'tradition', 'charisma' and 'legality' (Gerth and Mills, 1958,
pp. 78-9). If the authority of the imperial government was to be
seen as legitimate, this had to be effected within categories and
structures existing in the indigenous culture. In the 'native
states', authority was largely personal and, in Weber's terms, was
based on tradition, 'an established belief in the sanctity of
immemorial traditions' (ibid).

The 'durbar' was an indigenous institution. In this, the ruler
appeared in the presence of his immediate subordinates and all,
in the presence of their dependent subjects. It permitted those
in authority to communicate to their dependants and the dependants
to communicate with those in authority over them. Particularly in
pre-literate societies, the 'durbar', like the 'royal progress'
of an earlier age, acted as a visual symbol both of the presence
and power of the ruler and not least, of his continued existence.

By gathering the heads of the 'native states' in Delhi, a place for
centuries associated with the rulers of India, and by exhibiting them
in a subordinate position to the representative of the ruling power,
not only was the structure of authority demonstrated but the
tradition-based legitimacy of the indigenous elite was transferred
to the metropolitan power. The visual demonstration of this authority
by the display of military power also had important effects on those
participating as well as those who merely observed.

The principle underlying the durbar was that of *visual* display. It
was a display of power, the sources of power and the social and
political relationships which power confers. In this display, the
structure of political authority and the hierarchy of social prestige
were demonstrated in symbolic form. Such symbols were encoded in
set forms of behaviour, the size and number of persons and objects,
and the spatial relationships between them.

Insight into the nature of these symbols is provided by the principal
actor in the durbar of 1911. In his account, considerable attention
is given to symbolic forms of communication and the problems which
they present: whether the carriage of the head of state and 'King-
Emperor' should have six or four horses; his concern that the horse
on which he rides is larger than that of the 'King-Emperor';

the need for the latter to demonstrate, by learnt gestures appropriate
to the indigenous culture ('salaams') his role as the ultimate source
of power; problems presented by the relatively small stature of the
'King-Emperor'; the importance of particular forms of dress on
ceremonial occasions, and the necessity of allocating appropriate
distances between himself and members of the indigenous elite
(Hardinge, 1948, passim). Such symbolic forms of communication
clearly have important spatial implications. It is these which
make the durbars significant for the further development of Delhi.
Three durbars were held; the first, in 1877, to proclaim the
assumption of the title 'Empress of India' by the metropolitan
head of state; the second and third, in 1903 and 1911, to celebrate
the 'coronation' of new occupants of the imperial throne. As the
third occasion was attended by the 'King-Emperor' and 'Queen' it
provided the most extensive example of the ceremonial process.

The durbar of 1877 established the site. The area chosen lay
north-west of the Rajpur cantonment and the Ridge somewhat further
than the village of Wazirabad. The boundaries ran east-north-east
to take in the site of what was to become the Durbar Amphitheatre,
half a mile north of Dahirpur, over to Badlee on the Delhi-Amballa
Railway and down the Grand Trunk Road to the suburb of Sabzi Mandi.
The site was retained and enlarged on the two following occasions
(Figure 9.3).

The major spatial components were the tented camps of the indigenous
and colonial elites, the 'review ground' for the various durbar
activities, the 'amphitheatre' for formal ceremonial activity and
areas for servicing, roads, water supply, sanitation and power. The
base already existed in the cantonment road system and the road
network linking this and the Civil Lines to the city. This was
developed for the durbars of 1877 and 1903, with the colonial head
of state occupying the newly-built 'Circuit House'(later to become
the 'Government House' in the temporary capital of 1911-21 and
subsequently, the Registry of the University of Delhi).

Anticipating the future structure of New Delhi, the lay-out of the
Viceroy's camp of 1903 followed strict rules of socio-spatial
hierarchy. The central area formed the Viceroy's personal territory
and the remaining space accommodated his kitchens, immediate staff,
offices and ancillary services (Nilsson, 1973). The King's representative, the Duke of Connaught, was accommodated immediately
to the north of the Viceroy. To their immediate left,proportionately
smaller in size, was the camp of the Commander-in-Chief. Smaller
camps were next marked out for the Governors of Bombay and Madras,
and the Lieutenant Governors of Punjab, Bengal and Burma. More
distant and half the size, were the camps of those occupying roles
lower down the colonial hierarchy, the Chief Commissioners of Assam,
the Central Provinces and further away, the various Residents.

A similar structure characterised the lay-out of 1911. However,
unlike 1903, when some camps of the indigenous elite had been sited
in what is now the New Delhi area, 233 different camps occupied
some 25 square miles north-west of the Ridge(Hardinge,1948,p.42).

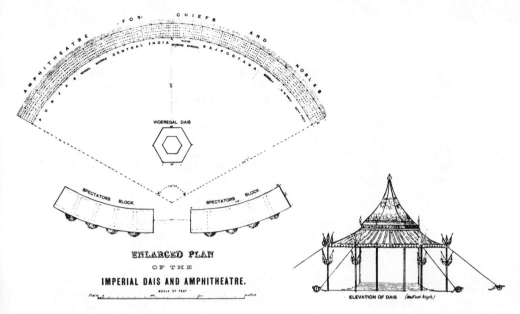

Figure 9.4

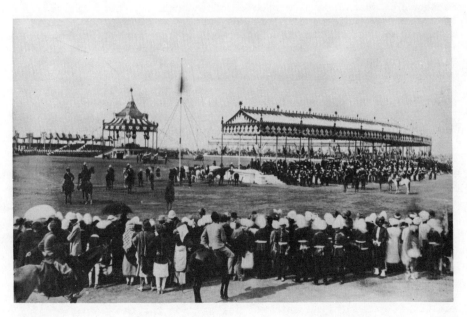

Figure 9.5

As the 'King-Emperor' was himself present in 1911, a larger area
of some 85 acres was necessary for the royal camp. Again
anticipating the hierarchies of New Delhi, the indigenous nobility
were accorded sites, their position and size appropriate to the
status of their occupants, near to, yet sufficiently distant from,
the source of prestige. The 30,000 troops, responsible both for
security as well as ceremonial, were strategically situated round
the perimeter of the durbar area, bounded by the river, Wazirabad,
Jagalpur, east to Mokandur, Balswa, Hyderpur and south to Wazirpur
and Sabzi Mandi (see Figure 9.3).

Given the visual function of the durbar, the next largest need
was for the 'review ground' covering an area equivalent in size
to that of the walled city. Here, and on the three polo grounds
laid out on the site of the old cantonment race course, were performed the particular recreational and ceremonial activities
associated with the colonial durbar: 'cavalry displays', 'tent-
pegging', 'football', 'hockey', 'cricket', 'fireworks', 'assaults-
at-arms', 'polo', 'massed band' performances, and the 'march past'.
In 1911 seating accommodation was provided for 100,000 spectators.
(In 1970 the polo grounds were occupied by the University Sports
and Police Grounds. According to the *Master Plan for Delhi*
(1962, vol.1,p.5), the 'residential colony of Maurice Nagar was
developed by the University on the same site where the original
staff quarters, called Rajpur quarters, of the Vice-regal lodge
existed, some of the barracks still existing around Miranda House,
Arts Faculty and the New Library buildings are reminiscent of the
police and military guards' residences').

The original amphitheatre was laid out in 1877 and modified for
subsequent occasions. The problem of recognising the relative
status of 100 indigenous rulers was resolved by a seating arrangement whereby all 'ruling chiefs' were largely equidistant from
the Vice-regal dais (I am indebted to Bernard Cohn for this insight.
Figures 9.4, 9.5).

The fourth requirement was the provision of transport and other
services for the main functional areas. By 1911 the development
of the rail and road system had permitted a far more extensive
demonstration to be undertaken than in 1877. Roads within the
city had been broadened, kept free of encroachments and maintained
for use by ceremonial processions. Outside the Fort, the *maidan*
provided a setting for the demonstration of political power (Figure
9.6). In the seclusion of the gardens within, social activities
associated with the durbar enabled the mixing of indigenous and
colonial elites (Figure 9.7).

With a budget of one million pounds for the occasion, preparation
over a year brought extensive developments to the skeleton services
earlier laid down. Within the 25-square mile area, 40 miles of
new roads were constructed in addition to 20 miles in the military
camps. 26½ miles of broad gauge and 9 miles of narrow gauge
railway were laid. The main railway station for the durbar of 1911

Figure 9.6

Figure 9.7

had 10 platforms, each 300 yards long. 50 miles of water mains and
30 miles of pipes were installed and electric power lines set up. The
amphitheatre, providing for 69 indigenous chiefs in 1871, and 100 in
1903, accommodated 200 in 1911. The entire durbar population,
accommodated under 10 square miles of tents, comprised some 250,000
people, the equivalent of the city of old Delhi(Hardinge,1948,p.29).

The new road system included the improvement of pre-1877 Alipur Road,
The Mall, Karnal Road, the Grand Trunk Road and the cantonment grid
system. New roads included 'Curzon Road', 'Chiefs' Road, two roads
leading to and from the amphitheatre, 'Princes' Road' and 'Kingsway',
'Spectators' Road', 'Military Road' and 'Polo Ground Road'. Within the
Civil Station, 'Club Road' was developed (see plans relating to *Delhi
Durbar*, 1902-3, *British Library*). As much of the railway was subsequently dismantled, the permanent results of this investment were the
roads and services: 'Kingsway Camp' provided for the tented accommodation of clerks working in the temporary capital of 1925. After 1947, the
area provided accommodation for refugees, 'colonies' of 'Harijans'
and municipal government employees.

10 SUMMARY

By the end of this second main phase of development, urban Delhi conformed to the classical model of 'native city', 'cantonment' and
'civil station'. The city population of some 233,000 was confined to
just over 1½ square miles of the walled city and the three major
suburbs of Paharganj, Sadr Bazaar and Sabzi Mandi (see Figure 9.8).
Cut off from expansion on the north, south and east, the only area for
growth was the west, where the gap in the ridge was being rapidly filled
by growing suburban development. This was described in 1913 as 'a
collection of mean houses occupied as a rule by lower castes'(Punjab
Government, *Gazetteer*, Delhi, 1913,p.220). According to Ferrell(1969),
Paharganj was mainly Muslim, with *kacha* (mud-brick) houses and shortly
to house building workers from New Delhi.More prosperous Punjabi
Muslims lived in Sadr Bazaar. In Sabzi Mandi, originally a vegetable
market, were some industries and the homes of factory employees(p.3).

With eight railways entering the city, its commercial and industrial
activity expanded. To the traditional crafts of silver, brass and
copperware, ivory, stone- and wood-carving, had been added newer industries: cotton spinning and weaving, flour milling, soap refining and
the production of chemicals. European goods, including glass and china,
were imported here and distributed throughout northern India (Punjab
Government, *Gazetteer*, 1913,p.220). The eastern section of the city
had changed little from the later 1880s.

> Daryaganj, the Fort, the public offices and the railway form an
> almost continuous line along the eastern and northern face of the
> city; and the angle between them is occupied by public gardens.
> The quarter thus occupied (by the Europeans) amounting to nearly
> half of the whole city, presents a comparatively open appearance
> and is distinctly marked off and separate from the denser proportion
> lying to the southwest and occupied by shops and dwelling house
> of the native population (ibid.,p.219).

Figure 9.8

To the north-west lay the European enclave of the Civil Lines, its
population neatly contained by the river and the Ridge. Here,
'the generality of houses are well built and suitably lit and
cooled by electric power; the roads are well kept and watered under
municipal arrangements' (ibid.). Here, on the two- or three-acre
compounds, with drive, stables and quarters at the rear for servants
and their kin, were less than 100 bungalows. Each family had its
own transport; neither tramway nor train came in sight. Here, well
away from its inhabitants, the 'aesthetic' qualities of the city
could be enjoyed.

> From the summit of the Ridge, the view of the station and
> the city is very picturesque; in the foreground, the houses
> and gardens of the English residents, thickly interspersed
> with trees, and in the distance, the city wall surmounted
> here and there by tall acacias, while over all rise the
> minarets of the Jama Masjid and the Fort (Punjab Government
> *Gazetteer*, 1883-4,p.183).

Metropolitan visitors could be accommodated at 'the most prominent
buildings in the Civil Lines' including the Club, 'the newly-
constructed Punjab Circuit House and Maiden's Hotel'. The area
of Daryaganj, previously favoured by Europeans, had been largely
abandoned. According to an observer in 1912, it was 'not a very
inviting locality, with houses and gardens look(ing) very shabby'
(Punjab Government, *Gazetteer*, 1913,p.219).

The third component was the cantonment which, though vacated in
1861, had been retained for future use. Indigenous troops had been
moved back there in 1905. As it was now clear that, with the
development of the Civil Station and suburbs outside the city, it
was not only the làtter which had to be defended (Gupta, 1971,p.76),
the remaining troops in the Fort were moved back to a site slightly
east of the old cantonment in 1910. Here were provided 'the
necessary residential quarters and lines, with a polo ground, race
course and golf links and also, the old cemetery' (Punjab Government,
Gazetteer, 1913,p.218).

On the limits of what had now become the metropolitan area of Delhi,
20 miles to the north and south of the old city and 10 miles to the
east, were the temporary shelters of a peripatetic government
inspectorate, the supervisors of roads, railways and canals. Within
this area were some 40 'rest houses', 'dak' or 'inspection bungalows'
'intended primarily for the use of officials on tour', though also
used by metropolitan tourists. Each stood in its own area of culturally modified territory and contained one 'sitting room'
(20' by 18'), two to three 'bedrooms', three or four 'bathrooms',
two other rooms and verandah. The outbuildings included stables,
cookhouse, coachhouse and accommodation for the *chowkidar* (Punjab
Government, *Gazetteer*, 1904, Table 29). With these enclaves of
cultural territory, the residential system of the colonial urban
settlement was complete.

Chapter 10

IMPERIAL DELHI 1911-47:
A model of colonial urban development

The caste system must be catching for there is in the English
community in India, a strong tendency to fall into groups
(John Law, *Indian Snapshots*, 1912,p.40).

Any general theory of the city must somehow relate the social
processes that go on in the city to the spatial form which
the city assumes (David Harvey, *Social Justice and the City*,
1973,p.23).

1 INTRODUCTION

The third phase in the development of colonial Delhi begins with
the decision to move the political and administrative capital of
India from Calcutta to Delhi in 1911.

As political and economic influence increased over the entire sub-
continent after 1858, a new, centrally-located capital was needed.
By 1911, the technological superiority of the metropolitan power
had made such a move feasible. Between 1867, when it was first
discussed (Thakore 1962,p.77),and the end of the century, a
communications system had been established in the form of roads,
railways, telegraph, telephone, printing presses and mail services.
By 1912 India was operating the first air mail service in the world.
Administrative centres could now be located independently of
'natural' communication links provided by rivers and coastal routes.

In explaining the development of Delhi between 1911 and the end of
colonial rule, the three main variables of colonialism, culture and
technology are equally important. The power structure of colonialism
was responsible for the basic decision to move. Within the new
capital, the distribution of power was responsible for reproducing
the same tripartite arrangement of 'native city', 'cantonment' and
the new 'civil station' of New Delhi. It also explains the existence of basic institutions in the city and its socio-spatial
structure. Cultural values and experience partly account for the
lay-out of the new city and for the quality of its urban environment.

Finally, imported technology, in the form of motorised transport
and electronic communication, determines the overall scale and
the system of communications within it.

2   THE TEMPORARY CAPITAL, 1911-21

The immediate need was for a temporary capital. A site already
existed in the Civil Lines, the developed area of which had been
extensively enlarged by the durbars of 1903 and 1911. Military
needs had already been met by the cantonment north-east of the
Ridge. The next requirement was accommodation for the head of
government and offices for his staff.

The local 'Circuit House', already converted for use by the 'King-
Emperor' in 1911, was now modified and re-styled as 'Government
House'. For other government needs, land, partly in the estate
of 'Metcalfe House', was taken over and, in 1912, a large
'Secretariat' constructed to accommodate the rapidly-growing
bureaucracy. New forms of transport were recognised in the provision
of 'garage accommodation' at the rear (*Delhi Report*, 1921-2,p.1).

The Delhi population was expanding rapidly. Between 1911 and 1921,
it increased from 232,837 to 304,420. Part of this growth was due
to the rising numbers of government employees who increased from
9,628 (with over 20,000 dependents) to 17,326 (with over 30,000
dependents) in the same period. Of this total population, the
number of metropolitan-born immigrants increased from 569 in 1911,
to 2,829 ten years later, thus forming about 2 per cent of the total
urban population. Of these, 78 per cent and 86 per cent respectively
were male (Ferrell, 1969,p.68).

This growth in the number of European males stimulated the provision
of 'European-style' accommodation, particularly in the form of
hotels, the extension of club facilities and the building of extra
bungalows in the Civil Lines. Accommodation specially constructed
for the 'Viceroy' during the 1903 durbar was now taken over and used
for the 'Swiss Hotel' (the gates still bore the plates of 'Curzon
House' in 1970). The largest hotel, 'Maiden's', was situated some
100 yards up Alipur Road and two others, the 'United Services' and
'Woodlands', moved from Kashmiri Gate into the Civil Lines during
this period. By 1919, there were some 140 bungalow-compound units
in the Civil Station (Figure 10.1).

Accommodation for the rapidly-growing ranks of government clerks
was made on the perimeter of the new temporary capital, the 'clerks'
quarters' being laid out at the northern and southern limits of
the old cantonment lines. To the north, at Timarpur, some 84 units
were grouped round three *maidans*. A stretch of open space and the
'Indian Cavalry Lines' separated the clerks from 'Government House'.
(The site of the 'Cavalry Lines' now forms Cavalry Lane on the
University campus). Quarters for press workmen lay higher up the
Ridge to the immediate east of the clerks (now the site of Balak
Ram Hospital). The second set of clerks' quarters lay next to the

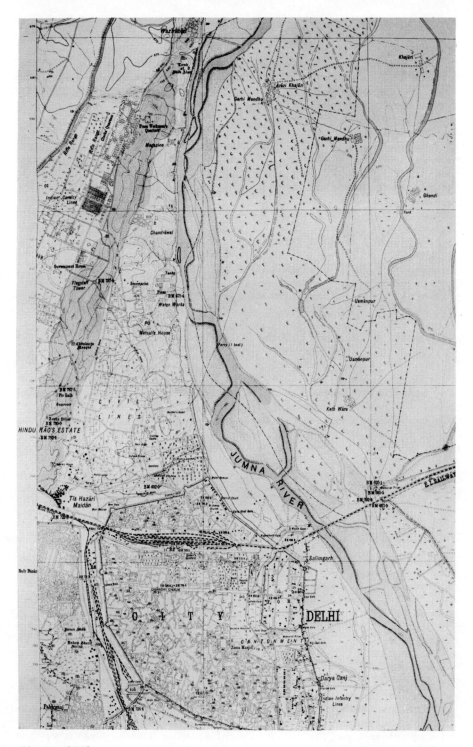

Figure 10.1

village of Rajpur; both areas were about one mile from the 'Secretariat'
Further temporary provision existed in the vast 'Kingsway Camp' of
some 1,000 tents pitched on the western side of the Najafgarh drainage
canal (see Sullivan, 1920,p.96).

The associational behaviour of the colonial community was centred
on the Delhi Club in Ludlow Castle, open to 'European gentlemen
received in general society' (Prasad, 1918,p.52) and the Roshnara
Club. The latter, located in an erstwhile Moghul garden bearing
the same name, combined the external forms of other (Dutch) colonial
powers with those of the colonial elite. Despite the temporary
nature of the capital, 'golf', a recreational activity increasingly
favoured by the leisure-oriented metropolitan middle-class, was
accommodated in Delhi's first golf-links, located at the south end
of the old cantonment. (This area was later occupied by four
institutes of Delhi University: Hindu and Hansraj Colleges, the
Institute for Economic Growth and the Sri Ram Institute for Industrial Relations). Other recreational provision had been made for
the cantonment, the durbars or the Civil Station. Thus, the cantonment race-course and three polo-grounds lay to the south and
south-west (now occupied by the police and university grounds).

Again anticipating developments in the new capital, the Civil Station
continued to be enclosed with a belt of protective territory. From
the village of Chandrawal, the river ran down the eastern boundary
to the north-east corner of the old city. Along the southern
boundary of the temporary capital, the Qudsia and Nicholson Gardens,
'Cemetery' the grounds of the 'Cecil' and 'Swiss Hotels', Police
Lines and Hindu Rao hospital provided a 'cordon sanitaire'. Moving
north-west to Rajpur, the 'Golf Links' and 'clerks' quarters' joined
up with the Najafgarh Canal and the Canal Road to provide an
effective frontier leading to the apex of the triangle at Wazirabad.

3 THE NEW COLONIAL URBAN SETTLEMENT LOCATED

The decision to move the capital was taken on political and administrative grounds. With a network of railways running to the main
regions of India, Delhi occupied a central position. The region's
historic associations with earlier Indian dynasties were seen as
recommending it to a population increasingly active in opposing
colonial rule. With the opening of the Delhi-Amballa railway in
1890, Delhi was now effectively linked with the hill station of
Simla, the alternative 'hot weather capital'.

The move decided, it remained for the site to be chosen. One considered was the culturally-modified territory on either side of
'the Ridge'. This suggestion was rejected by the metropolitan head
of state as 'the outcrop was hallowed by memories of the Mutiny
and was not to be built on' (Thakore, op.cit. p.86). Though various
other alternatives were considered, the site ultimately chosen,
suitable in terms of spatial needs, potentialities and wind direction
(prevailing winds come from the west and north-west) lay immediately
south of the old city. As the new capital was to be primarily a

centre of government, the two traditional institutions of colonial
rule had to be accommodated, the military in a cantonment, and the
administration in an expanded civil station. Estimated land
requirements were 15 square miles for the new cantonment and 12
square miles for the city, with a population of 30,000 and their
immediate dependents (subsequently changed to 65,000). In 1931,
the area of New Delhi occupied some 32 square miles (see also
Breeze, 1974, pp.12-13).

Given the site and extent of existing development, the lay-out of the
capital was based on two culturally-controlled decisions. Although
a small group of metropolitan 'planning' specialists were available
the final decision on siting was made at the local source of colonial
power. In choosing the site for his official dwelling, the'Viceroy'
adopted the same criteria as those of his predecessors in Delhi,
the 'Residents', some ninety years before. For reasons perceived
as 'historic' and 'visual', 'Government House' was located on the
highest point in the area, with 'views' to the dominant feature
of the old city, the Jama Masjid, in the north-east and the 'historic' site of the first Delhi settlement, Indrapastha, in the east.
In his own words,

> Two important decisions were taken: first, that the site should
> be on the southern side of Delhi, and second, that it should be
> at Raisina. It was I myself who decided the latter point....
> Having been informed that (the) committee of experts had
> selected and approved a site and that the lay-out had been
> flagged for my inspection and criticism, I went from Simla
> to Delhi....
>
> The moment I saw the selected site I realised its objections.
> It would be hot; it had no views; and it had no room for ex-
> pansion....
>
> (We) then mounted and galloped over the plain to a hill some
> distance away. From the top of the hill there was a magnificent
> view embracing old Delhi and all the principal monuments situated
> outside the town, with the river Jumna winding its way like a
> silver streak in the foreground at a little distance. I said
> at once to (the Commissioner of Delhi), 'This is the site for
> Government House', and he readily agreed (Hardinge, 1948,p.72).

(The site of Government House was later moved slightly to the west
and taken over by the Secretariat buildings).

Between these two points and the site of 'Government House' the
two organising axes of the city were aligned.

Apart from this visual link connecting the old and new cities, no
further attempt was made to integrate, at a physical-spatial level,
what now became two quite separate units. An alternative plan,
linking the two cities together, was not pursued (Nilsson,1973,p.45).

In the three decades between 1912 and 1947, four separate settlements, each distinguished by its own functional, cultural and
demographic characteristics, were to develop in the Delhi region.
The city, now pushing westwards into Sadr Bazaar, Sabzi Mandi and
what was to be a new suburb of Karol Bagh; the European cultural

enclave of the Civil Station; in the south, the new 'civil station' of New Delhi and south-west of this, the new cantonment (see Figure 1.1).

The relationship of this new cantonment to the new 'civil station' exactly reproduced the pattern of one hundred years before, though both were now on the opposite sides of the city. The new civil station of New Delhi lay separated and at a distance from the 'native city'. To the south-west, was the cantonment, out of sight over the Ridge yet strategically only one mile away. Conforming to earlier colonial urban models, the civilians lived outside and away from the 'native town', with the ultimate source of power, armed force, located slightly to their rear.

4   GOVERNMENT: THE MILITARY REQUIREMENT

The cantonment occupied some 17 square miles, its grid-iron lay-out following the basic principles of earlier models. To the south were the 'Maude', 'Shumran' and 'Sannaiyat Lines' for the indigenous troops, now known as 'Indian' rather than 'native'. Close by was a separate Indian Military Hospital. To the north, a mile away, were the Nicholson Lines, containing the British Infantry 'Barracks'.

Between these two concentrations of troops were the individual bungalow-compound units of some 120, mainly European, officers. A half-mile gap separated these from the lines of indigenous troops.

The main cluster of these compounds, located between 'The Mall' and 'Polo Road', contained some 30 units, each occupying one acre or more. Slightly to the north, some 35 bungalows were laid out on an area of half a square mile. Other senior officers' accommodation was on 'Wigram Road' where, along half a mile, six compounds, each with a 150-yards frontage, were situated.

Traditional cantonment institutions were reproduced in their appropriate place. Close to the indigenous troops was the *Sadr* (main) *Bazaar* and 'Cantonment Magistrate's Office'. Near the European troops, the 'Magazine', 'Church' and 'Cantonment Garden'. In the officers' residential area, the 'Club', the various 'officers' messes' and 'Brigade House'.

Apart from the low density of the officers' residential area and the strategic use of space to separate social and cultural groups, a belt of undeveloped land, between one and two miles wide, acted as a 'sanitary' and security zone round the entire built-up area of the cantonment. In addition, the spatial areas peculiar to military use were needed for rifle ranges, parade grounds, sports arenas, a 'military grass farm', cemetery as well as camping grounds for the use of visiting troops.

5   GOVERNMENT: THE CIVIL REQUIREMENT

The most substantial difference distinguishing the new from the old
city results, not from the *technology* but from the *technological
assumptions* underlying its construction.

In the thirty years prior to the city's foundation, five innovations,
all in the field of communications and transport technology, had been
developed in the industrialised societies of the West: the telephone,
automobile, cinematograph, radio and aeroplane. In addition, in the
early years of the twentieth century, the bicycle had been evolved as
a viable means of mass, personal transport. The scale, plan and
lay-out of the new imperial city were based on the assumption that
such technology existed.

Road-widths, intra-city distances, and residential areas were geared
to motorised transport. Distances, and communications between
members of the elite, assumed the presence of car and 'phone.
(The first manual telephone exchange had been established in the
Civil Lines in 1911 and another in the Kashmiri Gate area in 1923;
Delhi Report, 1923-4,p.19). The first automatic exchange was begun
in the new city in 1925-6 and another in 1937.

In 1913 there were 800 telephones in Delhi, and some 7,000 in 1947.
The total area covered by metropolitan Delhi in 1921 was 65 square
miles *(Delhi Report,* 1921-2. p.57). Subsequent increases in
numbers in relation to population growth are:

	Number of telephones	Population
1913	800	232,837 (1911)
1947	7,000	695,686 (1941)
1956	15,350	1,437,134 (1951)
1961	30,700	2,359,408 (1961)
1966	61,300	
1971	91,150	3,359,408 (1971)

(I am grateful to Professor P.V. and Dr Jaya Indiresan for this
information).

In the evolution of the city over the next two decades, an airport,
telephone exchange, cinemas and radio station, as well as a large
new government press, were to be the physical manifestation of a
technology imported by, and largely for, a governing elite. For
the supply of this technology, the capital depended on the metropolitan power. In this sense, New Delhi, both in its functioning
as well as its lay-out, represented a dependent, technological
appendage of a Western industrial state. Without this technology
it could function only by substituting manpower for tasks designed
for machine.

The new settlement was planned as a political, administrative and residential area. Little direct provision was made for industrial development (*Delhi Report*, 1927-8,p.45). Where this took place it was confined to the indigenous city and its suburbs.

The hexagonal pattern forming the basis of the planned area arose from the initial decision to run three axes from the residential site on Raisina Hill to the main mosque in the city, the site of Delhi's first settlement at Indraprastha and the Muslim tomb of Safdar Jang (Nilsson, 1973,p.82). The overall symmetry of the lay-out made reference to models of urban development conceived in earlier, politically autocratic capitals of Europe (such as Karlsruhe and Versailles). It was also characteristic of later Western 'town planning' models which had arisen in the later nineteenth century to assist in the accommodation of populations living in the indus-trialised town.

The two metropolitan representatives principally associated with the development of Delhi were both members of an upper middle-class elite. Their specialised knowledge of urban and residential development had previously been directed, in one case, to the production of dwellings for a wealthy upper class and, in the other, to aspects of urban development in colonial Africa (see entries under E. Lutyens and H. Baker in *Penguin Dictionary of Architecture*, 1966). Accounts of the development of Delhi frequently refer to the 'Baroque' ideas of its 'architect' and the 'garden city' principles on which the city was built. The use of these terms is misleading in the bi-cultural framework in which Delhi developed. So-called 'garden city' principles represent a rationalised application of the underlying values which had characterised conceptual models of settlement in the colonial society at least since the eighteenth century. Even in the metropolitan society, the so-called 'Garden City' of the early twentieth century was similarly a rational and conscious application of certain traditional values, shared by specific social groups and disseminated among a wider population. As attitudes to members of the indigenous society have been recorded, they are reproduced as illustrative of the perceived differences between the two cultures being accommodated in Delhi

> The natives do not improve much on acquaintance. Their very low intellects spoil much and I do not think it possible for the Indians and whites to mix freely and naturally. They are very different and even my ultra-wide sympathy with them cannot admit them on the same plane as myself (E. Lutyens, quoted in Nilsson 1973,p.72).

Some two decades later, in a comparable context, the metropolitan adviser appointed to draw up plans for the colonial capital of Lusaka (Zambia, but at that time 'Northern Rhodesia') wrote (c.1935)

> It would be a mistake to treat (the natives) as if they were Europeans. It would be ridiculous to expect them to accept the responsibilities of the white man, and it would be foolish to offer them those bodily comforts which they have never known and which generations and generations of habit have made necessary to the white man(S.D.Adshead, quoted in Collins, 1969).

The original site, south of the walled city, covered an area of some 32 square miles, and extended 4 miles from the southern wall. Apart from some 20 small villages which were engulfed, the boundaries carefully excluded all areas of densely populated settlement, including Paharganj and Sabzi Mandi.

As the first three government requirements of earlier European settlers in Delhi had been a cantonment, 'Residency' and accommodation for a small bureaucracy, a century later similar provision was made, albeit on a larger scale.

Government House was built on the highest point of the new site, its topmost point symbolically, like the 'Mutiny Memorial' before it, higher than the tallest indigenous structure in the vicinity (Nilsson, 1973,p.72). The site covered some two thirds of a square mile. Apart from accommodation for the 'Viceroy's staff', the house, completed and occupied in 1929, like all other bungalows in the city, was surrounded by gardens. Within this 'temple of imperial power' (Hussey, 1950,p.319) were those culture-specific social spaces required by the colonial elite: a 'durbar hall', three 'state drawing rooms', 'ballroom', 'billiard room', 'library', 'state dining room', 'Her Excellency's Sitting Room' and 'Her Excellency's Private Sitting Room', 'His Excellency's Private Staircase', large numbers of 'bed' and 'bathrooms' and similar divisions of space (ibid.,p.508). The vast compound was carefully railed off and planted with dense vegetation.

East of 'Government House' were two large offices accommodating the imperial bureaucracy, the north and south blocks of the 'Secretariat', completed in 1926. The remaining developed area was allocated almost entirely to the residential and institutional needs of the government and its accompanying network of roads. Only in 1919 did a change in the political relationship lead to a new unit of government, a 'Council of State' and 'Legislative Assembly' which therefore re-quired accommodation. The circular 'Council Chamber', by this time obliged to occupy a site similar in area to that of the principal European club, was symbolically inferior in size and elevation to both 'Government House' and the 'Secretariat' of the imperial bureaucracy.

6   THE EFFECTS OF CULTURAL CHANGE

Since the mid-nineteenth century, a steady process of acculturation had produced considerable numbers of 'Westernised' Indians whom the government increasingly employed in the army and subsidiary civilian roles. With the growth of this group, proficient both in the metropolitan language and culture, increasing demands were made by the indigenous society to recruit more of their number into govern-ment posts. Positions particularly sought were those of military officers and in the elite corps of administrators, the 'Indian Civil Service'.

Whilst increasing numbers were accepted into these two key spheres, particularly after 1920 (Gutteridge, 1963), it was an unstated assumption that much of their own cultural tradition, in terms of language, values, behaviour and life-style, were to be modified and that of the colonial culture adopted. As well as ideational aspects, this included such items as dress, the use of Western eating utensils, items of household 'furniture' as well as the type of residential accommodation and urban environment based, it should be noted, not on purely 'Western' or metropolitan models, but on the interpretation of these by the colonial elite.

In discussing the development of New Delhi, therefore, it is important to recognise that although the key decision-making positions of government were still monopolised by members of the metropolitan society, an increasing number of acculturated indigenes now filled senior government roles.

The largest spatial requirement arose from the residential needs of the colonial administrators, their immediate kin and the indigenous employees of government. The form and location of this was determined by occupational, social and racial criteria. For an understanding of these forms and their relationship to the social structure of the city, broader issues need to be considered.

7   RACE, PLACE AND SPACE: SOCIAL STRUCTURE IN THE COLONIAL CITY

The difficulties in describing the social structure of a culturally plural, colonial society have been well described by Smith (1965) and Rex (1970). This is especially the case in India with its added dimension of caste. In each cultural section of the society, different criteria of stratification apply, each based on different conceptions of social reality (see Béteille, 1967; Dumont, 1972).

The fact that representatives of two cultural traditions met, under the dominance-dependence relationship of colonialism, did not mean that one system of stratification 'replaced' or was 'absorbed' by the other. It was rather that, in certain places and situations, either system or a combination of both could operate simultaneously. A person's perception of his own status and the social structure of which he was a part depended not merely on the cultural section to which he belonged but also on his own place within it.

If we are to understand the socio-spatial structure of Delhi, some attention must therefore be paid to the nature of relationships in the colonial society and the criteria which helped to determine them.

Traditional Indian society is characterised by a system of stratification embodied in the notion of caste. The status of various castes and of individuals within them is often spatially expressed. In villages, lower-caste members frequently occupy areas on the perimeter and well-recognised norms govern both the distances between castes as well as their permitted movements within the village.

In the metropolitan society, stratification is based on a combination of ascriptive and achieved criteria. Here, birth, wealth, occupation and education are the most important attributes determining social 'class'. The social structure of the third culture, however, was different in that_the two principal organisations involved in the colonial relationship, the army and the government bureaucracy, were themselves both characterised by a high degree of functional differentiation and stratification.

Moreover, as members of the incoming culture were obliged not merely to recognise but also to work within what they perceived to be the highly stratified and caste-conscious social categories of the host society, it followed that their own awareness of status, and their notions of stratification, were magnified as a result of the contact between them. The colonial society which emerged from this contact was one whose members accepted the notion of a highly stratified society where each role carried its own status characteristics and conferred its relevant privileges.

It followed, therefore, that every member of the society, particularly metropolitan newcomers, had to be socially located. This was not simply for informal, social reasons so that each actor knew 'where he stood' in relation to others in the hierarchy. Much more prac-tical issues were involved. For example, should a newcomer arrive whose designated role did not fit into the known order of precedence, difficulties were experienced in allocating him the 'relevant' accommodation, pay or allowances. Was the British Royal Air Force corporal (Technical, Signals) equivalent in status to the Indian Office Superintendant (Railway Audit)? Did the Visiting Assistant Chaplain (Temporary) qualify for accommodation in the first- or second-class European hotel?

Arising from these and more important questions of status, it was logical that elaborate instruments should be developed to ensure that official hierarchies were known, recognised and observed in the ordering of social behaviour. For members of the army and government services, the most important of such instruments was the 'Warrant of Precedence' which laid down the hierarchy of official government roles. Where they occupied official posts, members of the indigenous society were obviously included within this.

The 'Warrant of Precedence' lists some 175 roles, classified into 61 basic positions. Taking those most likely to be permanently or temporarily resident in the capital city, a selection of them can be given, along with their numbered positions, as illustrative of the impact of colonial bureaucracy on the social structure of the city.

1   The Governor General and
      Viceroy
4   Commander-in-Chief
8   Members of the Governor
      General's Executive
      Council
11 President of the Legislative
      Assembly
14 Chief Commissioner of
      Railways
    General Officers Commanding
    Officers of the rank of
      General
20 Chief Judges
21 Lieutenant Generals
    Chief Commissioner of Delhi
23 Air Officer Commanding, RAF
      in India
    Members of the Railway Board
    Secretaries to the Govern-
      ment of India
    Vice Chairman, Imperial
      Council of Agricultural
      Research
24 Additional Secretaries to
      Government of India
    Members of the Central Board
      of Revenue
26 Consulting Engineer to the
      Government
    Director-General, Indian
      Medical Services
    Director-General, Posts &
      Telegraphs
    Major-Generals
27 Vice-Chancellors of Indian
      universities
29 Members of the Indian Civil
      Service of 30 years
      standing whose position
      but for this article
      would not be lower than
      Article 34
33 Accountants General Class I
    Brigadiers
    Chief Controller of Stores
    Director-General of
      Archaeology
    Chief Commissioner of Delhi
35 Private Secretary to the
      Viceroy
    Secretaries, Additional
      Secretaries and Joint
      Secretaries to Local
      Government

36 Chief Engineers
    Financial Adviser, Posts &
      Telegraphs
    Members of the Indian Civil
      Service and Indian
      Political Service of 23
      years standing
42 Deputy Secretaries to the
      Government of India
    Director General of
      Commercial Intelligence
    Director General of
      Public Information
44 Civilian Superintendant of
      Clothing Factories
    Deputy-Director-General,
      Indian Medical Services
    Colonels
    Superintending Engineers
46 Controller of Printing,
      Stamps and Stationery
48 Deputy-Director, Railway
      Board
53 Senior Chaplains, other
      than those already
      specified
56 Principals of major
      Government colleges
    Divisional Engineers and
      Assistant Divisional
      Engineers of 20 years
      standing
57 Under-Secretaries to the
      Government of India
    Librarian, Imperial Library
59 Majors
    Superintendants and Deputy
      Commissioners of Police
      of more than 15 but
      less than 20 years
      standing
61 Assistant Chief Controller
      of Stores
    Curator of the Board of
      Education
    Examiner of Questioned
      Documents
    Lady Assistants to the
      Inspector General, Civil
      Hospitals
    Assistant Secretaries
    Superintendants of Central
      Jails

Although such a 'Warrant' only applied to holders of official
positions in government, it none the less acted as a reference point
for 'non-officials' outside the government. All female members of
the community 'unless by virtue of holding an appointment themselves
they are entitled to a higher position in the table', took place
according to the rank assigned to their husbands *(Delhi and North
India Directory*, 1932,pp.7-19).

Whilst such a formally legitimised hierarchy is important in indicating
the social position of actors within the 'official' community, in
not including the total population of the city, it fails to give a
comprehensive picture. Criteria other than occupational rank,
therefore, need some consideration.

The most important of such criteria were ethnic and racial, distinctions being made between Europeans, Indians and Anglo-Indians,
(i.e. of mixed European and Indian descent). Such criteria did not
prevent certain of the indigenous society having comparable status
to higher-ranking Europeans. This was particularly the case for
those Indians, frequently highly Westernised in their attitudes
and behaviour, occupying senior government positions, for the
indigenous nobility, or for certain political leaders or indus-
trialists. However, 'other things being equal' such as rank,
seniority or socio-economic status, Europeans had precedence over
Indians.

The next most important distinction was between those occupying
official roles in the government and army, and the 'non-official'
community. Here convention had laid down certain levels of prestige.
Whilst the military had their own system of ranking, an army officer
whose official rank was otherwise similar to that of a government
official was none the less inferior in status. Within the army,
regiments were placed in a careful hierarchy (Allen, 1975,p.90).
Similarly, considerable status differences existed between the
different government services. The highest prestige was conferred
on members of the Indian Civil Service, below which were the Indian
Medical Service, Police Service, Forest Service, Engineering and
other services. A similar hierarchy existed between government
departments such as the Home, Foreign or Public Works. At the lower
levels of government were the Superintendants, Assistants, Stenographers and Clerks, the latter divided into first, second and third
divisions. It is clear,however, that even a third or 'lower division
clerk' with a permanent appointment, official designation, government
accommodation and pension rights, had considerable status in comparison
to any non-government employees. In all these various roles,
largely, though not entirely, filled by members of the indigenous
society, seniority acted as a further means of differentiation.

In the government-dominated context of Delhi, independent business
wealth had less influence in determining position in the social
hierarchy than in Bombay or Calcutta, where social structure and
criteria of differentiation were more influenced by economic factors.

Further differentiation was introduced by an 'honours' system, with
different 'orders' for members of each cultural section. In these,
a double level of distinction existed, both in the hierarchy of
various 'orders' - 'of the Garter', 'of the Bath', 'Star of India'
and also in the various ranks of appointment, the 'Knight Grand Cross'
'Knight' or 'Member'. For Hindus and Muslims, different titles were
introduced such as 'Rai Bahadur', 'Rai Sahib' and 'Khan Bahadur' and
'Khan Sahib'. Amongst the indigenous nobility, precedence was recognised by the number of guns fired in a 'salute'.

Amongst lower-ranking Indians working in government service, in
addition to occupational rank, pay and seniority, caste, status
of employer or employing department and educational qualifications
added further criteria for differentiation.

Outside military and government service, in terms of the perceptions
of the colonial community, other members of the indigenous population
were 'Indians' or 'natives'. Here, birth, title, wealth or
achievement were recognised criteria for establishing social position.
Caste, however, was not, for the colonial culture, an over-riding
indicator of status. Differentiation at these 'lower' levels was
based rather on what the colonial community perceived as 'character'
or 'moral qualities'. These would find expression in the distinctions made between Muslim, Sikh and Hindu, between Punjabis
or Madrasis, or between regionally located castes such as Jats
and Aggrawals.

The structure of the colonial society suggested here is that which
is likely to have been perceived by a European member of the elite.
The purpose of describing this in some considerable detail is not
only to provide insight into the atmosphere of social hierarchy
which prevailed in the capital city, but also,to suggest the social
structural background against which the physical-spatial forms of
the city emerged.

The contribution which the new capital made to this system of
stratification was to give it manifest physical and spatial expression. Distinctions hitherto informal or unarticulated were now
clarified in the ordered physical-spatial divisions of Delhi. The
surface of the earth and the built forms upon it were designed to
accommodate the conceptual model of a twentieth-century colonial
society.

8 THE RESIDENTIAL REQUIREMENT

Within the hexagonal grids, areas were allocated on criteria of race,
occupational rank and socio-economic status. Five basic types of
area were created: one for 'gazetted officers', mainly though not
entirely European, the second for European 'clerks'; a third was set
aside for indigenous 'clerks' and lower-ranking officials, and a
fourth, for members of the indigenous elite, the nobility of the
'native states'. The fifth area was 'non-official' space, occupied
by those with insufficient rank or status to qualify for a place
within the Imperial City (Figure 10.2).

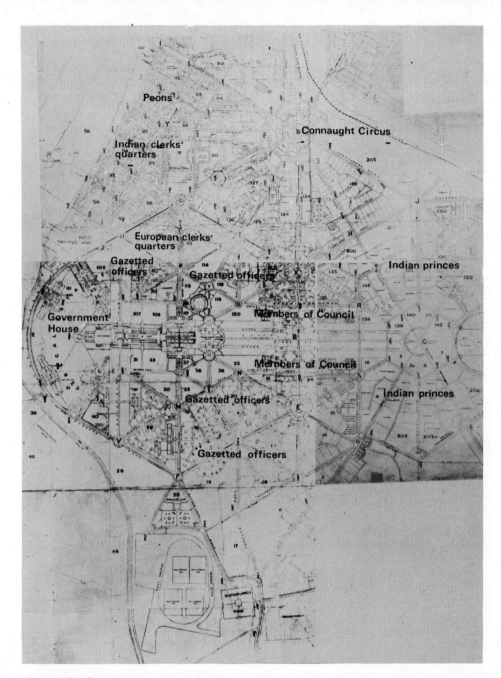

Figure 10.2

In each of these main sectors, accommodation, varying in size of
house and compound, was allocated according to status with the
highest-ranking positions, where possible, nearer to 'Government
House'. From the Viceroy, via the Commander-in-Chief, Members of
the Executive Council, senior gazetted officers, gazetted officers,
down to superintendants, peons, sweepers and *dhobis*, a carefully
stratified spatial order was integrated, both in terms of physical
distance and spatial provision, to the social structure of the city
(Thakore, 1962,p.122).

In front of the 'Secretariat' on either side of the 'Central Vista'
were the 'Honourable Members' of the 'Executive Council'. South of
the 'Vista', the entire area was occupied by 'gazetted officers'.
Officers of lower rank or less seniority, were located on the north
side of the 'Central Vista'.

At the eastern end of the central axis of 'Kingsway' was the 'Princes'
Park'. This, and the surrounding neighbourhood, contained the
extensive compounds of the indigenous elite. The fourth major section,
lying in the north-west between 'Reading Road' and 'Irwin Road', was
allocated to indigenous low-ranking officials. European clerks
occupied a smaller section immediately south of this. These sections
are discussed in detail below.

The status of any particular accommodation was communicated by one
or more of ten indicators: elevation, distance from Government House,
size of compound, size of dwelling, width of road, name of road,
name of area, number and index of house type (e.g. 'Block 4, 1E')
type and quantity of vegetation and the presence or absence of
various facilities. A beginning may be made with the social and
political meaning of nomenclature.

9   URBAN NOMENCLATURE AS A SYMBOL OF COLONIAL TAXONOMY

Thoroughfares were designated according to cultural-historical
criteria, their names derived from the folk heroes of the colonial
past. These included past and present heads of state as well as
political, military and administrative figures whose names were
linked with the development of the colonial society in India. Of
highest prestige were those places linked with the names of the
reigning head of state and of his immediate kin.

The most important ceremonial thoroughfare, between 'Government House'
and the symbolic monument of the reigning monarch situated in 'Princes'
Park' (King George V) was 'Kingsway'. Next in importance, bisecting
the first at right angles and linking the elite area of the city
to the main retailing centre, was 'Queensway'. Adjoining roads,
on either side of the 'Central Vista', containing the dwellings of
'Honourable Members' were respectively 'King Edward' and 'Queen
Victoria' Roads; the ceremonial space fronting 'Government House'
and the 'Secretariat' was 'King Edward Place'; the two roads leading
north and south towards it, 'Queen Mary's' and 'King George's
Avenues'. The three main interchanges were 'York Place', 'Windsor
Place' and 'Connaught Place'.

Next in importance in terms of proximity to Government House were those
thoroughfares designated by the names of leading civilian or military
figures instrumental in establishing colonial power in India, 'Hastings',
'Clive' and 'Dupleix' roads.

Further from Government House, though still marking residential areas of
social importance, were those thoroughfares designated either by the
names of previous indigenous rulers connected with Delhi (Tughluq, Lodi,
Sikandra,Shershah, Humayan, Akbar, Shahjahan, Aurangzeb, Jaisingh) or
of persons filling the pre-eminent political and social role in the
colonial society, that of 'Governor-General' or 'Viceroy' since the early
nineteenth century, as well as their wives (Cornwallis, Wellesley,
Dalhousie, Canning, Lytton, Curzon, Lady Hardinge, Chelmsford, Reading,
Irwin, Lady Irwin, Willingdon). Minor thoroughfares of less social
significance were designated by names of third-culture members connected either with the administrative development of the new capital or
with its physical construction (Hailey, Rouse, Keeling, Lutyens).

Neighbourhoods housing inhabitants lower in status such as those
occupied by clerks, both European and Indian, were designated by names
of leading military figures professionally active at the time the new
capital was constructed (Allenby, Baird, Foch, French, Haig, Joffre,
Pershing). Alternatively, the names were drawn from other military
figures whose activities were instrumental in establishing colonial
power in India (Havelock, Nicholson, Outram, Roberts, Taylor, Wilson,
Lake, Lawrence, Lumsden, Kitchener).

As the introduction of third-culture institutions had been reflected in
'Court Road' and 'Racquet Court Lane' of the Civil Station, so later
institutions were commemorated in 'Club Road', 'Race Course Road',
'Park Road', 'Parliament Street', 'Press Lane' and in the new canton-
ment, by thoroughfares leading to key functional units, 'Bath',
'Cemetery', 'Church', 'Gymnasium', 'Hospital', 'Polo' and 'Station'.

In 1942 some 60 per cent of all named major thoroughfares and residential places in the developed area of Old and New Delhi were designated
by a non-indigenous nomenclature. Of these 150, over half were names
of metropolitan sovereigns, military leaders, viceroys, governors-
general, and local administrators associated with the development of
colonial rule; 17 were associated with the particular institutions of
the urban third culture (cemetery, church, club, court, gymnasium,
hospital, hostel, hotel, library, park, parliament, polo, press, race-
course, racquet court, school, station); 6 had obvious associations
with the military aspects of its development ('Cavalry', 'Esplanade',
'Flagstaff', 'Lancer', 'Parade', 'Military Parade', 'Cantonment');
another 4, with the political processes of imperialism ('Coronation',
'Imperial', 'Princes', 'State Entry'). A few had topographical
connotations ('Hillside', 'Old Mill', 'Ridge','Underhill', 'Upper
Ridge', 'Wall', 'Boulevard', 'The Mall'). Only 3 had economic
connotations ('Factory', 'Farm', 'Market') and another 5 were associated
with the technology of communications and transport ('Canal', 'Chord',
'Electric', 'Grand Trunk' and 'Telegraph').

When one of the first acts of the newly independent state is to modify the nomenclature of its cities, the significance of such an analysis becomes apparent. An examination of this naming system gives insight not only into the degree of cultural dominance but also into the particular nature of that process: the military associations, the political system of empires and monarchies, the particular institutions involved, the high value placed by the colonial culture on the commemorative and symbolic use of military and political figures. The absence of names, either metropolitan, indigenous or of a more univer- sal origin, associated with the worlds of science, religion, education, technology, the arts, commerce and medicine, does not necessarily indicate the absence of institutions in these fields but rather, where they existed, their conscious subordination to the culture to which they belonged (e.g. the *Imperial* Agricultural Research Institute, the *Linlithgow* Library, the *Butler* High School, the *Lady Hardinge* Medical College). (See also Appendix 2).

10   HOUSING CLASSES IN THE COLONIAL CITY

The main residential area consisted of some 3,000 single-storey bungalows and quarters for 'officers, clerks and peons'. The average official compound consisted of a square or rectangular plot which, for 'gazetted officers', varied between one and three acres in size. It contained a centrally placed bungalow, one- or two-gated drive, garage and servants' quarters at the rear (Thakore, 1962,p.146).

In the original plan of 1912, the relationship of size to status in the official hierarchy had been

Members of Council	- 6 acres
Class I officers	- 5 acres
Class II officers	- 4 acres
Class III officers	- 3 acres
Class IV officers	- 3 acres
Others	- $1\frac{3}{4}$ acres

This scale was subsequently revised; sites allotted to the 'ruling princes' varied between 4 and 8 acres, for gazetted officers, 2 to $3\frac{1}{2}$ acres, and $\frac{1}{4}$ acre for Members of the Legislature. Residential sites leased out for private use ranged between 1 and 3 acres though these were subsequently reduced (ibid.,p.236).

The reproduction of the basic bungalow-compound unit, together with main and service roads, paths, the 'tan ride' (see below) and service area clearly meant very low residential densities. By 1940, within the main built-up area in the new city (bounded by Connaught Place, North and South Avenue, Roberts Road, Race Course Road, Club Road, Safdar Jang Road, Lodi Road, Golf Course Road, Pritviraj Road, Hardinge Road and Barakhamba Road) of some $4\frac{1}{2}$ square miles (about twice the size of the indigenous city with its 250,000 inhabitants) some 640 residential units had been laid out, each with its frontage of between 50 and 120 yards (see Figure 10.2).

Figure 10.3

Figure 10.4

Each bungalow-compound unit accurately conformed to the basic model
evolved by the colonial culture over the previous two centuries.
A contemporary record (1927) indicates a completed unit whose
official description, 'Gazetted Officer's Bungalow, Class C', aptly
demonstrates four of the many levels in the system of housing class
(Figure 10.3). Compounds were laid out with extensive lawns to the
front and rear, ample space on the side and with the drive providing
the appropriate visual experience on entry (Figure 10.4). As the
carefully planted vegetation rapidly reached maturity, each unit
became isolated from the next, providing, in the 'classical' dwelling
and modified grounds, a miniature 'estate' on the model of the
metropolitan 'gentry'.

In the north-west corner of the city, enclosed by Irwin and Reading
Roads, was the sector for the indigenous, lower-status assistants,
stenographers and clerks. As elsewhere, the size of the 'quarters'
varied according to the status of their inhabitants. Accommodation
was divided between 'orthodox' and 'unorthodox' Indians and took
the form of single-storey, quadrangular terraces facing on to a
central square.

Along the boundary demarcating the new from the old city and its
suburb of Paharganj, were the laundry, Mohammedan cemetery,
'Conservancy Depot', peons' quarters, and, further removed from
the centre of social power, quarters for the sweepers.

Accommodation for European clerical personnel lay south-east of
that for the indigenous clerks, along Irwin Road. For unmarried
European males, specially designed accommodation existed in the
'chummeries'.

The indigenous elite were located at the Eastern side of the settlement, their distance from the fount of authority compensated for by
the size of their individual territories. Grouped around 'Princes'
Park' were the 6- or 8-acre sites in each of which were the palaces
of the principal indigenous rulers. Along the boundary road of
Hardinge Avenue and Sikandra Road, on the north side of Kingsway,
official bungalows were allotted to indigenous members of the 'Council
of State' or 'upper house' of the newly formed legislature.

The relationship between size of dwelling and occupational status
was reflected in the allocation of resources. Bungalows for
'Honorary Members of Council' cost 89,000 rupees, those for 'gazetted
officers', between 40,000 and 44,000 rupees. 'Class I Married
European Clerks' Quarters' cost 8,600 rupees and 'Orthodox Indian
bachelor quarters' (with block rather than individual latrines)
3,200 rupees. Individual units in the 'peons' lines' cost 500 rupees.
A clear scale of values existed where the cost of housing one
'Honourable Member' was equivalent to that for 2 senior gazetted
officers, 10 married European clerks, 40 Indian clerks or 180 Indian
peons (Annual Progress Report, 1924-5,pp.15-41).

Because of the inter-locking of racial, social and occupational indices of stratification, a clear pattern of social and racial

segregation was established throughout the city. Beginning at
Government House, this followed an anti-clockwise direction running
round the centre and finishing on the boundaries of Paharganj. It
began as white (or pink) at Government House, continued - with the
addition of some acculturated, senior Indians - as white round the
south side of Kingsway, became increasingly brown on the north side
of the city until, with the addition of European and Anglo-Indian
clerks in the north-west, it shaded fully into brown in the Indian
clerks' quarters, and into darker shades, with the peons' and sweepers
section to their north. Symbolically, the 'Anglo-Indians', 'caught
between two strongly hierarchical cultures and looked down upon by
both' (Allen, 1975,p.90), were located outside the walls of the
indigenous city and on the perimeter of the imperial capital
(Figure 10.2).

11 STATUS IN THE CITY: SOCIAL AREAS

By 1925, the entire residential scheme was virtually complete. Five
years later, the prestige of each area had been established.

According to the *New Delhi Directory*, 1929-30 (Bhargava, 1930), just
under 3,000 government officials were living in New Delhi and the
Civil Lines in 1930. Of these, about 500 were 'senior officers',
about 350 of whom were European. The remainder were primarily Indian,
with a proportion of Anglo-Indians. Of the rest, 225 were of the
rank of 'Superintendant', some 883 were 'Assistants', 95 were
stenographers and 1,266 were clerks. In addition to listing all
government positions, together with the names of those occupying them,
Bhargava's 'Directory' also includes a separate list indicating the
addresses of all government employees. Though not fully comprehensive,
it permits the following analysis.

Taking the numbered ranks indicated in the 'Warrant of Precedence'
and plotting these against residential allocation, some insight
can be gained into the relative social status of each road in the
new imperial city. This suggests the following socio-spatial hierarchy

  1 York Place
     (Ranks 8-24; Additional Secretaries and above)
  2 Hastings Road
     (Ranks 8-26; Major Generals and above)
  3 York Road
     (Ranks 8-42; Deputy Secretaries and above)
  4 King George's Avenue
     (Ranks42-3; mainly Deputy Secretaries and Brigadiers)
  5 Dupleix Road
     (Ranks 36-46; Lieutenant Colonels and above)

followed by Clive Road, Akbar Road, Aurangzeb Road, Kushak Road and
Queensway for the higher ranks in the military and civilian
bureaucracy.

In this way, the roads can be ranked, with reasonable accuracy, throughout most of the capital area, from Ashoka Road, with its complement
of Assistant Secretaries, General Service Officers (Grade 2), (mainly
captains and majors) down to the clerical quarters in the north-west.
Irwin Road was largely confined to Indian Assistants, Stenographers
and Clerks. Allenby Road and Mahadeo Road, still in the European
section of the city, but adjoining the indigenous clerks' quarters,
accommodated Europeans of the ranks of Superintendant and Assistant,
Mahadeo Road mainly European assistants. Accommodation for low-
ranking European Assistants, Royal Air Force Corporals and clerks
was provided in the 'Chummeries'. Lawrence, Haig, Edward, Raja
Bazaar and other 'squares' were the province of Indian clerks, though
their place in the general hierarchy, distinguished by seniority and
pay, was recognisable from the difference in type of dwelling,
manifest in the house-number (e.g. 5C or 5D).

The nature of bureaucracy evident in these residential patterns is
best illustrated by indicating the occupational roles associated
with some of the various thoroughfares.(The house numbers are indicated alongside these roles).

York Place
1 Adjutant-General(Lt.General)
2 Director of Railway Audit
3 Additional Secretary (Home
     Department)
4 Auditor-General, Member of
     the Viceroy's Council
5 Member, Public Service
     Commission

King George's Avenue
1 Officer on Special Duty
     (Finance)
2 Joint Secretary (Home,
     Education and Land
     Department)
4 Officiating Joint Secretary
     (Home, Education and
     Land Department)
6 Secretary (Home, Education
     and Land)
8 Director, Civil Engineering
     (Railways)

Cantonment Road(later Irwin Road)
27D Assistant (Commerce)
28   Clerk
29D Assistant (Commerce)
32B Assistant (Commerce)
35   Superintendant (Commerce)
38   Stenographer (Finance)

Raja Bazaar Square
2D Assistant (Central Bureau
      of Revenue)
5D Assistant (Home Department)
5E Clerk (Foreign & Political)
5C Assistant (Military
      Secretary's Branch)

For the large, floating population of 'officers on special duty',
technical advisers and those not yet allocated housing, hostels,
clubs and hotels existed. The most prestigious of these were the
'Imperial Delhi Gymkhana Club', located between Club, Race Course
and Safdarjang Roads, and the 'Swiss', 'Cecil', 'Clark's' and
'Maiden's' hotels in the Civil Lines. With a small occupational
community of 3,000, consciousness of occupational rank in the working
environment was conveyed, by a multitude of symbols, to the residential
setting. In many cases, persons of equivalent rank, working in the

same department, lived in the same block of accommodation. Status
consciousness and the symbols by which it was known were as visible
as in the traditional caste-community of the indigenous village.

12   THE INSTITUTION OF RELIGION

Religious needs in the colonial and indigenous communities were
accommodated in appropriate places and forms. In the original plan
the official church of the colonial community had been placed
forward, and immediately left of Government House, occupying a
position symmetrically opposite the house of the Commander-in-
Chief which lay forward and to the right of the Viceregal residence.
In this arrangement, the symbolic significance of the relationship
between these three units is more easily perceived: the head of the
government is located prominently on the highest knoll. On his left,
the head of the religious system, to his right, the head of the
military system. The triangle connecting the heads of these three
core institutions of civil government, military organisation and
religion occupied a key position in the capital. (I am indebted to
Bijit Ghosh for this insight).

Other central parts of the city were made available to other
religious groups. 'Methodist' and 'Baptist chapels' were built.
A 'Roman Catholic' cathedral and convent, occupying an extensive
site, was opened in 1935. This was in a relatively low-status area
of the city on Irwin Road and lay between the residential sector of
the European, Anglo-Indian and Indian clerks. It accommodated the
estimated population of some 3,000 Roman Catholics in Delhi which,
in the early 1920s had consisted of 'soldiers, Europeans, Anglo-
Indians and pure Indians' *(Delhi Report*, 1921-2,p.67). Other central
city sites were made available to two metropolitan religious
organisations, the 'Young Mens' and 'Young Womens' Christian
Association' to establish premises offering temporary accommodation
(ibid.,p.35).

The needs of indigenous government employees were met by allocating
land situated on the boundary of their residential sector. Here,
the principal Hindu temple was erected, financed by a leading indigenous industrialist (the Birla Temple), its massive form providing an appropriate cultural symbol to the main area of indigenous
habitation. Close to the Birla Temple, were other indigenous places
of worship: the Mahabodi and Kalibari Temples, and, for Indian
Christians, a separate church of St Thomas. A Hindu cremation ground
and Muslim cemetery existed on the edge of the clerks' quarters. In
the same area, appropriately near the quarters of government employees
of mixed European and Indian descent, a separate cemetery was established for Indian Christians, the main Christian cemetery being in
Pritviraj Road, south-east of the European side of the city.

13   THE EDUCATIONAL REQUIREMENT

For the size of the new city, relatively little provision was made
for education. For the European population, their children 'at
home' or 'in the hills', this was hardly a priority. In 1931 it
was official government policy for European education to 'concentrate
schools in the hills' (ibid.,1930-1,p.116). In the early stages of
the capital, the European population had been mainly one of unaccompanied males. The number of European children had been insufficient
to keep even a small 'station school' going in the Civil Lines 'the
schools would have had more children had not some ladies started
classes in their bungalows'(ibid.,1929-30,p.67). In 1924, there
were only 40 European children to cater for and these were accommodated
by the religious associations of the community, in so-called 'Convent'
schools. As the number grew to 134 by 1932 another 'Convent School'
was begun (ibid.,1924-5,p.16). In terms of the influence of the
metropolitan society on the educational institutions of the indigenous
culture, 1924-5 is of interest in that 'it was marked by the increased
number of students who have actually gone abroad - five students
proceeded to England' from among the 1,015 students in Delhi
University in that year. The Students' Advisory Committee was
dealing with 20 applications for overseas education a year (ibid.,
see also 1932-3,p.117).

In this context, it is less surprising that the original spatial
allocation for educational institutions in the city, of two large
sectors south-east of Connaught Place (Thakore, 1962,p.118) was
subsequently withdrawn on grounds of economy. The university,
temporarily established in the temporary 'Government House' and old
Civil Station cantonment in 1922, was subsequently allotted to this
site on a permanent basis. The sector in the new city, earlier
earmarked for secondary schools and the university,was taken over
for government housing. (After its foundation in 1922, the University
remained uncertain of its permanent location or the extent of its
facilities for the next few years. In 1928 the temporary Vice-
regal Lodge (earlier the Punjab Circuit House) was permanently
handed over to it and the various Indian states asked to contribute
towards providing residence halls for students. By 1931, the
university had 2,033 students (*Delhi Reports*, 1924-5, 1927-8,
1928-9, 1931-2). By way of comparison, forty years later it had -
including 'corresponding' students - over 83,000).

Where educational provision was made for the indigenous inhabitants,
it was established, logically enough, in the old city. Here, by the
1920s, some 200 primary schools were supported from government sources,
although almost all of them existed in rented premises (ibid.,
1921-2,p.66). Similarly, the main institutions of higher education,
both of indigenous and 'missionary' origin, were likewise in the old
city before being moved to the Civil Lines site. (These included
Hindu College, the Arabic College, St Stephens' and Tibbia College).

The major exceptions to this pattern were the one school and two
colleges located in the new cultural enclave of New Delhi and oriented,
appropriately, to culturally new forms of education. In 1921, an

official report referred to the 'Modern School' in Barakhamba Road,
'a preparatory school on Western lines for the sons of the wealthy
classes' (ibid., 1921-2,p.65). 'Lady Irwin' and 'Lady Hardinge
Colleges' were equally oriented to Western forms in the area of
female medical education. By 1935, there was 'a very large demand
from Indian parents' for admission to the schools run primarily for
European children, although prevailing regulations kept their numbers
down to a proportion of 15 per cent of the total (ibid., 1934-5,p.124).

14   ECONOMIC INSTITUTIONS

In contrast to the residential provision in the city, retailing and
marketing took second place. In the two decades between 1911 and
1931, the economic needs of the colonial community continued to
affect sections of the old city rather than the new. This was
particularly so in the traditional European enclave of Kashmiri Gate.

The use of the Civil Station as the temporary capital reinforced this
trend. As the station itself typically provided few facilities (the
European 'drapers', 'milliners', 'dress-makers' and 'lingerie') the
neighbourhood of Kashmiri Gate emerged as an area of specialised
Western trading. The influx of Europeans between 1911 and 1921, low
in number though high in status, was followed by institutions to
meet their needs. By 1931, Kashmiri Gate had become the principal
entrepot for the diffusion of Western goods and services into Delhi.
Here, mainly for a European population whose members stayed for one
or two 'tours', were retailers supplying culture-specific needs of
residence, clothing, diet and recreational and social behaviour:
five furniture stores, 'cabinet makers', 'monumental sculptors and
coffin makers' ('tombstones erected in all parts of India'), two
tailors, a shoe shop ('for best English shoes'), chemists, con-
fectioners, a dairy farm, mineral water suppliers, and two wine and
spirit stores ('under European management'). Particular recreational
needs were catered for with three 'sports outfitters', two arms and
ammunition shops, a 'saddler', motor supplier, three photographic
dealers, and a European-owned catering firm offering 'afternoon teas,
parties, dinners, suppers and banquets supplied and catered for in
the best style under European supervision'. A jeweller's and 'art
and curio store' catered for surplus wealth and specialised services
such as those of the accountant, commercial agent, auctioneer (essential for the disposal of furniture on the completion and commencement
of a 'tour'), two banks and a hairdresser were also available.

For goods and services peculiar to the itinerant nature of government
roles, specialised services were available. The 'English Warehouse'
offered 'furniture hired out, houses furnished' and the 'Western
Stores, General Merchants and Importers of High Class Provisions'
supplied the various equipment required by the eating, adornment,
social and ceremonial behaviour of the colonial community, including
'crockery, glass-ware, cutlery, toilet requisites, fancy goods,
camp furniture, EPNS novelties'. Seasonal rituals were catered for
in the importing of 'Christmas season presentation goods, toys and
crackers'; other firms 'under European management' catered for the

specific needs of the itinerant official, fulfilling multiple functions
as 'House and commission agents, builders, decorators, estate agents,
rent collectors, loaders and unloaders, rickshaw and servant
suppliers' (see advertisements in Bhargava, 1930 and also *Delhi and
North India Directory*, 1932).

For less frequent needs, or those more easily supplied by the indigenous population, the main retailing outlets were in Chandni Chowk
and other parts of the old city where 'oriental perfumes, cloth and
silk' were purchased. Other favoured marketing areas lay, like
Kashmiri Gate, on the edge of the old city, the frontiers dividing
old from the new (Burn Bastion, Egerton and Nicholson Roads).

The new marketing centre, established mid-way between old and new
cities (Figure 10.5), was slow to start and only gradually attracted
any but the largest of concerns. The lay-out, visual characteristics
and scale of 'Connaught Place' conformed to the cultural norms of the
new capital. As transport was always available to the New Delhi
residents, Connaught Place was located some two to three miles from
the elite residential areas. It comprised a circular 'shopping parade'
divided into various blocks. In contrast to the narrow, tightly-knit,
linear bazaars of the indigenous city, adapted to pedestrian needs,
the spacious, circular lay-out of Connaught Place, with its colonnaded
frontage, tree-lined pavements and extensive perimeter distances,
was geared to the needs of the new, car-driving elite of New Delhi
(Figures 10.6, 10.7). Chauffeured cars could be driven to the store
into which the customer could walk and be attended to by the numerous
assistants. From here, a drive further round the place, to the
'Empire Stores' or a suitable restaurant, would complete the afternoon's activities.

> Usually a friend of mine drove me to shop in Delhi; her car was
> much bigger than mine. In the back she took two bull terriers...
> to guard any parcels.
>   Not infrequently we stopped for 'elevenses' at Davicoes (in
> Connaught Place), an excellent patisserie, which provided hot
> chocolate and cream and rich cakes, and not only that but gossip
> as well (Stokes-Roberts, 1959,p.66. The period described was in
> the early 1930s.).

Retailers from the old city were slow to take up premises here, de-
terred by high rents and the seeming dependence on the European,
Westernised Indian and government service population of the city.
Earliest to come were government departments such as the Railways
and Post Office, and large metropolitan firms and organisations,
previously based in Calcutta. By 1930, those European and Indian
retailers particularly catering to the Western and Westernised market
had moved in: banks, upholsterers, caterers, chemists, cloth merchants,
drapers and dressmakers, some five general merchants, three hair-
dressers, an insurance company, a firm of architects, three 'milliners',
a tobacconist, winesellers, a music shop, furniture suppliers, photographers, stationers and Western food stores. (Some retailers, such
as the 'music shop' selling 'pianos' and 'sheet music' were almost
entirely dependent on the patronage of the immigrant community. With
its departure, the 'music shop' led a precarious existence, its inside

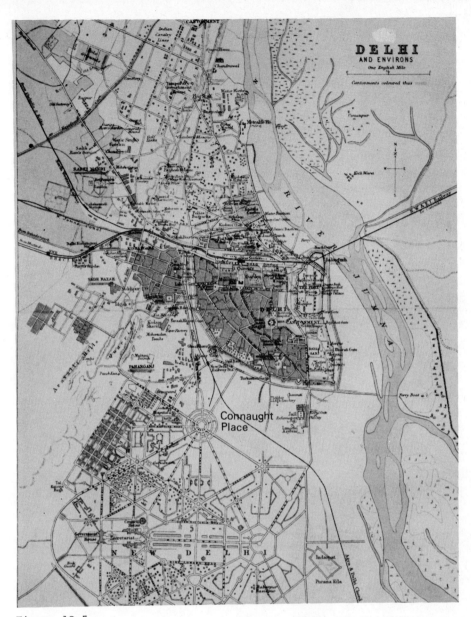

Figure 10.5

Figure 10.6

Figure 10.7

walls still, in 1970, adorned with pictures of the musical folk heroes
of earlier colonial decades - Harry Roy, Geraldo, Evelyn Laye, Albert
Sandler. Its economic future was saved, not by a revived interest in
the music of the West, but of the East, and patronised by Western
visitors).

Other smaller shopping areas, less important for the European
population but relying on trade from lower-status government employees,
were situated near the clerks' quarters, in Panchkuin Road, Baird Road,
Round Market and Gole Market. Here were located the main suppliers of
pedal cycles. Motor car suppliers were appropriately in Kashmiri
Gate, Queen's Gardens and Underhill Road in the Civil Station.

The establishment of these shops had important cultural effects. With
the European and Westernised Indian elite acting as reference groups
for everyday social behaviour such as were associated with eating,
sitting, sleeping, entertaining and other leisure activities, growing
numbers of the indigenous population, having access to the necessary
artefacts of cutlery, crockery, chairs, tables, curtaining, upholstery,
increasingly purchased these and incorporated them into their own
forms of behaviour.

As the adoption of such material artefacts of the colonial culture
increased, traditional life-styles were changed. House forms, previously adapted to indigenous values and behaviour, were increasingly
affected by those of the dominant newcomer. Increasingly, two styles
of behaviour developed, to be adopted for relevant situations. One,
suited to the traditional environment, involved the wearing of loose-
fitting, traditional clothes, sitting cross-legged on the floor,
eating with the fingers, consuming traditional foods and cooking with
traditional metal vessels. The other, appropriate for the Western
or European environment of New Delhi, involved the wearing of tight-
fitting, European dress, sitting on chairs, at a table, eating with
metal implements, utilising extensive numbers of vessels, consuming
unaccustomed forms of food and participating in new forms of social
behaviour.

An institution which did much to foster such change was the hotel,
of which many were built in the early development of the new capital.
Each hotel, however, catered primarily for either an indigenous or
European clientele, and was situated in the appropriate area of the
city. Apart from the 'Imperial' on Queensway and the 'Marina' in
Connaught Place, the other major European hotels were, 'under European
management' in the Civil Lines: the 'Alexandra', 'Clarke's', the
'Swiss', the 'Cecil', 'Woodlands' and 'Maiden's' 'situated in the
best position opposite the Club... and owned and *managed* by an
Englishman of long Indian experience' (Murray, 1913, advertisement).
For the indigenous population, the 'Delhi Punjab Hindu Hotel' had
opened in 1911 ('with open courtyards to all rooms'), the 'Sharma'
in 1912, and the 'Vishnu Hindu', 'Rajmahal', 'Hindu', 'Royal Hindu'
and 'Ibrahim Bombay', some years later (Prasad, 1918, advertisements).
By 1935, the distinctive provision for members of each culture was
sufficiently taken for granted for guides to list two sets of hotels:
those 'under European management and those under Indian management'.

Adopting the social categories of the metropolitan culture an indigenously produced guide announced that 'Delhi claims sufficient
and good accommodation for all races' (Arora, 1935,p.94).

Apart from the economic needs of the local European population the
new capital also accommodated nation-level institutions. Three of
these, the airport, 'All-India Radio Station' and the 'Imperial
Agricultural Research Institute' all depended on the diffusion of
science and technology from the metropolitan society, mainly since
the foundation of the capital.

15   SOCIAL INSTITUTIONS

Accommodation for the associational behaviour of the colonial
community followed previously established patterns. A wider variety
of institutions, however, was now made available.

The foremost of these, catering for the large numbers of unaccompanied
males in the capital, were the two clubs, the 'Imperial Delhi
Gymkhana' and the 'Chelmsford'.

Of these, that with highest prestige was the 'Gymkhana', located in
the elite residential sector of the city, south-east of Kingsway.
Membership was confined to Europeans. The 'Gymkhana', opened in
1928, had twenty-four residential units which, with its 'spacious
grounds... and tennis courts' formed 'one of the main attractions
of New Delhi, apart from supplying a long felt want' *(Delhi Report,*
1928-9,p.60). In addition, it offered a swimming pool, extensive
gardens, bars, billiard room, library, reading room, dining and
dancing facilities as well as easy access to surrounding facilities.
Within half a mile were the race-course, three polo grounds, the
Commander-in-Chief's residence, the Willingdon airport, and the main
residential area of senior gazetted officers. The Chelmsford Club,
somewhat lower in status, had both European and Indian members and
lay slightly north of the 'Central Vista'.

Over the years, the concept of the club had become increasingly
popular with members of the indigenous population. For decades
excluded from membership of the 'English Clubs', they started their
own. The 'New Delhi Club', had been established early in the development of the new city and was located at the south end of the
Indian clerical enclave. Like the 'Talkatora Club' in 'Park Lane'
it had a membership mainly of indigenous government officers. The
'Madras Club', located in 'Block 95' of the 'Orthodox Chummeries',
was patronised mainly by South Indians. On the edge of Queen's
Gardens, now largely abandoned as an area of European pursuits,
members of a Westernising Indian society set up their own institutions,
the 'Bench and Bar Club', 'Chartered Bank Club', 'Municipal Club',
and 'Northern Railway Club', where all the officiating officers
were Indian (Prasad, 1918).

A further social need was accommodation in the event of illness. Because of their demographic characteristics, controlled environment and availability of resources, the colonial community was less in need of this than were members of the indigenous society. Where sickness occurred, senior-ranking officials were treated in the spacious surroundings of their bungalows. Where more specialised treatment was required, the 'Willingdon' and 'Irwin' hospitals existed in the new city. Other hospitals, founded either by missionary or voluntary institutions, were located in the indigenous city. The 'Hindu Rao' hospital, located in the first European suburban 'mansion' in the Civil Lines dating from 1828 was, despite its name, appropriately reserved for members of the colonial community.

16   THE ACCOMMODATION OF RECREATIONAL ACTIVITIES

Recreational provision was based on the traditional, institutionalised activities of the colonial culture, now expanded by technological innovations diffused from the metropolitan society. As many of these pursuits involved considerable numbers of people situated in any one place at a given time, or alternatively, movement within a given area, extensive spatial demands were made by them on the capital.

One set of recreational activities was linked to the use of the horse, an animal whose role in the governmental, social and recreational activities of the third culture has so far been ignored.

Despite the fact that by 1920 the automobile had made the horse obsolete as a system of elite, personal urban transport in most of the cities of the West, values long inherent in the colonial culture continued to place horse-related pursuits at the centre of recreational life. Moreover, because of the high proportion of military and civilian officials among the population of Delhi, whose professional role required equestrian skills, the provision of facilities to acquire them can be seen as an essential need. A military member of the community refers to 'the tyranny of the horse, which was regarded as... (an) object of worship... one lived and talked horses'. According to another informant, female members 'were perpetually jumping on and off horses' (Allen, 1975,pp.95,111).

Of the various activities taking place in the 'Delhi Season', the two most important were the 'Annual Imperial Horse Show' and the 'Annual All-India Polo Tournament' (Arora, 1935,p.99). Other horse-related activities included those recreational pursuits common to the elite of the metropolitan society; in Delhi, these were the meetings of the 'Delhi Hunt', the competitions at the Delhi Race-Course and the daily activity of 'riding'.

The provision for these activities, pursued by the European and indigenous elite of the city, had important effects on its lay-out. In the south of the city, the race-course, in use from 1926, enclosed four polo grounds and occupied about half a square mile to the south of the Gymkhana Club. Less usual, and possibly unique to the city of Delhi, was a 'tan ride', a specially constructed roadway, running parallel to the main avenues in the city, for use in daily equestrian exercise (this went along Ridge Road, Roberts Road, King George's Avenue, Dupleix Road, Aurangzeb Road, Queensway to Connaught Place). Stables as well as garages were provided in the larger of Delhi compounds

Activities such as the 'Horse Show' and meetings of the 'Delhi Hunt' also provided the occasion for the associated forms of social be- haviour, the 'Horse Show Ball' and 'Annual Delhi Hunt Ball'. Such 'balls' were held in different venues, including the clubs, the 'officers' mess', the Civil Station hotels and hired accommodation in Connaught Place.

With the concentration of government officials in Delhi and the more efficient communication network provided by rail, air, car and tele- phone, entertaining and inter-dining increased in importance as a recreational pursuit of the community. The relatively low cost of food and the availability of labour for domestic service, encouraged a practice long favoured in the colonial community. Now, with a purpose-built environment, institutionalised forms of eating could be freely pursued: breakfast on the verandah, 'morning coffee', 'lunchtime receptions', 'afternoon tea', the 'garden party, 'drinks' and 'dinner' all ensured that the one- to three-acre compound had frequent use through the cooler months of the year.

The garden provided a constant place of recreation, for the cul- tivation of plants, the growing of vegetables, bird-watching and relaxation through the exercise of visual, aural and olfactory senses. (Significantly, the only book to have been written in recent years by a British High Commissioner on his experiences in India is M. Macdonald's *Birds in my Indian Garden* (1960)).

Having established the large number of extensive compounds in the new city, mechanisms were developed by which the new values needed for the continuation of this environment would be institutionalised in the indigenous population. In 1922 an 'Annual Flower Show and Vegetable Show' was instituted, with the express object of 'giving an impetus to private gardening in the city' *(Delhi Report,* 1921-2,p.33).

Recreational activities popular among middle and upper classes in the metropolitan society were also introduced. This was especially the case with 'tennis', 'cricket' and 'golf'. Club grounds were made sufficiently large for 'tennis courts' and 'swimming pools'. 'Tennis courts' were also provided in the larger compounds as well as in Kudsia Park and Queen's Gardens, where they were maintained by the Metropolitan Council.

To replace the golf links opened near the old cantonment in the late nineteenth century, a much larger course was laid down. This, situated between Wellesley, Cornwallis and Lodi Roads, covered an area of over half a square mile. By 1935, it was perceived by govern- ment officials as 'a usual centre of attraction for the public', the monthly number of players being just over 400 (ibid.,1934-5,p.54).

During the cooler months, riding, walking and the occasional picnic were possible in the area of the Ridge, west of the city. This, subject to an intense programme of arboriculture, had become designated as 'Reserved Forest', not available for further urban development. On the highest points on the Ridge, at Malcha, Raisina and Kushak, 'views' were marked on the map. Here, joining the Upper Ridge Road to Reading Road at the foot, was a further recreational area transferred from the metropolitan environment, 'Lovers' Lane'.

By 1931, the diffusion of recreational pursuits from the colonial culture was sufficient for the Municipal authority to maintain 18 tennis courts, 5 football grounds, 5 hockey pitches and two cricket grounds. Cricket, increasingly adopted by the acculturated elite, was particularly favoured. With the erection of the 'Willingdon Pavilion' it was the object of Delhi and District Cricket Club to make Delhi 'the home of cricket in India' (ibid.,1931-2,p.14).

New forms of technology extended the scope of recreational pursuits. Cinemas had been introduced, both in the old and new city, those patronised by Europeans being in Kashmiri Gate (the 'Capitol' and 'Roxy') and Connaught Place ('Plaza' and 'Regal') and for the indigenous community in Chandni Chowk (the 'Krishna'). By 1920, motorised transport had made possible the steep ascent up to the particular Delhi hill stations of Simla, Mussoorie and Kasauli. In the following two decades, car-ownership among the elite was to become sufficiently widespread for the nearest hill stations to become the object of 'week-end' visits, as well as the long-term summer stay. With the introduction of the aeroplane and opening of 'Willingdon Airport' near Safdarjang's tomb, the Delhi Flying Club added a further dimension to elite recreational pursuits.

   'Balls, picnics, and parties', as an American song says, is the
   keynote of high official life in Delhi, the winter capital, and
   in Simla, the summer capital. During the so-called cold-weather
   season in Delhi, life is just one whirl of gaiety. Horse Show
   week is particularly marvellous. Balls, picnics and parties;
   visitors come from miles around. The American tourists in comic
   topees travel hundreds of miles from Bombay... Indian princes
   bringing magnificent jewels leave their native States to add
   splendour to Delhi. European women in the latest Parisian
   creations; Indian princesses in gorgeous saris; officers in their
   colourful mess jackets; the jingle of spurs; the throb in the
   throttles of expensive motor-cars; the pawing and stamping of
   four-legged thoroughbreds; cricket matches, picnics, gymkhanas,
   colourful life. Against this kaleidoscopic background the Government of India carries on (Greenwall, 1933,p.161).

17   SOCIO-SPATIAL STRUCTURE IN THE CITY: A COMMENT

The Delhi which had been created was one built for two different worlds, the 'European' and the 'native', for the ruler and the ones who were ruled. This notion of dualism is the starting point for any explanation of the size and structure of the city.

Like the early cantonments, Delhi was built on the principle of
duplication, of providing separate and different provision for each
cultural section in the city. Thus, where the cantonment had 'British
barracks' and 'native lines', the colonial city had 'Imperial Delhi'
and the 'native town'.

The principle of duplication did not stop at the local level. To
conform to cultural preferences, the 'cold weather' capital 'on the
plains' was duplicated by a 'summer capital' 'in the hills'(Simla).
Within the city, further duplication of space arose from the need
to accommodate cultural behaviour at different seasons of the year.
Thus, the activities of the colonial community had to be accommodated
both outside and inside the house and unlike the indigenous courtyard
house, the bungalow did not provide sleeping space on the roof. The
spatial areas which resulted from this duplication of provision and
the cultural factors which governed their size were made possible
by the distribution of power. Whilst a combination of technology
and economic forces were pushing urban forms *upwards* in the metropolitan society, in the city of Delhi, colonialism was forcing them
outwards. When time is short, space is conserved. When time is
plentiful, space is consumed. In the industrialised West, people
increasingly saved time: in the colonial East, Europeans spent it,
consuming extensive urban space in the process.

Though each bungalow-compound unit was similar to those of the Civil
Station of the past, the lay-out of Imperial Delhi was different.
The Civil Station had grown gradually, by accident, over the years.
Relatively haphazard and unarranged, it was an informal provision
for a community, expressed in a cultural way.

New Delhi, however, was very different. The measured, symmetrical
grid was evidence of three levels of colonial control. It expressed
total control over the environment, with the power to define boundaries and order the spaces within them; it represented total control
over the social structure, the power to order precedence, create
communities and control social relations between them. Third, it
expressed total control over the process of allocation; once the
places were created they would be filled according to plan.

In this way, an abstract 'social structure' existing in the mind and
expressed in behaviour, was literally concretised into reality by the
physical-spatial forms on the ground. Only in the very last years of
colonial rule did the colonial power begin to have second thoughts on
the lay-out of the city (Breeze, 1974,p.19).

In the elite area south of the 'Vista' factors additional to the
political and cultural accounted for the further consumption of space.
Delhi, in common with other colonial societies (see Balandier,
1951,p.46) had large military and civilian communities whose European
population was predominantly male, relatively young, with few children
and fewer old. Apart from the very young, children were either 'at
Home' or 'in the hills'. The aged or those who might possibly have
been so, were either 'at Home' or were dead. Because all military
and civilian personnel were medically tested before being put into

service, the population was healthy, active, even athletic. Consequently, the lack of schools, nurseries and hospitals was compensated by ample provision for horse-riding facilities, gardens, polo grounds and facilities for social interaction like the club. For these and other reasons, the place of the Central Business District in many colonial settlements was occupied by the club, golf links and race-course (see p.280).

Moreover, as this pre-selected population was characterised by middle-class values and behaviour, their environment was adapted to suit. The senses had been educated and modelled according to metropolitan taste. 'Visual' experiences were important and 'nature' had to surround every house. Such 'ex-urban' ideologies with their notions of seclusion and isolation combined with deference to reference groups 'at Home' to make the elite area of Delhi into a series of 'private spaces', each an individual unit in itself. These values were essentially those of an urban middle and upper class for whom the dichotomy between urban and rural ('town' and 'country') had long been apparent. Such attitudes were as typical of those professionally concerned with the 'design' of New Delhi as those who lived there.

It is worth noting that the fundamental distinction between 'town' and 'country' in metropolitan categories of environment does not, even for 'Westernised Indians', exist in relation to the Indian environment. Neither the term 'country', least of all 'countryside', with the connotations they carry in Britain, exist as environmental categories, except perhaps for a minute elite. Depending on social and economic background, environmental categories are expressed in different ways. Amongst English-speaking Indians (already an indicator of socio-economic status, the number comprising not more than 5 per cent of the total Indian population), those actors temporarily leaving the city would indicate the *place* to which they are going, i.e. 'I am going to Baroda' or frequently, 'to my village' or 'my native place'. The reason for this is clear: journeys are made primarily for reasons of business and kinship matters. The notion of 'holidays' is not one, as in the modern industrial society, of 'getting away from it all', of changing a stressful urban environment for beaches, 'landscapes' or 'nature' but of re-joining kin, and discussing matters such as marriage arrangements, financial problems, the education of siblings. Only occasionally do 'Westernised' Indians of higher status 'go to the hills' or more usually, 'to a hill station'. No one ever spends a 'weekend in the country' because neither'weekend' nor 'country' (in the metropolitan sense) exists. Yet the elite residential areas of Delhi were essential 'country' or at least 'suburban' environments.

Further insights into these basic distinctions can be gained from even a cursory examination of orientations to time in contemporary English-speaking India. References to time are to dates of the month rather than days in the week. 'The meeting will be on the 17th' or 'he gave it me on the 9th' are used where the English practice would be to say 'The meeting will be next Wednesday' or 'a fortnight tomorrow' or 'a week last Friday'. The difference springs from the strong notion of 'weekend' in the industrial society which, dependent on the individual, may be from 'Saturday lunchtime' (or noon), 'Saturday morning' ('breakfast'), or 'after work on Friday' (17.00) to 'Sunday evening' or 'Monday morning' and the different quality or 'characteristics' associated with days in the week. For such notions to be used in India is to invite constant reinterpretation of statements on both sides: 'I'll give it you on Thursday' is greeted by 'that will be on the 17th'; the Indian will say, 'I'll telephone you on the 12th' to which the English response is 'that will be Tuesday?'

An examination of such notions of time current in contemporary Indian society gives important insights, first, into the ordering of time into divisions and their relation to place in the metropolitan society. The notions of the 'weekend' and 'holidays' were bound up with the conceptualisation and categorisation of environment. The concept of a 'vacation', implies not only a change in activity but a change in environment which, in the metropolitan society, meant to a non-urban setting, characterised by culturally preferred landscape items such as 'the sea', 'nature' and 'the country'. For the member of the colonial community the nearest to this was 'the hills'. It is these concepts which come closer to conveying a clearer understanding of the reproduction of 'country' characteristics in the New Delhi environment.

Though separate, the two cities inter-acted and were inter-dependent. As the new monopolised the old, the old serviced the new. Each became a reference point for the other. Within the physical-spatial forms of the new city, the behaviour of the indigenous inhabitants was rapidly adapted to its use. Along with the new forms and spaces came the equipment to fill them - at the domestic level, chairs for dining, relaxing, writing and conversation; beds for sleeping; tables for eating, storing or display. In addition came cutlery, tableware, clothing and *almirahs* (cupboards) and trunks to accommodate them all. Vehicles were needed to move from one distant place in the city to another.

With these material changes in culture came changes in life-styles and social behaviour; in postures for sitting, eating, sleeping, resting, excreting and, to a lesser extent, forms of associational behaviour. With the equipment and its use, the specialised areas of the new house types came into use. The city provided opportunity to break from traditional patterns, its dwellings encouraged new nuclear family structures and the specialisation of internal space permitted new forms of socialisation to occur.

As new occupational roles were created - secretary, sweeper, supervisor or servant - people came into the city to fill them, accepting as part of the process the environment in which they were contained. The status of the son of a Banya shopkeeper living in a rural village in Punjab was exchanged for that of a Lower Division Clerk, residing in D4, Block 3, Outram Square. The son of the Bengali Brahmin teacher became Assistant Secretary (Home Department) living in a Type II bungalow in Ashoka Road. The stratification system of the Indian village was not replaced by the social and spatial structure of the city but was overlaid by it, making the degree of differentiation much more complex.

Associational and recreational behaviour adapted to the new environment. Clubs emerged and metropolitan games were taken up. Spaces set aside for cricket and tennis were utilised and hotels found favourable use. The bicycle became a symbol of social and spatial mobility.

In these and other ways, the multi-functional spaces of the tightly knit old city were replaced by the specialised, single-function spaces of the new. The forms of the city established, the equipment and behaviour were introduced to make it work.

As a 'counterfactual' thesis one might ask what would have happened in Delhi had 'colonial development' not taken place.

Two propositions can be suggested. First, the choice of site for Imperial Delhi was very largely dictated by the total spatial area of even terrain perceived as necessary for the new capital. If this capital was to be within the immediate vicinity of and accessible from Shahjahanabad (and not across the river) the site ultimately chosen was the only possible area of sufficient size which could be used in the particular culture-specific way in which the city was eventually built.

It is clear from the foregoing pages that cultural as well as political factors accounting for spatial use in Delhi determined its size. Had other colonial cultures provided a capital they might have simply taken over and enlarged the indigenous city, built a second city close by in a smaller area and with higher densities, or of course, built one further away, over a larger area and at much lower densities than the New Delhi which was actually constructed.

Second, on the basis of comparison with walled cities in non-industrialised societies unaffected by colonial experience, and of the walled city in what became the industrialised countries of Europe, the other alternative pattern for Delhi's 'non-colonial' development would have been a gradual process of extra-mural accretion around three sides of the city wall. This process had in fact begun during the first decades of the nineteenth century.

18   EFFECTS ON THE INDIGENOUS CITY

The impact of these developments on the old city between 1920 and 1940 was more indirect than direct. The interest in modernisation and renewal expressed at the end of the previous century was now transferred to the new capital whose development absorbed the funds for urban development in the region. The four main local authorities which were created (Old Delhi Municipal Committee, Civil Lines 'Notified Area', New Delhi Municipal Committee and New Delhi Cantonment) effectively divided the cultural areas of the city.

By 1931, the 7 square miles of the old city and its suburbs contained a population of almost 350,000, 28 per cent of the increase in the previous decade directly due to the building of New Delhi (Jagmohan 1975,p.29). In the 9 square miles of the Civil Station and durbar

area, were some 16,000 inhabitants. To the south, the 33 square miles
of New Delhi contained about 65,000 people; in the cantonment over
the ridge, less than 9,000 inhabitants occupied 16½ square miles
(Bopegamage, 1957,p.36).

The difference in densities implied by these figures reflected
different urban systems created on totally different principles.
Having constructed a culturally-modified environment, the colonial
authority had now to maintain it. The vast spatial areas had to be
planted, watered and protected. Government gardens as well as hundreds
of bungalow compounds had to be maintained. Miles of roadway and the
'tan ride' had to be kept up. The broad avenues and the spacious
gardens in the Civil Lines were also not forgotten. In 1929, 86,000
rupees was spent on a scheme for supplying unfiltered water in the
Civil Lines, 'a crying need in the area. The occupiers of bungalows
have to pay heavy bills for filtered water for gardening purposes
and have been clamouring for an unfiltered supply'. In the same year,
some 87,000 rupees was spent on the 'metalled and painted roads in
the Civil Lines' (Delhi Report, 1929-30,pp.40-1).

This is not to say that funds were not available for the old city.
Some 800,000 rupees, for example, had been spent in 1927-8 on
improving the drainage system and one million rupees was spent the
following year on the water supply. Other minor improvements were
attempted. Nevertheless, the differences in access to resources,
as well as expectations and traditions in the two cities, is marked
by the stark differences in vital statistics from them both. Between
1921 and 1931, birth rates in the walled city were between 42 and 57
per 1,000; in the Civil Lines, about 18-22 per 1,000 and in 1932,
in New Delhi, 28 per 1,000

Infant mortality in the walled city ranged from 174 to 253 per 1,000.
In 1913 it had been 346 and in May 1929 it was 512. In the Civil
Lines it was below 10 and in New Delhi in 1932, 82. Death rates
in the old city were between 30 and 47 per 1,000, in the Civil Lines
15-20, and in New Delhi, 9 per 1,000.

Whilst the vastly different demographic structure of each area does
not permit a genuine comparison to be made between these figures,
it is clear that in comparison to any external indices prevailing at
the time, there were startling differences in living standards
(ibid., 1920-30).

As in the previous century, proposals were made to demolish the wall
between the Ajmir and Delhi Gates to relieve congestion in the city.
The proposal was turned down by the central government in 1929
(ibid.,1929-30,p.33). Instead, the area south of the wall was levelled
and grassed over for sports grounds and 'intervening spaces planted
with ornamental and flowering shrubs' (ibid.,1928-9,p.61) effectively
dividing the populations of the two cities. In 1931 the more southern
part of this area was re-developed to provide accommodation for
municipal and government employees (Thakore, 1961,p.188): even then,

Figure 10.8 Elite residence in the colonial culture: Madras first quarter, nineteenth century

Figure 10.9 Elite residence in the colonial culture: Delhi, second quarter, twentieth century

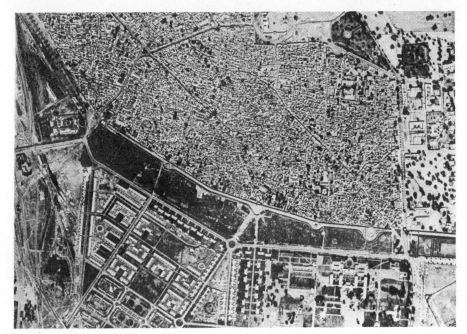

Figure 10.10

Figure 10.11

a strip 1½ miles long and 100 yards wide was preserved as a barrier of social and cultural space between the old and new environments. The wall remained till the end of colonial rule, demolished only in 1950 (ibid.).

19   IMPERIAL DELHI: THE LAST DECADE

At the close of the Second World War, with two years of dependent status still to run, the colonial city of Delhi maintained its separate parts.   Each had its own boundaries and distinctive social and cultural worlds.

At the historic centre was the old city, densely populated, over-crowded and in comparison to the new, with extremely poor conditions of health.   The wall and a 100-yard strip of open ground outside it separated the city from the new settlement to the south (Figure 10.10). The old, undeveloped intra-mural cantonment of Daryaganj and the 'esplanade' east of the Fort, acted as barriers to contain the population to the rear of the Jama Masjid.

In the colonial settlement of New Delhi, the trees were reaching full height.   A cultural landscape existed to the taste of a European colonial elite.   The values and political relationships of the past had continued to structure environments to the present (Figures 10.8, 10.9).

From the 'Viceroy' and 'Commander-in-Chief' downwards, the life styles were those of a colonialised metropolitan elite.   The 'Viceroy's House' faced east, down the 'Central Vista', the church, forward to the left, and the 'Secretariat' blocks in front (Figure 10.11).   To the south in their private estates, lived the members of a governing elite.   North of the 'Viceroy's House' were 'quarters' for the indigenous clerks.   From the circular 'Council Chamber' behind the 'Secretariat', a road led to the shopping centre of 'Connaught Place'. In the distance, hardly visible in the haze yet with a clear line marking the boundary around it, lay the 'native city'.   Only the war and rumours of indigenous rule had delayed completion, interfering with original plans.   Open spaces around the 'Secretariat' had been built over with temporary blocks, to be removed at the end of the war. When this arrived, the acres of visual space could be utilised for ceremonial use.   At the centre of these, fulfilling its visual role, was the 'Central Vista'.   Here could be celebrated victory in an imperial war.

In 'Princes' Park', within sight of earlier cities, elite palaces and the monument to a previous king, imperial troops were assembled for the performance of ceremonial roles (Figure 10.12).   From here to the processional close, lay an avenue a mile and a half long, a tract of colonial territory contrived for ritual display (Figure 10.13).

This broad expanse formed the northern tract of a 'green belt' en-circling the elite residential sector of the city.   Around this area, south of the 'Vista', a ring of mainly recreational space

Figure 10.12

Figure 10.13

was maintained. Moving round from west to east, this comprised the
'Reserved Forest' on the Ridge, open ground by the cantonment, the
'race-course' and 'polo grounds', 'Willingdon airport', the 'Safdar
Jang garden', 'government nurseries' at Jor Bagh, 'Lady Willingdon
Park', the 'Lodi Golf Links', 'Princes' Park' and the 'Irwin
Amphitheatre and Stadium' linking up to the 'Central Vista'. Carefully cultivated, watered and maintained, the 'green belt' lowered
dust levels in the summer heat and, by accident or design, acted
as a barrier against unnecessary intrusion from 'outside'. The
whole was neatly bounded by the railway.

Behind the Ridge, out of sight, lay the cantonment; north of the
old city, the historic Civil Lines, an area increasingly favoured
by a Westernised indigenous elite. Only to the west, and increasingly on the opposite bank of the Jumna, was the indigenous
city permitted to expand.

Within these inter-dependent, interacting areas of a single city
were distinct social and cultural as well as physical-spatial
environments, each with its own values, behaviour and relationships. Ih Delhi, colonialism, with its 'dimensions' of political
power, culture and technology, had created a classical colonial city.

20 EPILOGUE

The transformation of the physical-spatial structure of Delhi
between 1947 and the present day - a period equal in length to
that between 1918 and the end of colonial rule - forms no part
of a study on 'colonial urban development'. Such a subject awaits
further research and a separate monograph.

In this epilogue, therefore, only brief and tentative comments are
suggested, based mainly on studies already made (Rao and Desai,1965;
Bopegamage, 1957; Thakore, 1962; Mitra, 1968; Jagmohan, 1975).

The most important factor affecting Delhi's post-colonial development has been its immense growth in population. In thirty years
between 1941 and 1971 it has expanded by almost three million, one
of the fastest growing city populations in the world.

Growth of Delhi between 1901 and 1971 (Census of India, 1971)

Year	Actual population	Absolute growth in in a decade	Per cent growth in a decade
1901	214,115		
1911	237,944	23,829	11.13
1921	304,420	66,476	27.94
1931	447,442	143,022	46.98
1941	695,686	248,244	55.48
1951	1,437,134	741,448	106.58
1961	2,359,408	992,274	64.17
1971	3,629,842	1,270,434	53.85

The immediate cause of this phenomenal growth resulted from one of
the last acts of colonial rule, the 'partition'of India and Pakistan.
Between 1947 and 1952, over 300,000 Muslims left Delhi and 500,000
Sikhs and Hindus moved in, an overall gain of over 200,000. Between
1941 and 1951, the population more than doubled in size, from less
than 700,000 to well over 1.4 million.

No city in the industrialised world, even at the height of growth
rates in the nineteenth century, has had to cope with such rapid
increases and with such comparatively few resources. The sheer
accommodation of numbers has been an unparalleled achievement. In
1971 the population was well over $3\frac{1}{2}$ million.

The accommodation of these migrants and the increase from natural
growth, has rapidly expanded the built-up area of the city. The
boundaries of 1947 have been massively extended.

Yet at the core of this region, what Bopegamage wrote in 1957 is
still to a large extent true today, 'In recent years, new hotels,
government blocks, private houses and buildings of all kinds have
sprung up, though there has been no major change in the pattern
of the city' (p.17).

The problems which the inheritors of this structure perceive have
frequently been stated. One most often mentioned is that of gross
differences in density and the different levels of amenity provision.

Ten years after Independence, the walled city, with 10 per cent of
the built-up area of Greater Delhi, had 60 per cent of its total
population; New Delhi with 28 per cent of its area, had 17 per cent
(Rao and Desai, 1965,p.30). Vast differences in population densities
characterised different parts of the city. In Old Delhi, gross
densities were 106,197 persons per square mile, in New Delhi, 9,472,
in the Civil Lines, 9,248 and in the Cantonment, 1,909 persons per
square mile (ibid.,p.31). In 1961 certain wards of the old city
had over 1,100 persons per acre (*Census of India,* District Census
Handbook, 1961). These figures indicated, among other things,
different living standards, life-styles, incomes, behaviours, expectations, opportunities as well as cultural traditions. A 1975
estimate of the average gross density of Old Delhi suggests 487
people per acre, with certain wards still having the highest density
distribution in the world (Jagmohan, 1975,p.33).

The vast growth in the responsibilities of government and the need
to create employment for migrants to the city, have led to the increase in government establishments, administrative centres and
research institutes. As in the capital city of all so-called 'new
nations', the growth of the international community has been large.

New cultural centres have arisen, conference halls have been erected
and industrial estates set up. Housing schemes, public and private,
have mushroomed all round the city. With a large proportion of its
population of school age, the number of schools, colleges and other
educational institutions have been expanded. Hotels have arisen to

cater for the rise in the tourist trade. The advantage which the
government has had in owning a large part of the urban land and
therefore being in a position to control development has, however,
other aspects. Of these, the most prominent is that of taking
responsibility for the manner in which development occurs. As
the government is by far the largest employer in Delhi and provides
housing for the majority of its employees, it carries the heaviest
burden for promoting continuity or change in the social and urban
structure of Delhi. One of the most recent statements by the Vice
Chairman of the Delhi Development Association, is a plea for
'rebuilding Shahjahanabad', the old city, and integrating the two
divided cities into one (Jagmohan, 1975).

How such developments are taking place, however, and the policies
formed within a post-colonial and culturally autonomous setting,
are themes for other research.

PART FOUR

Chapter 11

COLONIAL URBAN DEVELOPMENT:
Some implications for further research

Every man is, in certain respects,

  like all other men,
  like some other men,
  like no other man.

C. Kluckhohn and H.A. Murray,ed., *Personality in Nature, Society and Culture.* 1953, p.53).

1   INTRODUCTION

At the outset, two sets of inter-related themes were proposed. One of these related to the impact of colonialism on urban development. Central to this issue is an examination of the kind of structures and relationships existing between metropolitan and colonised society, structures which permit a particular distribution of resources and which enable the values of one culture to be embodied in the urban forms of another. In this theme, the dominance-dependence relation-ship of colonialism has been used as a major explanatory variable.

The other main theme has been concerned with the impact of cultures on environments, and particularly, how cultural and social factors influence urban form. In this theme, the main explanatory variables have been those of cultural values and world-views.

In the particular context discussed, it is clear that both themes and variables are not mutually exclusive but inter-related. In the dominance-dependence situation of colonialism, where culture contact exists, all changes in values and behaviour do not necessarily result from nor do they depend on the particular structure of authority. Similarly, in any instance where environments are modified according to the values of a cultural group, there is a power relationship or authority structure within which decisions are made.

The problem arises when attempting to distinguish between the relative importance of these two variables, the 'power structure of colonialism' and 'cultural values'. This study has shown how, for the colonial

community, cultural values and world-views combined with a particular
structure of power to produce both culture-specific and situational
environments. They were situational in that they resulted from
culture contact within a particular power situation, at a particular
time and with particular forms of technology available. In his review
of the major schools of thought aimed at explaining urban social and
spatial patterns, Sjoberg (1965a, pp.170-8) draws attention to the
influence of technology, cultural values and social power. Referring
to the impact of science and technology on the city, he concedes that
'considerable data have accumulated suggesting that cultural values
and power factors... may induce major distortions in the ideal or
actual patterns resulting from technological change' (ibid. p.170;
see also Wheatley, 1963). In the case of colonial urban development it is clear that the form of 'social power' referred to here
as the dominance-dependence relationship enabled a particular culture
to use its own forms of science and technology to establish a distinct
social and spatial environment. In short, environments manifest the
distribution of social power and express it in a culture-specific way.

It is worth adding that the relative importance of culture and power
variables in a social situation involving culture contact, and not
necessarily an 'environmental' one, has wider applicability in the
investigation of human behaviour.

Of the many theoretical and empirical questions posed by a study of
this kind, only a limited number can be discussed below. The first
of the two themes raises obvious applied or 'policy' issues in
relation to the post-colonial city. How far do such structures
persist in the ordering of urban development? To what extent does
'dependent' urban development continue? What social or physical-spatial
problems does the de-colonised city pose?

Questions raised by the second theme are of a more theoretical and
methodological nature. What is the relationship between environment
and social or individual behaviour? How are environments used as a
means of social control or social and cultural communication? What
methods are appropriate for examining the distribution of environmental
values in any society of culture? It is the task of this final
chapter to take up these and related issues.

2   DEPENDENT URBAN DEVELOPMENT

If economic independence follows only slowly on political autonomy,
cultural independence lags even further behind. New elites have
been influenced by metropolitan values; the apparatus of the colonial
state is not easily dismantled or changed. Between the metropolitan
and de-colonised society, information flows tend to persist; the
exchange of persons goes on. Having for years been linked to metropolitan social, political and cultural models, the de-colonised
society finds their replacement a task not easily achieved.

Educational structures and content, developed over decades, are not
revised overnight. In many cases, the knowledge required for new
curriculae simply does not exist; for years, cultures have been
interpreted through the eyes of the dominant power or, in some cases,
not investigated at all. Their histories have been pre-empted, their
cultural traditions subordinated to the values and purposes of a
European colonial power. Only slowly, therefore, are imperial
structures eroded and cultural colonialism undermined.

In the planning of education, welfare or science, national goals have
to evolve. In the field of urban development, new institutes and
policies must meet new national needs; for these, information is
required which in many cases does not exist. Research is needed and
the results incorporated into strategies for economic and social
development. Community studies are required and cultural traditions
made known.

Whereas in India such developments have long since occurred, in
nations more recently 'un-yoked' they are still in the early stages
of growth. The shortage of professional skills combines with links
to what was previously the metropolitan power - or political com-
petitors elsewhere - to ensure that cultural colonialism persists.
Through 'aid' or the international structure of trade, the transfer
of values goes on. Financed by 'development agencies', 'foundations'
and the previous metropolitan power, 'development models' have been
provided by planning teams from all over the world. Colonial
settlements in Africa persist as environments for new kinds of
elites (see, for example, White, 1948; Dyer, 1963; Trevallion, 1966;
Lock, 1967).

In such cases, it is not surprising that the values of a metropolitan
elite find congruence with those of a culturally similar colonial
past. Cultural categories are assumed to be universal, particularly
those relating to environments. Latent values are stimulated by
relics of the imperial past.

Thus, metropolitan advisers on the development of Kaduna, Northern
Nigeria (financed by the metropolitan 'Ministry of Overseas
Development') found that, in 1967

> Kanta Road, after 50 years, now reaps the benefit of imaginative
> tree planting by the early pioneers and is perhaps the most
> attractive and unspoiled of Lugard's Avenues. Originally named
> after him it still contains his headquarters now used as an
> officers' club. In a city so spread out as Kaduna, shade trees
> along its extenuated major and minor roads are an inestimable
> boon. The plan proposes to plant new trees on a large scale
> throughout the existing and proposed road network.

The original plan of the city, with its strict segregation into
European and non-European residential areas, large, centrally-located
race course, golf-course, spacious compounds and 'native' and
'European' cemetery, had been conceived in 1917 by F.D. Lugard in
his role as 'Governor-General' of the 'protectorate' of Northern
Nigeria. Fifty years later, metropolitan advisers found that the
'Lugard Bridge', 'a small and elegant iron suspension bridge...

brought to Kaduna from Zunguru, Lugard's headquarters before 1917
(and) re-erected in the Government Gardens, (gave) access to a
pleasant woodland walk along the north bank of the river' (Lock,
1967, pp. 182, 206). Kaduna in the 1960s, like Lagos, still retained
the race course as the central focus in the city. To the north of
the city was sited the 'proposed military cantonment'(ibid).

Such advisers make their own cultural appraisals, operating with
metropolitan categories of perception which are both irrelevant
and patronising: 'The solid simple architecture of the North (of
Nigeria) is designed to keep life cool indoors and to give an
inviting and sympathetic softness of form inside. While the facing
slurry is still wet, deft fingerwork produces a variety of straight
and sweeping patterns conferring subtle texture and a human touch
to an otherwise monotonous wall surface' (ibid.). In another 'expert's'
report produced in 1973 for a Middle Eastern state, there was,
according to an indigenous observer, 'a mediocre housing survey with
many photographs of open desert and romantic pictures of Bedouin
children and animals' *(Architects' Journal,* 12 December 1973, p.456).

If such blatant examples of cultural imperialism are now less likely
to occur, new modes of dependence arise in the transfer of 'models'
and 'techniques'. The term 'tropical architecture' has long been a
misnomer on two accounts: first, in implying that the major influences
on built form are climatic rather than social and cultural; second,
in ignoring the relationship of economic, cultural and political
dependence, inherent in colonialism, which has permitted such
'architecture' to occur. The term 'colonial architecture' was more
accurate and honest.

Where political circumstances have changed, new economic relationships
encourage cultural dependence in a different form. Oil rich states
of the Middle East, anxious to 'modernise' traditional societies in
years rather than decades, look round for professional advice. Multi-
national and metropolitan companies are only too willing to assist.
Yet in the process of importing the high-technology environments of
the West, little thought is given to the consequences, whether in
terms of energy consumption, the need for skilled manpower to maintain
them or, most important of all, the disruption of social and cultural
institutions which is involved. Thus, whilst increasing concern is
felt about the energy-consuming urban environments of the industrialised West, the organisations responsible for creating them
eagerly reproduce similar environments in the industrialising Middle
East. It is evident from professional comment that cultural
imperialism,in 'the present exploitation of developing countries in
the Middle East', is producing 'meaningless Arabianised versions of
living patterns that are entirely European in their cultural values'
(ibid.; also 13 August, 17 September, 17 October, 1975).

Whilst this particular situation is unique, the solution to such
problems in the less affluent, post-colonial societies is neither
simple, nor, for each society or city, is it the same. Communities
need housing; employment must be generated and environmental decisions
made. In making such decisions, the relevance of external models and

experience is limited. With regard to norms about 'density', space
standards or larger questions of 'over-urbanisation' (Sovani, 1966;
Bose, 1971), external models are not only irrelevant but even
dysfunctional.

Levels of urbanisation, space standards and the quality of urban life
have historically been a consequence resulting from what is desirable
and what is attainable at any particular time and within a particular
economic, political and cultural context. Irrespective of the social
and cultural variables which govern all norms of behaviour (including
spatial standards), the notion of socially or 'nationally' applied
norms cannot be considered outside the much larger issue of social
process and political development. The institutionalisation of norms,
whether they relate to housing or law, is governed by what is socially,
culturally and politically acceptable. Norms (such as those relating
to 'density' and 'over-crowding') cannot be discussed regardless of
social and political processes, nor what are perceived as social and
economic priorities. If this study has any relevance for these issues
it is in showing how one particular colonial culture organised its own
autonomous environment according to its prevailing norms and values.

The larger questions of dependent urban development lie beyond the
scope of this study. In the classical colonial situation, urban
centres were established in the colonised society and used as
entrepot ports. By these, the institutions of capitalism were
extended, the ports used as collecting and exporting points for
indigenous materials and goods and as a means of extending the
metropolitan market system. The physical structure of capitalism
was introduced into colonised territories with the city as the centre
of productive life; this substituted for a system of villages which
had previously served largely self-sufficient agricultural communities
(Cox, 1971, p.389 . See also Frank, 1971b).

In the metropolitan society, industrialisation generated urbanisation.
In the colonial society, the urbanisation which took place was dependent on the industrialisation of the metropolitan economy. The effect
of this was to disrupt traditional market structures and economic
systems, establishing new spatial relationships which were linked
to the metropolitan power (Friedmann, 1972). In most cases, the
colonial city was divorced from its hinterland, becoming an appendage
of the metropolitan economy. (The work of S. Amin, A.G. Frank and
others influential in the development of dependency theory is discussed in Oxaal et al. (1974) and Brookfield (1975).)

In the metropolitan capital were established those institutions of
government, economy, law, education, culture or science on which
the colonial society was obliged to depend. Apart from government,
the most important of these were economic: banks, insurance and
shipping companies, industrial concerns, exchanges and markets.
They were also educational, scientific and cultural. Here, in the
universities and other institutes, research was undertaken, teachers
trained, and army officers, engineers, doctors or lawyers socialised
into metropolitan norms. In the metropolitan centres of learning,
knowledge of the colonial societies was developed and institutes

established by which such knowledge could be further diffused.   In
the metropolitan capital, the influence of colonialism on urban
development is manifest in those institutions which were located
there but not in the colonial society itself; for example, in London
and its environs, institutions of government in the 'India Office',
'Colonial Office', parliament buildings; Haileybury School, founded
for the training of Indian administrators, the older universities,
for the education of the Indian Civil Service, Sandhurst, for the
training of army officers, the School of Oriental and African Studies,
for the education of linguists.   In the realms of science, technology,
medicine and law, the Imperial College of Science and Technology, the
London School of Hygiene and Tropical Medicine, the Inns of Court;
in culture, the British Museum, India Office Library; in finance, the
myriad banks, insurance, shipping and other commercial concerns
located in 'the City' whose financial interests were (and are) in
Africa and the East.

3   THE POST-COLONIAL CITY

In the past three decades, over seventy states, mainly in Africa and
Asia, have gained political if not economic independence, half of
them previously dependent on Britain.   In many of the urban centres
of such states, the physical-spatial characteristics of the colonial
city to a greater or lesser extent remain.   One of these is the
fundamental distinction between its various parts, particularly
between that of what was once the 'colonial settlement' and the
'indigenous city'.

In the provision of amenities, the colonial settlement was built, not
merely to the specifications of the 'modern' city but to the requirements of a colonial elite.   Whether in relation to the supply of
roads, recreational space, water, power lines, sewers, housing,
shopping and hotels, the concentration was in the European immigrant
sector.   The indigenous city, in contrast, was characterised by gross
underprovision of these amenities.

Yet irrespective of these objective differences, it is the symbolic
meaning of these distinctions which had, in retrospect, the greatest
effect.   In one of the most damning indictments of colonialism,
The Wretched of the Earth, Frantz Fanon focusses on the segregated
city as epitomising the entire colonial relationship.
> The colonial world is a world divided into compartments... of
> native quarters and European quarters, of schools for natives
> and schools for Europeans; in the same way we need not recall
> apartheid in South Africa.   Yet, if we examine closely this
> system of compartments, we will at least be able to reveal the
> lines of force it implies.   This approach to the colonial world,
> its ordering and its geographical layout will allow us to mark
> out the lines on which a decolonized society will be reorganised.
>   The colonial world is a world cut in two.   The dividing line,
> the frontiers are shown by barracks and police stations.   In the
> colonies it is the policeman and the soldier who are the official,
> instituted go-betweens, the spokesman of the settler and his
> rule of oppression...

The zone where the natives live is not complementary to the zone
inhabited by the settlers.... The settler's town is a strongly
built town, all made of stone and steel. It is a brightly lit
town; the streets are covered with asphalt, and the garbage cans
swallow all the leavings, unseen, unknown and hardly thought
about.... The settler's town is a well-fed town, an easygoing
town; its belly is always full of good things. The settler's
town is a town of white people, of foreigners.

The town belonging to the colonized people, or at least the
native town, the Negro village, the medina, the reservation, is
a place of ill fame, peopled by men of evil repute. They are
born there, it matters little where or how; they die there, it
matters not where, nor how. It is a world without spaciousness;
men live on top of each other, and their huts are built one on
top of the other. The native town is a hungry town, starved of
bread, of meat, of shoes, of coal, of light. The native town is
a crouching village, a town on its knees, a town wallowing in
the mire. It is a town of niggers and dirty Arabs. The look
that the native turns on the settler's town is a look of lust,
a look of envy.

For Fanon, the central fact about this 'world divided into compart-
ments... inhabited by two different species' is that of race.

When you examine at close quarters the colonial context, it is
evident that what parcels out the world is to begin with the
fact of belonging to or not belonging to a given race, a given
species. In the colonies, the economic substructure is also a
superstructure. The cause is the consequence; you are rich
because you are white, you are white because you are rich. That
is why Marxist analysis should always be slightly stretched every
time we have to do with the colonial problem (pp.37-40, Grove
Press, New York 1968).

In the immediate post-independence years, despite modifications, in
most cities the basic pattern has often remained. As a result of the
initial structuring of inequalities, whether in terms of housing,
services or spatial standards, newcomers to the city reinforce the
old structural pattern. Thus, low-income migrants have tended to
filter in to the old (indigenous) city and its environs where kinship networks, marginal employment as well as an environment which
is both culturally familiar and functional in providing temporary
shelter, continue to attract them.

On the other hand, new elites flow into the expanded area of the old
colonial settlement. The wealthy leave the old city to take up
residence in the new. In this area, new shopping centres, banks,
airline terminals, hotels, tourist offices and houses for visitors
and diplomats are built. Here are the facilities, amenities and
culturally familiar environments which make such visitors feel at
home. Thus, urban development begun with the de facto or implicit
recognition of racial inequality and discrimination would appear
not only to continue to divide rich from indigenous poor but also,
in many ex-colonial cities round the world, representatives of the
rich countries from those of the poor. This would seem to be as
true in Indonesia (Wertheim, 1964), the Phillipines (personal

communication, John Useem), and in many African states as it is in India

For the external observer, the most obvious aspect of difference in
amenity relates to the availability of space. According to Wertheim,
in Bandung, where Europeans once represented 12 per cent of the
population, they occupied 52 per cent of the residential space.
Indonesians, representing 77 per cent of the population, occupied
44 per cent of the space (p.182). The phenomenon is sufficiently
widespread in many 'twin cities' of India for one geographer to construct a typology of Indian cities with this as a major operational
component (Brush, 1968).

A further characteristic of this particular form of city relates to
its economic and technological demands. Here, a historical comment
is relevant.

The 'natural' growth of cities has been closely related to the development of science, technology, economic resources and social and
political organisation. Until the eighteenth century, with the in-
vention of mechanically propelled vehicles and especially, the later
nineteenth century, with the introduction of railways, the motor car,
public transport and electronic means of communication, urban settlements were relatively small, compact communities, their size limited
to intra-urban distances traversed on foot or by the combination of
human and animal power.

The exceptions to this were in authoritarian political systems where
political coercion and the distribution of power gave rise to cities
where manpower was substituted for technological means of communication.
As examples, one might quote Karlsruhe, Versailles and, in the
twentieth century, colonial New Delhi.

With the removal of autocratic power, and without the technology and
energy base which keeps the sectors of comparably large cities in
contact with each other - motor vehicles, subways, buses, tramways,
telephones, television - and where administrative and political
institutions of local government are still relatively undeveloped,
the 'expanded city' becomes an anachronism in two different ways.
Its far-flung, spatially separated parts belong, on one hand, to an
imperial system now past. On the other, they belong to a stage of
urban development which has evolved from and relies upon, high levels
of technology, adequate supplies of energy, economic prosperity and
institutions of urban government. This is a situation which, for
many transplanted cities in the ex-colonial world, has yet to be
reached (cf. Jagmohan, 1975,pp.39,89).

The physical-spatial forms which characterised colonial urban development would appear to place immense strains on the economic resources
of the post-colonial city. Because colonial administrators wanted
'views', status, privacy and a particular cultural environment, water
pipes, sewers, telephone wires, cables, roads and transport routes
have to be perhaps five times as long as they need be, even today, if
the 'colonial' environment is still maintained. With regard to the
economics of time and energy, low-income workers resident on the edge

of the elite areas have to travel across acres of 'colonial space' in
order to reach centrally located work-places. Unlike the elite, who
have access to private transport, they must travel on foot, bicycle
or public transport. Because levels of technology are relatively
low and skilled maintenance in short supply, the public transit
system is immensely overloaded. Thus, productivity is affected not
only by the hours lost in travelling but also by the sheer physical
strain of waiting and travelling in climatic conditions considerably
more extreme than those experienced in Europe.

Other observers have commented on the patterns of stratification and
social structure emerging in some such ex-colonial cities. According
to McGee, Singapore, in 1967, remained a city 'planned by Europeans
and inhabited by non-Europeans whose residential distribution continues to reflect the intentions of the European rulers to an amazing
degree' (p.72). How far this is characteristic of other ex-colonial
cities, only individual studies can show. Certainly, at 'independence', the new occupants of the city inherited a physical-spatial
structure tailor-made to reproduce a system of 'housing classes' and
stratification identical with the old.

Whether or not new elites moved into old colonial elite dwellings and
areas, the spatial and residential norms characteristic of these areas
act as a referent. It would seem that the colonial bungalows of New
Delhi still function as major symbols of status whether occupied by
foreign diplomats, business elites or government ministers. Indeed,
it is likely that the entire 'Western' city acts as a dysfunctional
model in the promotion of indigenous urban development.

In a similar way, planners have drawn attention to the 'military
space' of cantonments occupying large tracts of land often close to
the main city, usually held and administered by a different local
authority. It has been suggested that this not only inhibits
development within its boundaries but acts as a further wedge in
driving commercial or residential development far from the centre
of the city.

If it is accepted that the ideas and models of modern industrial
society generally understood under the inadequate label of 'modernisation' were introduced into many colonial countries by the vehicle
of British imperialism, it could also be argued that the first model
of modern urban residential life, in most cases that of a 'suburban
elite', was also introduced as part of the same process. In India,
this model, characterised by low-density, low-rise development was
quite contrary to previous urban traditions, determined by indigenous
family structure, the urban economy, prevailing technology as well as
cultural institutions. Moreover, the models and theory developed in
the colonial third culture in India were diffused to other areas of
colonial rule.

Thus, Lord Lugard, instrumental in colonial settlement in Africa,
born in India and serving in the Indian army, recommended in 1909
that 'compounds' in the 'European Reservation' in Northern Nigeria
should be :

100 yards in depth, 70-100 yards of frontage (i.e. from 1½
to 2 acres) enclosed by a live hedge, mud wall or substantial
fence. Within this area, ornamental and shade trees and dhub
grass will be planted. Houses will be about 20 yards from the
frontage road. Servants' quarters and stables will be at least
50 yards to the rear (1906,pp.416-22).

In Murray's handbook, *How to Live in Tropical Africa* (1895), the
'Indian bungalow' is described as 'the one perfect house for all
tropical countries'. The 'dak bungalow' with its 'spacious living
room... large teakwood table and inviting lounge chairs... a cabinet
of cutlery, china and glass, all clean and in perfect order.... The
bedrooms with adjoining baths and... a boy... to make the punkah
pull' travelled as far as China (Andrews, 1918,p.319). In the
rubber estates of Malaya, 'the manager's bungalow is held to be an
index of the prestige and prosperity of the company. On estates
where there are other white men beside the manager, the bungalows
of all such people are patterned after that of the manager' (Jain,
1970,p.335). In East Africa, Kendall (1955) states that 'the standard
plot of 50 by 100 feet was borrowed from Indian towns and after 1915
came to prevail in most commercial areas of Uganda'(p.126).

The most explicit account of the diffusion of colonial urban development, however, comes from Mabogunje (1968b) writing of Nigeria

The advent of Europeans to Ibadan in 1893... introduced alien
ideas of urban existence as well as alien institutions to the
(urban) scene. Since most of those institutions tended to be
space-oriented, it was inevitable that they could not be integrated
into, or contained within, the old city. They had therefore to
find new locations, beyond the limits of the existing built-up
area. First to come were the administrators, with their ideas
of specialised roles in a hierarchy of authority. At the bottom
were the messengers, the clerks, the chief-clerks and so on; at
the top were the Assistant District Officer, the District Officer,
the Provincial Officer, the Resident and the Governor. With each
of these ranks went not only a residence but an office, often
separate from the residence. The latter represented a major
departure from traditional pattern. It meant increased space
consumption within the city and it began the process of a major
separation of place of work from place of residence. Eventually,
it was to impose on Ibadan the familiar modern city problem of
journey to work.

The importance of the change wrought by the arrival of the
European (was that) status in the new urban tradition was based
on achievement - initially on the degree of skill in reading and
writing; advancement within the system was based on standards
of efficiency, higher education and higher output of work. As
soon as the Residency was opened at Ibadan, it attracted a group
of Africans from Lagos who had had, since the 1860's, the benefit
of European education. With the arrival of each new institution -
the railways, the commercial houses, the banks, the agents of
central government - the numbers of these people continued to
increase, and they tended to settle around the new institutions
which attracted their service.

This group of literate Africans filled mainly the clerical and executive posts in their various establishments. Above them in the administrative class there was usually a diverse group of Europeans. The English dominated the political administration, as well as transport and a part of commerce. The Germans, French and Italians were restricted almost exclusively to commerce. In all cases, the expatriates tended to claim exclusive rights of residence in certain parts of the city and thus began the tradition of 'residential reservations' (pp.39,41).

With the colonial era, a style and pattern of urban residence was introduced and increasingly adopted, becoming a reference model for the indigenous population, and both before and after the end of the colonial period, taken over by the indigenous elite in all colonial societies (see, for example, Tandon, 1961,pp.236-7; Majogunje, 1968b,p.42). According to some observers, this model, with its liberal spatial norms, has resulted in a rapidly accelerating scramble for land, an inflation of house and land prices, a dispersal of urban activities and, for the urban poor, further concentration in the poorer and generally older parts of the city or alternatively, dispersal to the perimeters of the built-up area.

At another level, the symbolism embodied in the colonial landscape also poses problems. In national capitals, there is 'the vexing problem of making... foreign buildings and institutions look and feel that they belong to the new nation and not its colonial predecessors' (Southall, 1971,p.58). The dismantling of statues and the renaming of streets not only raises acrimonious debate between sections lobbying for their own candidates to replace artefacts of the colonial era; ironically, for the non-indigenous visitor, the empty plinth or the indigenous street name (often in indigenous script) on a colonial facade serves only to emphasise that the built form as well as the entire urban lay-out belong not simply to an alien, but to a colonial culture. Thus, as Davies (1969,p.14) writes, 'Notwithstanding references in publicity literature to 'The Garden City' it is doubly outdated in Lusaka as the visual expression of a colonial or imported way of life.

In recent years, New Delhi has been presented as a 'tourist attraction' for travellers from East and West, considerable expenditure being made in 'beautifying' the ex-colonial city. Little research has been promoted, however, into the perceptions of such tourists and the images which the juxtaposition of old and new city project. In the opinion of one such visitor, the remnants of Imperial Delhi should be seen along with the remains of other great urban centres in Asia, such as Angkor Wat or Mohenjo-Daro, as a classical example of modern colonial archaeology. The greatest 'tourist attraction' unwittingly bequeathed by the process of colonial urban development would appear to be the 'neglected' old city which, like the indigenous cities of Morocco in French colonial Africa, has been preserved by what Professor Janet Lughod calls the 'serendipity of conservation' (personal communication, 1973).

As this study has shown, the colonial culture established its own
environment, an environment which goes far deeper than 'statues' and
'street names'. It was one which reflected the values, not of the
metropolitan but of the colonial society, values which modernisation
and democratic control in the metropolitan society made increasingly
irrelevant. Hutchins(1968), for example, suggests that members of
that society who went to India from the late nineteenth century did
so partially in order to obtain those benefits which economic,
political and social change 'at Home' made increasingly difficult to
find: domestic service, generous space standards, freedom from increasing industrial and environmental stress, recreation and the life
of a rapidly vanishing age . And whilst this study has concentrated
on the built environment of the colonial third culture, it is clear
that such a culture encompassed *all* aspects of life: the city, as
Fanon has patently shown, was its most representative artefact. The
task for the inheritors of the colonial city is one of investing it
with a new set of social, cultural and political properties and of
giving it a new symbolic meaning representative of the society of
which it is now a part.

How far these or other issues are perceived as 'problems' by such
post-colonial societies and not simply by 'external' observers is a
matter for internal decision. What is clear, as Brookfield (1975,
p.209) has said, is that 'development study... concerned with the
great inequalities of our age and their reduction' (one may add,
in any society, or between any societies) demands 'an immense
expansion of ideas in both space and time and its incorporation
into a new understanding of man's changing environment and relation
to environment'.

4   THEORETICAL AND RESEARCH IMPLICATIONS

Earlier studies have examined *formal* systems of social and racial
segregation enforced by physical barriers, pass controls and the
like (see Kuper et al., 1958). Little investigation has so far
been made of *informal* controls - either intentional or unintentional
in nature - which have effectively restricted free movement, particularly in a situation of cultural pluralism, between different
parts of a city (Langlands,1969). Banton (1971) has shown, for the
ruling white minority in Africa, how important self-segregation was
as a means of exercising supervision over the activities of its own
members. This not only protected the white minority's monopoly of
power but also made the immigrant more dependent upon the approval
of other members of his racial category. Physical segregation had
other important functions.
> From a psychological position, any European... was in an exposed
> position. All the social scaffolding which in his home society
> was built round the values taught to children and many of the
> social controls which supported the cultural norms, had been
> removed. Where whites were few in number, considerable deter-
> mination was required to maintain at all times the norms and
> thereby the prestige of the imperial culture. To help him in
> this a man might institutionalise his own behaviour, creating
> personal customs and routines that reminded him of the expectations

of absent others: the idea of the explorer or administrator
dressing for dinner in the African bush is not really so foolish
as it may seem to the stay-at-home. A club or a clique of friends
may provide the individual with a similar kind of support and a
means of supervising the behaviour of people identified with him
and whose misconduct might therefore redound upon himself.   The
social exclusiveness of minorities needs to be seen in this
light (p.269).

The physical-spatial unit of the bungalow-compound complex, as much
as the larger cultural environment of the civil and hill station,
had a similar function to the club. Apart from their strategic or
'sanitation' functions, the culturally modified territory of the
colonial third culture had an important role to play in providing
social and cultural reassurance to its occupants and distinguishing
them from those living in the other culture areas of the 'native
city'.

Yet wittingly or unwittingly, the existence of these physically
separated culture areas was instrumental in furthering the process
of what Mitchell (1966) has referred to as 'categorisation': 'The
pattern of behaviour between races because of the social distance
between them, becomes categorical. Thus, any person recognised as
a member of a particular race is expected to behave in a standardised
way' (p.53).   Referring to the same process, Kuper (1971) has written
    People in any society project their own concepts, based on their
    own cultural premises, onto a particular universe... though it
    is difficult to examine these other concepts and universes in
    their own right... the notions are contained largely in language,
    the social side of speech. Each social universe is represented
    by its own notions and when people of different universes come
    into contact with each other their culturally different notions
    set the pattern for their classification of each other(p.305).
For these reasons the colonial city has considerable importance for
the whole understanding of 'urbanism' and urbanisation. It contra-
dicts a basic assumption of 'urbanism', that spatially compact people
merge, interact and, as a result, develop new values and relationships. It is as likely that inhabitants of separate areas are
socialised into separate communities, each with its own identity,
and the whole generating categorical relationships and stereotypes.

The use of socially and culturally created environments has been
remarked upon in other studies of the colonial city phenomenon. To
oversimplify, the indigenous city becomes associated with 'traditional'
and the colonial settlement, or 'Western' city, with 'modern' behaviour. Each area is invested with symbolic value and is used to
communicate social and cultural identities.

Thus, Pons (1969, pp.11,31,261) has described how, in what was once
a Belgian colony in Africa, the social and physical environment of
the 'European town' acted as a check on potentially hostile behaviour
of indigenous inhabitants. The 'European town', the African residential areas and the rural tribal hinterland were conceptualised, by
members of the indigenous African society, as different social worlds,

each associated with different degrees of 'civilisation' and therefore
having appropriate behaviour for each. In India, a move from the 'old
city' to a 'bungalow-compound' in the Civil Lines, along with the
changed behaviour which such physical-spatial environments required,
was an accepted means of communicating new social, cultural and
political identities(for example, Nanda,1962,pp.30-1).

In contemporary Hyderabad, Duncan (1976) has shown how the 'ostentatious
display' of residential environments in the new city is perceived by
inhabitants of the old as manifesting a loss of 'traditional values
of modesty'. Both old and new elites 'use the same terms to describe
the people living in the other landscape as they used to describe
the landscape itself'.

The contrast in environments manifest in the colonial city was also a
result of 'nativism' on the part of both the dominant as well as the
subordinate groups which arose in the culture contact situation. The
nativism of the colonial community was largely unconscious and of a
perpetuative rather than *revivalistic* type, in which elements from
the metropolitan culture were unconsciously exaggerated as a buttress
to maintain cultural and social identity. This is as true of environments as it is of behaviour (Linton,1943).

It is not only these theoretical issues which have relevance for the
examination of social and cultural factors in environment in the
metropolitan society. In the understanding of race relations,
Rex (1973) has rightly argued that race problems are 'primarily
linked with the phenomenon of colonialism' (especially pp.75-92).
In dealing with such problems we are concerned not simply with 'local'
or even 'national' situations in London, Birmingham or New York, but
with the stereotypes which emerge or have emerged from a global
colonial system. On one hand, such stereotypes are directly or
indirectly acquired by members of the metropolitan society from experience in colonial territories (ibid.,p.87). The role which colonial
third-culture members played in mediating between the two societies
and in acting as agents by which the two cultures are interpreted and
images conveyed has never been properly examined. Equally neglected
are the stereotypes developed in colonial and ex-colonial societies
by the indigenous members themselves and the very real social and
physical realities of racial and residential segregation characteristic
of colonial urban development.

At a more theoretical level, the issues raised in the previous pages
pose problems of a different kind. Acts of perception are a product
of the cultural milieu of the person perceiving; they rest on his
previous experience and training, his motivation at the time and the
social situation and context in which he acts. Values expressed in
perception are both socially and culturally learnt. It has been the
object of this study to make explicit this question of values, and
to bring the visual, physical and spatial more consciously into the
study of urban social structure and behaviour. It equally implies a
need to bring the psychological, social and cultural into the study
of the visual, physical and spatial.

All environments are essentially ethnoenvironments, made meaningful to their observers in terms of the social and cultural categories with which they are perceived. If contemporary attitudes to environment are to be understood, then research must identify such categories as they are expressed in everyday speech and records, and in the shared, taken-for-granted knowledge on which people decide and act. In examining the attitudes of people to an environment in the past, this study has attempted to identify the relevant values and categories by reference to the written, graphic and photographic records of the actors' perceptual experience and to relate these to the environments produced.

In terms of method, the study has also attempted to show that historical data not only can but must be used to enlarge our theoretical understanding of the city (Eyles, 1974,pp.43-4; Bailey, 1975,pp.47,110). Conversely, an explicit theoretical framework is needed to interpret historical data. The history of the city, in particular, can draw with profit on a wide-ranging theory and methodology developed by cognate disciplines (Cohn, 1970,pp.46-7).

The urban consequences of colonialism and the multi-cultural city present problems in two different realms. One is that of the environmental decision-maker, and his task of making urban structures responsive to the aspirations and activities of those for whom the city exists.

The other is that of the social scientist for whom the city presents problems of understanding, and the identification of the human, social and cultural phenomena of which the total reality consists. Such phenomena are identifiable only within a comparative, cross-cultural and multi-disciplinary perspective. The two spheres of interest are not exclusive, but complementary.

ILLUSTRATIONS AND SOURCES

As all illustrations are referred to in the text, captions have
generally not been added except where additional information is
needed. The following list indicates the location of the subject-
matter and the date of the illustration where these are known.
Except where otherwise stated, photographs are by the author and
were taken in 1970.

The majority of the illustrations are reproduced with the kind permission of the India Office Library, London; these are noted as IOL,
followed by the album number for photographs and, if from the drawings
collection, by the reference number.

Thanks are also due to the Institute of Royal Engineers Library,
Chatham (6.4), the National Army Museum, London (5.3, 6.8, 9.4),
Professor S. Nilsson (4.8b), the Radio Times Hulton Picture Library
(7.6) and the Town and Country Planning Organisation, Delhi (8.1)
for their help in supplying and their permission to use the illustrations indicated.

Facing Figures
page

4	1.1	Based on Survey of India, *Delhi Guide Map*, 1969 (2nd edn)
6	1.2	Dariba, off Chandni Chowk, Old Delhi.
6	1.3	Chandni Chowk, Old Delhi, looking west.
8	1.4	Pritviraj Road, New Delhi.
8	1.5	Vijay Chowk and Central Vista (previously Prince Edward Place), New Delhi.
8	1.6	Jan Path (previously Queen's Way), New Delhi.
11	1.7	Ramakrishnapuram, Outer Ring Road, New Delhi.
11	1.8	Outer Ring Road, Ramakrishnapuram, New Delhi.
47	3.1	Map of Kanpur, *Imperial Guide to India*, 1904.
46	3.2	Circuit House, Civil Lines, Varanasi, Uttar Pradesh.
76	4.1	Residency, location unknown, late nineteenth century (IOL,Ph.10/11).
76	4.2	Possibly Peshawar, 1920s (IOL,PH.66/1,p.27).
84	4.3a	Lawrencepor, Punjab, 1873 (IOL,WD,1470).

Facing page	Figures	
84	4.3b	Possibly Delhi, c.1943 (IOL,Ph.18/A).
87	4.4a	Lahore, 1920s (IOL,Ph.39,p.1).
87	4.4b	Ambala, late nineteenth century (IOL,Ph.154,p.134a).
92	4.5a	Calcutta, 1868. Caption: 'Alipore Road, Calcutta, 1868, 26 October. A Chummery. Mr Miller, Mr Wilson, Mr Ball, Mr Ingram' (IOL,Wb 268).
92	4.5b	Alexandra Place, New Delhi, c.1969.
98	5.1	Allahabad, 1930, *Imperial Gazetteer of India*, Atlas, 1931,p.64.
98	5.2	Agra, 1930, ibid. p.58.
100	5.3	Bangalore, c.1850. Caption: 'Officers' Houses and Lines, 14th N.I. at Bangalore'.
100	5.4	Godwin, G., *Town Swamps and Social Bridges*, 1859 (Leicester University Press, reprint edn, 1972),p.36.
111	5.5	Agra, 1868. Map of Agra City and Cantonment (IOL).
111	5.6	*Royal Commission on the Sanitary State of the Army in India*, 1863, Minutes of Evidence, p.178.
113	5.7	Ibid., Abstract of Station Returns, p.418.
113	5.8	*Royal Commission on the Sanitary State of the Army in India*, 1863, Minutes of Evidence, p.323.
127	6.1	South India, early twentieth century (IOL,Ph.148, p.40).
127	6.2	Varanesi, Uttar Pradesh.
132	6.3	Sehore (now Madya Pradesh), 1927 (IOL,Ph.1/3/C 1925-33).
132	6.4	Government of India, *Military Engineer Services Handbook*, vol.2, Buildings and General, part 2, Architecture and Design, 1925.
136	6.5	*Delhi Sketch Book*, 1853, p.35; Hyderabad Residency (IOL,Ph.17/4,p.12); Brock, W. *Sanitary Houses and Bungalows*, in Board of Trade (Patents Office). Specifications of Inventions printed under the Patents, Designs and Trade Marks Act, 1883, vol.64, 13001 to 13,200; Madras, 1880s (IOL,Ph.148,p.34).
138	6.6	Jhabua (now Madya Pradesh), c.1935 (IOL,Ph.223/4,p.7).
138	6.7	Location unknown, c.1943 (IOL,Ph.18/A,p.5).
141	6.8	Location unknown, c.1885 (National Army Museum 0/PH 5301-6).
141	6.9	Rajkot, Kathiawar, Gujrat, 1913. Caption: 'Mrs Wood's Garden Party'. The male participants are being led, blindfold, by the female, round flagged markers. (IOL,Ph.1/1/C 1912-19).
141	6.10	The continuation of the 'reception', and the use of the complex to accommodate it, is illustrated in this photograph taken in Delhi, 1969.
144	6.11	Location unknown, 1865 (IOL,WD2887).
144	6.12	Tilak Marg, New Delhi (previously Hardinge Avenue).
153	6.13	Location unknown (IOL, no ref.).
153	6.14	Bangalore, 1930s (IOL,Ph.304)
165	7.1	*Delhi Sketch Book*, 1851.
165	7.2	Viceregal Lodge, Simla, 1895 (IOL,Ph.15/1,p.70).

DELHI NOMENCLATURE

The following list indicates the original nomenclature of major roads
and other locations with their post-Independence names (as in 1972).
(CL = Civil Lines; C = Cantonment).

Allenby Road	Dr Bishamber Das Rd
Albuquerque Road	Tees January Marg
Alipur Road(CL)	Shamnath Marg
Baird Road	Bangla Sahib Marg
Cavalry Lines(CL)	Cavalry Lane
Central Avenue(CL)	Sardar Patel Marg
Circuit House Road(CL)	Vishvavidyalaya Marg
Circular Road (south of old city)	Jawaharlal Nehru Marg
Circular Road (north of old city)	Gokhale Marg
Clive Road	Thyagaraja Marg
Commissioner Road(CL)	previously behind Maiden's Hotel
Coronation Road(CL)	Banda Bahadur Marg
Curzon Lane	Balwant Rai Mehta Lane
Curzon Road	Kasturba Gandhi Marg
Daryganj Road	Ansari Marg
Delhi-Muttra Road	Bahadurshah Zafar Marg

Edward Park	Netaji Subhash Park
Elgin Road	Netaji Subhash Marg
Factory Road	Ring Road: by Gwalior Pottery
Flagstaff Road	Dhwaja Marg
Garstin Bastion Road	Shardhanand Marg
Government House	see Viceroy's House
Hardinge Avenue	Tilak Marg
Hamilton Road	Zorawarsingh Marg
Havelock Road	Kalibari Marg
Hotel Road(CL)	previously near Swiss Hotel
Irwin Road (first known as Cantonment Road)	Baba Kharak Singh Marg
Ibbetson Road	Ashram Marg
Keeling Road	Tolstoy Marg
King Edward Road	Maulana Azad Marg
King Edward Place	Vijay Chowk
King's Way(CL)	Bhai Parmanand Marg
Kingsway	Raj Path
Kitchener Road	Sardar Patel Marg
Lady Hardinge Road	Shaheed Bhagat Singh Marg
Lancer Road(CL)	east of Lucknow Road
Linlithgow Road	Dr K.S. Krishnan Road?
Lovers' Lane	Shankar Road: eastern end joining Mandir Lane
Ludlow Castle Road(CL)	Raj Niwas Marg
Lutyens Road	Lawrence Road
Metcalfe Road	by Metcalfe House
Military Parade Road	

Minto Road	Vivekanand Marg
Mutiny Memorial Road	Rani Jhansi Marg
Nicholson Road	Gokhale Marg
Old Mill Road	Rafi Marg
Original Road	Desh Bandu Gupta Marg; eastern end
Overbridge Road	Desh Bandu Gupta Marg
Panchkuin Road	Panchkuin Marg
Princes' Park	Fifteenth August Maidan
Princes' Road(CL)	Jahanara Marg
Probyn Road	Vikramaditya Marg
Queen's Road(Old Delhi)	Shyama Prasad Mukherji Marg
Queen Mary's Avenue	Pandit Pant Marg
Queen Victoria Road	Dr Rajendra Prasad Marg
Queen's Gardens(Old Delhi)	Mahatma Gandhi Park
Queensway	Jan Path
Qutb Road	Aurobindo Marg
Rajpur Road	Rajpur Marg
Reading Road	Mandir Marg
Ridge Road	Rani Jhansi Road
Roberts Road	Teen Murti Marg
Rouse Avenue	Deen Dayal Upadhyaya Marg
Spectators' Road(CL)	branches northwest off north end of Bhai Parmanand Marg
State Entry Road	between Chelmsford Road and Northern Railway Line
Upper Bela Road	Mahatma Gandhi Marg
Viceroy's House	Rashtrapati Bhavan

Wellesley Road   Dr Zakir Husain Marg

Wigram Road(C)   Mandir Marg

York Place   Motilal Nehru Place

By 1972, the process of 'de-colonising' the road names of Delhi
had changed some 50% (70 out of 151) of the more obvious colonial
names existing in 1947. The expansion of the metropolitan area
and the consequent increase in the use of indigenous names reduced
the proportion to about 25% of the whole (some 81 out of 332) in
1972. The area of the city with apparently the least name changes
between 1947 and 1972 was the cantonment. The principal 'colonial'
road names remaining in 1972 included the following (data from India
Tourist Development Corporation, *Delhi City Map*, 1972.).

Albert
Alexander Place
Baird Place(C)
Baird Lane
Barron
Boulevard(CL)
Brassey Avenue
Butler(CL)
Campbell(C)
Canal(CL)
Canning
Canning Lane
Cassels(C)
Cavalry(C)
Cavalry Lane(CL)
Cemetery(C)
Chelmsford
Church(C)
Church (New Delhi)
Church (Old Delhi)
Club
Connaught Circus
Connaught Lane
Cornwallis
Court(CL)
Dalhousie

Doctor(s') Lane
Dupleix
East Avenue
Electric Lane
Esplanade
Farm
Golf Course
Grand Trunk
Gymnasium(C)
Hailey
Hailey Lane
Hastings
Hastings Lane
Hillside
Hospital(C)
Hostel
Imperial Avenue(CL)
King George's Ave
Kirby Place(C)
Kitchener
Library
Library Avenue
Lothian
Lucknow(CL)
Lytton
Lytton Lane

Magazine(CL)
Market Lane
Maude(C)
Nicholson(C)
North Avenue
Parade(C)
Park St
Polo(C)
Press
Press Lane
Race Course
Racquet Court Lane(CL)
Ratendone
School Lane
South Avenue
South End
Station(C)
Telegraph
The Mall(C)
The Mall(CL)
Thompson
Underhill(CL)
Upper Ridge
Wellesley
West Avenue
Willingden Crescent
Windsor Place

BIBLIOGRAPHY

The bibliography is divided into three sections. Section A includes the more important general works of reference; Section B, the sources, both primary and secondary, from which the historical data are derived, though excluding those references indicated in Section C. Section C lists the main reference works used for the case-study of Delhi.

SECTION A

Abu-Lughod, J. (1965), 'Tale of Two Cities: the Origins of Modern Cairo', *Comparative Studies in Society and History*, 7, 429-57.

Abu-Lughod, J. (1971), *Cairo: 1001 Years of the City Victorious*, Princeton University Press.

Amin, S. (1974), *Modern Migrations in Western Africa*, Oxford University Press.

Anderson, J. (1971), 'Space-time Budgets and Activity Studies in Urban Geography and Planning', *Environment and Planning*, 2, 353-68.

Anderson, M. (1971), *Family Structure in Nineteenth Century Lancashire*, Cambridge University Press.

Aries, P. (1962), *Centuries of Childhood*, Cape, London.

Asad, T., ed. (1973), *Anthropology and the Colonial Encounter*, Ithaca Press, London.

Bailey, J. (1975), *Social Theory for Planning*, Routledge & Kegan Paul, London.

Balandier, G. (1951), 'The Colonial Situation: A Theoretical Approach' in Wallerstein, I. (1966), 34-61.

Banton, M., ed. (1966), *The Social Anthropology of Complex Societies*, Tavistock, London.

Banton, M. (1971), 'Urbanisation and the Colour Line' in Turner, V. (1971), 391-9.

Basak, R. (1953), 'The Hindu Concept of the Natural World' in Morgan, K.W. (1953), 83-116.

Beattie, J. (1966), *Other Cultures: Aims, Methods and Achievements in Social Anthropology*, Routledge & Kegan Paul, London.

Beckinsale, R.P. (1970), *Urbanisation and its Problems*, Blackwell, Oxford.

Bernstein, H. (1971), 'Modernisation Theory and the Sociological Study of Development', *Journal of Development Studies*, 7, 141-60.

Béteille, A. (1969), *Castes, Old and New: Essays in Social Structure and Stratification*, Asia Publishing House, London.

Béteille, A. (1967), 'Race and Descent as Social Categories in India', *Daedalus*, 96 (Spring).

Bharati, A. (1973), 'Actual and Ideal Himalayas: Hindu Views of the Mountains', paper presented to the IXth International Congress of Anthropological and Ethnological Sciences, Chicago, August-September, 1973.

Bhardwaj, S.M. (1973), *Hindu Places of Pilgrimage in India: A Cultural Geography*, University of California Press, Berkeley.

Bidney, D. (1968), 'Cultural Relativism' in *International Encyclopaedia of Social Sciences*, Macmillan, New York, 543-7.

Board, C. et al. (1969), *Progress in Geography*, 1, Edward Arnold, London.

Board, C. et al. (1971), *Progress in Geography*, 3, Edward Arnold, London.

Board, C. et al. (1974), *Progress in Geography*, 6, Edward Arnold, London.

Boas, F. (1934), 'Geographical Names of the Kwakiutl Indians' in Hymes, D.H. (1964), 171-81.

Bose, A. (1970), *Urbanisation in India: An Inventory of Source Materials*. Academic Books, New Delhi.

Bose, A. (1971), 'The Urbanisation Process in South and South East Asia' in Jakobsen and Prakesh, ed. (1971), 81-110.

Braibanti, R., ed. (1966), *Asian Bureaucratic Systems Emergent from the British Imperial Tradition*, Duke University, North Carolina.

Breeze, G. (1966), *Urbanisation in Developing Societies*, Prentice-Hall, New Jersey.

Breeze, G., ed. (1969), *The City in Newly-Developing Countries*, Prentice-Hall, New Jersey.

Bright, W. (1968), 'Language and Culture' in *International Encyclopaedia of Social Sciences*, Macmillan, New York.

Brookfield, H.C. (1969), 'On the Environment as Perceived' in Board C., et al. (1969).

Brookfield, H.C. (1975), *Interdependent Development*, Methuen, London.

Brush, J.E. (1962), 'The Morphology of Indian Cities' in Turner, R., ed. (1962), 52-70.

Brush, J.E. (1968), 'Spatial Patterns of Population in Indian Cities', *Geographical Review*, 58, 362-91.

Brush, J.E. (1970), 'The Growth of the Presidency Towns' in Fox, R.G., ed. (1970), 91-114.

Burgess, E.W. and Bogue, D.J., eds (1964), *Contributions to Urban Sociology*, University of Chicago Press.

Buttimer, A. (1969), 'Social Space in Interdisciplinary Perspective', *Geographical Review*, 69, 417-26.

Castells, M. (1972), *La Question Urbaine*, Francois Maspéro, Paris.

Chalklin, C.W. and Havinden, M.A., eds (1974), *Rural Change and Urban Growth*, 1500-1800, Longmans, London.

Chapin, F. Stuart (1968), 'Activity Systems and Urban Structure',
    Journal of the American Institute of Planners, 34, 1.
Cohn, B.S. (1970), 'Society and Social Change under the Raj',
    South Asian Review, 4,1, 27-49.
Cohn, B.S. (1971), *India: the Social Anthropology of a
    Civilisation*, Prentice-Hall, New Jersey.
Collins, J. (1969), 'Lusaka: The Myth of the Garden City', *Zambian
    Urban Studies*, Zambian Institute of Social Research.
Cosgrove, I. and Jackson, R. (1972), *The Geography of Recreation
    and Leisure*, Hutchinson, London.
Cox, O.C. (1971), 'The Question of Pluralism', *Race*, 12, 385-400.
Craik, K.H. (1973), 'Environmental Psychology', *Annual Review of
    Psychology*, 24, 403-22.
Cressey, P.F. (1956), 'Ecological Organisation of Rangoon', *Sociology
    and Social Research*, 40, 166-9.
Cross, M. (1971), 'On Conflict Theory, Race Relations and the Theory
    of the Plural Society', *Race*, 12, 477-94.
Cruise O'Brien, R. (1972), *White Society in Black Africa: The French
    in Senegal*, Faber & Faber, London.
Davidoff, L. (1973), *The Best Circles: Society, Etiquette and the
    Season*, Croom Helm, London.
Davis, D.H. (1969), 'Lusaka, Zambia: Some Town Planning Problems in
    an African Capital City at Independence', *Zambian Urban
    Studies*, Zambian Institute for Social Research.
De Briey, P. (1970), 'Urbanisation and Under-development',
    Civilisations, 15, 4, 2-14.
Douglas, M. (1973), *Rules and Meanings*, Penguin Books, Harmondsworth.
Dumont, L. (1972), *Homo Hierarchicus*, Paladin, London.
Duncan, J.S. (1976), 'Landscapes and the Communication of Social
    Identity' in Rapoport, A., ed. (1976) forthcoming.
Dyer, H.T. (1963), *Mombasa Master Plan*, Municipal Council, Kenya.
Emerson, R. (1968), 'Colonialism' in *International Encyclopaedia
    of Social Sciences*, Macmillan, New York.
Evans-Pritchard, E.E. (1956), *The Nuer*, Clarendon Press, Oxford.
Eyles, J.D. (1974),'Social Theory and Social Geography' in Board,C.
    et al. (1974), 27-88.
Fabrega, H. Jr, (1972), 'Medical Anthropology' in Siegel,B.J.,
    ed. (1972), 167-229.
Filkin, C. and Weir, D. (1972), 'Locality' in Gittus, E., ed.(1972),
    106-58.
Firth, R. (1951), *Elements of Social Organisation*, Watts, London.
Foster, G.M. (1960), *Culture and Conquest: America's Spanish Heritage*,
    Wenner-Gren Foundation, New York.
Fox, R.G., ed. (1970), *Urban India: Society, Space and Image*,Monograph
    and Occasional Paper Series, no.10, Program in Comparative
    Studies on Southern Asia, Duke University.
Frake, C.O. (1969), 'The Ethnographic Study of Cognitive Systems' in
    Tyler, S., ed. (1969), 28-41.
Frank, A.G. (1971a), *The Sociology of Development and the Under-
    Development of Sociology*, Pluto Press, London.
Frank, A.G. (1971b), *Capitalism and Under-development in Latin America:
    Historical Studies of Chile and Brazil*, Penguin Books,
    Harmondsworth.

Friedmann, J. (1968), 'The Strategy of Deliberate Urbanisation',
        Journal of the American Institute of Planners, 34, 6, 364-73.
Friedmann, J. (1972), 'The Spatial Organisation of Power in the
        Development of Urban Systems', *Comparative Urban Research*,
        1, 5-42.
Furnivall, J.S. (1944), *Netherlands India: A Study of Plural Economy*,
        Cambridge University Press, London.
Furnivall, J.S. (1948), *Colonial Policy and Practice*, Cambridge
        University Press, London.
Gerth, H.H. and Mills, C.W., eds (1958), *From Max Weber: Essays in
        Sociology*, Galaxy Book, Oxford University Press, New York.
Ghana Ministry of Housing, Town and Country Planning Division (1958),
        Accra: A Plan for the Town, Government Printer, Accra.
Gillion, K.L. (1968), *Ahmedabad: A Study in Indian Urban History*,
        University of California Press, Berkeley.
Ginsburg, N. (1965), 'Urban Geography in Non-Western Areas' in Hauser
        P.M. and Schnore, L., eds (1965), 311-47.
Ginsburg, N. (1973), 'From Colonialism to National Development:
        Geographical Perspectives on Patterns and Policies',
        Annals of the Association of American Geographers, 63, 1-21.
Gist, N.P. (1958), 'The Ecological Structure of an Asian City:
        Bangalore, an East-West Comparison', *Population Review*,
        2, 1, 17-25.
Gittus, E., ed. (1972), *Key Variables in Social Research*, Heinemann,
        London.
Glacken, C.J. (1967), *Traces on the Rhodian Shore. Nature and Culture
        in Western Thought from Ancient Times to the End of the
        Eighteenth Century*, University of California Press, Berkeley.
Goffman, E. (1970), *Asylums*, Penguin Books, Harmondsworth.
Goffman, E. (1971), *The Presentation of Self in Everyday Life*,
        Penguin Books, Harmondsworth.
Goodenough, W.H. (1971), *Culture, Language and Society*, Addison-Wesley
        Module in Anthropology, 7.
Goodey, B. (1971), *Perception of the Environment*, Centre for Urban
        and Regional Studies, University of Birmingham.
Goodey, B. (1972), *A Checklist of Sources on Environmental Perception*,
        Centre for Urban and Regional Studies, University of
        Birmingham.
Greenberger, A.J. (1969), *The British Image of India: A Study in the
        Literature of Imperialism*, Oxford University Press, London.
Gutteridge, W. (1963), 'The Indianisation of the Indian Army,
        1918-1945', *Race*, 4, 39-48.
Hall, E.T. (1959), *The Silent Language*, Doubleday, New York.
Hall, E.T. (1966a), *The Hidden Dimension*, Doubleday, New York.
Hall, E.T. (1966b), 'The Anthropology of Space', *Architectural
        Review*, 140, 835, 163-6.
Hallowell, I. (1967), 'The Self and Its Behavioural Environment' in
        Hallowell, I., *Culture and Experience*, University of
        Pennsylvania Press,
Harvey, D. (1973), *Social Justice and the City*, Edward Arnold,
        London.
Hauser, P.M. (1965), 'Observations on the Urban-Folk Continuum and
        Urban-Rural Dichotomies as Forms of Western Ethnocentricism'
        In Hauser, P.M. and Schnore, L.F., eds (1965), 503-17.

Hauser, P.M. and Schnore, L.F., eds (1965), *The Study of Urbanisation*, John Wiley, New York.

Hazlehurst, L.W. (1970), 'Urban Space and Activities' in Fox, R.G. ed. (1970), 186-98.

Herskovitz, M.J. (1966), *Cultural Anthropology*, Knopf, New York.

Herskovitz, M.J. (1973), *Cultural Relativism*, Vintage Books, New York.

Hobsbawm, E.J. (1969), *Industry and Empire: An Economic History of Britain Since 1750*, Penguin Books, Harmondsworth.

Horvath, R.V. (1969), 'In Search of a Theory of Urbanisation: Notes on the Colonial City', *East Lakes Geographer*, 5, 69-82.

Horvath, R.V. (1972), 'A Definition of Colonialism', *Current Anthropology*, 13, 1, 45-57.

Hoselitz, B.F. (1962), 'The Role of Urbanisation in Economic Development: Some International Comparisons' in Turner, R., ed. (1962), 157-81.

Hoselitz, B.F. (1969), 'The Role of Cities in Economic Growth of Under-developed Areas' in Breeze, G., ed. (1969).

Hymes, Dell, H., ed. (1964) *Language in Culture and Society*, Harper, New York.

Jain, R.K. (1970), *South Indians on the Plantation Frontier in Malaya*, Yale University Press, New Haven and London.

Jakobsen, L. and Prakash, V., eds (1971), *Urbanisation and National Development*, Sage Publications, Beverly Hills.

Johnson, E.A.J. (1970), *The Organisation of Space in Developing Countries*, Harvard University Press, Cambridge, Mass.

Kasperson, R.E. and Minghi, J.V., eds (1969), *The Structure of Political Geography*, Aldine, Chicago.

Kay, G. (1967), *A Social Geography of Zambia*, University of London Press.

Kendall, H. (1955), *Town Planning in Uganda*, Crown Agents, London.

Keyfitz, N. (1961), 'The Ecology of Indonesian Cities', *American Journal of Sociology*, 66, 4, 348-54.

Kiernan, V.G. (1969), *The Lords of Human Kind: European Attitudes to the Outside World in the Imperial Age*, Weidenfeld & Nicolson, London.

King, A.D. (1970), 'India's Lost Libraries', *Hindustan Times*, 26 July.

King, A.D. (1973a), 'The Bungalow: the Development and Diffusion of a House-type', *Architectural Association Quarterly*, 5, 3, 5-26.

King, A.D. (1973b), 'Social Process and Urban Form: the Bungalow as an Indicator of Social Trends', *Architectural Association Quarterly*, 5, 4, 4-21.

King, A.D. (1976), 'Cultural Pluralism and Urban Form: the Colonial City as a Laboratory for Cross-Cultural Research' in Rapoport, A., ed. (1976), forthcoming.

King, A.D. (1976), 'Values, "Science" and Settlement: A Case Study in Environmental Control' in Rapoport, A. ed. (1976), forthcoming.

Kluckhohn, C. and Murray, H.A. (1953), *Personality in Nature, Culture and Society*, Jonathan Cape, London.

Kuper, H. (1971), 'Colour, Categories and Colonialism: the Swazi Case' in Turner, V., ed. (1971), 286-307.

Kuper, H. (1972), 'The Language of Sites in the Politics of Space' *American Anthropologist*, 74, 3, 411-25.

Kuper, L., et al. (1958), *Durban: A Study in Racial Ecology*, Cape, London.

Kuper, L. and Smith, M.G. eds (1969), *Pluralism in Africa*, University of California Press, Berkeley.

Langlands,B. (1969), 'Perspectives on Urban Planning for Uganda' in Safier, M. and Langlands,B. (1969).

Laslett, P. (1965), *The World We Have Lost*, Methuen, London.

Laslett, P. (1972), 'Mean Household Size in England Since the Sixteenth Century' in Laslett, P. (1972), 125-58.

Laslett, P., ed. (1972), *Household and Family Structure in Past Time*, Cambridge University Press.

Learmonth, A.T.A. (1973), 'Towards a Spatial Model of the South Asian City' in Open University, *The Process of Urbanisation*, Open University Press, Bletchley, 73-112.

Levi-Strauss, C. (1963), *Structural Anthropology*, Basic Books, New York.

Lewandowski, S. (1975), 'Urban Growth and Municipal Development in the Colonial City of Madras, 1860-1900', *Journal of Asian Studies*, 34,2.

Linton, R. (1943), 'Nativistic Movements', *American Anthropologist*, 45, 230-40.

Lloyd, P.C., et al. (1967), *The City of Ibadan*, Cambridge University Press, London.

Lock, Max & Partners, (1967), *Kaduna 1917-1967-2017. A Survey and Plan of the Capital Territory for the Government of Northern Nigeria*, Faber & Faber, London.

Lowenthal, D. and Prince, H.C. (1965), 'English Landscape Tastes', *Geographical Review*, 55, 186-222.

Mabogunje, A. (1968a), *Urbanisation in Nigeria*, University of London.

Mabogunje, A. (1968b), 'The Morphology of Ibadan' in Lloyd, P.C. et al. (1968), 35-52.

McCoughlin, J.B. (1970), *Urban and Regional Planning: A Systems Approach*, Faber, London.

McGee, T.G. (1967), *The Southeast Asian City*, Bell, London.

McGee, T.G. (1971), *The Urbanisation Process in the Third World: Explorations in Search of a Theory*, Bell, London.

McMaster, D. (1970), 'The Colonial District Town in Uganda' in Beckinsale, R.P., ed. (1970), 330-51.

Malinowski, B. (1945), *The Dynamics of Culture Change*, Yale University Press, New Haven.

Mannoni,O. (1956), *Prospero and Caliban. The Psychology of Colonisation*, Methuen, London.

Manzoor Alam, S. (1972), *Metropolitan Hyderabad and its Region: A Strategy for Development*, Asia Publishing House, London.

Martin, G. (1971), 'Introduction' to Granville, A.B., *Spas of England and Principal Sea-Bathing Places*, (1971, 1st edn 1841), Adams & Dart, Bath, v-xxi.

Martin, P. (1972), 'Concepts of Human Territoriality' in Ucko, P.J., et al. (1972), 427-45.

Maunier, R. (1949), *The Sociology of Colonies: An Introduction to the Study of Race Contact*, Routledge & Kegan Paul, London.

Michelson, W. (1970), *Man and His Urban Enviroment: A Sociological Approach*, Addison-Wesley, London.

Mitchell, J.C. (1966), 'Theoretical Orientations in African Urban Studies: Methodological Approaches' in Banton, M.(ed.)(1966).

Mitchell, N. (1972), *The Indian Hill Station: Kodaikanal*, University of Chicago, Department of Geography Research Paper, 141, Chicago.

Mittal, A. (1971), 'Patterns of Interaction and Group Formation in a Government Employees' Colony in Delhi', *Sociological Bulletin*, 20, 39-53.

Morgan, K.W. (1953), *The Religion of the Hindus*, Ronald Press, New York.

Murphy, R. (1957), 'New Capitals of Asia', *Economic Development and Cultural Change*, 5, 3, 216-43.

Murphy, R. (1969), 'Traditionalism and Colonialism: Changing Urban Roles in Asia', *Journal of Asian Studies*, 29, 1, 67-84.

Nakamura, H. (1964), *The Ways of Thinking of Eastern Peoples: India, China, Tibet, Japan*, East-West Center Press, Honolulu.

Naqvi, H.K. (1968), *Urban Centres and Industries in Upper India, 1553-1803*, Asia Publishing House, Bombay.

Neale, R. (1974), 'Society, Belief and the Building of Bath' in Chalkin, C.W. and Havinden, M.A. (1974), 253-80.

Ness, G.D. (1970), 'The Malayan Bureaucracy and its Occupational Communities', *Comparative Studies in Society and History*, 12, 179-87.

Nicholson, M. (1959), *Mountain Gloom and Mountain Glory: The Development of the Aesthetics of the Infinite*, Cornell University Press, New York.

Nicholson, N. (1955), *The Lakers*, Robert Hale, London.

Nilsson, S. (1968), *European Architecture in India, 1750-1850*, Faber & Faber, London.

Nilsson, S. (1973), *The New Capitals of India, Pakistan and Bangladesh*, Scandinavian Institute of South Asian Studies, Monograph Series 12, Sweden.

O'Brien, P. (1975), 'Theories of Dependency' in Oxaal, I., et al. (1975).

Otley, C.B. (1973), 'The Educational Background of British Army Officers', *Sociology*, 7, 265-84.

Oxaal, I. et al. (1975), *Beyond the Sociology of Development*, Routledge & Kegan Paul, London.

Palmier, L.H. (1957), 'Changing Outposts: The Western Communities in South East Asia', *Yale Review*, 47, 405-15.

Panikkar, K.M. (1965), *Asia and Western Dominance*, Allen & Unwin, London.

Parsons, T. et al. (1961), *Theories of Society*, Free Press of Glencoe, New York.

Parsons, T. (1966), *Societies: Evolutionary and Comparative Perspectives*, Prentice-Hall, New Jersey.

Patmore, J.A. (1970), 'The Spa Towns of Britain' in Beckinsale, R.P. (1970), 47-69.

Pimlott, J.A.R. (1947), *The Englishman's Holiday*, Faber & Faber, London.

Plumb, J.H. (1973), *The Commercialisation of Leisure in Eighteenth Century England*, University of Reading.

Polgar, S. (1962), 'Health and Human Behaviour: Areas of Interest
        Common to the Social and Medical Sciences', *Current
        Anthropology*, 3, 2, 159-205.
Pons, V. (1969), *Stanleyville: An African Urban Community Under
        Belgian Administration*, Oxford University Press, London.
Prince, H.C. (1971), 'Real, Imagined and Abstract Worlds of the Past',
        in Board, C. et al. (1971), 1-86.
Qadeer, M.A. (1974), 'Do Cities "Modernise" the Developing Countries?
        An Examination of the South Asian Experience', *Comparative
        Studies in Society and History*, 16, 3, 266-83.
Rapoport, A. (1969a), *House Form and Culture*, Prentice-Hall, New Jersey.
Rapoport, A. (1969b), 'Some Aspects of the Organisation of Urban
        Space', *Response to Enviroment*, Student Publications of the
        School of Design, North Carolina State University, 121-40.
Rapoport, A. (1970), 'The Study of Spatial Quality', *Journal of
        Aesthetic Education*, 4, 4, 81-96.
Rapoport, A. (1971), 'Some Observations on Man-Environment Studies',
        Architectural Research and Teaching, 2, 4-16.
Rapoport, A. (1973), 'Some Perspectives on Human Use and Organisation
        of Space', *Architectural Association Quarterly*, 5, 3, 27-37.
Rapoport, A. ed. (1976) forthcoming, *The Mutual Interaction of Man
        and His Built Environment: A Cross-Cultural Perspective*,
        World Anthropology Series, Mouton, The Hague.
Razzell, P.E. (1963), 'Social Origins of the Officers of the Indian
        and British Home Army, 1758-1962', *British Journal of
        Sociology*, 14, 248-60.
Redfield, R. and Singer, M. (1954), 'The Cultural Role of Cities',
        Economic Development and Cultural Change, 8, 1, 53-73.
Redick, R.W. (1953), 'A Demographic and Ecological Study of Rangoon,
        Burma', in Burgess, E.W. and Bogue, D.J. eds (1964), 31-41.
Reiss, A.J., ed. (1964), *Louis Wirth on Cities and Social Life*,
        University of Chicago.
Rex, J. (1967), *Race, Community and Conflict*, Oxford University Press,
        London.
Rex, J. (1970), *Race Relations and Sociological Theory*, Weidenfeld
        and Nicholson, London.
Rex, J. (1973), *Race, Colonialism and the City*, Routledge & Kegan
        Paul, London.
Ribeiro, D. (1968), *The Civilisational Process*, Smithsonian Institute,
        Washington.
Robertson, A.F. (1970), 'African and European Social Clubs in Rural
        Ghana', *Race*, 12, 2, 207-18.
Romney, A.P. and d'Andrade, R.G., eds (1964), 'Transcultural Studies
        in Cognition', *American Anthropologist*, 66 (3), part 2.
Rowe, W.L. (1973), 'Caste, Kinship and Association in Urban India'
        in Southall, A., ed. (1973), 211-50.
Safier, M. and Langlands, B.W.(1969), *Perspectives on Urban Planning
        for Uganda*, Department of Geography, Makerere University
        College, Uganda.
Sapir, E.A. (1912), 'Language and Environment', *American Anthropologist*,
        14, 2, 226-42.
Sapir, E.A. (1949), *Selected Writings in Language, Culture and
        Personality*, ed. Mandelbaum, D.G., University of California.
Schwerdtfeger, F. (1972), 'Urban Settlement Patterns in Northern
        Nigeria', in Ucko, P.J., et al. (1972), 547-556.

Scotch, N.A. (1963), 'Medical Anthropology' in Siegel, B.J. ed. (1963).

Segall, M.H., et al. (1966), *The Influence of Culture on Visual Perception*, Bobbs Merrill, Indianopolis.

Scheflen, A.E. (1976), *Human Territories: How We Behave in Space-Time*, Prentice-Hall, New Jersey.

Sharma, U. (1971), *Rampal and His Family: The Story of an Immigrant*, Collins, London.

Shibutani, T. (1955), 'Reference Groups as Perspectives', *American Journal of Sociology*, 60, 562-9.

Siegel, B.J. ed. (1963), *Biennial Review of Anthropology*, Stanford University Press.

Siegel, B.J. ed. (1972), *Biennial Review of Anthropology*, Stanford University Press.

Singh, R.L. ed. (1971), *India: A Regional Geography*, National Geographic Society of India, Varanasi.

Sjoberg, G. (1960), *The Pre-Industrial City*, Free Press, New York.

Sjoberg, G. (1965a), 'Theory and Research in Urban Sociology' in Hauser, P.M. and Schnore, L.F. (1965), 157-90

Sjoberg, G. (1965b), 'Cities in Developing and in Industrial Societies' in Hauser P.M. and Schnore, L.F. (1965), 213-64.

Smith, M.G. (1965), *The Plural Society in the British West Indies*, Oxford University Press.

Sopher, D.E. (1967), *The Geography of Religion*, Prentice Hall, New Jersey.

Southall, A. (1971), 'The Impact of Imperialism upon Urban Development in Africa' in Turner, V. ed. (1971), 216-55.

Southall, A., ed. (1973) *Urban Anthropology: Cross-Cultural Studies of Urbanisation*, Oxford University Press, London.

Sovani, N.V. (1966), *Urbanisation and Urban India*, Asia Publishing House Delhi.

Spate, O.H. and Learmonth, A.T.A. (1965), *India and Pakistan: A General and Regional Geography*, Methuen, London.

Spencer, J,E. and Thomas, W.L. (1948), 'The Hill Stations and Summer Resorts of the Orient', *Geographical Review*, 39, 4, 637-51.

Stambouli, F. (1971), 'Système Social et Urbanisation: Aspects de la Dynamique Globale de l'Urbanisation de la Ville de Tunis', *Revue Tunisienne de Science Sociale*, 8, 27, 31-63.

Stea, D. (1969), 'Space,Territory and Human Movements' in Kasperson, R.E. and Minghi, J. V. eds (1969), 216-55.

Sturtevant, W.C. (1964), 'Studies in Ethnoscience' in Romney, A.P. and d'Andrade, R.G. (1964), 99-131.

Swanson, M.W. (1969), 'Urban Origins of Separate Development', *Race*, 10, 31-40.

Timms, D.W.G. (1971), *The Urban Mosaic*, Cambridge University Press.

Trevallion, B.A.W. (1966), *Metropolitan Kano: Report on the 20 Year Development Plan*, 1963-83, Newman Neame Ltd., for the Greater Kano Planning Authority.

Turner, R., ed. (1962), *India's Urban Future*, University of California Press, Berkeley.

Turner, V., ed. (1971), *Colonialism in Africa, 1870-1960*, Cambridge University Press, London.

Tyler, S., ed. (1969), *Cognitive Anthropology*, Holt, Rinehart & Winston, New York.

Ucko, P.J., et al. (1972), *Man, Settlement and Urbanism*, Duckworth, London.

Unni, K.R. and Oakley, D. (1965), *The Rural Habit*, School of Planning and Architecture, New Delhi.

United Nations, (1971), *Climate and House Design*, New York.

Useem, J. and R., (1967), 'The Interfaces of a Binational Third Culture: A Study of the American Community in India', *Journal of Social Issues*, 23, 1.

Useem, J. and R. and Donoghue, J. (1963), 'Men in the Middle of the Third Culture: The Roles of American and Non-Western People in Cross-Cultural Administration', *Human Organisation*, 22, 169-79.

Wagner, P.L. (1962), 'Themes in Cultural Geography' in Wagner P.L. and Mikesell, M., eds (1962).

Wagner, P.L. and Mikesell, M., eds (1962), *Readings in Cultural Geography*, University of Chicago.

Wallerstein, I., ed. (1966), *Social Change: The Colonial Situation*, John Wiley, New York.

Weber, M. (1966), *The City*, Free Press, New York.

Wertheim, W.F. (1964), *Indonesian Society in Transition*, W. van Hoeve, The Hague.

Wheatley, P. (1963), 'What the Greatness of a City is said to be: Reflections on Sjoberg's "Pre-Industrial City"', *Pacific Viewpoint*, 4, 2, 163-88.

Wheatley, P. (1969), *City as Symbol*, University College, London.

White, L.W.T., Silberman, L. and Anderson, P.R. (1948), *Nairobi: Master Plan for a Colonial Capital*, HMSO, London.

Whorf, B.L. (1956), *Language, Thought and Reality*, Chapman and Hall, London.

Wilcox, P. (1969), Review of Pahl, R.E., *Readings in Urban Sociology* (1968), *Social Forces*, 48, 2, 286.

Wirth, L. (1927), 'The Ghetto' in Reiss, A.J., ed. (1964), 84-98.

Wirth, L. (1938), 'Urbanism as a Way of Life' in Reiss,A.J., ed.(1964).

Withington, W.A.(1961), 'Upland Resorts and Tourism in Indonesia: Some Recent Trends', *Geographical Review*, 51, 418-23.

Worsley, P. (1964), *The Third World*, Weidenfield & Nicolson, London.

SECTION B

Addis, A.W.C. (1910), *Practical Hints to Young Engineers Employed on Indian Railways*, E. and F.N. Spon, London.

Allen, C. (1975),*Plain Tales from the Raj: Images of British India in the Twentieth Century*, Andre Deutsch and British Broadcasting Corporation, London.

Anand, Mulk Raj, (1968), *Morning Face: An Autobiographical Novel*, Kutub, Bombay.

Andrews, R.C. and Y.B. (1918), *Camps and Trails in China*, Appleton, New York.

Anon., (1854), 'Notes of Four Months Residence on Mount Aboo in 1851', *Saunders Monthly Magazine*, 3, 4.

Anon., (1905), *My Garden in the City of Gardens*, John Lane, London.

Archer, E. (1833), *Tours in Upper India and in Parts of the Himalaya Mountains*, 2 vols, Richard Bentley, London.

Archer, M. (1955), 'Indian Paintings for British Naturalists',
        Geographical Magazine, 28, 220-30.
Archer, M. (1962), 'India Revealed: Sketches by the Daniells',
        Appollo (November), 689-92.
Archer, M. (1963), 'Birds of India', *Geographical Magazine*, 36, 470-81.
Archer, M. (1964), 'Georgian Splendour in South India', *Country Life*,
        130, 728-31.
Archer, M. (1966), 'Aspects of Classicism in India: Georgian Buildings
        in Calcutta', *Country Life*, 132.
Archer, M. (1967), 'British Painters of the Indian Scene', *Journal
        of the Royal Society of Arts*, 854-79.
Archer, M. (1969), 'Benares and the British', *History Today*, 19, 405-10.
Baikie, R. (1834), *Observations on the Neilgherries etc.*, Baptist
        Mission Press, Calcutta.
Becher, A. (1930), *Personal Reminiscences in India and Europe, 1830-88*,
        Constable, London.
Bevan, H. (1839), *Thirty Years in India*, 2 vols, Pelham Richardson,
        London.
Brown, H. (1948), *The Sahibs: The Life and Ways of the British in
        India as Recorded by Themselves*, Hodge, London.
Buckland, C.T. (1884), *Sketches of Social Life in India*, W.H. Allen,
        London.
Butler, I. (1969), *The Viceroy's Wife: Letters of Alice, Countess of
        Reading, India, 1921-25*, Hodder & Stoughton, London.
Census of India, (1961), *District Census Handbook, Delhi*.
Clark, S. (1864), *Practical Observations on the Hygiene of the Army
        in India*, Cox, London.
Cohn, B.S. (1962), 'The British in Benares: a Nineteenth Century
        Colonial Society', *Comparative Studies in Society and
        History*, 4, 169-208.
Cohn, B.S. (1966), 'Recruitment and Training of British Civil
        Servants in India, 1600-1800' in Braibanti, R., ed. (1966),
        87-140.
Compton, J.M. (1968), 'Open Competition and the Indian Civil Service,
        1854-76', *English Historical Review*, 83, 265-84.
de Vere Allen, J. (1970), 'Malayan Civil Service, 1874-1941:
        Colonial Bureaucracy-Malayan Elite', *Comparative Studies
        in Society and History*, 12, 2, 149-78.
Delhi Sketch Book, vols 1-6, 1850-5, Delhi Gazette Press.
Duncan, A. (1888), *The Prevention of Diseases in Tropical and Sub-
        Tropical Campaigns*, Churchill, London.
Edwardes, M. (1969), *Bound to Exile: The Victorians in India*,
        Sidgewick & Jackson.
Falkland, Lady, (1930), *Chow-Chow: A Journal Kept in India, Egypt
        and Syria, 1857*, Eric Partridge, London.
Firminger, T.A.C. (1918), *A Manual of Gardening for Bengal and
        Upper India*, Thacker and Spink, Calcutta.
Goument, C.E.V. (1921), *Roorkee Treatise on Civil Engineering*,
        Allahabad.
Government of India, (1887), *Cantonment Regulations*, under Acts
        XX11, 1864, 1870, Act 111, 1880. Government Printer,
        Calcutta.
Government of India, (1924), *Cantonment Regulations*, under Acts
        XX11, 1864, 1870, Government Printer, Calcutta.

Government of India, (1899), *Cantonments Code*, Government Printer,
        Calcutta.
Greenwall, H.J. (1933), *Storm Over India*, Hurst & Blackett, London.
Hardinge, Lord (1948), *My Indian Years*, 1910-16, John Murray, London.
Hutchings, F.G. (1967), *The Illusion of Permanence: British
        Imperialism in India*, Princeton University Press.
'Indicus' (1919), 'Indian Reforms and the Station Club', *Contemporary
        Review*, 116, 321-6
Karve, D.D. (1963), *The New Brahmins*, Cambridge University Press.
Kincaid, D. (1973), *British Social Life In India, 1608-1937*,
        Routledge & Kegan Paul, London.
King, H. (1875), *Madras Manual of Health*, Government Printer, Madras.
Law, J. (1912), *Indian Snapshots*, Thacker & Spink, Calcutta.
Lawrence, Lady (n.d.), *Indian Embers*, George Ronald, Oxford.
Lambert (1879), *The Golden Guide to London*, no publisher, London.
Lugard, Lord (1970), *Political Memoranda 1913-18*, Frank Cass, London.
        (3rd edn, earlier edns, 1906, 1919).
Macdonald, M. (1960), *Birds in My Indian Garden*, Cape, London.
Mackenzie, J. (1929), *Army Health in India*, Bale, London.
Markandaya, K. (1966), *A Handful of Rice*, Hind Pocket Books, Delhi.
Martin, J.R. (1868), *Sanitary History of the Army in India*,
        reprinted from *The Lancet*, London.
Meadows, S.D. (1931), *Modern Eastern Bungalows and How to Build Them*,
        Thacker's Press and Directories, Calcutta.
Moore, W.J. (1862), *Health in the Tropics or Sanitary Art Applied
        to Europeans in India*, Churchill, London.
Murray, J. (1872), *Handbook for Travellers in India*, John Murray,
        London.
Murray, J. (1882), *Handbook of the Bengal Presidency*, John Murray,
        London.
Murray, J. (1895), *How to Live in Tropical Africa*, Philip & Son,
        London.
Murray, J. (1904), *Imperial Guide to India*, John Murray, London.
Murray, J. (1913), *Handbook for Travellers in India, Burma & Ceylon*,
        John Murray, London.
Murray, J.A.H. (1888), *A New English Dictionary on Historical
        Principles*, Clarendon Press, Oxford.
Nanda, B.R. (1962), *The Nehrus, Motilal and Jawaharlal*, Allen and
        Unwin, London.
Orwell, G. (1955), *Burmese Days*, Secker and Warburg, London.
Panikkar, K.M. (1970), *Asia and Western Dominance*, Allen and Unwin,
        London.
Panter-Downes, M. (1967), *Ooty Preserved: A Victorian Hill Station
        in India*, Hamish Hamilton, London.
Parliamentary Committee (1858), *Report of the Parliamentary
        Committee on Colonisation and Settlement (India)*,
        Parliamentary Papers, Session 3, Vll, 1.
Pfeil, K. (1935), 'Die Indische Stadt'. Leipzig (unpublished,India
        Office Library).
Platt, K. (1923), *The Home and Health in India and the Tropical
        Colonies*, Baillière, Tindall & Cox, London.

Reeder, D.A. (1965), 'Capital Investment in the Western Suburbs of
        Victorian London', dissertation for the degree of Ph.D.,
        University of Leicester.
Renbourne, E.T. (1961), *Life and Death of the Solar Topi: Protection
        of the Head from the Sun,* War Office, Directorate of
        Physiological and Biological Research, Report 117.
Reynolds, R.A. (1937), *White Sahibs in India,* Secker & Warburg,
        London.
Richards, F. (1965), *Old Soldier Sahib,* Faber, London.
Ricketts, L.E. (1912), 'English Society in India', *Contemporary
        Review,* 101, 681-6.
Royal Commission (1863), *Royal Commission on the Sanitary State of
        the Army in India,* Report from the Commissioners, Parliamen-
        tary Papers, XIX, 1.
Russell, W.H. (1860), *My Diary in the Years 1858-9,* 2 vols, Routledge,
        Warne & Routledge, London.
Sleeman, W.H. (1915), *Rambles and Recollections of an Indian Official,*
        Oxford University Press, London (first published, 1844).
Smith, H.P. (1883), *Glossary of Terms and Phrases,* Kegan Paul, London.
Spear, P. (1963), *The Nabobs,* Oxford University Press, London.
Spear, P. (1965), *A History of India,* Penguin Books, Harmondsworth.
Steevens, G.W. (1899), *In India,* Blackwood, London.
Sterndale, R.C. (1881), *Municipal Work in India: Hints on Sanitation,
        General Conservancy and Improvement in Municipalities,*
        Thacker and Spink, Calcutta.
Stocqueler, J.H. (1853), *The Military Encyclopaedia,* W.H. Allen,
        London.
Stokes-Roberts, E. (1910), *Some Practical Points in the Design and
        Construction of Military Buildings in India,* Government
        Printer, Calcutta.
Stokes-Roberts, E. (1959), *Eastern Kaleidoscope,* P.R. Macmillan,
        London.
Tagore, D. (1916), *Autobiography,* Macmillan, London.
Tandon, P. (1961), *Punjabi Century, 1857-1947,* Chatto & Windus, London.
Thompson, E. (1938), *An Indian Day,* Penguin Books, Harmondsworth.
Times of India, (1930), *The Indian Yearbook,* Times of India Press,
        Bombay.
Trevelyan, G. (1894), *Cawnpore,* Macmillan, London.
Voyle, G.E. (1876), *A Military Dictionary,* William Clowes, London.
White, G.F. (1838), *Views Chiefly among the Himalaya Mountains...
        taken in 1829, 1831, 1832,* Fisher, London.
Wilson, E. (1974), *Gone with the Raj,* George Reeve, Wymondham.
Woodruff, P. (1965), *The Men Who Ruled India,* 2 vols, Cape, London.
Yule, H. and Burnell, A.C. (1903), *Hobson-Jobson. A Glossary of
        Colloquial Anglo-Indian Words and Phrases,* John Murray,
        London.

Extensive reference has been made to the Western Drawings Collection,
India Office Library, as well as its large photographic archive.   The
paintings and drawings are catalogued in:
Archer, M. (1969), *British Drawings in the India Office Library,*vol. 1
        (Amateur Artists), vol. 2 (Official and Professional Artists),
        HMSO, London.

Archer, M. (1972), *Company Drawings in the India Office Library*, HMSO, London.

SECTION C

Ahmad, A. (1969), *An Intellectual History of Islam in India*, Edinburgh University Press.
Andrews, C.F. (1929), *Zakah Ullah of Delhi*, Heffer, Cambridge.
Annual Progress Reports for the New Capital Project at Delhi, 1924-5 to 1927-8, Government of India Press, Delhi.
Anon. (1865), 'Delhi in 1835' in *The Tourists Guide from Delhi to Kurrachee*, Lahore.
Arora, R.C. (1935), *Delhi: Imperial City*, Unique Literature Publishing House, Aligarh.
Bhargava, J. (1930), *New Delhi Directory, 1929-30*, Model Press, Delhi.
Bhatia, S.S. (1956), 'Historical Geography of Delhi', *Indian Geographer*, 1, 1, 17-43.
Bopegamage, A. (1957), *Delhi: A Study in Urban Sociology*, University of Bombay.
Breeze, G. (1974), *Urban and Regional Planning for Delhi-New Delhi*, Princeton University Press.
Chopra, P. (1970), *Delhi. History and Places of Interest* (Delhi Gazetteer), Delhi Administration, Delhi.
Cole, H.H. (1872), *Architecture of Ancient Delhi*, Arundel Society, London.
Cooper, F. (1863), *Handbook for Delhi*, R. Williams, Delhi.
Delhi Administration (1921-), *Report on the Administration of Delhi Province*, Central Government Press, Delhi. (years 1921-2 to 1931-2).
Delhi Archaeological Society (1850), *Journal of the Archaeological Society of Delhi*, Delhi Gazette Press, Delhi.
Delhi Development Authority, (1961), *Master Plan and Work Studies for Delhi*, 2 vols, DDA, Delhi.
Delhi and North India Directory, Publicity Bureau, Lahore, 1932.
Delhi Durbar, 1902-3, plans and documents relating to, (British Library), 1903.
Delhi Durbar of 1911, notes written to accompany a series of lantern slides (British Library), 1911.
Fanshawe, H.C. (1902), *Delhi: Past and Present*, Murray, London.
Ferrell, D.W. (1969), 'Delhi, 1911-22: Society and Politics in the New Imperial Capital of India', dissertation for the degree of Ph.D., Australian National University, Canberra.
Fonseca, R. (1971), 'The Walled City of Delhi', *Ekistics*, 31, 182, 72-80.
Government of India (1903), *Coronation Durbar, Delhi. Official Directory*.
Government of India (1961), *Census of India, District Census Handbook*.
Gupta, N. (1971), 'Military Security and Urban Development: A Case Study of Delhi, 1857-1912', *Modern Asian Studies*, 5,1,61-77.
Gupta, S.K. (1968), 'Scale and Use of Open Spaces in Old and New Delhi' (thesis submitted in partial fulfilment for the Postgraduate Diploma in Town and Country Planning), School of Town and Country Planning, Delhi University.

Harcourt, A. (1866), *The New Guide to Delhi*, G.A. Savielle, Allahabad.

Harcourt, A. (1873), *The New Guide to Delhi*, Victoria Press, Lahore.

Hearn, G.R. (1906), *The Seven Cities of Delhi*, Thacker, London.

Hussey, C.E.C. (1950), *The Life of Sir Edwin Lutyens*, Country Life, London.

India Tourism Development Corporation (1973), *Guide to Delhi*, ITDC, New Delhi.

Jagmohan (1975), *Rebuilding Shahjahanabad: The Walled City of Delhi*, Vikas, Delhi.

Keene, H.G. (1882), *Handbook for Visitors to Delhi*, Thacker & Spink, Calcutta.

Mitra, A. (1968), *Delhi: Capital City*, privately printed, Delhi.

Monk, F.F. (1935), *A History of St Stephen's College, Delhi*, YMCA Publishing House, Calcutta.

Punjab Government (1884), *Gazetteer of the Delhi District, 1883-4*, Calcutta Central Press, Calcutta.

Punjab Government (1904), *Punjab District Gazetteer, Delhi Statistical Tables*, Government Printer, Lahore.

Punjab Government (1913), *Punjab District Gazetteer (Delhi District)*, Government Printer, Lahore.

Prasad, H. (1918), *Encyclopaedic Indian Directory*, Encyclopaedic Indian Directory Co., Allahabad.

Rao, V.K.R.V. and Desai, I.P. (1965), *Greater Delhi: A Study in Urbanisation, 1940-1957*, Asia Publishing House, New Delhi.

Roberts, A.A. (1847), 'Population of Delhi and Its Suburbs, etc., 1847'. Appendix A in *Selections from Public Correspondence from the Government of India, Northwest Provinces*, 1-5, part III, 1, Government Printer, Agra.

Spear, P. (1945), *Delhi: A Historical Sketch*, H. Milford for Oxford University Press, Bombay.

Spear, P. (1951), *Twilight of the Moghuls: Studies in Late Moghul Delhi*, Cambridge University Press.

Stephen, C. (1876), *The Archaeology and Monumental Remains of Delhi*, Thacker & Spink, Simla.

Sullivan, D.D. (1920), *Here is Delhi*, Delhi.

Thakore, M.P. (1962), 'Aspects of the Urban Geography of New Delhi', dissertation for the degree of Ph.D., University of London.

MAPS AND PLANS RELATING TO DELHI

Except where otherwise stated, these have been consulted in the India Office Library, London. Reference numbers are given in brackets.

(1800) 'Plan of Dehly Reduced from a Large Hindostanny Map of that City' (Town and Country Planning Organisation, Delhi, Subs. TCPO).

(1807) Sketch of the Environs of Delhi, F.S. White, Surveyor (TCPO).

(1808) Environs of Delhi (E VII 16).

(1812) Plan of Native Delhi (TCPO).

(1840) District of Dehlee (E VII 13).

(1848) District of Dihlee (E VII 14).

(1849-50) Fort and Cantonment of Delhi (E VII 18).

(1850?) Delhi (Plan of the City). A native map with names in the
        vernacular character (E VII 17).
(1857) Delhi and Environs during the Siege, 1857 (E VII 22).
(1857) Fort and Cantonment of Delhi (E VII 19).
(1867-8) Delhi Cantonment, City, Civil Station and Environs (O V 1 (A)).
(1905) Cantonment and Civil Lines (O V 1).
(1911) Coronation Durbar (O V 1 (B)).
(1912) Delhi and Vicinity (O V 1 (I)).
(1912) Punjab and U.P. Delhi District (O V 1 (E)).
(1913) Plans of Government House (O V 2).
(1919) Delhi and Vicinity (O V 1 (F)).
(1920) Delhi and Vicinity (O V 1 (C)).
(1927) Tourist Map of Delhi (O V 1 (3)).
(1927-8) Imperial Delhi, index Plan of Lay-out.
(1939-42) Delhi Guide Map, Survey of India.
(1959) Delhi Guide Map, Survey of India.
(1969) Delhi Guide Map, Survey of India.
(1972) Delhi City Map, Survey of India and India Tourism Development
        Corporation.

NAME INDEX

SUBJECT INDEX